Policy and Change in T

Policy, Planning and Critical Theory

Series Editor: **Paul Cloke**
St David's University College, Lampeter, UK

This major new series will focus on the relevance of critical social theory to important contemporary processes and practices in planning and policy-making. It aims to demonstrate the need to incorporate state and governmental activities within these new theoretical approaches, and will focus on current trends in governmental policy in Western states, with particular reference to the relationship between the centre and the locality, the provision of services, and the formulation of government policy.

Forthcoming titles in this series include

The Global Region: Production, State Policies and Uneven Development
David Sadler

Beyond the Housing Crisis
Mark Goodwin

People, Place, Protest: Making Sense of Popular Protest in Modern Britain
Michael J Griffiths

Policy and Planning for International Agriculture
Richard Le Heron

Gender, Planning and the Policy Process
Jo Little

Selling Places: the City as Cultural Capital, Past and Present
C Philo and G Kearns

Uneven Reproduction: Economy, Space and Society
Andrew Pratt

Policy and Change in Thatcher's Britain

Edited by

Paul Cloke
St David's University College, Lampeter, UK

PERGAMON PRESS
OXFORD · NEW YORK · SEOUL · TOKYO

UK	Pergamon Press plc, Headington Hill Hall, Oxford OX3 0BW, England
U.S.A.	Pergamon Press, Inc, 660 White Plains Road, Tarrytown, New York 10591, U.S.A.
KOREA	Pergamon Press Korea, KPO Box 315, Seoul 110–603, Korea
JAPAN	Pergamon Press Japan, Tsunashima Building Annex, 3–20–12 Yushima, Bunkyo-ku, Tokyo 113, Japan

---

First edition 1992

Library of Congress Cataloging-in-Publication Data

Policy and change in Thatcher's Britain/edited by Paul Cloke
p. cm. — (Policy planning and critical theory)
1. Great Britain—Social policy. 2. Great Britain—Social conditions—1945– 3. Great Britain—Economic policy—1945– 4. Great Britain—Economic conditions—1945– 5. Critical theory.
I. Series.
HN385.5.P58 1992 361.6′1′0941—dc20 91–33813

British Library Cataloguing in Publication Data

Cloke, Paul J. (Paul John), *1953–*
Policy and change in Thatcher's Britain.
(Policy, planning & critical theory)
I. Title II. Series
354.41072

ISBN 0–08–040647–5 Hardcover
ISBN 0–08–040648–3 Flexicover

Printed in Great Britain by BPCC Wheatons Ltd, Exeter.

Contents

Contributors

PETER AMBROSE
School of Cultural and Community Studies
University of Sussex

DAVID BANISTER
Bartlett School of Architecture and Planning
University College, London

DAVID BYRNE
Department of Sociology and Social Policy
University of Durham

PAUL CLOKE
Department of Geography
St. David's University College
Lampeter

LINDA McDOWELL
Faculty of Social Sciences
Open University

MARK GOODWIN
Department of Geography
St. David's University College
Lampeter

RON MARTIN
Department of Geography
University of Cambridge

TIMOTHY O'RIORDAN
School of Environmental Sciences
University of East Anglia

Contributors

MAGGIE PEARSON
Department of General Practice
University of Liverpool

ROD RHODES
Department of Politics
University of York

DAVID SADLER
Department of Geography
University of Durham

PETER TAYLOR
Department of Geography
University of Newcastle-upon-Tyne

NIGEL THRIFT
Department of Geography
University of Bristol

PETER WILLIAMS
Centre of Housing Management and Development
University of Wales College of Cardiff

Preface

The day that Margaret Thatcher relinquished power in Britain is one of those key time–space moments when most people will remember exactly where they were when they heard the news. I was sitting having breakfast with Owen Furuseth and his family in Charlotte, North Carolina, at the time, and the local press judged the event worthy of only a few column inches under the heading "Iron Lady Finally Cracks". To my personal chagrin, I missed out on all of the detailed media coverage in Britain, but in terms at least of populist image this was the end of an era. It was as if very few had been able to be neutral about Mrs Thatcher, her governments and her policies. Strong support was registered in opinion polls and ballot boxes (although her winning share of the popular vote was surprisingly lower than many might have imagined). She was given hard-edged but admiring titles (such as "iron lady") and to some extent she adapted to the myth as well as creating it. Equally vehement dislike also ruminated within the country, spreading alternative (and far less complimentary) titles around in the undercurrents of society. In a more witty than damning contribution, for example, Adrian Plass (1988) points out that Maggie Thatcher is an anagram of GET RICH TEAM HAG.

Just as the Thatcher era was very real in populist terms, so it has been the subject of significant intellectual and academic attention. The phenomenon of Thatcherism has been analysed at length in search not only of an understanding of the anatomy of the politics employed by Thatcher, but also of an answer to the question of whether those politics were vested solely in her leadership or whether broader ideologies provided the driving force to her regime. These issues are becoming somewhat clearer now she has gone, and John Major struggles to fill the void with new forms of ideology or pragmatics.

It is not our intention here to offer yet another account of the politics of Thatcherism. There are already such accounts available which have performed this task with great distinction. Andrew Gamble, for example, in his book *The Free Economy and the Strong State* (1988) clearly points out the contradictory nature of the political phenomenon of Thatcherism:

> Thatcherism has been such a contradictory phenomenon in government because of the basic practical and theoretical uncertainty about the kind of degree of state restructuring that it sought. Creating a "free economy" commanded wide support in the Conservative party when it was interpreted to mean lower taxes, lower public expenditure, less nationalisation, weaker trade unions, less government regulation and control, and more equality. But a free economy was also understood by some to mean a state strong enough to intervene actively in all institutions of civil society to impose, nurture and stimulate the business values, attitudes and practices necessary to re-launch Britain as a successful capitalist economy (p. 232).

Taking us on even further, Bob Jessop, Kevin Bonnett, Simon Bromley and Tom Ling in their book on *Thatcherism* (1988) link Thatcherism with post-Fordism in that the politics of this era have exacerbated spatial and social distinctions in Britain so as to bring about a politically exclusionary strategy of two nations.

> The primacy of the political class struggle in Thatcherite policy is often astonishing. Whereas the last Labour government tended to subordinate political strategy to economic crisis-management, the Thatcher governments have often treated economic policy as a subfield for the politics of hegemony . . . . The general rationale seems to be that if the government can modify the balance of forces in the short term, it will gain sufficient time to restructure society, and to allow a market-generated recovery (pp. 29–30).

This book uses such accounts as a partial foundation on which to build a series of accounts of how the ensemble of economic, social, political and cultural relations in Britain have been changed during the Thatcher era, and of how particular policy arenas have been affected by such changes.

As the first book to be published in the *Policy Planning and Critical Theory* series, it is seemly that the authors here variously use aspects of critical social theory to inform their analysis of particular policy themes. Accordingly, the book is simply divided into four sections. In the first, Nigel Thrift specifically parallels the directions taken in social theory with the directions taken by the Thatcher governments. He clearly shows that not only does critical social theory inform our interpretation of Thatcherism, but Thatcherism has made such demands on social theory as to insist on changing theoretical agendas.

The second section seeks to present accounts of the changing political and governmental relations which have occurred during the Thatcher era. In a series of essays, Peter Taylor, Rod Rhodes, Mark Goodwin and Peter Ambrose explain and analyse the context in which state apparatus in the form of policy-making and planning has been employed. Necessarily there is not complete agreement between the authors here either on the theoretical approaches necessary for an understanding of changing relations, or indeed on the evaluative outcomes of those changes. Nevertheless, this section serves to stress the obvious (but sometimes forgotten) necessity to look beyond immediate policy arenas in search of why and how policy changes occur.

In the third section, there is a series of essays which seek to illustrate the particular outworkings of those changing relations under Thatcherism, in particular systematic or spatial policy arenas. This grouping does not pretend to be a complete or all-embracing overview of all policy arenas impacted on by Thatcherism. Rather, what is intended here is to illustrate the policy effects of Thatcherism in some areas which are important and recognizable both to contemporary social science and more generally. Thus Ron Martin, Peter Williams, David Banister, Maggie Pearson and Tim O'Riordan analyse key policy sectors while David Byrne and myself write on Thatcher's city and Thatcher's countryside respectively.

Finally, the fourth section allows scope for David Sadler and Linda McDowell to offer some more overarching commentaries on the major economic and social changes which have characterized Britain under Thatcher. Both stress the unevenness of development, with Sadler's emphasis being on spatial divisions of labour and McDowell's emphasis on gender division of labour. Their conclusions, however, merge with those expressed in other chapters as Linda McDowell writes:

> The net result is that Britain in the early 1990's is a significantly more unequal society, than it was ten years earlier and indeed, than it has been for several decades.

This sentence summarizes the mood of many contributions to this book.

I would like to thank many people who have been associated with the production of this book including: Geraldine Billingham at

Pergamon; Caron McKee in Lampeter; the growing and very supportive band of human geography colleagues at St. David's University College; and Viv, Elizabeth, William and Holly the collie.

PAUL CLOKE

Lampeter

References

Gamble, A. (1988) *The Free Economy and the Strong State: The Politics of Thatcherism*. Macmillan, London.

Jessop, B., Bonnett, K., Bromley, S., and Ling, T. (1988) *Thatcherism*. Polity Press, Oxford.

Plass, A. (1988) *Clearing Out the Rubbish*. Minstrel, Eastbourne.

1

Light Out of Darkness? Critical Social Theory in 1980s Britain

NIGEL THRIFT

Introduction

This chapter is an attempt to document some of the theoretical legacies of the political history of Britain in the 1980s; I want to show the extent to which context produced text. This is not, however, a full-blown account. Thus, the chapter does not pretend to be a comprehensive history of the intellectual twists and turns of British academe in the 1980s. That would occupy more space than I have here and, in any case, such an account already exists (Anderson 1990a, b). Nor is it a paper which moves as much as it might outside the shores of Britain, which is not to deny that the impulses of world economy, society and culture have increasingly made their presence felt in Britain, or that social theory is increasingly a global business. It is simply a way of limiting the context so that a text can be produced. What the paper does try to do is show how political puzzles can generate substantial intellectual shifts.

Accordingly, the paper is in three parts. The first part documents very briefly some of the key flashpoints in Britain's economy, society and polity in the 1980s: the stuff from which challenges to prevalent social theory were made. The second part documents some of the accounts that a (very broadly defined) "left" offered of these shocks, concentrating on the spheres of the economy, state and civil society, and the environment. The third part describes the way in which these short-term accounts were transformed into longer-term theoretical gains, paying particular attention to both the strengths and weaknesses of these transformations. The paper concludes with a call for more attention to be paid to the structuring of civil society as a pressing political and theoretical issue.

1. Shock after Shock

For many on the left in Britain, the miners' strike of 1984/85 had it all. Unambiguously working class communities were under siege from a determinedly free market government. The future of a state-owned industry was at stake. The strike was a direct challenge to so many of the Thatcher government's most cherished principles; the sanctity of the public sector borrowing requirement, the curtailment of union power, even the privatization of state-owned assets. The strike was also a direct challenge to the Labour Party. Would it reconsecrate itself to the pursuit of a vision of Britain held since 1945? Would it uphold the importance of production, the role of the party as the standard bearer of the working class, the importance of nationalized industries, and so on? The strike was, of course, comprehensively defeated. By 1985 the miners' union had been crushed and the British coal industry began a slide into near-oblivion.

In direct counterpoint to this event the same years saw the City of London growing in prominence in Britain. A frenzy of deregulation, culminating in "Big Bang" in 1986, was meant to guarantee the position of the City as one of the world's premier financial centres. No more than three hours drive from the valleys of Wales and their entrenched mining communities could be found a world where the telephones worked properly, where money was counted in millions of pounds, not tens of pence, and where suits, rather than overalls, were the normal garb. The "productive" economy of working for money seemed to be losing out to the casino economy of making money (Thrift and Leyshon 1991).

If this schizophrenic economy was setting the left questions it could not answer, so was the state of the state and civil society. The Falklands War of 1982 showed that the nation state could still sponsor overseas adventures and get considerable popular support for doing so: nationalism was not a spent force. The state apparatus itself showed signs of becoming ever more centralized (in the process snuffing out local left redoubts like the GLC) and it also showed alarming flashes of out-and-out authoritarianism. But the confidence of the left was, of course, hit hardest by the general election defeats of 1979, 1984 and 1987. Given that the Conservative Government only received around 40 per cent of the vote in each election, and given the influence of the SDP, especially in the 1984 elections, these defeats still showed that the left was not touching the electorate in the way that it needed to to gain power.

At least part of the reason for this state of affairs was the diversity of British civil society. It was not so much that there was an increase in the number of social groupings (this had chiefly occurred in the 1960s), nor that the divides between social groupings had become greater—nineteenth-century Britain was probably as or more socially fractured. Rather, each social grouping was finding a voice. For some on the left, who framed everything in terms of class politics, the political atmosphere was quiescent. But it would be more accurate to say that politics in Britain in the 1980s was as tumultuous as before but was not organized on orthodox political lines: the political system and politics were out of alignment. The fact was underlined by the race riots of the early 1980s and the Salman Rushdie affair in the late 1980s. It was underlined once more by the growing power of the women's movement in all areas of life. It was underlined, yet again, by the rise of numerous environmental movements.

Thus, in each sphere of society—the economy, the state and civil society—the left was faced with the same challenge: had the economy, the state and civil society all moved out of true or had the left? The answers were not easy to come by.

The impact of each and everyone of those shocks was increased by their geographical interpellation. Thus the different bases of the economies of the coal-mining areas and the City of London were seen by many as symbols of two nations; they represented the continued growth of a north-south divide (Townsend and Lewis 1989, Martin 1989, Smith 1989), a national economy and an international economy, the decline of production and the growth of services industries, and so on. Similarly the increasingly centralized and authoritarian state was seen by many as an English state expressing the power of London, a state whose writ did not run in Wales or Scotland or Northern Ireland. The election defeats revealed a similar polarizing pattern with the elections in the south becoming increasingly a Conservative: Alliance battle, with Labour a poor third, whilst in the north elections were increasingly a Conservative: Labour battle, with the Alliance lagging behind (Johnston *et al.* 1988). As a result, the Labour Party could gain few electoral benefits from further advances in the north, and was finding it hard to make any headway in the south. Civil society similarly showed strong spatial patterning which in many cases proved to be constitutive. In other words, spatial frames and spatial metaphors saturated left thinking about social change. They were integral to the way that problems were posed and answered.

2. Accounts of Change

How then did the left account for these social changes? One thing is certain: it did not just cleave to the old verities, as changing accounts of the economy, state and civil society, and the environment all show.

The Economy

So far as the economy was concerned, most debates revolved around *two* features of the British economy which the Thatcher years had drawn into sharp focus. One was the economy's continuing relative decline as a result of the weakness of many modernizing forces. No one, to the left or right, disputed the need for some form of structural change to restore the economy's fortunes. The Thatcher government offered the freeing of entrepreneurial spirit, overseen by a strong state. The left found it easy to criticize this economic strategy, less easy to devise alternatives. The second feature was the British economy's degree of internationalization. Britain is a remarkably internationalized economy by comparison with other national economies. In 1988, for example, Britain was the world leader in foreign acquisitions. It also possessed the highest ratio in the world of foreign acquisitions to gross domestic fixed capital formation. In manufacturing industry, foreigners own or control just over 20 per cent of total production and one in seven workers is now employed in a foreign-owed firm (Auerbach 1989). By the year 2000 Japanese companies will account for one-tenth of Britain's manufacturing output (*The Economist* 22 September 1990: p. 33). Thus, it is no surprise that the reasons for economic decline and the importance of the international economy became the most important features of work by the left. The rethinking took three chief forms.

The first of these was an attempt to retheorize the restructuring of production as a *microeconomic process*. Most especially, this effort tended to concentrate on the restructuring of the *labour process* and *labour markets* (e.g. Atkinson 1985, Rubery 1987), summarized in the phrase "labour market flexibility". For the most part this line of thinking was simply a careful attempt to begin to understand the rapid restructuring of labour but it can also be taken as an inquiry into the long-term costs to the overall economy of the extension of the interests of capital.

The second form of rethinking consisted of an attempt to document Britain's role in the changing world economy, especially through the notion of Britain's role in a new "post-Fordist" *macroeconomic regime of accumulation* that would replace the old Fordist regime of mass production and consumption. This was a model with its roots in the work of Aglietta in the 1970s which was then expanded upon (and changed to a considerable degree) in the work of other members of the French regulation school like Lipietz and Boyer (Dunford 1990). It was adopted with enthusiasm by many on the left in the mid-1980s but by the late 1980s considerable doubts were being expressed about some aspects of the approach (Jessop 1990, Sayer 1990).

The third form of rethinking consisted of work on the relative efficacy of plan and market. This work had a practical imperative in that the government was committed to the extension of the free market into all walks of economic life. But it also had a theoretical imperative, a mixture of the discussions on planning in centralized economies generally (especially centred around Nove's *The Economics of Feasible Socialism*) and attempts to formulate a convincing case for more government intervention in the British economy on the German or Japanese model.

These three forms of rethinking came together in a fourth, overarching theory of industrial change which suggested that the world economy, and Britain within it, were moving towards a new regime of flexible accumulation.

> With the crisis of mass production, new flexible technologies and productive processes were introduced based on the optimisation of economies of scope rather than of scale economies. New Marshallian flexible industrial districts are becoming the spearhead of economic growth. . . . They are characterized by a decentralised production system and a highly flexible labour market, locally integrated but organisationally disintegrated, specialising in particular market niches and using new mechanisms of shop-floor labour organisation, logical organisation of the production process (such as just in time) and labour management (Swyngedouw 1989: p. 36).

This fourth form of rethinking synthesized all the previous three adding together work on flexible labour markets, the regulation approach and thinking on plan versus market (in that it took much of its impetus from the markets and hierarchies approach to be found in modified neoclassical economics). But it went further than this, by adding in a *meso-economic* level, the *mode of regulation*, conceived as an ensemble of norms, institutions, organizational forms, social networks and patterns of conduct which guides the regime of accumulation and promotes compatibility in a system under stress, found most especially in the guise of the state and the financial system. Thus, the debate on reasons for economic decline and the importance of the international economy started to move away from a purely economic analysis.

In geography in Britain, these concerns were chiefly expressed through work on restructuring theory and localities. Restructuring theory was formulated against a background of extensive spatial change in the fabric of the British economy and society, such as the decline of manufacturing in large cities (especially London), the decentralization of population and employed from large cities, the rapid increase in women in the labour force in certain parts of the country, the rise of industries like banking and finance, especially in the South East of England, and, most recently, the transformation of some inner city areas by financial capital. Each of these changes affected the organizational base of the left to different degrees in different places (usually adversely, it has to be said).

Restructuring theory was concerned simply with how this spatial unevenness was caused by the processes of capitalism. It was a task which at first may have seemed relatively straightforward, but it soon became clear that the structuralist pedigree of much of the early work could lead too easily into the trap of reductionism and most particularly to the elimination of:

> its own theoretical object. If taken literally, it had the effect of reducing all spatial effects to non-spatial social relations. The spatial disappeared, being ultimately "entirely social". There was something wrong with a Marxist geography that obliterated space and denied geography any genuine existence. This reductionism was inconsistent with the aim of the restructuring approach to situate and explain specificities, rather than eliminate them (Lovering, 1989: p. 210).

Thus it was that an interest in "localities" became prominent from 1984 onwards (Massey 1984a, b, Cooke 1989, Duncan and Savage 1991), an idea which was intended to redress the reductionism of the previous approach of restructuring. Studies of localities would show the range of differential responses to international economic restructuring, and the constitutive nature of these different responses on that process of restructuring. Theoretically, they would demonstrate the importance of space as an active part of social process. Practically, they would put people on the ground to see what was happening. Further, locality studies would have to be an empirical exercise, to begin with, because in the new non-reductionist climate it was realized that geographical outcomes could no longer be seen as predictable or determinate.

Locality studies, then, were intended to focus both theoretical and political attention. That they have subsequently become identified as the progenitors of a new movement in human geography is an interesting example of social processes of academic "spectacularization" at work in the US, but it should not be allowed to direct attention from their original genesis as a modest, but absolutely necessary, step towards understanding the changes in British economy and society as spatially constituted as well as constitutive. As Massey (1991: p. 280) puts it:

> It is true that the current programme of locality studies was proposed for reasons which were historically specific. They arose from the situation *then* and *there*. And moreover that situation was not one only, or even primarily defined by academic/intellectual debate. It was a situation defined by what was happening in society more widely, and by important questions which were raised as a result of those changes. Such a history, in other words, does not imply that locality research, the study of particular places, should in some more general sense, always and everywhere, be the focus of human geographical enquiry. Sometimes we may want to study particular localities for particular strategic reasons. Most often, indeed, we may find that other focuses of research will be more important.

Seen in this way, many of the subsequent criticisms of locality research (e.g. Smith 1987) were misdirected. The constant tendency to muddle up the concrete and the locality (as if only localities were concrete), the easy assumption that studying localities somehow means fetishising them, the tendency to brand locality studies as exercises in unbridled empiricism; these were all straws in the wind.

The State and Civil Society

Through the 1980s Britain's state apparatus became ever more centralized. Old corporatist modes of government, based on bargaining between organized interests (Gamble 1988), were discredited. They were replaced, according to many analysts, by a "strong state" motivated by the Thatcherite project of reversing long-term economic decline, weakening the social democratic concensus and pursing a cold war in international politics.

In the early 1980s the British state, and issues of the state more generally, received considerable attention from the left. However, by the mid-1980s interest in the state had waned (but see Giddens 1985). The chief debate tended to take place around notions of a "strong state" (Gamble 1988), and the state as a pivot of a new mode of regulation (Jessop 1990). In some senses, this comparative lack of attention to the state is a surprise. After all, as Hall (1988: p. 279) pointed out, there are many unanswered questions:

> Our critique of statism remains at an extremely primitive level. If the state is no longer to be the monolithic caretaker of socialism, what is it? What are the institutional forms of a responsive (rather than prescriptive state?). Or a regulative (rather than a centralising state?). Of a state whose function is not to curtail but to expand civil society and the democratic character of social life? . . . Can the left abandon the ideas of the rational planning of resources and the rational choice between priorities in a society of scarcity . . . ? Can we combine a greater use of the market mechanism with greater regulation . . . ?

The study of the state was displaced from centre stage by the study of civil society. Partly this was, in fact, connected to theorizing the state: there was a clear need to think through a form of society in which the state was not an ever-expanding monolithic entity but a more diverse and democratized presence. It was also the result of a "cultural turn", a synthesis of practical/political and theoretical concerns, for what was most clear was that developments in an increasingly plural civil society had outrun the ability of those on the left to explain them. Most particularly, there was the problem of how the Thatcherite project had been allowed to succeed. To many on the left Thatcherism seemed to have won the "struggle for popular identities" (Hall 1988: p. 282). It seemed to understand popular aspirations better than the left which was still locked into an old equation of the welfare state and the working class.

Therefore, if the shocks to the left administered by the changes in forms and state of the economy were substantial, those administered by civil society were probably even greater. The first of these shocks was the nationalism engendered by the Falklands War.

> To anyone brought up on the war poets—standard reading in an English school—and associating naval expeditions with gun-boat diplomacy and the rhetoric of national glory with *1066 and All That*, it seemed that the country had gone mad. The drowning of 500 Latin American sailors was treated as a national triumph, the sacrifice of British lives as a restoration of national greatness. The "tall, wiry" men with silvery grey hair and "boyish" good looks were once again in command (Samuel 1989: p. x).

The reaction of the left to this new state of affairs was to turn to issues of meaning and culture, and especially to the construction of "Englishness" (Colls and Dodd 1986). In particular, attention was given to the importance of the study of the invention of "national" traditions (Hobsbawn and Ranger 1983) and, using Anderson's (1983) seminal phrase, the creation of "imagined communities", "imagined because the members of even the smallest nation will never know most of their fellow members, meet them, or even hear them, yet in the minds of each lives the image of their communion" (Anderson 1983: p. 15). As time went by, however, something of a division opened up between those for whom an affirmative national tradition could exist, at least in principle, as a radicalized sense of belonging drawing on particular historical ideas and events and those for whom any kind of idea of national belonging was anathema, "the special inheritance of a popular soul by definition undefeated and forever struggling towards the light" (Nairn 1988: p. 380). Whichever the case, the extraordinary three volume work edited by Samuel (1989), *Patriotisms,* shows the degree to which nationalism concerned the left in the 1980s.

A similar cultural concern also surfaced in work on race. That work had began as a documentary account of the racial divides of Britain, but already in the 1970s it had become concerned with cultural issues, especially as a result of the work of the CCCS in Birmingham. In the 1980s the literature on race increasingly dwelt on notions of racialization and especially the construction of racialized nations of national identity. Thus in history,

> in order to integrate . . . black historians we found ourselves forced to reinterpret earlier passages in national history; we had to take more seriously what was originally no more than a rhetorical flourish: the proposition that Britain is a land peopled by minorities and that the English, except as a figment of the patriotic imagination, do not exist (Samuel 1989: p. xiii).

The most influential book of the 1980s on race, Gilroy's (1988) *There Ain't No Black in the Union Jack,* precisely showed the new connections between work on nationalism and racism. Work on gender similarly began to follow these new avenues of approach. The 1980s had started with the dual systems approach being most popular in which women's oppression was seen as being the result of the articulation of class (capital) and gender (Hartmann 1978). By the end of the 1980s this kind of approach had been discredited and had been replaced by an approach which stressed notions of culture and subjectivity (Lovell 1989), work that was grouped under the heading of the social construction of gender and sexuality.

> For the moment, women, still had a problematic place in both social and psychic representation. The problem for women of women-as-signs has made the self-definition of women a resonant issue within feminism. It has also determined the restless inability of feminism to settle for humanist definitions of the subject, or for materialism's relegation of the problem to determinations of class only (Kaplan 1986: p. 62).

Such work on nationalism, race and gender clearly had to have an effect on the left shibboleth of class.

As with the other social dimensions, work on class became increasingly cultural, a tendency that had begun with Thompson's *The Making of the English Working Class*, and was cemented by Stedman-Jone's (1980) *Languages of Class*. But, this work on class and culture tended to bring class down from the pedestal on which the left had placed it. Class became one of a number of different structuring forces in society and not necessarily the most prominent one. Some were willing to go further. Thus Gilroy (1988: p. 245) concludes that:

> if . . . struggles (some of which are conducted in and through "race") are to be called class struggles, then class analysis must itself be thoroughly overhauled. I am not sure whether the labour involved in doing this makes it either a possible or a desirable task. The liberating rationality which informs these struggles has found new modes of expression which stress what can be called neo-populist themes. They appeal directly to "the people". By contrast, the political languages of class and socialism have been so thoroughly discredited by labourism at home and "actually exiting socialism" abroad that they may be completely beyond recuscitation.

For those who still accepted the need for a language of class—as fact and fiction—problems still remained. In particular, it was clear that the nature of class was changing. A "service class" of managers and professionals was growing in importance, basing their power on monopolization of educational credentials as well as work and labour market situations (Abercrombie and Urry 1983, Lash and Urry 1987, Thrift and Williams 1987). Gender was also being seen as increasingly crucial to the formation of class. Thus, the number of highly-paid women professional and managerial workers was growing (Crompton and Sanderson 1990) and so were the number of low-paid part-time women workers (Beechey 1986).

What, then, were the common components of these four different dimensions of society that the left fixed upon? The first was the attention paid to discourses and textuality in the construction of human beings. That is, it was assumed that people were born into and out of discourses and could contribute to them even when they died through the trace of texts. By the end of the 1980s such work had become the norm, chiefly through the influence of French poststructuralist social theorists like Foucault on genealogy and power–knowledge relations, Derrida on deconstruction, Lyotard on the libidinal economy, and Baudrillard on fatal strategies.

This component was related to a second common component, the need to understand the formation of identity. In particular, the left developed the idea that identity is fractured. It consists of a "promiscuous variety of belongings" (Samuel 1989: p. xv) like nation, race, gender and class which are only partly related to each other by "technologies of the self".

The third common component, springing out of the previous two, and from the increasingly authoritarian pressures exerted by the "strong state", stressed the importance of redefining the public community through the notion of citizenship. This was the chief way in which the left approached the problem of democracy (Hirst 1989). Work on nationalism and politics increasingly stressed the legal and political constitution of citizens (Gamble 1988). Work on race became increasingly involved with notions of citizenship (Smith 1988). Work on gender, influenced especially by the work of Pateman (1986, 1989), showed how civil society was a male construct, implicity and explicity devaluing women's rights (Benton 1988). Women are defined in the first place "by sexual differences, as wives and mothers, daughters and spinsters" (Samuel 1988: p. xiv). Finally, work on class looked more and more closely at citizenship as a means of securing political influence for the dispossessed by defining a basic bundle of citizenship rights (Burnett 1988). In other words, the intention was to redefine British democracy, making it more plural in response to an increasingly plural society and making it more accessible to those with fewer political resources.

As these new components arrived in the work of the left, so they began to be pieced together into explanations of the left's political failure. Perhaps the most influential of these explanations at the beginning of the 1980s characterized Thatcherism as "authoritarian populism". This was a notion first advanced by Hall in the late 1970s (see Hall 1988). It was a development of the Gramscian notion of hegemony, on to which was grafted the work of other writers like Lacan and Foucault. According to this analysis Thatcherism was successful because it had established "a hegemonic discourse . . . (which) plays upon and resonates with elements of the identities, daily experiences and beliefs which people already have". It was able to do this because subjects do not have fully fixed loyalties and beliefs nor internally unified and coherent ideologies. Instead their identities are fractured, multiple and contradictory, so that space exists for ideological struggle (Jessop *et al.* 1988: p. 42).

One problem, of course, was the elusive nature of this definition of hegemony. In practice, did authoritarian populism consist of "a new form of state; the ideological complement to a more directly disciplinary form of state; or the specific conjunctions of class struggles?" (Jessop *et al.* 1988: p. 43). In Hall's writings, this was unclear. More to the point, it had to be asked whether hegemony existed at all. After all, little more than 42 per cent of the electorate voted for the Conservatives in each of the three elections that they won, while survey after survey has shown that many parts of the Thatcher programme that were held most dear had no widespread public support (Hirst 1989).

Thus, by the middle of the 1980s other cultural explanations were being tried. One of the most persuasive was that consumption was to blame; it was diverting attention from grappling with capitalism. Thus work on consumption in the 1970s and early 1980s was concerned with consumption sector cleavages, usually those around home ownership, which were leading to the fragmentation of class politics. But perhaps the most pervasive images were drawn from Jameson's (1984) development of Baudrillard, presenting British society as in the grip of an orgy of superficial and surficial consumption, a kind of postmodern semiotic feeding frenzy, characterized by hyperconformist differentation and a general hypnotic asociality. These images were only sharpened by the consumption boom in Britain in the mid-1980s.

Unfortunately, the strategy of blaming the voter/consumer, with its 1930s mass consumption critique overtones, did not bear closer examination. Detailed empirical and theoretical work on television, advertising and consumer culture showed that consumption was part of a complex and contradictory process of symbolic work (Bourdieu 1984, Featherstone 1991). Commercial consumption was not a slavishly conformist process of passive reception.

> Commercial cultural forms have helped to produce an historical present from which we cannot now escape and in which there are many more materials—no matter what we think of them—available for necessary symbolic work than ever there were in the past. Out of these came forms not dreamt of in the commercial imagination and certainly not in the official one . . . Commerce appears twice in the cultural argument, as that which is to be escaped from and that which provides the means and materials for alternatives (Willis 1990: p. 19).

The fact of the matter was that Britain in the 1980s was as combative as ever; material and symbolic struggles still raged as they had before (Thrift and Forbes 1981). The problem was that these struggles had moved away from the left's traditional terrain.

Geography was a crucial element of these debates on state and civil society. It made an appearance in three main ways. First, more and more attention was paid to the geography of discourse and textuality. On one level, this simply meant an appreciation of the contextual dimension of discourses and texts (Thrift 1985, 1986, 1990). On another level, more and more attention was given to the constitutive powers of geographical metaphors, rhetorics and so on. For example, in the case of gender, the distinction between public and private has come under intense scrutiny (Rose 1990).

The second appearance of geography was around the issue of identity. Identity is clearly based, to a degree, on territory. For example, Gilroy (1988: p. 243) notes the strong symbolic boundaries of the territories of rioters.

> The strong association of identity and territory which is revealed is also expressed in the language of community employed by riot participants. This language suggests that area-based notions of group solidarity provided an important unifying factor for crowd behaviour. Community was a strong theme in subsequent local political organising around the issue which had generated the riots.

Third, there was the geography of citizenship; "within a nation state, the rights to work, pursue a chosen lifestyle and participate in political decisions are all socially differentiated, and may impinge in different ways on the structuring of society and space" (Smith 1989: p. 150). In other words, the right to citizenship is spatially as well as socially variable and this has constitutive implications.

In geography itself, these issues tended to cluster around three chief problematics. The first of these, associated especially with the work of Jameson (1984) and Harvey (1985, 1989, 1990) concerned a change in the representation of space and time, resulting from processes like the growth of telecommunications that "revolutionise the objective qualities of space and time" (Harvey 1989: p. 240). Harvey takes this "time–space compression" to be at the heart of postmodern experiences. The second problematic has been the locality. Writers like Cooke (1990) and Jackson (1991) have been concerned to push locality research into this cultural sphere. Finally, more and more attention has been paid, since the original, seminal "radical cultural geography issue" of *Antipode* (1983), to notions of landscape, as a key spatial metaphor, as a means of fostering local, regional and national identity, and as a key to notions of citizenship (Cosgrove and Daniels 1988).

The Environment

The environment has become an issue of significance for the left only comparatively recently in Britain compared with a number of other countries such as Germany. The left is now trying to regain the environmental high ground (the Communist Party, for example, has now sworn to follow the path of "ecological economics"), but this has not proved an easy task because of the theoretical legacy the left inherited.

As Benton (1989) makes clear, Marx and many subsequent Marxists tended to assume that there were no realities that were invulnerable to human intentionality, partly because of an understandable political reluctance to give ground to the Malthusians, and partly because of a tendency to magnify the transformative powers of capitalism. Now we know that the realm of necessity does not keep expanding. We also know that the limits of necessity vary from one society to another.

> What is required is the recognition that each form of social/economic life has its own specific mode and dynamic of inter-relation with its own specific contextual conditions, resource materials, energy sources, and naturally mediated unintended consequences (Benton 1989: p. 77).

But Benton's notion of forms of social/economic life tends to be restricted to aspects of political economy. As Urry (1990: p. 4) points out, there is a need to recognize:

> changing *cultural* configurations which transform what is actually taken to be "nature", what is "natural", in each society (such as the preference for deciduous rather than coniferous forests); and changing *political* definitions of how and why certain aspects of the physical and/or built environment are worth preserving or are deemed suitable for destruction—how nature is in a sense politicised.

Thus Urry points to widespread changes in the way that nature is currently read (thus humans are increasingly viewed as part of nature rather than distinct from it, Western science is increasingly viewed with suspicion, nature is increasingly regarded as having rights and people as yet unborn are regarded as having general rights of inheritance) and changes in political activity concerning the environment (O'Riordan 1989).

In geography, this work has crystallized around two notions. The first of these, chiefly an outgrowth of political economy, is the study of *political ecology*, "the attempt to identify the social and environmental causes of environmental degradation, resource depletion and maldistribution of benefits and liabilities" (Emel and Peet 1989: p. 61). The second notion, chiefly an outgrowth of the turn to culture referred to above, is the study of *landscape*. The meanings of environments can be created, extended, altered and elaborated in many ways according to dominant modes of representation and interpretation and the rise of the study of landscape is an acknowledgement of the importance of studying these modes in all their diversity (Cosgrove and Daniels 1988).

Apocalypse Now?

By the end of the 1980s, some were forecasting the demise of everything that the left held dear. In the pages of *Marxism Today* especially, "new times" had been reached. A new all-singing, all-dancing postmodern world had hoved into view to which the only answer was a kind of Star Trek Marxism, boldly going where no one had gone before. Thus, after years of "huffing and puffing" the left was "clearing the decks" for a "reconstruction" that would take account of a new form of "disorganized", "flexible" or "post-Fordist" capitalism.

> Our world is being remade. Mass production, the mass consumer, the big city, big brother state, the sprawling housing estate, and the nation state are in decline. Flexibility, diversity, differentation, mobility, communication, decentralisation and internationalisation are in the ascendant. In the process our own identities, our sense of self, our own subjectivities are being transformed. We are in transition to a new era (*Marxism Today*, October 1988, p. 3).

In other words, elements of the left were intent on transferring the post-Fordist model of economy and state into society as a whole (Jessop 1991).

The events in eastern Europe and the Soviet Union only seemed to set the seal on this change. The world geopolitical map was being remade and old cold war certainties were disappearing. The world, or so it seemed, had shifted into another gear. Whether this is actually the case still remains to be seen. Certainly, there are good reasons to doubt that a new form of capitalism has come into existence. And, as Halliday (1990: p. 23) has pointed out,

> the demise of communism does not necessarily change the left's agenda. The central question is (still) whether and how far there does exist an alternative to the predominant model of capitalism and, if so, what social agencies can be mobilized democratically to create and maintain it.

What does seem clear is that in the rush to acknowledge the wide ranging changes that were taking place, parts of the left were in danger of simply simulating those changes in theory. What was missing was an audit of what might count as advances in understanding. It is this that I now try to provide.

An Audit

In the next section I want to conduct an audit of British critical theory in the 1980s. I want to consider the degree to which the events outlined above and the short-term theoretical reactions to them, were converted into longer-term theoretical gains. In what ways did critical theory make fundamental and lasting advances, and what issues has it still to face up to?

Let us commence the audit with the positive advances. So far as the economy is concerned the left finally faced up to two issues of the greatest theoretical importance. The first was an issue of scale and scope. The large is no longer considered to be automatically impressive; indeed in many accounts quite the opposite. Where economies and organizations were often described in hierarchical terms, they are now often described as "flat". The left, with its research into flexible labour processes and labour markets, new methods of lean production, clusters of small firms and new forms of inter-firm co-operation, has undoubtedly been at the cutting edge of research into changes in modern economies. Theories of post-Fordism or disorganization have tried to capture these changes in broad terms and even if they have sometimes gone too far—one of the chief criticisms of much new work is that it too often ignores the parts of economies which are not at the cutting edge—they have still provided valuable heuristics.

Second, as privatization has bitten, so the left has faced up to the issues of plan and market. In Britain, this has meant much more emphasis is now places on so-called market socialism and on the operation of "quasi-markets" in public organizations (Estrin and Le Grand 1990). In line with theories of regulation, "regulatory regimes" (Tomlinson 1990) have become a critical part of this interest. Indeed the worry now for some on the left is that "the market" is being essentialized:

> The market is seen as part of the *principles* of the form of social organisation, and can function as a principle because it is an essence, i.e. can determine the key features of a society's function irrespective of any particular institutional characteristics. This is surely what the market cannot do. There is no such thing as "the market", but only markets, whose effects are determined by the agents who operate in them, their forms of calculation, their relations to other agents, and the legal and moral framework in which they operate (Tomlinson 1990: p. 43).

In the sphere of state and civil society, the gains have probably been even more impressive. Most particularly, no one now believes that class is the be-all and end-all of social life or that social life, culture and politics are necessarily organized on class lines. The rise of other social groupings based around race, gender, the environment and so on, means that social life and social conflict have become more pluralistic, structured by a wider variety of interests, and involve very many different "enemies". There is a consequent realization that the possibilities for radical collective action can spring equally from the organizational possibilities provided by "race" or "gender" or "the environment" as they can from narrowly-based class politics (Gilroy 1988).

At the same time, and partly the result of this new emphasis on the plurality of civil society, the importance of discourse and textuality is now established. Most particularly, the importance of reflexivity is constantly asserted, most especially in the matter of the conditioning of description. Writers on the left are now much more aware of the disciplinary traditions from which they have emerged, of the presence in their texts of manifold references, of the fact that their texts are narratives that are full with metaphors, tropes and other devices to create aesthetic effects which strengthen rhetorical impacts. Texts are now "looked *at*, as well as through . . . are seen to be made, and made to persuade" (with the result that) "those who make them have rather more to answer for" (Geertz 1988: p. 138). Equally, the importance of the constitution of self and identities has become a major focus of work, both referring back to the study of discourse and textuality and extending it into new pastures, without losing sight of the fact that "our identities are still constituted through social hierarchy and cultural differentiation, as well as through those processes of division and fragmentation described in psycho-analytic theory" (Kaplan 1986: p. 63).

A third important advance has been across economy, state and civil society, and the environment. It is the increasing importance of globalization coupled with an increasing attention to the local (Urry 1990, Robertson 1990). Society can no longer be conceived of almost exclusively as the bounded nation state; its bounds have moved out to encompass the world.

> This century has seen a drastic explosion of mobility, including tourism, migrant labour, immigration and urban sprawl. More and more people "dwell" with the help of mass transit, automobiles and airplanes. In cities on six continents foreign populations have come to stay—mixing in but often in partial, specific fashions. The "exotic" is uncannily close. Conversely, there seem to be no distant places left on the planet where the presence of "modern" products, media and power cannot be felt. An older topography of experience and travel is exploded. One no longer leaves home confident of finding something radically new, another time or space. Differences are encountered in the adjoining neighbourhood, the familiar turns up at the end of the earth (Clifford 1988: pp. 13-14).

But as societies have become more global, so the local may well have become more important at one and the same time. Thus "as spatial barriers diminish so we have become more sensitized to what the world's spaces contain" (Harvey 1989: p. 294). The race is on to make places seem different from one another.

A fourth important advance has been the increasingly attention paid to the role of space. From the work of Giddens in the early 1980s (Giddens 1984) and Mann in the mid-1980s (Mann 1986) to later work on postmodernism, space has been a key referent in contemporary social theory. Massey's slogan of 1984, "geography matters", still holds. Society is constructed through space as space is constructed through society and that fact makes difference: societies will never be seen again as integrated wholes but always and everywhere as unevenly interconnected mosaics.

Finally, and to summarize the gains, theory is much less confident than it once was: critical theory has become much more humble in its aims and, much more sensitive to *difference*. This can be demonstrated in a number of ways. First there is much greater awareness that critical theory (and its practitioners) are a part of the historical order, and have to be situated in it (Bourdieu 1988, 1989). The conditions of knowledge are now acknowledged in theoretical work; they have become a part of theory (Thrift 1979). In particular, texts are seen to be a vital part of the formation of subjectivity and of power relations. Second, and as a partial consequence, there is more authorial self-doubt: "neither presumption of innocence nor benefit of doubt is automatically accorded; indeed, save for correlation co-efficients and significance tests, they are not accorded at all" (Geertz 1988: p. 139). Authors are fractured subjects, just like readers (Henriques *et al.* 1984). Third, there is a fitting modesty to many "truth" claims, a modesty that is increasingly influenced by post-structuralist criticisms of originary concepts, binary metaphysics, and theoretical schemas that try to colonize the world (Norris 1990, 1991). Even Habermas, when it comes down to it, is only willing to assert, rather modestly, that "what it is to live well is somehow secretly embedded in that which makes us most distinctively what we are: language. The good life shadows our every discursive gesture" (Eagleton 1990a: p. 408). These changes do not, perhaps, paint the most alluring picture of modern critical theory. As Geertz (1988: p. 139) puts it, "half-convinced writers trying to half-convince readers of their (the writers) half convictions would not on the face of it seem an especially favourable situation for the production of works of very much power". But the successes in the 1980s of theoretical approaches like critical realism (Bhaskar 1989), which recognize the grounds of their being, and the continued production of interesting and important works of social theory, suggest otherwise. Of course, it is possible to go too far, promoting a cult of difference, of the heterogeneous, which ultimately shows a scant regard for difference (Eagleton 1990b), but that has been a characteristic of French rather than British critical theory.

These, then, are the gains of British critical theory in the 1980s. But there have also been a series of problems and challenges that critical theorists have not taken sufficiently to heart. Therefore, I now want to move to the debit side of this audit.

So far as the economy has been concerned, two challenges have not been taken up wholeheartedly and the result has been that critical economic theory remains a lopsided project. The first of these has been a retreat from consideration of the processes of concentration and centralization implicit in the existence of the large firm. At a point in time when large firms have become more important than ever, many theorists seem to have decided that they are in decline. Of course, large corporations have become more decentralized, "flatter" and "leaner" than they once were. The declining size of factories (but not so far of offices), the increase in strategic alliances, the increased use of subcontracting, all of these have contributed to this process. Further, it has become much clearer that large firms co-exist with other forms of industrial organization. But the fact remains that these flatter, more diffuse large firms still exert enormous and unequal *power*—and we need to understand the way that they do this. Perhaps, as Jameson (1990: p. 244) points out, "the utterly outmoded doctrine of monopoly capital may be just the image we need . . . to track the system into its most minute recesses and crannies". Certainly, as Jameson points out, the search for the new decentralized monopoly capital is important, even though it will not end at "the grim and windowless headquarters we thought we were looking for". The second challenge, still to be fully faced, concerns the primacy of production. The majority of the *theoretical* work done on the economy in the 1980s by the left in Britain was on the transformation of the productive economy. The issue of the "non-productive" industries involved in distribution, circulation, exchange and consumption has received much less theoretical attention, as has the issue of the industries connected with the production, circulation, exchange and consumption of money. This bias to production fits clearly into the Marxist tradition of emphasizing production and demonstrating suspicion of trade and money, a tradition which, in fact, is much older than Marx.

> One particularly prominent strand in Western discourse, which goes back to Aristotle, is the general condemnation of money and trade in the light of an ideal of household self-sufficiency and production for use.... Profit-oriented exchange is (regarded as) unnatural; and is destructive of the bonds between households. Prices should therefore be fixed, and goods and services remunerated in accordance with the status of those who provide them. Money as a tool intended only to facilitate exchange is naturally barren, and, of all the ways of getting wealth, lending at interest—where money is made to yield a "crop" or "litter"—is "the most contrary to nature".
>
> Aristotle's writings re-surfaced in the Western World in the thirteenth century and were taken up by Thomas Aquinas through whom they achieved a new renown. His influence on the economic thought and attitude of the Middle Ages was, as Polanyi observes, quite as great as that which Smith and Ricardo were to exercise on the thinking of a subsequent epoch, and his authority was invoked in support of the Church's profound disquiet about material acquisition ... one of the major problems was that the merchant apparently created nothing while the usurer earned money even as he slept. "The labourer is worthy of his hire" but it was not at all clear that the merchant and the money lender laboured. It was essentially this idea of material production as the source of value which prompted Tawney to remark that the last true descendant of the doctrines of Aquinas is the labour theory of value. The last of the school men was Karl Marx (Parry and Bloch 1989: pp. 2-3).

Of course, in the British case, there is good reason to emphasize production, but there is just as pressing a need to work out theoretically how the "non-productive" activities fit in. This need was made more pressing in the late 1980s when Britain passed through a consumption boom based on the efficiency of its non-productive industries and the inefficiency of many of its productive ones, with ultimately disastrous consequences. There is still only a very limited amount of *theoretical* work by critical theorists that allows this task to be carried through, specifically the work of writers like Ingham (1984) and Anderson (1987) which, for all its flaws, (see, for example, Daunton 1990) does at least address the issues.

The second problem is associated with the turn to discourse and textuality. In the case of discourse I believe the problem is the overwhelming emphasis on language as the metaphor for communication (Hunt 1989, Chartier 1985). In one sense, it may be that the meaning of language simply needs to be broadened out, so that it includes not only writing but also visual images, music, smell; discourse in its fullest sense (Potter and Weatherall 1987). To a degree this has been happening as the new interest in "landscape" and "figural" communication (e.g. Lash 1990) makes clear. But in another sense, this incremental strategy may be inadequate. As Levin (1988: p. 29) puts it:

> The fact is we don't even know if we know all the ways of thinking and perceiving and we certainly don't now much about the ones we have so far attempted to classify. Language is muddled up with everything else the body does and there is no general reason—even a pragmatist one—to isolate it and declare this is what we're all about, the rest is conceptually insignificant.

Seen in this way, the new emphasis on the body is a hopeful step in the right direction, pointing as it does to the spatiality of communication. But what concerns me most about these different ways of framing discourse, as an expanded notion of language or as something different to language, is that they lack a developed theoretical framework which amalgamates people and the object world in the contexts which so often give communication its (unspoken) meaning. Hagerstrand's attempt to create an ecology of position through time—geography still seems to me to be useful here in that it points to the need to analyse context theoretically in order to understand how categories, identities, selves and intentuality constantly shift, and vice versa. (I think Hagerstrand was trying, to use one of Raymond Williams' phrases, to create a "particularism" rather than simply a catalogue of *difference*. The problem is to make this into what Williams called "a militant particularism", one which recognizes lines of power and conflict that are involved in contexts.) Perhaps the most interesting work currently being done in this area concerns deaf people's visual language of "sign", which is explicitly spatial in character, and which is much more carefully keyed into context (Sacks 1989). This "grammaticization" of space may well repay further study.

In the case of textuality, many authors have taken their cue from post-structuralist authors, most particularly Derrida, who stress the socially constituted nature of texts, and point to the equal importance of writing and speech (Dews 1987). Thus Derrida describes a shimmering, nomadic play of meaning that is always unstable and undecidable in which meaning constantly escapes "individual" presence. Notwithstanding a number of protestations to the contrary (Doel 1991), in the end it seems to me that Derrida does let the world become a generalized text with all the problems that this engenders.

But there is another way. Most particularly this is to be found in the extensive historical and anthropological work on literacy and the interface between the oral and the written, between speech and writing, (see Goody 1989, Chartier 1987, Ong 1982, Vincent 1989, Furet and Ozouf 1982) as well as in the sociological work on the reception of texts, especially that of Bourdieu. This work regards the texts of Derrida, Foucault and others as something of a simplification (if that is possible) "of the process by which works take on meaning" (Chartier 1989: p. 161), as not producing sufficient emphasis on the symbolic work of reading, as not giving enough attention to the productions of texts, as not paying enough attention to "the text itself, the object that conveys the text, and the act that grasps it" (Chartier 1989: p. 161). This body of work also emphasizes the fluidity and complexity of meaning, but it does so in a way which is historically *and* geographically situated. Texts are not everywhere in all times, rhizomatically reproducing themselves.

> We have a choice between two models for making sense of texts, books and their readers. The first contrasts discipline and invention, presenting these categories not as antagonistic but as an interrelated pair. Every textual or typographical moment that aims to create, control and constraint always secretes tactics that tame or subvert it, conversely there is no production or cultural practice that does not rely on materials imposed by tradition, authority, or the market and that is not subjected to surveillance and censures from those who have power over words or gestures. . . .
>
> Discipline and invention most be considered, but so must distinction and divulation. This second pair of interdependent ideas enables us to posit an understanding of objects and cultural models that is not reductive to a simple process of diffusion, one generally thought to descend along the social ladder. The processes of imitation or vulgarisation are more complex and more dynamic and must be considered, above all, as struggles of competition. In these struggles every divulgation, conceded or won, produces simultaneously the search for a new distinction (Chartier 1989: pp. 173–174).

Third, there is the problem of reflexivity. The turn to the light industry of literary theory in so many of the social sciences (in anthropology, social history, sociology, human geography) and the consequent privileging of culture has had many benefits (Thrift 1982). But, it can go too far. For example, in anthropology, a discipline under real threat, we find the emergence of a postmodern ethnography (Clifford and Marcus 1986), a practice which often seems in danger of worshipping reflexivity, with the attendant risks of falling over into aestheticism: much of the writing is, as even Geertz (1988: p. 137) admits, "pumped up and febrile". Granted, the easy realism of some previous anthropological texts is no longer an option but neither is the replacement of the act of description by a self-referential constipation.

Postmodern ethnography also draws attention to other tendencies that have arisen from the increasing tendency of relexivity. The first of these is the "spectacularization" (Friedman 1989) of texts by authors: texts become self-referential agonies to be worn as badges of courage; authority becomes a performance art. The second is what seems to be an increasing "spectacularization" of authors (ironically, usually running contrary to the messages of many of these authors' works concerning the death of the author). This is particularly the case in the English-speaking world at present where texts by foreign authors are much more likely to be translated when they are bizarre. Thus Moi (1987: p. 6) points to the lack of translation of French feminist writing that is rooted in historical and social reality because such texts "are perceived as lacking in exotic difference". In other words, the turn to reflexivity may be vital but there are real dangers. Spencer's (1989: p. 162) ironically understated judgement on postmodern ethnography can be generalized:

> A critic once likened the music of the great Afro-American composer, Thelonius Monk to the feeling of "missing the bottom step in the dark", that brief moment of vertigo when the familiar and unexpected drops away. I suspect most anthropologists aspire to a similar ability to upset the apple-cart of cultural expectation (but . . .) this ability cannot be reduced to recipes and formulas from the light industry that is American literary criticism: as Sperber says: "ideally . . . each anthropologist should rethink the ethnographic genre". In the end, though, we may also need to rethink the style of anthropological work as well as the style of anthropological writing.

A third problem is the way in which it seems that history is being abandoned for fear of being tarred with the brush of historicism. This problem reaches its apogee in Soja's (1989) "spectacularization" of geography where historicism is broadly defined as "an overdeveloped historical contextualization of social life and social theory that actually submerges and particularizes the geographical and spatial imagination" (p. 15). Quite clearly, the power of geography has been overlooked in the study of social life, and in social theory, but there is an equal problem of going too far the other way and ignoring "the extraordinary importance and power of historiography" (Soja 1989: p. 15). The problem (which some will no doubt connect with the nature of the postmodern world) has manifested itself in a number of ways.

The first of these is what often seems like an inflating currency of unsubstantiated statements about the nature of modern societies. Since practically every statement made about postmodern societies comes into this category, I will take only two. Thus, first of all, Harvey (1989, 1990) insists that heightened time–space compression provokes ephemerality, confusion, disruption, fragmentation and "a turn to aesthetics" (p. 328). One has to ask, quite seriously, how such claim could ever be evaluated (Massey 1991), but, if it could, I am not at all sure that such a conclusion would be reached. Second, Lash (1990), in common with many other authors, insists that we have reached an age of "figural" discourse in which images have taken over from texts and narratives. Again, one has to ask how such a claim might be validated. Again, I am not sure that such a conclusion might be reached in historical terms (what of medieval societies, for example, where images were a major currency). The list could go on but it seems clear that there is a real danger that assertions drawn from the experience of middle class cultural elites will be taken as general realities.

A second manifestation is the sense in which most modern work in social science now seems to have forked into either micro-studies or massive transhistorical adventures. The result is that the sense of history or geography falls between the two paths. This is why the work of authors like Michael Mann, and of movements like the new regional geography, are so important: they keep a hold on history *and* geography (Anderson 1990). The third manifestation consists of the way in which certain segments of the community can simply be painted out of history. Acknowledgement of difference has lead to curious indifference over the fate of certain sections of the community. For example, any survey of the 1980s has to note the way in which the respectable white working class often seemed to have been marginalized in the writings of the left "deemed (to be) beyond the pale, lost to socialism, and . . . therefore . . . dumped in favour of other groups who more easily seem to recognise and rebel against their claims" (Walkerdine and Lucey 1989: p. 13; see also Bianchini 1987).

To conclude, any audit of long-term advances in British critical theory in the 1980s would, I think, be positive. These advances have been outlined. The problems that have arisen have chiefly come from forgetting that texts do not just have to be *interpreted*, they also have to be *interrogated* within their social, historical and geographical context.

Conclusions

If there was one thing that took the British left by surprise in the 1980s it was the way in which the sheer ebullience and inventiveness of civil society had outrun its theoretical and practical preconceptions and prescriptions. The left responded with a programme of theoretical work, much of which has been outlined above, which helped to lead it towards a "politics of diversity" that would enable it to encompass non-class political groupings. Geography was a crucial part of this move, both because of its increasing political importance, and because of the growing awareness of its theoretical importance as the ground of difference.

But one might well argue that this programme of theoretical work has not been sufficient. If the key practical, theoretical and moral issue for the left is a "struggle for popular identities" (Hall 1988: p. 282) then the problem is that the left still has relatively little grasp of processes of identification/longing/belonging. Currently, the study of socialization and the theory of agency/social action which must underpin it is still too often based on relatively little in the way of coherent theory: rather, there are islands of understanding set in seas of ignorance.

This theoretical project must encompass at least the three Cs of context, childhood and community, as part of a more general enquiry into how identity is formed and maintained.

The first C is context. What has been most noticeable about work in the early 1980s that called for a contextual dimension is that it was subverted in the late 1980s. Context was radically reduced to (i) simply a localized piece of space within which processes unfold (locality studies), (ii) a physical setting for social interaction (in Gidden's terms, a locale), (iii) any illustrative empirical study (Smith 1989). But context was meant to be the pivot of a theory of social agency, showing the way in which "people", understood as "cultural artefacts", consist of a series of dialogical personas constituted in and by particular settings, and in turn constituting these settings. The term was meant to point to the need to study processes of autobiography, memory, self-formation and identity as inherently geographical: places are people as much as people are places. Meaning does not exist without context (Folch-Serra 1990).

Second, and following on from this, there is a need for more research on *childhood*. So many longings, and belongings are formed in childhood, and become innate predispositions to act and interpret situations in particular ways. Yet we know surprisingly little about this process, even after decades of social psychology. In particular, there is a pressing need for more work on how children construct accounts of the state, money, and history (Walkerdine 1989). This will start to help us to support Steedman's (1986) and Walkerdine and Lucey's (1989) calls to focus on the social bases of imaginative life and the ways that they are crippled. As Steedman puts it in the introduction to the best book to arrive from the British left in the 1980s, *Landscape for a Good Woman*,

> This is a book about stories; and it is a book about things (objects, entities, relationships, people) and the way in which we talk and write about them: about the difficulties of metaphor. Above all, it is about people wanting these things, and the structures of political thought that have labelled this wanting as wrong (Steedman 1986: p. 23).

In other words, we need to step into fantasy, and childhood may be the best way to approach it. I do not mean by fantasy "the irrational" which, as Jameson (1990: p. 237) points out, has simply "become the dumping ground for anything one wishes to exclude", but the identification of desire and its interpretive devices.

Third, and finally, we must turn to *community* again. It seems to me that we still know surprisingly little about what community is in the modern world, defined as an association of shared interest and feeling. This is the case in a number of ways. First, most of the work on communities has been work on "forced" communities, especially working class communities of the last two centuries where community could certainly be positive but was often defensive. We need to know more about the myriad "unforced" communities which have come together voluntarily—from ecologists to stamp collectors. One indicator of this is the *Directory of British Associations*. It now lists more than 6,500 organizations, a 76 per cent rise on the 3,700 entries in the first edition printed in 1965 (*Financial Times*, 22 September 1990,

p. viii). Although we can hazard guesses (including a general rise in education qualifications, the explosion of consumer culture, and the growth of the service class), there is no work that currently enables us to understand the reasons for this increase. Second, we need to know the forms communities can take, why people identify with them, and the degree of commitment people show to them. One of the remarkable things about modern societies is the sheer number of communities that have come into existence and the multiplying membership of them. Yet no one would know from the writings of British left that the fastest growing social movement in Britain today is Evangelical Christianity. Third, we need to know how geography intervenes and helps to constitute these communities, communities which are now rarely based on defined pieces of territory in ways that they once were. We know surprisingly little, for example, about how modern telecommunications has affected human sociability (Meyrowitz 1985; Kirby 1989, Thrift 1990).

These three priorities are important precisely because the left has become isolated from British civil society. As Campbell (1988: p. 38) puts it:

> We think of politics as being meetings. It speaks volumes that political culture in Britain has become, as one of my local MPs told me, a case of going to 400 meetings a year. Now what kind of human being is that? No cooking, no nappy changing . . . He's probably proud of the squalor in which he lives, because that is a testament to his political commitment. Now, I'm being trivial here, but actually what people do as political action is, they read, they buy, they refuse to buy, and they commit all sorts of acts which are about participation in a culture. Its only nutcases in ever-declining political organisations who think that the only political act is to go to a meeting.

As they used to say: only connect. Now the message is: only reconnect, but reconnect with a pluralistic world. That requires finding a particularism which can be universalized and in this, as in much else, Eagleton (1990: p. 414) points the way to a genuine oppositional imagination:

> The final purpose of our universality, of our equal rights to participate in the public definition of meanings and values, is that the unique particularities of individuals may be respected and fullfilled. Particularity returns again at a "higher" level: difference must pass through identity if it is to come into its own, a position distinctly abandoned by much contemporary theory. It is not a matter of what Raymond Williams calls a "militant particularism"—of those currently categorised as "other"—women, foreigners, homosexuals—simply demanding recognition for what they are. What is it to "be" a woman, a homosexual, a native

> of Ireland? It is true, and important, that such excluded groups will already have developed certain styles, values, life-experiences which can be appealed to now as a form of political expression; but the more fundamental political question is that of "demanding" an equal right with others to discover what one might become, not of assuming some already fully-fashioned identity which is merely repressed. All "oppositional identities" are in part the function of oppression, as well as of resistance to that oppression, and in this sense what one might become cannot simply be read off from what one is now . . . the universal, then, is not some reaction of abstract duty set sternly against the particular; it is just every individual's equal right to have his or her difference respected, and to participate in the common process whereby that can be achieved.

In other words, in Britain now, the chief imperative is to find out how, why, with what and where people belong: what their economic, social and cultural resources are and how they wield them. This is a necessary first step to establishing a new notion of collectivity, one which is not associated with uniformity and subordination but is "active, demanding and creative" (Campbell 1988: p. 39). It remains to be seen whether this will occur.

Acknowledgements

I would like to acknowledge the many helpful criticisms made of a first draft of this paper at the Nordic Institute of Social Geographers' annual conference in Joenssuu in September 1990.

References

Abercrombie, N., and Urry, J. (1983) *Capital, Labour and the Middle Classes* Allen & Unwin, London.
Anderson, B. (1983) *Imagined Communities* Verso, London.
Anderson, P. (1987) Figures of descent, *New Left Review*, No. 161.
Anderson, P. (1990a) A culture in contraflow—I, *New Left Review*, No. 180.
Anderson, P. (1990b) A culture in contraflow—II, *New Left Review*, No. 182, pp. 85-137.
Antipode (1983) Special issue on radical cultural geography, *Antipode*.
Atkinson, J. (1985) Flexibility: planning for an uncertain future, *Manpower Policy and Practice* Vol. 1. Gower, Aldershot.
Beechey, V. (1986) *A Matter of Hours*, Croom Helm, Beckenham.
Benton, T. (1989) Marxism and natural limits: an ecological critique and reconstruction, *New Left Review*, No. 178, pp. 51-86.
Best, M. H. (1990) *The New Competition*. Polity Press, Cambridge.
Bhaskar, R. (1989) *Reclaiming Reality*, Verso, London.
Bianchini, F. (1987) GLC R.I.P.: Cultural policies in London, 1981-1986, *New Formations*, **1**: 103-117.
Bourdieu, P. (1984) *Distinction*. Routledge & Kegan Paul, London.
Bourdieu, P. (1988) *Berkeley Journal of Sociology*.

Bourdieu, P. (1989) *Homo Academicus*. Polity Press, Cambridge.
Campbell, B. (1988) Clearing the decks, *Marxism Today*, October, pp. 34-39.
Chartier, R. (1987) *The Cultural Uses of Print in Early Modern France*. Princeton University Press, Princeton, N.J.
Chartier, R. (1989) Texts, printings, readings. In Hunt, L. (ed.) *The New Cultural History*. pp. 154–175. University of California Press, Berkeley.
Clifford, J.C. (1988) *The Predicament of Culture*. University of California Press, Berkeley.
Clifford, J.C., and Marcus, C. (eds) (1986) *Writing Culture*. University of California Press, Berkeley.
Colls, R., and Dodd, P. (1986) *Englishness. Politics and Culture 1880-1920*. Croom Helm, Beckenham.
Cooke, P. (ed.) (1989) *Localities*. Unwin Hyman, London.
Cosgrove, D., and Daniels, S. (eds.) (1988). *The Iconography of Landscape*. Cambridge University Press, Cambridge.
Crompton, R., and Sanderson, K. (1990) *Gendered Jobs and Social Change*. Unwin Hyman, London.
Daunton, M. (1990) Gentlemanly capitalism and British industry 1820–1914 *Past and Present*, No. 122, pp. 119–158.
Dews, P. (1987) *Logics of Disintegration*. Verso, London.
Doel, M. (1991) (In) stalling deconstruction, *Environment and Planning D. Society and Space*, **9** (forthcoming).
Duncan, S., and Savage, M. (eds.) (1991) Special issue on "Localities", *Environment and Planning A*, **23** (2).
Dunford, M. (1990) Theories of regulation, *Environment and Planning D. Society and Space*, **8**: 297-321.
Eagleton, T. (1990a) *The Ideology of the Aesthetic*. Blackwell, Oxford.
Eagleton, T (1990b) *The Significance of Theory*. Blackwell, Oxford.
Emel, J., and Peet, J.R. (1989) Resource management and natural hazards. In Peet, J.R., and Thrift, N.J. (eds.) *New Models in Geography*, Vol. 1, pp. 49-76.
Estrin, S. and Le Grand, J. (1990). *Market Socialism*. Unwin Hyman, London.
Featherstone, M. (1991) *Consumer Culture and Postmodernism*. Sage, London.
Folch–Serra, M. (1990) Place, voice, space: Mikhail Bakhtin's dialogical landscape, *Environment and Planning D. Society and Space*, **8**: 255-274.
Friedman, J. (1987) Beyond otherness or: the spectacularisation of anthropology, *Telos*, **71**: 161-170.
Furet, F., and Ozouf, J. (1982) *Reading and Writing*. Cambridge University Press, Cambridge.
Gamble, A. (1988) *The Free Economy and the Strong State*. Macmillan, London.
Geertz, C. (1988) *Works and Lives. The Anthropologist as Author*. Polity Press, Cambridge.
Giddens, A. (1984) *The Constitution of Society*. Polity Press, Cambridge.
Giddens, A. (1985) *The Nation State and Violence*. Polity Press, Cambridge.
Gilroy, P. (1988). *There ain't no Black in the Union Jack*. Hutchinson, London.
Hall, S. (1988) *The Hard Road to Renewal. Thatcherism and the Crisis of the Left*. Verso, London.
Halliday, F. (1990) The ends of Cold War, *New Left Review*, No. 180, pp. 65-73.
Hartmann, H. (1979) The unhappy marriage of Marxism and feminism: towards a more progressive union. *Capital and Class*.
Harvey, D.W. (1989) *The Condition of Postmodernity*. Blackwell, Oxford.
Harvey, D.W. (1990) Between space and time. *Annals, Association of American Geographers*, **80**, 418–432.
Henriques, J. *et al.* (1984) *Changing the Subject*. Methuen, London.

Hirst, P. (1989) *After Thatcherism.* Oxford University Press, Oxford.
Hobsbawm, E., and Ranger, T. (eds.) (1983). *The Invention of Tradition.* Cambridge University Press, Cambridge.
Hunt, L. (ed.) (1989) *The New Cultural History.* University of California Press, Berkeley.
Ingham, G. (1984) *Capitalism Divided.* Macmillan, London.
Jackson, P. (1991) Mapping meanings: a cultural critique of locality studies, *Environment and Planning A*, **23**: 215-228.
Jameson, F. (1984) Postmodernism, or the cultural logic of late capitalism, *New Left Review*, No. 146, pp. 52-92.
Jameson, F. (1990) *Adorno and Late Marxism.* Verso, London.
Jessop, B. *et al.* (1988) *Thatcherism: a Tale of Two Nations.* Polity Press, Cambridge.
Jessop, B. (1990) Regulation theories in retrospect and prospect. *Economy and Society*, **19**: 153–216.
Jessop, B. 1990, Bonnett, K., and Bromley, S. (1990) Farewell to Thatcherism? Neo-liberalism and new-times, *New Left Review*, No. 179, pp. 81-102.
Johnston, R. J., and Pattie, C. (1989) *Dividing Britain.* Longman, London.
Kaplan, C. (1986) Pandora's box: subjectivity, class and sexuality in socialist-feminist criticism. In Green, G., and Kahn, C. (eds) *Making a Difference.* Methuen, London.
Kirby, A.W. (1989) A sense of place, *Critical Studies in Mass Communication*, **6**: 322-326.
Lash, S. (1989) *Sociology of Postmodernism.* Routledge, London.
Lash, S., and Urry, J. (1987) *The End of Organised Capitalism.* Polity Press, Cambridge.
Levin, C. (1988) Richard Rorty and postmodernity, *Canadian Journal of Political and Social Theory*, **10**: 25-36.
Lovell, J. (ed.) (1989) *British Feminist Thought.* Blackwell, Oxford.
Lovering, J. (1989) The restructuring debate. In Peet, J.R., and Thrift, N.J. (eds.) *New Models in Geography*, Vol. 1, pp. 198-223 Unwin Hyman, London.
Mann, M. (1986) *Sources of Social Power.* Cambridge University Press, Cambridge.
Martin, R.L. (1989) Regional imbalance as consequence and contrast in regional economic renewal. In Green, F. (ed.) *The Restructuring of the UK Economy*, pp. 80-100 Harvester Wheatsheaf, Hemel Hempstead
Marxism Today (1988) New times, *Marxism Today*, October 1988.
Massey, D.B. (1984a) Industrial location, *ESRC Newsletter*, No. 51, supplement, p. xv.
Massey, D.B. (1984b) *Spatial Divisions of Labour.* Macmillan, London.
Massey, D.B. (1991) The political place of locality studies, *Environment and Planning A*, **23**: 267-281.
Meyrowitz, J. (1985) *No Sense of Place.* Oxford University Press, New York.
Moi, J. (ed.) (1987) *French Feminist Thought.* Blackwell, Oxford.
Nairn, T. (1988) *The Enchanted Glass. Britain and its Monarchy.* Radius, London.
Norris, C. (1990) *What's Wrong with Postmodernism?* Harvester Wheatsheaf, New York.
Norris, C. (1991) *Spinoza and the Origins of Modern Critical Theory.* Blackwell, Oxford.
Nove, A. (1988) *The Economics of Feasible Socialism.* Allen & Unwin, London.
Ong, W. (1982) *Orality and Literacy.* Methuen, London.
O'Riordan, J. (1989) The challenge of environmentalism. In Peet, J.R., and Thrift, N.J. (eds) *New Models in Geography.* Vol. 1 pp. 77-102 Unwin Hyman, London.

Parry, J., and Bloch, M. (eds.) (1989). *Money and the Morality of Exchange.* Cambridge University Press, Cambridge.
Pateman, C. (1986) *The Disorders of Women.* Polity Press, Cambridge.
Pateman, C. (1989) *The Sexual Contract.* Stanford University Press, Stanford.
Potter, J.B, and Weatherall, (1987) *Discourse and Social Psychology.* Sage, London.
Robertson, R. (ed.) (1990) Special issue on global culture. *Theory, Culture and Society,* **7**: Nos. 2-3.
Rose, G. (1990) The struggle for political democracy: emancipation, gender, and geography. *Environment and Planning D. Society and Space,* **8**: 395-408.
Rubery, J. (1987) Flexibility of labour costs in non-union firms. In Tarling, R. (ed.) *Flexibility in Labour Markets.* Academic Press, London.
Sacks, O. (1989) *Seeing Voices.* University of California Press, Berkeley.
Samuel, R. (ed.) (1989) *Patriotism.* Vol. 1. Routledge, London.
Sayer, A. (1990) Post-Fordism in question, *International Journal of Urban and Regional Research.*
Smith, D. (1989) *North and South.* Pelican, Harmondsworth.
Smith, N. (1987) Dangers of the empirical turn: some comments on the CURS initiative, *Antipode,* **19**: 59-68.
Smith, S.J. (1989) Society, space and citizenship: a human geography for the "new times", *Transactions of the Institute of British Geographers,* No. 14, pp. 144-156.
Soja, E.W. (1989) *Postmodern Geographies.* Verso, London.
Spencer, J. (1989) The new ethnography, *Man.*
Stedman Jones, G. (1980) *Languages of Class.* Cambridge University Press, Cambridge.
Steedman, C. (1986) *Landscape for a Good Woman.* Virago, London.
Steedman, C. (1990) *Childhood, Culture and Class in Britain.* Virago, London.
Swyngedouw, E. (1989) *Environment and Planning D. Society and Space.*
Thompson, E.P. (1968) *The Making of the English Working Class.* Penguin, Harmondsworth.
Thrift, N.J. (1979) The limits to knowledge. Australian National University, Australian National University Seminar Paper.
Thrift, N.J. (1985) Flies and germs; a geography of knowledge. In Gregory, D., and Urry, J. (eds.) *Social Relations and Spatial Structures,* pp. 404-430 Macmillan, London.
Thrift, N.J. (1986) Little games and big stories. In Hoggart, K., and Kofman, E. (eds.) *Politics, Geography and Social Stratification* pp. 175-226 Croom Helm, Beckenham.
Thrift, N.J. (1990) For a new regional geography 1. *Progress in Human Geography,* **14**: 272-279.
Thrift, N.J. (1991) For a new regional geography 2. *Progress in Human Geography,* (forthcoming).
Thrift, N.J. and Forbes, D.K. (1981) A landscape without figures, *Political Geography Quarterly,* **3**: 7-21.
Thrift, N.J. and Leyshon, A. (1991) *Making Money.* Routledge, London.
Thrift, N.J. and Williams, P. (eds.) (1987) *Class and Space.* Routledge & Kegan Paul, London.
Tomlinson, J. (1990) Market socialism. A basis for socialist renewal? In Hindess, B. (ed.) *Reactions to the Right,* pp. 32-49 Routledge, London.
Townsend, A., and Lewis, J. (1989) *The North–South Divide,* Paul Chapman, London.
Urry, J. (1990) Globalisation, localisation and the nation-state, *Lancaster Regionalism Group Working Paper 40.*

Vincent, D. (1989) *Literacy and Popular Culture*. Cambridge University Press, Cambridge.
Walkerdine, V. (1989) *The Mastery of Reason*. Routledge, London.
Walkerdine, V., and Lucey, H. (1989) *Democracy in the Kitchen*. Virago, London.
Willis, P. (1990) *Common Culture*. Open University Press, Milton Keynes.

2

Changing Political Relations

PETER TAYLOR

Writing of changing political relations in contemporary Britain is to chronicle the phenomenon called Thatcherism. The (now ex-) Prime Minister of Great Britain has a politics named after her, the accolade of her very own "ism". Minogue (1987: p. x) humorously refers to this as a "career grade", noting that others have their names converted to adjectives—Churchillian, Bennite—but only Mrs Thatcher's name has been converted to a noun. As has been pointed out often, this is the first time that this has happened to a British Prime Minister, but it seems to me to be even unique among leaders of liberal democracies, certainly no US President has yet to spawn an "ism".

Whatever this Thatcherism may be, most serious commentators describe it as much more than political relations *per se*. Thatcherism cannot be discussed without reference to the economic theory of monetarism, for instance, and the term itself originates from analysts who emphasize its ideological dimension as a "hegemonic project". Hence the call by Jessop *et al.* (1988, 56) for "rounded approaches" to Thatcherism that give due weight to economic, ideological and political aspects of the phenomenon. This call must be heeded if we are to develop an understanding of the contemporary British scene. Nevertheless, Thatcherism is fundamentally a set of political actions. They are, no doubt, responses to economic circumstances and their collective motive may be designated in ideological terms, but at the heart of Thatcherism is an attempt to restructure political relations. Hence whilst not ignoring other dimensions, this essay will concentrate upon the politics of Thatcherism without, it is hoped, doing too much damage to the broader essence of the phenomenon.

Question: Which Conservative Prime Minister, speaking at the Party Conference following an electoral victory secured on a promise of using market forces to stem Britain's economic decline, told the party faithful: "We are returned to office to change the course of history of this nation—nothing less"? *Answer*: Edward Heath in 1970, of course. The circumstances and rhetoric are quintessentially Thatcherite and yet Heath is the nemesis of Thatcher, his government was the example to be avoided when the Conservatives returned to power in 1979. This indicates that at the very least we must not treat Thatcherism uncritically as a distinctive politics of the 1980s. In the first section of the chapter we review the meanings of Thatcherism and consider the debates surrounding the term. Our route out of this large literature is to take what may be termed a world-systems political geography approach. In part two we step back and view Thatcherism more generally in the context of changing political relations throughout core zone of the capitalist world-economy. We are then in a position to identify what may be singular in the case of Britain and the Thatcher phenomenon: We treat Thatcherism as the latest particular feature of Britain's politics of decline, a response to what I shall term post-hegemonic trauma.

Having set up Thatcherism in terms of general historical social science theory, the final three parts of the chapter interpret the changing political relations in the light of the theory. Part three deals with the politics of power in terms of how Thatcherism is remoulding the British state and undermining past practices. This is the basis for its radical credentials—it is "revolutionary" in intra-class terms in its attack of one part of the traditional British establishment. But it is counter-revolutionary, of course, in inter-class terms and this is the subject of part four. We describe the politics of support and the "two nation" basis of Thatcherism. Finally, in a short conclusion, we consider the implications of these two politics and argue that their combination in Thatcherism may be a highly unstable mix that can create a territorial crisis of the state. Thatcherism has done what the right always feared the socialists might do: unmask the true power of the British state.

Thatcherism

"Thatcherism", complain Jessop *et al.* (1988: p. 5) "seems to have acquired almost as many meanings as there are people who mention it." These range from celebrations of the individual herself to Marxist analyses of a new hegemonic bloc. We do not have to suffer reading adulatory biographies of Mrs Thatcher to find the former: right-leaning political scientists can be quite sycophantic in this context. Minogue and Biddess's book of essays on Thatcherism, for instance, concludes with Finer (1987: p. 140) lamenting in celebration: "I do not believe that in our lifetime we shall ever look upon her like again." But curiously some highly critical Marxist analysis of Thatcherism has been interpreted in a similar manner. Jessop *et al.* (1988: p. 69) refer to Gramscian interpretations as an "ideological celebration of Thatcherism", a sort of back-to-front sycophancy. This allows Gould and Anderson (1987: p. 40) to sneer: "Marxist intellectuals in Britain seem to have 'Thatcherism' on the brain."

What is happening here? Certainly at a superficial level it would seem that writers on opposite sides of the political spectrum interpret the success of Mrs Thatcher and her government as representing a major transformation in British politics. This reading of recent history serves its proponents in their debates *within* their respective corners of the political spectrum. Both on the right and left the celebration of Thatcherism is a rejection of the postwar social democratic consensus. The phenomenon of Thatcherism is used by both sides to prevent any political return to the flawed politics, both right wing and left wing, that are perceived before 1979. What is the political substance behind this unholy convergence?

Friends and Enemies

The celebration of Mrs Thatcher on the right is to be expected. After losing 4 out of 5 elections before 1979 the Conservative Party reasserted itself as the "natural" party of government in the 1980s. But Mrs Thatcher was always more than just a winner. The failure of the Heath government between 1972 and 1974, when it was defeated by trade union power, brought a major reappraisal on the right of British politics. The result was Thatcherism. After the trauma of the Heath government, the Conservative Party was vulnerable to New Right analyses (Gamble 1988, 1989). In this argument the success of the trade unions was merely a dramatic example of a more general problem of democracy. Politics in Western democracies had become a political market in which consumers did not pay the price of their consumption. Competing interests forced parties in their search for votes to bid against one another in a spiral to economic disaster. In Britain the inevitable crisis predicted by this argument was manifest in the 1970s. The result was what the political scientists identified as Britain's ungovernability (Tivey 1988: p. 98) due to government "overload" (King 1975). The solution was to withdraw the state from this political bazaar and base economic policy, not on interest group bargaining, but on control of the money supply. Monetarism and a state dealing only with its "proper" function of maintaining order and protecting property were the theoretical ideal. But such a change in behaviour needed a change in ideology. Conservatives had to learn to rid themselves of "bourgeois guilt" (Minogue 1988) for social inequalities that had made them susceptible to social democratic arguments. Stripped of their guilt, Conservatives could allow the market and not the state to be the great distributor by rewarding enterprise and penalizing dependence. In this argument, therefore, Thatcherism is a crusade that has saved both the Conservative Party and Britain from the crisis of the 1970s. It has broken through the logjam of the social democratic consensus and produced a new era of British politics.

Many enemies of Thatcherism would agree with the last sentence. The earliest theoretical assessments of Thatcherism came from writers in *Marxism Today* who actually coined the term for posterity. This latest New Left (Eurocommunist) group were the first to develop a theoretical interpretation of Mrs Thatcher's Conservatives as more than a party under an unpleasant leader with a new shrill rhetoric. Their analysis of "authoritarian popularism" can be traced back to the January 1979 issue of *Marxism Today* and has been developed to become possibly the most popular interpretation of Thatcherism (Hall and Jacques 1983).

In this Marxist analysis the postwar social democratic consensus is concealing the contradictions of modern capitalism and the 1970s represent a conjuncture when the old social formation is falling apart. Any such period provides an opportunity for all social groups to establish a new position in a reconstructed social formation. Mrs Thatcher's Conservatives have seized that opportunity. While the Labour government in the late 1970s were trying once again to make the unworkable work, the Conservatives embarked on a project to move on to a new political terrain of their choosing. In Gramscian terms this is an "organic" change in the social formation. It requires a direct attack on existing social norms and their replacement by a new vision and an alternative common sense. In this case public expenditure and trade unions become popular enemies allowing a class politics of monetarism and patriotism to be constructed. According to this argument a new "historic bloc" is being created which overturns working class gains obtained under social democratic regimes of the past (both right and left). But all is not lost. The left can learn from Thatcherism; it is a necessary stage that must be suffered to educate people of the easy fallacies of social democracy. As Thatcherism disposes of the latter the outlook for its opponents on the left is consequently improved.

The above descriptions of two contrary yet converging interpretations of Thatcherism are highly simplified statements that cover in just a few paragraphs a large literature. I have concentrated on early treatments of Thatcherism and both positions have been further developed. Nevertheless, the key point, celebratory convergence, stands. In what follows I explore the complexities of the phenomenon of Thatcherism, but this should not be treated as direct criticism of the above positions. Given my omission of much subtlety of New Right and New Left arguments, I would stand accused properly of a straw man critical exercise. My purpose below is not to contrast the complexity with my simple treatments of the previous arguments but to move beyond the celebration of Thatcherism towards an alternative perspective for locating political relations in Britain in the 1980s.

Paradoxes and Dilemmas

Writers of all persuasions agree that we must avoid treating Thatcherism as a great political monolith. Rather it has a range of characteristics some reinforcing one another but others seemingly contradictory. Marquand's (1988: p. 160) list of "four dimensions" of Thatcherism is a useful starting point. First, Thatcherism is a response to the collective despair of continuing national decline—a sort of "British Gaullism". Second, Thatcherism is a vehicle for the promotion of economic liberalism. Third, there is a moral dimension, often entitled "Victorian values", which encompasses respect for authority and tradition as a revolt against the "social liberalism" of the 1960s. Finally, the fourth characteristic is personal to Mrs Thatcher and emphasizes her charismatic leadership with its populist overtones. Each dimension is related to every other one in many different ways. Together they consist of the phenomenon of Thatcherism, but they most certainly do not constitute a coherent ideology.

Paradoxes within Thatcherism are easy to identify as Marquand (1988) points out. The most discussed is that between free market and strong state which lies at the heart of Gamble's (1988) analysis. There is also the fundamental contrast between the neo-liberal internationalism and the Gaullist-like nationalism. And, of course, the popularism rests uneasily with Conservative traditional modes of governing. Each of these paradoxes has given rise to different interpretations of Thatcherism. There are "revisionisms" of position from both right and left which involve changing both the temporal and spatial bases of the two "contrasting and converging" interpretations presented previously.

The most interesting revisionism from the right can be found in the work of Bulpitt (1983, 1986). He concentrates on traditional Conservative statecraft and is able to find a consistent pattern of practices from 1880 which includes Thatcherism. Certainly there was a break in 1979, but only so as to *re-establish* Conservative statecraft in the new circumstances. This statecraft is based upon a distinction between "high politics" and "low politics" with the Conservatives insulating the former from popular influences by conceding ground in the latter. In this argument even Keynsian macroeconomic management is compatible with Conservative statecraft if it remains as high politics. This "autonomy of the centre" was undermined by the more interventionist government policies after 1961. Bulpitt refers to these changes as "pseudo" or "post" Keynsian policies when an ethos of technocratic modernization affected both main parties. Hence in this "world turned upside down" for the Conservatives, between 1961 and 1979, high politics was subjected to pressures from various interest groups to make the country ungovernable in Conservative terms. Monetarism enters the picture as a means of rebuilding the relative autonomy of the centre lost since 1961. Hence Mrs Thatcher's government continues in a Conservative tradition that stretches back to the beginning of popular government in Britain.

Once back in control of high politics things did not turn out as expected however. In the original theory the autonomy of the centre was to be complemented by an autonomy of the periphery. But the latter, especially in local government, soon threatened the newly established high politics. Reciprocal autonomy was quickly abandoned. At the same time the effects of the monetarist policy were found to be much more severe than anticipated. The beginnings of period of international economic stagnation meant that British austerity measures proved to be economically disastrous on a whole range of indicators. The government quickly learned that, as Bulpitt (1986: p. 37) neatly puts it, "monetarism in one country" was impossible. Hence the major change in economic policy from 1981 which has been subsequently criticized by the New Right. Nevertheless, the break with 1961 to 1979 "post-Keynsian" policies was completed to reassert a high politics safe in Conservative hands.

There are certain similarities between Bulpitt's arguments and the criticisms Jessop *et al.* (1988) make in the left's debates over the authoritarian popularism thesis. They insist, for instance, on recognizing that important changes have occurred in "the dynamic of Thatcherism" during its application as political practice. They also contest the common interpretation of the postwar social democratic consensus. Rather than emphasizing the break in 1961, however, they develop the international context theme alluded to by Bulpitt.

Jessop *et al.* (1988) argue that the standard interpretation of the postwar consensus is fatally flawed because it omits the crucial external element. There was a domestic consensus on Keynsian economics and the welfare state to be sure, but in addition the City as an international financial centre was prioritized while Britain was locked into an expensive Atlantic alliance system. It is these "external aspects" of the postwar consensus that were "the dominant factors" in the postwar settlement:

> A combination of structural constraints and political decisions taken in the mid-forties entrenched the British economy into a destructive mode of growth. Essentially Britain acquired a position within the international division of labour which privileged financial capital and externally-orientated commercial and industrial capital and weakened domestic capital (Jessop *et al.* 1988: p. 164).

Even in the 1960s, for all its modernization policies, this externally orientated position continued to be privileged over domestic social democratic needs. The end result of this postwar settlement was the "disintegration of the UK economy as a nationally integrated national space" (Jessop *et al.* 1988: p. 165). Hence it is hardly surprising that the Conservatives found they could not operate "monetarism in one country" after 1979.

Jessop and his colleagues consider that this argument counts against considering Thatcherism as a distinctive break from the past. Rather the government's economic liberalism reinforces and accelerates the internationalizing project they trace back to 1945. But therein lies an "intriguing dilemma". By favouring interests with an international orientation, the Conservatives may deprive themselves of a national political base. This is Marquand's Gaullist versus economic liberalisms paradox identified earlier. For Jessop *et al.* (1988: p. 173), however, it is not a practical paradox since the Gaullist option of economic restructuring is not open to any British government: "there is simply no significant bloc of domestic UK capital that might provide the base for such a strategy".

The arguments in this section have downplayed the distinctiveness of Thatcherism and have directed our attention to the particular features of the British state and its external relations.

Let us use these insights to retheorize the phenomenon of Thatcherism using a fresh perspective wherein the state and its external relations are moved to centre stage.

World-Economy and New Politics

We will take Jessop *et al.*'s (1988: p. 161) advice that "the international dimensions of the British state under Thatcherism need much greater attention". Such a call is by no means restricted to writers of the left, of course. The "realism" or "facing up to the facts" that supporters claim for the Thatcher government has always had an important international element: "In the end, whatever the rhetoric, parties have to respond to the same realities, especially economic realities (and even more especially, international economic realities)" (Gould and Anderson 1987: p. 41). We are going to develop this idea from a particular critical perspective. The unusual feature of our approach is that we will not be viewing the problem as external constraints on the state. Rather we will look in on the state from the perspective of this great "external" or international dimension. We will view the world-economy as the fundamental unit of social change.

A Family of New Politics

The world-economy, Wallerstein's (1983) "historical capitalism", is an integrated hierarchical social system that has been global in extent since about 1900. It is integrated through a myriad of commodity chains linking many series of production nodes from raw material extraction through to final consumption. It is hierarchical because of different forms of social relations found at the various production nodes that can be most generally divided into core and peripheral in nature. This "uneven development" allows us to identify core and periphery zones within the world-economy and we concentrate on the former in the remainder of this discussion. In addition, the development of the world-economy is not a smooth process. There are a series of growth periods alternating with relative stagnation. Of the various cycles that have been identified the Kondratieff waves of approximately fifty years duration are what will concern us here. The important point is that such cycles are system-wide, they affect all countries, although not necessarily in exactly the same way.

The politics of the world-economy is, of course, balkanized: There is not one core state but many competing against one and other. In this competition and in the internal management of their territories all governing politicians have to cope with economic circumstances beyond their control—the cycles. During "A phases" of growth the problems of government and resulting modes of statecraft will be very different from the "B phases" of stagnation. In short there will be a series of "new politics" in each country as politicians grapple with the changing material situations. I have argued elsewhere (Taylor 1982: pp. 275-276) that these new politics are not themselves matters of party competition. Rather *all* major parties in a country adapt to a new situation by modifying their policies to fit a new agenda.

There is a very good evidence for this broad view of political change in the form of numerous "coincidences" in political developments across different states. The very origins of modern party-based liberal democracy occurred in many countries in the decades before 1900, for instance. It would be highly unlikely that each case was autonomous of the others. An even more striking example is the rise of "welfare states" of various forms in core states in the Kondratieff A phase that was the "postwar boom" (*c*. 1945-1970). This seems to be a clear case where the new material circumstances at the global level facilitated the new politics of social democracy by providing the opportunity for its establishment. This is not to say that there was anything automatic about it, but clearly we are not looking at a simple autonomous process when we study, say, the rise of the British welfare state. The world-economy is enabling and constraining and governing politicians create their particular country's version of a "new politics" within the "family" of such politics devised during each change in the world-economy.

How does this analysis fit the current B phase since *c*. 1970? Two political reactions to the economic change can be identified: First a period of political instability (1970s) followed by a contrasting period of stability (1980s). In the 1970s governments in many countries were perceived as failures as popular expectations built up in the A phase could no longer be satisfied. The 1970s were a period when governments were rarely re-elected for a second term. It is all change in the 1980s. "Strong" governments emerge in many countries and are often dominated by powerful leaders. Reagan, Mitterand, Kohl and Thatcher all had no trouble in being re-elected. Times had changed as the voters attune to a new agenda that is "realistic" towards the new economic circumstances.

What is the essence of this latest new politics? Domestically there is a reversal of the social democratic and corporatist policies that had developed since 1945. Cutting government expenditure and attacking trade unions seem to be key elements of the new politics. This fits Thatcherism very well, of course, and can be easily extended to "Reaganomics" in the USA. In fact Mrs Thatcher and President Reagan are often seen as ideological soulmates in a New Right offensive across the world. But in our model this ideological basis for the new politics takes a back seat to the world-system constraints. A test of our position can be conducted by looking at left wing governments in the 1980s. Spain, Greece, Australia and New Zealand have all elected and re-elected socialist and Labour governments under strong personal leadership in the 1980s. The key point is, however, that their domestic policies are very similar to "Thatcherism" and "Reaganomics". Possibly the major challenge to trade union power by any government in the 1980s was that of the Spanish socialist government. Furthermore, New Zealand has had possibly the most severe cost cutting expenditure programme, Rogernomics, named after its "Thatcherite" Labour economics minister. Generally, therefore, irrespective of the ideological hue of the government similar sets of domestic policies have emerged across a range of countries in the core of the world-economy.

Interestingly enough, foreign policies among this group of countries seem to have diverged from previously similar "Western" stances. On the right the 1980s began with Mrs Thatcher and President Reagan stirring up the "second Cold War". On the left there was resistance to this militarism for parties both in and out of government. New Zealand's anti-nuclear policy led to the breaking up of the ANZUS defence group and in Europe both Greek and Spanish socialists were intially seen as anti-American over US bases and NATO membership respectively. It seems it is in foreign policy that left wing governments chose to express their radicalism after the domestic sphere was ruled out of court by the new politics. But no lasting damage was done to the Western alliance. Spain and Greece were soon brought into line and remote New Zealand was safely ignored. And all the time "socialist France", after its initial "socialist experiment", was pursuing the new domestic politics with a nuclear-based foreign policy at least as vigorously as either Thatcher or Reagan.

Despite the strong evidence for this world-economy and new politics approach presented above, we must be careful not to overstate the case. Certainly if one had used the previous "B phase" and focused on the "strong governments" of the 1930s the range of "new politics"—from Nazi Germany to New Deal USA—is very great. This highlights the point that the enabling and constraining world-economy most certainly does not determine any given new politics for all countries to adopt. Even in the more homogenous family of contemporary new politics there will be, inevitably, much variety below the general similarities I have described above. There is an important sense in which every state's politics is unique within a global tendency towards a new politics. This is pre-eminently the case for Britain.

New Politics in a Situation of Post-hegemonic Trauma

I have previously used the world-economy and new politics approach to describe the changes in British political agendas since World War I (Taylor 1982, 1989). Basically the one and a half global Kondratieff waves to the present are reflected in a symmetrical sequence of political responses in Britain. The two B phases are represented by first a "politics of crisis" when the country seems ungovernable (1920s and 1970s) to be followed by a "politics of national interest" which finds a right political solution as the Labour Party splits and is pushed back to its heartlands (1930s and 1980s). In between the A phase is first represented by the social democratic consensus (late 1940s and 1950s) to be followed by a technocratic modernizing politics (1960s)—Bulpitt's post-Keynsian interventionist departure—that attempted to stem Britain's continuing relative economic decline.

What this political story lacks is a proper appreciation of the special nature of Britain in the world-economy. In another paper (Taylor 1989b) I have tried to describe Britain's unique role in the twentieth century in world-systems terms as a case of post-hegemonic trauma. What I mean by this is that from its position of nineteenth-century predominance—both economically and politically—Britain has been on a trajectory of relative decline throughout this century. This is not just any case of decline, the heights of dominance reached—hegemony—continue to inform the collective mentality of the society. To a large degree, therefore, the basic problem confronting all British politicians in the twentieth century has been how to package and sell the country's reduced international circumstances to a population with memories of world domination. Tivey (1988) describes stages in the development of the politics of this problem. By the end of the nineteenth century an optimistic scenario prevailed consisting of belief in mass democracy and social reform in Britain coupled with providing the benefits of empire to the less fortunate peoples of the world. Prior to 1914, however, this social imperial project was under stress at home. Nevertheless, there was continued belief that the country still controlled its own destiny: "No one thought that (Britain) was seriously constrained by the pressure or hostility of the rest of the world" so that "British practices and policies could, by and large, be determined internally" (Tivey 1988: pp. 36–37). By 1939 the picture had turned around. Britain had lost control of outside forces and was thus no longer in control of her own destiny (Tivey 1988: p. 46). This is a fundamental change in British politics. Instead of politicians believing that "wherever general principles (of democracy, liberty, socialism) might lead, then British practice could follow. . . . Political vision became more and more strategic, pragmatic, instrumental" (Tivey 1988: p. 115). This is most clearly illustrated, as may be expected, in foreign policy.

The different roles that Britain has adopted in the international system in the twentieth century each reflect different ways of coming to terms with decline. Even late nineteenth-century imperialism—the greatest empire the world has ever seen—can be interpreted as a substitution of political power for failing economic power. After 1945 and with the demise of empire, the main alternative role to maintain Britain's global influence was the special relationship with the new dominant power, USA. This "hegemony's mate" position corresponds to the external constraints that dominate the social democratic consensus in Jessop *et al.*'s (1988) argument. Certainly Britain can be implicated in the construction of the Cold War as a geopolitical order where her global concerns and experience would be fully valued (Taylor 1990a). But by the 1960s Britain had to settle for a regional role as part of the European Community. This immense climb down was made possible because of the economic success of the original EC countries relative to Britain. Unfortunately Britain joined the EC as economic stagnation set in and by the 1970s was commonly viewed as the "sick man of Europe". No wonder the British public had become disillusioned with their politicians.

Enter Thatcherism. Mrs Thatcher, so her supporters say, has put the Great back into Britain. Combinations of previous roles are brought together with a final amalgam of global grandeur. From the search for a new generation of "Victorian entrepreneurs" to save the British economy to the naval-led imperial victory in the Falklands/Malvinas War—the Empire strikes back—visions of nineteenth-century greatness are rekindled. With the coming of the second Cold War the Iron Lady was able to get back Britain's place on the world political agenda as a nuclear power to be reckoned with. The special relationship with the USA returned with the Thatcher–Reagan mutual appreciation society. Finally in Europe the "sick man" was converted to the indomitable negotiator for Britain's interests. To properly understand Thatcherism, therefore, we must see it as a particular new politics where the international dimension—"turning Britain around" no less—has been of unusual importance.

The legacy of post-hegemonic trauma has been used as an opportunity by Mrs Thatcher's government in foreign policy, in domestic policy it is more of a constraint. When the Labour government created the welfare state after 1945 it was not just producing any social democratic consensus. For a short time it had a vision of itself as leader of a social democratic world, a "third way" between the extremes of capitalist America and communist Russia. The idea that Britain's welfare state was the best in the world persisted long after the credibility of a third way had vanished in the Cold War. The current manifestation of this would seem to be the tenacious respect the British people continue to have for their National Health Service. Politically this remains beyond the pale, even for an ultra-privatizing Thatcher government. It illustrates how complex are the relations between the politics of power and the politics of support in contemporary Britain.

Politics of Power: Thatcherism and the British State

At first sight the politics of power of Mrs Thatcher's government is basically the same as that of previous Conservative administrations. The party continues to be funded by donations from private sector business and in return provides conditions conducive to profit taking. Taxation changes, the many privatization projects and relaxation of capital flow control are key Thatcher policies that work for the party's paymasters. As previously argued, the international neo-liberalism does not reflect a major change in Britain's economic orientation, since all British governments have been committed to a liberal world economy since the Bretton Woods agreement in 1944. The Thatcher government extension of the policy has created, however, one of the key paradoxes of this politics:

> Today, the national traditions to which Thatcherism appeals point not towards a renewal of Britain's old economic supremacy, but towards subordination to stronger economies and multinational firms (Marquand 1988: p. 170).

The increasing mismatch between British capital and the British territorial economy will produce potential contradictions between the Conservatives politics of power and politics of support which will one day come to a head, but which Mrs Thatcher has merely accelerated rather than created.

It is another sphere of the politics of power that Mrs Thatcher's government has had a profound and distinctive influence. The British state and its apparatus are, as has often been pointed out, unique. For Nairn (1977) the British state is an anachronism, a semi-modern legacy of a by-gone age. In this argument the state itself is inherently conservative and has managed to tame all challenges through the 1970s. Whereas previous modernization projects, notably those of the 1960s, failed to overcome state inertia, Thatcherism has involved what Dahrendorf (1988: p. 198) calls "the insidious process of deinstitutionalization": The state apparatus has not blocked Thatcherite policies.

The Buffer State Apparatus

The origins of Thatcherism lie in the failures of past British governments which had generated, by the 1970s, serious questions of political legitimacy. Hence the interpretation of the problem as a constitutional crisis (Hirst 1989, Graham and Prosser 1988), Britain's first since 1911. The British state, so long admired for its fabled gradualism, seemed to be coming apart at the seams. The best index of this change in attitude can be found in the work of Samuel Beer who originally wrote to celebrate the stability of Britain's political practices (1965) but returned to report disintegration into ungovernability (1982).

A key feature of the British state is that it operates through its so-called "unwritten constitution". This may have facilitated political stability by providing a flexibility for state elites in periods of social change and challenge. The important feature, however, is the lack of a formal balance of powers within the state. Sovereignty lies squarely with Parliament, which in practice means the party that controls the House of Commons. This extreme concentration of power has been traditionally mediated through a layer of apolitical institutions lying between government and citizen. Hence surrounding all British governments there has been a ring of "political buffers" that have curbed full application of the potential "elective dictatorship" by government through Parliament. These informal aspects of the unwritten constitution have relied upon consensus among the political elite as to what constitutes appropriate and legitimate behaviour. In this way British socialism has been deradicalized, according to Milband's

(1973) famous thesis, into a mere parliamentary shadow termed labourism.

The civil service has been a central buffer in this process. Unlike most other countries it is overtly non-political through all grades so that government's top advisers in all state departments have not been government appointees. The same advisers normally serve governments of different parties. Beyond the civil service there have been a wide range of institutions nominally independent of government that allow a degree of autonomy to services that are publicly funded. The BBC is a typical example and has never been viewed as a "state" broadcasting organization. Through the twentieth century a wide range of such institutions have arisen to oversee various areas of policy from positions of relative autonomy. Along with Royal Commissions set up to investigate particular policy issues in a non-political way, these intermediate institutions have come to be associated with a broad British establishment—"the great and the good"—who have had, not surprisingly, disproportionate influence on the British political consensus.

This practical balance of power beyond Parliament has always been potentially fragile, since its constitutional guarantees are by definition inadequate—all intermediate bodies may be manipulated or even abolished using a simple majority in the House of Commons. In fact it was Lord Hailsham (1978), Mrs Thatcher's first Lord Chancellor, who popularized the term "elective dictatorship" when in opposition. It is hardly surprising, therefore, that "Mrs Thatcher has clearly recognized that an unwritten constitution is no restraint at all if you have a secure majority" (Hirst 1989; p. 50).

Creating a Naked State

The constitutional crisis on which Mrs Thatcher rode to power has not been confronted by any explicit constitutional reform (Graham and Prosser 1988: p. 13). Rather there have been massive informal changes in the balance of power within the British state. If the cause of the crisis was the threat to the relative autonomy of the centre, as many Conservatives believed, then the attack on local authorities and trade unions makes very good sense despite the break from traditional support for local government autonomy. As we have already noted, Bulpitt (1986) argues that initial intentions for reciprocal autonomy between centre and periphery soon gave way to the extension of the centre. The important point for our argument here is that this extension went far beyond the locus of Labour opposition in the periphery. The list of victims is quite daunting. Promotion of civil servants has become subject to direct intervention by Mrs Thatcher, appointments to bodies such as the BBC are no longer politically balanced, other bodies such as in higher education and the health service have been abolished and replaced by management boards drawn from business circles. And of course Mrs Thatcher never found it necessary to institute any Royal Commissions. As one commentator would have it the "great and the good" have become the lost tribe of British politics (Kavanagh 1990: p. 293)! No wonder Bulpitt (1986: p. 38) concludes that "There is no doubt that this abandonment of the reciprocal autonomy stance marked a major break with old Conservative statecraft."

This is where we come to Thatcherism's claims to be a radical political movement (Gould and Anderson 1987: p. 50). As Kavanagh (1990: p. 292) has put it: "Although leader of the Conservative party she is pre-eminently an anti-establishment figure." The symbolic proof of this was the vote of 2–1 by the Oxford University Congregation not to award their most famous graduate, Mrs Thatcher, an honorary degree. She remains the only Oxford-educated prime minister not to be so honoured. Mrs Thatcher's supporters revel in such situations. Gould and Anderson (1987: p. 45) describe the "establishment opposition" thus:

> It receives support from many quarters—from the egalitarian High Tables of Oxbridge, from "highly respected and independent" research centres, from quality journalism, from the House of Lords, yes, even among the Bench of Bishops.

This allows Kavanagh (1990: p. 288) to argue that class analysis (i.e. Marxism) is inadequate for understanding Thatcherism.

We obtain a very different perspective in terms of a politics of power analysis. In all capitalist states this politics is pre-eminently a matter of intra-class politics, about control of the state apparatus. In this context the Thatcher government has abandoned consensus statecraft for a new political elite statecraft. Mrs Thatcher has used the potential extreme power that Britain's unwritten constitution gives to an elected government. Lord Hailsham was afraid that a left wing socialist government would take advantage of this constitutional situation, but in the event it is a right wing government that has destroyed the buffers. What has been revealed is not a pleasant sight: a naked state at the behest of elective dictatorship. No wonder Kavanagh

(1990: p. 293) is concerned for the future of this British state:

> In so far as the actions since 1979 have politicized areas hitherto relatively immune to such considerations they provide pretexts for a future Labour government to intervene in these spheres.

The "great and the good" are already responding with calls for constitutional change (Hirst 1989) and certainly Labour's past government record would seem to suggest a return to consensus statecraft when it returns to power. But once unveiled, can the naked state really be fully clothed again? Thatcherism's lasting achievement may well turn out to be its transformation of the British state, the creation of a new politics of power.

The Politics of Support: Thatcherism and Two Nations

Marquand (1988: p. 171) has designated Thatcherism to be both "revolutionary and counter-revolutionary". The so-called "revolutionary" element relates to the changing politics of power we have just described. In terms of the politics of support Thatcherism remains profoundly counter-revolutionary. The 1970s crisis of the British state went beyond corporatism to indict the party system itself. Mrs Thatcher's crusade, therefore, has involved a rhetoric for destroying the party system that has dominated Britain in the twentieth century by elimination of the Labour Party as an electoral force. But we must be careful in placing too much emphasis on rhetoric. At the height of the social democratic consensus and after three consecutive Conservative victories, Lord Hailsham proclaimed the end of British socialism in 1959. In any case the Labour Party has been pushed back to its heartlands but no further. Furthermore, it can be argued that Unionism—traditional one-nation Conservatism—has been as much a victim of Thatcherism as its electoral opponent Labourism (Gamble 1989: p. 13). Hence, although superficially the British party system has survived the 1980s intact—the competition for government remains Conservative versus Labour—below the surface there have been changes that may have just as profound implications for future political relations as the deinstitutionalization in the politics of power.

Electoral Puzzles

Both major political parties continue to have a socially biased politics of support in keeping with their origins. As a populist,

Mrs Thatcher has pursued some policies that have been directed at the middle of the social spectrum to consolidate her support. An important element of her electoral success has been the attraction of more affluent working class voters from Labour. But we should be careful not to interpret these electoral successes as a process of successful political mobilization. Overall the Conservatives under Mrs Thatcher have generally attracted less votes than under her predecessors. Her success is more to do with the "demobilization" of her opponents by their political divisions. But there are changes occurring that are much more important than where the cleavage between the parties occurs on the national social spectrum.

The three general election victories of the Conservatives under Mrs Thatcher have been extensively analysed and it is not possible to review this work here. Some conclusions of one of the major analysts are of particular interest to our arguments, however. Crewe (1988) talks about these particular general elections doing "considerable damage" to existing theories of voting behaviour (p. 27) and the relationship between voting and survey data being "a puzzle" (p. 44). Basically it is very difficult to find a Thatcherite public in opinion surveys that is large enough to sustain a Thatcherite government in office. The electorate's support for the National Health Service and its preference for Labour in this context is just the most well-known failure to spread Thatcherite ideas. Crewe (1988: p. 38) shows, for example, that throughout the Thatcher governments support for cutting taxes has declined as support for spending more on basic services has increased (after the 1979 there was an exact balance between these two positions, by 1987 six times more people favoured the latter over the former). These results are quite spectacular and fully warranting Crewe's designation as a puzzle.

What is happening in this politics of support? Crewe retreats to the issue of the superior statecraft of Mrs Thatcher—competence to govern—as an answer. The dominance of Mrs Thatcher's style of leadership as an issue coupled with matching the economic cycle to the political cycle is no doubt very important. Another reason that is rarely discussed is the fact that survey data—publicly expressed opinions to strangers—is very different in kind from casting a vote in a ballot. Borrowing from Myrdal (1972), we might expect a degree of "public social democracy" coinciding with "private Thatcherism". Obviously many of the two-thirds of the electorate who preferred more services to less taxes in 1987 must have voted Conservative.

There is one overwhelming feature of the three Thatcher general elections that makes national modelling of political behaviour suspect and that is the spatial polarization of voters that has occurred. Although there may be some dealignment socially, in spatial terms supporters of the two main parties have never been further apart. Models and survey analyses that ignore the vast differences across the country in the effects of government policy and the consequent responses of voters must be fatally flawed. Two nations are an integral element of Thatcherism.

Two Nations

We must be careful in attributing electoral polarization to Mrs Thatcher's government. Labour has been becoming more urban and more northern since the 1950s. Nevertheless, there has been a qualitative change in the territorial structure of the politics of support under Mrs Thatcher. Her political attack on Labour institutions has inevitably had a differential impact across the country. Furthermore, the regions of Labour strength have generally suffered in the redistribution aspects of government policy. They have registered a collective sense of being neglected and left behind as the rest of the country goes forward. Thatcherism is seen as a threat to the identity of large parts of the country.

Gamble (1989: p. 14) describes this two nation process as a series of opposites: the nation of the future versus the nation of the past, the nation of independence and self-reliance versus the nation of dependence and subsidy, the nation of the employed and prosperous versus the nation of the unemployed and poor. Thatcherism for the "other nation" is quite straightforward:

> The nation of subsidy and dependence is no longer to be propped up: it is to be reconstructed. The South is to swallow the North (Gamble 1989: p. 14).

Jessop *et al.* (1988: pp. 87-89) consider this to be a "two nations project" whereby the Thatcher government has been able to build up its privileged nation of "good citizens" and "hard workers" as the support base of its political hegemony. Instead of the social democratic horizontal cleavage based upon class, this is an attempt to construct a new vertical cleavage which opposes "productive" to "parasitic". Given the uneven development of Britain and the simple plurality electoral system, this has enabled the government to be returned to power on the basis of support across a wide swath of southern Britain. It can be considered, in short, a "southern government" formed by a new regional party. Such sentiments are strongest in Scotland, but can also be found throughout all regions beyond "the South". Questions such as "should *their* government impose policies *we* did not vote for on *our* region?" indicate the new legitimacy issue that arises from a two nations strategy. Short-term electoral success may lead to longer term political disaster in a new legitimacy crisis.

After Thatcherism: a Territorial Crisis in a Naked State?

After setting the record as the longest serving British prime minister in the twentieth century, the question that was being generally asked is what happens after Mrs Thatcher? In the short term the answer under the new leadership of John Major is still working itself out. In the medium term—which is what the concept of Thatcherism is all about—the legacy of the Thatcher government is quite problematic. Although the thrust of its policies have looked very distinctive when viewed solely from a British perspective, when seen in a broader geographical context we have shown that Thatcherism's political agenda is part of a family of "new politics" found across the core of the world economy. This agenda is not even the property of the right. Nevertheless, there are unique features of Thatcherism relating to its location in Britain.

In the context of British political relations Thatcherism does constitute a transformation from past practices. As we have argued in the politics of power the buffers have been removed and in the politics of support two nations have been created. It is the combination of these two processes, aptly captured in the titles of two books—Graham and Prosser's (1988) *Waiving the Rules* and Johnston *et al*'s (1988) *A Nation Dividing*?—that dominates any consideration of the legacy of Thatcherism. Will there be a territorial crisis in this naked state? Thatcherism has set up this Unionist's nightmare as a genuine possibility. Perhaps Nairn's (1977) *Break-up of Britain* was two decades ahead of its time. Alternatively our world-economy approach suggests a different scenario. A new A phase of the world-economy will generate different material circumstances allowing a new agenda to be constructed. In this next family of new politics the distinctive British version, in its rejection of Thatcherism, may finally expunge the harking back to past national greatness from our politics. The end of the Cold War—Britain's final major contribution to a geopolitical world order—can signal a final acceptance of an "ordinary" status for Britain. The question is open as to what form of political relations will be constructed in a new Britain in a new Europe.

References

Beer, S.H. (1965) *Modern British Politics*. Faber, London.
Beer, S.H. (1982) *Britain Against Itself*. Faber, London.
Bulpitt, J. (1983) *Territory and Power in the United Kingdom*. Manchester University Press.
Bulpitt, J. (1986) The discipline of the new democracy: Mrs Thatcher's domestic statecraft, *Political Studies*, **34**: 19-39.
Crewe, I. (1988) Has the electorate become Thatcherite? In Skidelsky, R. (ed.) *Thatcherism*. Chatto & Windus, London.
Dahrendorf, R. (1988) Changing social values under Mrs Thatcher. In Skidelsky, R. (ed.) *Thatcherism*. Chatto & Windus, London.
Finer, S.E. (1987) Thatcherism and British political history. In Minogue, K. and Biddiss, M. (eds.) *Thatcherism: Personality and Politics*. Macmillan, London.
Gamble, A. (1988) *The Free Economy and the Strong State: The Politics of Thatcherism*. Macmillan, London.
Gamble, A. (1989) Thatcherism and the new politics. In Mohan, J. (ed.) *The Political Geography of Contemporary Britain*. Macmillan, London.
Gould, J., and Anderson, D. (1987) Thatcherism and British society. In Minogue, K. and Biddiss, M. (eds.) *Thatcherism: Personality and Politics*. Macmillan, London.
Graham, C., and Prosser, T. (eds.) (1988) *Waiving the Rules: The Constitution under Thatcherism*. Open University Press, Milton Keynes.
Hailsham, L. (1978) *The Dilemma of Democracy*. Collins, London.
Hall, S., and Jacques, M. (eds.) (1983) *The Politics of Thatcherism*. Lawrence & Wishart, London.
Hirst, P. (1989) *After Thatcher*. Collins, London.
Jessop, B., Bonnett, K., Bromley, S., and Ling, T. (1988) *Thatcherism: A Tale of Two Nations*. Polity Press, Cambridge.
Johnston, R.J., Pattie, C.J., and Allsopp, J.G. (1988) *A Nation Dividing? The Electoral Map of Great Britain, 1979-1987*. Longman, London.
Kavanach, D. (1990) *Thatcherism and British Politics: The End of Consensus?* 2nd edition. Oxford University Press.
King, A. (1975) Overload: problems of governing in the 1970s, *Political Studies*, 23: 284-296.
Marquand, D. (1988) The paradoxes of Thatcherism. In Skidelsky, R. (ed.) *Thatcherism*. Chatto & Windus, London.
Minogue, K. (1987) Introduction: the context of Thatcherism. In Minogue, K. and Biddiss, M. (eds.) *Thatcherism: Personality and Politics*. Macmillan, London.
Minogue, K. (1988) The emergence of the New Right. In Skidelsky, R. (ed.) *Thatcherism*. Chatto & Windus, London.
Myrdal, G. (1969) *Objectivity in Social Research*. Random House, New York.
Nairn, T. (1977) *The Break-up of Britain*. New Left, London.
Taylor, P.J. (1982) The changing political map. In Johnston, R.J. and Doornkamp, J.C. (eds.) *The Changing Geography of the United Kingdom*. Methuen, London.
Taylor, P.J. (1989a) *Political Geography: World-economy, Nation-state and Locality*. Longman, London.

Taylor, P.J. (1989b) Britain's changing role in the world-economy. In Mohan, J. (ed.) *The Political Geography of Contemporary Britain.* Macmillan, London.
Taylor, P.J. (1990) *Britain and the Cold War: 1945 as Geopolitical Transition.* Pinter, London.
Tivey, L. (1988) *Interpretations of British Politics.* Harvester Wheatsheaf, New York.
Wallerstein, I. (1983) *Historical Capitalism.* Verso, London.

3

Changing Intergovernmental Relations[1]

R.A.W. RHODES

Introduction

The 1980s were a decade of turmoil for local government and all other species of government beyond Westminster and Whitehall. This chapter presents a panoramic survey of the relationships between central government and sub-central governments (SCG) during the postwar period. It is not confined to the 1980s and the legislation of the three Thatcher parliaments for one simple reason: it is possible to explain developments in the 1980s only with reference to earlier years. Consequently I have broken this study into the following periods:

1945-61: stable external support system, economic and welfare state growth and *apolitisme*.

1974-79: unstable external support system, economic decline and incorporation.

1979-83: economic recession, bureaucratic control and politicization.

1983-87: economic recovery, abolition and stand-off.

1987-90: economic instability, a new central operating code and fragmentation.

The next section of the paper describes each of these five periods before in the third and final section I attempt a summary explanation of trends in intergovernmental relations (IGR) in the 1980s.

1945-61: Stability, Growth, Apolitisme

Strictly speaking, the years 1945-51 should be treated as the period of postwar reconstruction and the subsequent decade as one of growth. Any such division on economic grounds masks, however, other substantial continuities; with the benefit of hindsight the period is significant for what did not happen. Nationalist parties were conspicuous only for their electoral weakness. Conflict between central and local government was spasmodic and had a certain novelty value. If any concern was expressed it focused on the loss of functions by local government and the growing dependence of local authorities on central grant; the cry of centralization rent the air. Nonetheless, a number of developments should be noted.

First, the period was one of external stability, low unemployment, low inflation and relatively high growth rates. The economic surplus provided the means, whilst the central elite ideology provided the motive, to create the welfare state, and local government was the prime vehicle for the delivery of its services. Central departments in Britain were and have remained non-executant units of government. They have "hands-off" control of such major services as housing, education and welfare. Thus, if the period 1961-74 was to see the rate of growth accelerate, this period saw the foundations being laid for that development.

The second major development was the increasing use by government of *ad hoc* agencies, or non-departmental public bodies. The best known of these agencies is, of course, the National Health Service, but the period also saw the removal of public utilities (e.g. gas, electricity) from local government to the newly created nationalized industries.

Third, the period saw the increasing prominence of professionals as part of the structure of government; they became institutionalized. Accountants, lawyers, engineers and public health inspectors consolidated their position, and teachers, social workers and planners arrived on the scene. For the most part, career advancement was solely within the public sector, and professional work organization and the departments of local government were identical. The expansion of the welfare state went hand in hand with the extension of professional influence and the emergence of functional politics.

Fourth, central funding of local services was "consolidated". In 1946-47, 24 per cent of central funding was in the form of general grants: that is, money *not* assigned to specific services. By 1961, this figure had risen to 68 per cent. Central departments with responsibilities for particular services might have been expected to resist such an erosion of their influence—and indeed the (then) Ministry of Education did oppose such consolidation in 1929. However, there was little central resistance to block or general grants in this period because "other constraints on local government emerged in Britain alongside the growth in the grant system, so that specific grants became less necessary in the influencing of local service delivery" (Page 1981: p. 22). These constraints included the development of the legal framework of services; the vertical coalition of professionals in central and local government with shared values about (and responses to) service delivery; and, finally, the creation of vested interests by the specific grant so that producers *and* consumers supported service expenditure (Page 1981: p. 23).

Fifth, the period is distinguished by *apolitisme*. There are a number of strands to this argument. First, party colonization of sub-central governments was incomplete, and, for example, the numerous *ad hoc* agencies were subject to otiose forms of accountability. Second, a substantial proportion of local councils were controlled by "Independents", not the political parties. Third, the incursion of party politics into local government was resented and resisted; after all, "there's only one way to build a road". Fourth, even when the parties did control local authorities, there was little difference between them, and control could be purely nominal with little or no impact over and beyond the election. Decision-making was the preserve of committee chairmen and chief officers. Above all, IGR were characterized by professional bureaucratic brokerage and the relative weakness of political linkages between centre and periphery. (For a more detailed discussion see Bulpitt 1983: pp. 146-155.)

Finally, the interests of the periphery were managed by a strategy of accommodation. Scottish interests were accommodated by both the growth of expenditure and the gradual expansion of the functions of the Scottish Office. The same strategy of economic and administrative growth was applied to local authorities. To a significant degree, sub-central and central interests were united in the development of the welfare state and the pursuit of economic growth. The consolidation of functional politics was founded on consensus and quiescence.

1961-74: "Stop-Go", Modernization, Protest

Harold Wilson's aspiration to modernize Britain and generate economic growth through "the white heat of the technological revolution" had been anticipated by the Macmillan–Maudling experiment with planned growth from 1961. Along with the introduction of national planning, regional planning and a new national budgetary process came a more interventionist style of government and extensive reform of the machinery of government at every level. Britain was to be modernized.

Nevertheless, consultation and bargaining remained the normal style of intergovernmental relations. For most of the period local service spending was buoyant. Central governments of both parties kept an eye out for the electorally damaging implications of any slippage by local government in areas of key importance. For example, slum clearance and rehousing were policies pushed by central government departments for most of the 1960s, as was the reorganization of secondary schooling from the mid-1960s until the mid-1970s. A whole series of expectations about reasonably consensual dealing between Whitehall and local councils was embodied in the concept of "partnership". Ministers often went out of their way to choose mode of implementing policy that maximized voluntary local authority co-operation.

The bargaining phase lasted throughout the Heath government's period of office, despite some selective attempts by the Conservatives to develop more stringent controls. With some determination, the government forced through changes in council housing finances against strong resistance (including, in 1972, an attempt by the Labour council at Clay Cross to refuse implementation of rent increases imposed by the government). But elsewhere the government was cautious. Sales of council housing were successfully obstructed by all Labour councils. And although a full-scale reorganization of local authorities was put through against much opposition from councils destined to lose many of their powers, the two-tier system which the government adopted was more popular with existing councillors than previous Labour proposals for unitary authorities had been. Moreover, having decided on the principles of reform, the government was prepared to bargain over such "details" as the allocation of the planning function. Nowhere is evidence of bargaining clearer than in the determination of the level and allocation of central grant. Through their national representative organizations, local authorities were able to gain small but significant changes in both the total and the rate of growth of central grant. For local government, therefore, the period witnessed a mixture of centrally initiated reform and consultation.

Modernization intensified conflict between central and sub-central units of government. Central intervention provoked confrontations in the fields of education and housing. But given the scale of institutional change, the increase in conflict was modest. In part, protest was limited by the pre-existing structure of IGR. Local access to national political elites was relatively weak, whereas professional actors were key advocates of the reform (see Rhodes 1986a: ch. 6). Perhaps most important, the centre "factorized" the problem of reform. Thus, there were separate reorganizations of local government in Scotland, England and Wales and London; of particular functions (e.g. water, health); and of the centre's decentralized arms (e.g. regional economic planning councils and the Welsh Office). At no time was the reform of IGR comprehensively reviewed, and key aspects of the system were ignored altogether (e.g. finance). The central strategy of factorizing encouraged a fragmented response, dampened the level of protest and, in the case of water and health, simply served to reinforce professional dominance. The strategy of factorized modernization had few obvious economic benefits.

If this period saw the continued differentiation of functional politics, it also saw major conflicts in the arena of territorial politics. For example, the rise of Scottish and Welsh nationalism after 1967 represented a substantial threat to the consensus which had governed territorial politics in Britain.

Explanations of the rise of nationalism abound. The factors which caused the resurgent electoral performance of the SNP include: the decline of the UK economy, loss of confidence in British government, institutional weakness, the relatively greater economic decline of the regions, cultural differences, nationalist feelings and specific issues or grievances—for example, North Sea oil, membership of the EEC. There is corresponding disagreement on the importance of these factors.

Nationalism was not a phenomenon unique to the 1960s and early 1970s. It has been a persistent feature of the British political landscape reinforced by separate educational, legal, religious and governmental systems. Nor can such popular expressions of nationalism as a separate international football team, a national flag and a national anthem be omitted from the list of distinctive characteristics. However, the strength of Welsh and Scottish nationalism has been overstated. Rose (1982: p. 88) has pointed out that "By fighting elections, Nationalists register the weakness of their support in their own nation." The "problem" to be explained is *not* the rise of nationalism but why the centre in this period took the challenge so seriously. In other words, the issue to be explored is the constraints upon and the weakness of central government. In addition, the increasing salience of nationalism cannot be divorced from that of other social cleavages. The combined effects of central weakness and social differentiation were to become marked from 1974 onwards.

Above all, the attention accorded to nationalism in this period should not obscure the substantial continuities in SCG. The policy networks remained paramount in the expansion of welfare state services; the centre remained politically insulated from local elites; and, in Urwin's (1982: p. 68) phrases, "tolerance and indifference", "the concern to accommodate demands within the prevailing structure" and "an *ad hoc* attempt to resolve a specific complaint or demand" continued to characterize central attitudes and actions.

The key feature of intergovernmental relations in this period was not crisis but instability. Economic pressures were mounting, the central strategy of institutional modernization was bearing no obvious fruit, and the incidence of conflict and protest was increasing. The onset of economic decline was to alter the picture markedly.

Any explanation of the development of SCG in this period must encompass external instability, economic growth and a central elite ideology based on the mixed economy welfare state. The expansion of the welfare state led to increased functional differentiation and the institutionalization of the professions. The resulting policy networks, or professional-bureaucratic complexes, lie at the heart of a system of functional politics which marginalized local political elites. Britain was a "dual polity" (Bulpitt 1983: pp. 64-65 and ch. 5) characterized by the insulation of national from local political elites: functional politics came to dominate territorial politics.

However, there were stresses and strains within the system of functional politics. Economic growth and the subsequent occupational restructuring fostered class de-alignment. Traditional social cleavages re-emerged (e.g. nationalism) and functional politics generated sectoral cleavages. Moreover, Union had established a unitary state with multiform institutions, and the expansion of the welfare state had further fragmented service delivery systems. This complex of organizations became the locus within which the conflicts of a social structure characterized by multiple cleavages were played out. Economic growth and functional politics did not herald the homogeneous society but increased the degree of social and political differentiation. Functional politics fostered a territorial reaction.

It is important to remember that the politicization of intergovernmental relations has roots in an era of relative stability and prosperity. With deepening economic decline, an increasingly unstable external support system and a shift in central elite ideology, there was a quantum leap in politicization. In addition, the problem-solving capacity of the system began to experience ever-intensifying difficulties.

1974-79: Instability, Economic Decline, Incorporation

Three factors are particularly important for understanding developments in this period. First, the economic decline of the UK was accelerated by an unstable external support system. This instability was both economic—the escalation of world commodity prices, most notably oil prices—and political—UK dependence on international bodies and corresponding inability to take independent action. Confronted by massive inflation, the government had to seek a substantial loan from the IMF which required drastic cuts in public expenditure. Second, the reorganization of local government stimulated the spread of party politics and the virtual demise of the "Independent". Third, the 1974 elections produced a minority Labour government followed by an overall Labour majority of four. These knife edge situations generated imperatives to negotiate with minority parties to preserve a working majority. This conjunction of external economic disruption and political fragility called forth central strategies of incorporation for English local authorities and factorizing for nationalist political demands.

The Labour government clearly made a sustained effort to introduce a kind of top level, overall "corporatism" into its dealings with local government. Its innovation was to try to incorporate the powerful local authority associations (and their joint bodies) and reach a consensus about local government spending. For the first time, Whitehall set up a forum in which to discuss the long-run future of local spending with the local authority associations. This Consultative Council on Local Government Finance (CCLGF) was also remarkable in that it brought the Treasury and local authority representatives into face-to-face contact for the first time, and explicitly integrated the planning of local spending into the Public Expenditure Survey (PES) system. The government hoped that by involving the local authority associations in policy-making affecting local government it would be able to persuade them of the "realities" of the economic situation, and thus enlist their support in the battle to keep down the growth of local spending. In the Treasury's view, the objective of the CCLGF was "effective control", and if it was not achieved, "other measures would have to be considered" (Layfield Committee 1976: p. 327).

It is difficult to say how effective the CCLGF was in meeting this aim. Many of its members claim that it was successful in getting the local authority associations to persuade their members to behave with restraint. However, there were also other forces working in the same direction, including cash limits on central grants to local authorities and the swing in mid-term elections to Conservative-controlled authorities committed to expenditure restraint. But whatever else it accomplished the CCLGF symbolized a shift of influence within local government away from service-oriented councillors and officers (for example, the education policy community) and towards local politicians and finance directors more concerned with "corporate planning", increased efficiency and financial soundness. In effect, the CCLGF was an attempt by Whitehall to build up the influence of national community of local government, so that it would be better able to control the rest of the local government system in return for consultation and a direct voice in future planning (for a full account see Rhodes 1986a: ch. 4).

Other types of SCG were also "incorporated" and, in the case of the nationalized industries, they were explicitly part of the "Social Contract". The threat from nationalist politics produced an inconsistent response from the centre. Labour's majority was slight, and negotiations with third parties (including the SNP) were necessary to maintain a working majority. The government's problems in having to continuously manufacture a working majority were compounded by the parlous state of the British economy. The lack of economic growth denied the government the compromises, so typical of functional politics, of marginal improvements in service provision. Both inflation and unemployment rates rose, and "stagflation" replaced "stop–go" as the key dilemma of the British economy. In these circumstances, "cuts" in public expenditure were a high priority and the post-war consensus on the mixed economy welfare state began to crumble. Between 1976-79 the Labour government introduced a species of monetarism, the Conservative opposition was taking a decisive step towards social market liberalism, and the belief in salvation through institutional modernization was collapsing on its transparent failures. Whether these shifts are seen as a loss of confidence in government or the loss of confidence by governing elites, the period was one of reassessment and search for new directions. Moreover, the government was now denied the usual escape route of adventures in "high politics". Britain's role in the world had contracted and the country was vulnerable to externally generated instability. Attention was not easily distracted from domestic economic ills. The Labour government did not have its "Falklands" to rescue its public esteem. Devolution was, therefore, a policy bred of central weakness rather than nationalist strength. Certainly the policy was much disliked by both ministers and civil servants. The legislation bears all the hallmarks of antagonistic reluctance, being both internally inconsistent and ambiguous.

The first point to note about the government's response to the problem of nationalism was that it pursued separate policies in Scotland and Wales. There was a policy (of sorts) for England. "Organic change" or the redistribution of functions between the different types of local authority three years after a major reorganization was first mooted in a devolution White Paper and preoccupied the Secretary of State for the Environment between 1977-79. There was still no grand design for the reform of territorial politics, just a strategy of factorizing or a series of *ad hoc* responses.

Second, the government was determined that the doctrine of the supremacy of Parliament would not be challenged. Throughout the centre insisted, for example, on the retention of all powers of economic management. However, it is probably a mistake to suggest that constitutional issues were at stake. Political survival was the key consideration for a "minority" party government; the centre was to concede as little as possible commensurate with the Labour Party retaining power.

Third, although the growth of central intervention took a very poor second place to the devolution debate at the time, the changes in the form of that intervention were particularly significant. The definition of the centre's responsibility for economic management had stressed aggregate control. For local government, this responsibility encompassed the level of central grant to local government. Since 1975-76 this responsibility has been unilaterally redefined. Local *expenditure* (not grant) was explicitly included in the PES, the anticipated level of expenditure for individual local services was identified, and general guidance on the level of rate increases was proffered. In other words, central government was intervening to regulate local expenditure. It had not been so targeted before. Hereafter, the control was to become more specific.

Ostensibly a period of dramatic transformations, the years

1974-79 reaffirmed the resilience of the Union. After the defeats in the referenda, nationalist politics were weaker in 1979 than at any time in the past decade. But there had been important changes. If the new forms of central interventions in IGR were not newsworthy, they had the potential for transforming the system. That potential was soon to be realized.

1979-83: Economic Recession, Control, Politicization

If this period had a single theme, it was the search by central government for more effective instruments of control over the expenditures of sub-central government. Control was not, however, the only development of significance. The government sought to restrict the size of the public sector by privatization. Although its "progress" under this head was initially slow, nonetheless it became a distinctive feature of Conservative policy. Control and privatization can be seen as an attack on the public sector, as a means for curtailing its role in British society. A third feature of government strategy was the proliferation of non-departmental public bodies which served to expand the public sector and make it more complex.

Local government railed vigorously against being both controlled and bypassed by the use of non-departmental public bodies. As relations between the two levels of government deteriorated, so there were marked changes in behaviour. In short, the consultation so distinctive of the mid-1970s, was replaced by bureaucratic direction and confrontation. Successive Secretaries of State for the Environment adopted a unilateral style of decision making, and the more normal consultative mode was forsaken. Both sides demonstrated an increasing willingness to resort to litigation to resolve their differences. With Labour taking political control at the local level, local government responded to unilateralism with recalcitrance. An increasing number of Labour controlled local authorities demonstrated a willingness to defy the government's edicts on expenditure. In the vast majority of local authorities risk avoidance strategies became the dominant characteristic of the budgetary process; that is, local councils sought ways and means for reducing the uncertainties surrounding central grant.

The outcome of this new style of central local relations was a series of unintended consequences, the most serious of which, from the central government's point of view, was the need to make constant changes in the grant system in order to gain effective control. The government's explicit objective that *local* income and expenditure should conform with *national* decisions proved elusive.

Relations with SCG deteriorated because the Conservative Government sought to control public expenditure as part of its monetarist strategy for managing a national economy suffering from high inflation. Local expenditure is a significant proportion of total public expenditure, and its reduction was therefore a prime government objective. Although such a reduction served economic objectives, it was primarily part of a broader political strategy for restructuring the welfare state. In accordance with its avowed commitment to social market liberalism, the government also sought to expand the role of the market in the provision of services and to reduce government involvement.

The achievements of the new system can be described, at best, as mixed. It is clear that cuts were not as severe as they were widely perceived to be. Between 1979-80 and 1982-83 total public expenditure rose as a proportion of GDP, and central government's own proportion also increased sharply. The big spenders were not for the most part local government services, and some local services declined dramatically, e.g. housing. The Conservatives cut substantially the centre's contribution to local services; the proportion of net current local expenditure financed by block grant fell from 61 per cent to 56 per cent, whilst the proportion of expenditure financed by specific grants rose. The number of local government employees fell by 4 per cent in the same period. Most dramatically, local capital expenditure was subject to stringent regulation and was reduced by some 40 per cent in real terms from an already severely reduced base. And yet, in spite of the "cuts", local current expenditure *increased* between March 1979 and March 1983 by 9 per cent in real terms.

In short, as had been the case under the previous Labour government, local government was a prime target in the resource squeeze whilst, ironically, the Conservatives presided over an increase in both total public expenditure and local current expenditure.

Strategies for Scotland and Wales in this period were variations on the same themes. Scotland appears to have been used as the "test-bed" for legislation for England. Most of the grant innovations were introduced in Scotland first; for example, the Secretary of State for Scotland was empowered to reduce the grant to an individual local authority if he thought its expenditure was "excessive": a power not available to the Secretary of State for the Environment until 1985. A Welsh Consultative Council on Local Government Finance was introduced to implement the new grant system. This innovation had initially been proposed as part of the Labour government's devolution package. It now reappeared as a means of control, *not* devolution. *Both* cases provide a wonderfully clear example of the centre employing a factorizing strategy and using institutional reforms to solve its own problems.

With the increasingly apparent failure of successive governments to manage the mixed economy, the postwar consensus on intervention, ownership and the welfare state began to founder. In its place, the "New Right", focused on the money supply, the PSBR and the minimal state, emphasized reductions in public expenditure and the contraction of the welfare state. This "resource squeeze" intensified competition between policy networks determined to preserve their turf. Clients were mobilized, and direct contact with local political elites was established. The "hands-off" character of the dual polity was replaced by a command territorial operating code. This change was particularly obvious in the changes made to the system for distributing grant to local authorities; but it was also evident in the efforts to reduce the number of quangos and in the investment and pricing controls over the nationalized industries. But direction was a high cost strategy. At first, the centre had channelled its political contacts through an intermediate tier of representation based on the national community of local government. Increasingly, this channel was replaced by face-to-face contact between ministers and individual (or small groups of) local authorities. Ministers were dragged into conflict with the "over-spending" local authorities. The politicization of local politics had spilt over into IGR. The costs in time and even loss of political face were mounting. To make matters worse, the policy failed. The new central elite ideology had not countered economic decline with a reduction in the size of the public sector but it had intensified the politicization of SCG and generated a policy mess wherein nobody achieved their objectives.

Moreover, the changes in SCG exerted a feed back effect on national government policy. Thus, expenditure controls fell largely on local capital expenditure and, in effect, became cuts in the private sector, e.g. the construction industry, thereby contributing to the de-industrialization of the British economy and rising unemployment. Government action intensified economic decline, which in turn increased the pressure on the welfare state, in particular in social security payments to the unemployed. Policy networks had the capacity to resist the pressure for reduced expenditure and, coupled with strident protest from client groups, welfare state expenditures continued to rise. This increase threatened the government's monetary targets, intensified the search for means to control public expenditure and generated yet more recalcitrance in SCG. The resultant policy mess casts doubt on the efficacy of the command operating code of central elites.

1983-87: Recovery, Abolition and Stand-off

After four years of direction and control, the Conservatives faced a choice in 1983 between intensifying bureaucratic direction and a more conciliatory mix of strategies designed to win compliance. The government chose to intensify direction. IGR seemed to be entering a new phase of explicit centralization.

The government's first step was to abolish the Greater London Council (GLC) and the metropolitan county councils (MCCs) because they were Labour dominated, high spending and at odds with the government's view of the world. Their functions were transferred to a range of bodies including central departments, quangos, private companies, joint bodies, joint committees, district councils/London boroughs. The new system is both fragmented and complex (for details see Hebbert and Travers 1988 and Leach and Davis 1990). It is also important to note that a significant proportion of these agencies are not directly or indirectly elected. For example, only 33 per cent of the expenditure on local services in London is by the directly elected London boroughs.

After removing the "over-spending" GLC and MCCs, the government added a second prong to its attack: the introduction of rate capping. However, imposing a ceiling on the amount of tax a local authority could raise affected only a small number of authorities and made only a marginal contribution to the reduction of total local authority expenditure. Between 1983 and 1987 local current expenditure continued to rise in real terms by some 11 per cent. The government returned to the fray announcing that it would introduce the community charge, better known as the poll tax (HMSO 1986). However, the Green Paper made little immediate impact. The government wanted to secure a third term of office before resuming its attack on the "problem" of local government. There was a stand-off, made possible by the relative improvement in Britain's economic fortunes. Grant settlements were more favourable to local authorities. Volume targets were abolished. The increase in expenditure continued. "You can't throw money at problems, money isn't the answer. . . . But there is one exception to the rule. You could throw money at a General Election" (Jenkins 1989: p. 280). The brakes were off. More important, the radical government had lost its sense of direction. The local government stand-off is one instance of this drift in government policy and, perhaps, it could be said to epitomize the government's second parliament.

The failure of centralization and direction as an effective strategy for local government is clearly illustrated by the phenomenon of repetitive legislation. Repetitive legislation is the process whereby laws are made and remade throughout a parliament because of the high degree of uncertainty surrounding their viability. The sheer volume of local government legislation in the 1980s is evidence of this process; there were some 40 Acts of Parliament directly affecting local government, especially local government finance.

Instability, which was already a feature of the system, was intensified by both repetitive legislation and the complex, fragmented structure of the conurbations. Both the Audit Commission (1984) and the Comptroller and Auditor General (1985) concluded that the grant system was causing inefficiency and ineffectiveness in local government.

Although local authorities remained willing to challenge the centre in the courts, the main response to the waves of legislation took the form of political campaigns. The GLC and the MCCs mounted professional public relations campaigns against their abolition. Rate-capped councils mounted a united campaign up to the deadline for making a rate where upon they capitulated. Conservative control of the county councils was eroded to the extent that 25 out of 46 English and Welsh counties had no party in overall control. The new urban left flourished in metropolitan areas (Gyford 1985). Eventually even the government conceded that there had been "a worsening of the relationship between central government and the moderate and responsible local authorities" (HMSO 1986: p. 5). Given that local authorities were recalcitrant tools, the government turned to a variety of other agencies in order to achieve its objectives. The Manpower Services Commission (MSC, latterly the Training Agency) rather than local education authorities was used as the vehicle for the government's programme to improve vocational education in and out of schools. In the inner cities, the government deployed enterprise zones, free ports and urban development corporations as the means for economic regeneration. The abolition of the GLC and the MCCs proliferated agencies whilst contracting out increased the involvement of the private sector in service delivery.

The importance of these changes cannot be underestimated. They left few policy areas as the exclusive domain of a single agency. Organizational interdependence is ubiquitous. Effective policy implementation requires interorganizational co-operation. By proliferating agencies, bypassing local government and restructuring its relationships with non-departmental public bodies, the government created obstacles to co-operation and increased policy slippage. The range of agencies involved in the delivery of services increased substantially. The predilection for a command style over consultation was linked to policies which fostered structural differentiation, thereby dissipating authority between agencies.

However, although the thrust of the legislation between 1983-87 was undeniably centralizing, the extent to which it increased the capacity of the centre to realize its objectives should not be overestimated. Economic recovery, reduced levels of unemployment and the receipts from privatization paid for the tax cuts whilst public expenditure was stabilized as a proportion of GNP. Conservative policies contained the seeds of their own ineffectiveness. Repetitive legislation and the politicization of IGR generated a complex, ambiguous, unstable and recalcitrant system. Policy networks were a source of dynamic conservatism, slowing the pace of change. The command style was evidence of a faulty operating code. The government failed to recognize that Britain was a dual polity in which centre and locality were insulated from each other and opted for a strategy which required hands-on control of the sub-central system. The resultant policy mess, in which no level of government could attain its objectives, was inevitable. Policy towards local government was in limbo. Local authorities were battered, bowed but not yet broken. The "revolution" was just around the corner.

1987-90: Instability, a New Code and Fragmentation

The legislative programme of the third Conservative parliament may have been as prolific as its two predecessors but it was qualitatively different. The objective was still control but command was no longer the strategy. Some of the lessons of the previous two terms had been learnt. The narrow fixation on local expenditure gave way to a set of broader themes designed to restructure local government and provide a new territorial operating code for the centre. There were three key themes: accountability, competition and consumerism.

The Local Government Finance Act 1988 abolished domestic rates and replaced them with a flat rate charge paid by all adults. The non-domestic rate was replaced by a uniform business rate set by the centre. The grant system was (ostensibly) simplified. The aim of the poll tax was to reinforce the link between the receipt of, and paying for, services. Everybody was to pay something towards the cost of local services. Accountability was also reinforced for particular services. For example, the Education Reform Act 1988 gave parents more control over schools and delegated financial responsibility to school governors.

Although it is too early to draw any definite conclusions about the results of the move towards greater accountability, the immediate consequences of the poll tax are obvious: demonstrations, backbench disquiet, poor government performance in the opinion polls, defeat in local elections and massive subsidies to local authorities to reduce poll tax levels and thereby limit possible electoral damage. The politicization of IGR continued apace. Moreover, this list does not fully reveal the extent of the government's problems; for example the full impact of the business rate remains to be felt because of transitional arrangements. The costs of abolishing the poll tax and introducing the council tax are high. To compound the difficulties still further, the government was pursuing conflicting objectives. For example, the link between local services and paying for them was obscured by both subsidies to reduce the increase in bills and by capping poll tax. In effect, if voters did not vote to reduce local expenditure, then the government stepped in to levy the "correct" level of taxation. Accountability had to give way to the need to reduce expenditure. And amidst all the changes and controversy, local current expenditure continued to rise!

The government has always favoured contracting-out and the Local Government Act 1988 legislates for its introduction in refuse collection, street cleaning, catering, the cleaning of buildings, grounds and vehicle maintenance. The introduction of such competition may not lead to a vastly increased role for the private sector but it does reduce levels of pay and conditions of work for the workforce even when the service continues to be provided by the local authority.

Allied to accountability and competition is the concept of citizens as customers, not as clients. Customers not only pay for the service—the link to accountability—but they are also demanding—the link to competition. Thus, the Housing Act 1980 gave tenants the right to buy their council houses and the Housing Act 1988 extended tenants' choice, giving them the right to choose a landlord other than the local authority. In education also, parental choice has been extended. Parents may choose between LEA schools, City Technology Colleges and Grant Maintained Schools. It is clear that the sale of council houses has been a popular and successful policy, although the latest package does not seem to offer the same prospects (Rhodes 1991).

Since its first parliament, it is clear that the government sought to control the expenditure of individual local authorities. Repetitive legislation merely served to multiply unintended consequences. Frustrated by the failure of its command strategy, the government retaliated by abolishing and capping "over-spenders" to discover that it still had not achieved its goal of cutting local expenditure. Instability, ambiguity and confusion, not "cuts", were the products of its actions. The relationship between central and local government was a policy mess. No level of government could attain its objectives. A stand-off ensued in which the government re-thought its strategy and returned with a "revolutionary" programme of reform.

If the government has failed to achieve its major objectives, and if the overall result is a policy mess, nonetheless the record is not one of unrelieved gloom for the Conservatives. Elements of the government's several policies have been successful. For example, its ideological messages about consumer choice and competition have had some impact. The government has also derived marked political benefits from policies such as the sale of council houses. The outcome of the "revolutionary" programme is unclear. The record doe not inspire confidence. The prognosis has to be cautious, however, reflecting not only the fact that the government has had some success but also its persistence.

The three themes of accountability, competition and consumerism can be summarized in the phrase "the enabling authority". In other words, local authorities have ceased to be the sole providers of services. They now work with and through a range of bodies. To ensure that the services are provided efficiently there will be increased competition and greater responsiveness to consumers. The role of the local authority will be to manage contracts and to regulate contractors. Service provision at the local level will become highly differentiated with central agencies, local authorities, other sub-central agencies (such as the NHS), private companies and the voluntary sector all playing an important role. The intention is that the centre will no longer play a command role because control will be an inevitable product of competitiveness, accountability and responsiveness in a differentiated sub-central system.

There are, however, contradictions in the programme of policies. In some respects the reforms may have a centralizing effect. Up to 75 per cent of local authority income is now centrally determined. Similarly, there seems to be a centralizing trend in particular policy areas: for example, the introduction of the national curriculum in education. Nonetheless, there is clear evidence of decentralization. For example, the introduction of local management schemes in education decentralizes financial management to schools and their governors. The government has proliferated agencies and thereby increased its problems of co-ordination and control. It could be argued that the strategy is to erode the powers of local government by centralizing some functions (e.g. the national curriculum) and decentralizing others to markets or citizens (e.g. school finances). But the evidence for this interpretation is also contradictory. For example, local authorities have been given increased responsibilities for child care and their responsibility for community care is to be enlarged. The reason for this catalogue of contradictions is as simple as it is important. I have tried to describe recent changes in a systematic way, but consistency is not a feature of the government's programme. I have imposed a set of *ex post facto* rationalizations on a disparate and at times contradictory set of policies. None of the Acts post-1987 follows a consistent or simple set of principles.

Explanation

In order to understand the likely outcome of the local government reforms of the 1980s, it is necessary to explore the interaction between national economic problems, party ideology, party politics, bureaucratic tradition and bureaucratic politics.

Interventions in IGR do not reflect the government's concern with the state of local government but with the perceived imperatives of national economic management. In the case of the Conservative government, concern with inflation, the public sector borrowing requirement and the level of public expenditure shaped policy on local government. Although the Labour Party may have had a similar definition of the economic problem between 1975-79, the Conservative Party's response to Britain's relative economic decline was distinctively shaped by ideology.

The control of local expenditure may have been a long-standing concern of the Treasury, but the policies on privatization and the poll tax and the scale of contracting out are distinctively Conservative. They also reflect the thinking of the New Right and its various think tanks. Economic problems provided the stimulus to intervene. Party ideology shaped the form and extent of that intervention. Political parties give expression to ideology and are a major source of policy initiation, a counterweight to the inertia of Whitehall and interests institutionalized in policy networks. They are also the focal point of conflict. Conservative policies have politicized and polarized IGR. The Labour Party has a majority on a substantial and increasing proportion of local councils. Local government has been simultaneously an area in which the electoral fortunes of the Labour Party have been revived, the test bed for socialist policies, and the main source of opposition to the government. Local government has been a pawn in this increasingly polarized national party political arena.

The Conservative Party may have initiated a range of policies but intent and result diverged markedly. The government either did not anticipate, or ignored, the constraints imposed by the dual polity and by policy networks. The dual polity exemplifies the non-executant tradition of administration and the political insulation of centre from locality. The government was determined to intervene and to control individual local authorities. It adopted a command or bureaucratic operating code. It either failed to understand, or chose to ignore, the simple fact that British government is differentiated and disaggregated: the unitary state is a multi-form maze of interdependencies. As a result, it lacked the hands-on means to impose its policies: the organizational infrastructure of field agents to supervise implementation. It also politicized relationships with local government thereby eroding the latter's "responsibility ethic" or predisposition to conform to government expenditure guidelines. Failure was built into the original policy design.

To compound the problem, the professional-bureaucratic complexes at the heart of British government—the policy networks—were a brake on the government's ambitions. Policy making in British government is dominated by function specific networks comprising central departments, professions and other key interests. Outside interests are institutionalized in government, relationships are routinized, the policy agenda is stable and conservative with a small "c", and policy change is incremental. These networks, especially the professions, were "handbagged" by the Thatcher government. Unfortunately, their co-operation was integral to the effective implementation of policy. A pattern of authoritative pronouncements by the centre followed by policy slippage in implementation became all too common. The dynamic conservatism of the policy networks illustrates the recurrent tension in British government between authoritative decision making and interdependence.

The history of local government is compounded of multiple contradictions—economic, political and organization. Monocausal explanations are inadequate. Policy making for local government has generated a policy mess because of the failure to appreciate that disaggregation, differentiation, interdependence and policy networks are central characteristics of the British polity.

"The Enabling Authority" may represent a new territorial operating code for the centre. The success or otherwise of the recent wave of government policy on local government remains to be seen. One point is, however, clear. The system remains unstable. The Conservatives will require a fourth election victory and another Parliament to successfully implement its reforms. Few would have believed in 1979 that British government, with its long-standing tradition of a strong executive, would still be seeking to control its local government system after a decade of legislation. If there has been centralization, it is at the cost of central effectiveness. If, as some commentators allege, the 1980s witnessed the demise of local government, the patient's death is a very slow one. There are no winners in this particular game. Everybody loses. The term "policy mess" most accurately captures the indeterminacy of the policy outcomes.

Note

1. This paper incorporates extracts from Rhodes (1988: pp. 371-387). I would like to thank Unwin-Hyman for permission to re-use this material. Lack of space has led me to focus on developments in local government. I have deliberately excluded Northern Ireland and a thorough analysis of the sub-central government should devote more space to non-departmental public bodies and the policy of privatization. For a discussion of these topics the reader should consult Rhodes (1988). My thanks to Keith Alderman (York) for his comments on the first draft of the chapter.

References

Audit Commission for Local Authorities in England and Wales (1984) *The Impact on Local Authorities' Economy, Efficiency and Effectiveness of the Block Grant Distribution System*. HMSO, London.

Bulpitt, J.G. (1983) *Territory and Power in the United Kingdom.* Manchester University Press, Manchester.

Committee of Public Accounts (1985) *Operation of the Rate Support Grant System.* Seventh Report, Session 1985-86, HC 47. HMSO, London.

Gyford, J. (1985) *The Politics of Local Socialism.* Allen & Unwin, London.

Hebbert, M., and Travers, T. (eds.) (1988) *The London Government Handbook.* Cassell, London.

HMSO (1986) *Paying for Local Government.* Cmnd 9714. HMSO, London.

Jenkins, P. (1989) *Mrs Thatcher's Revolution.* Pan Books, London.

Layfield Committee (1976) *Report of the Committee of Inquiry into Local Government Finance.* Cmnd 6453. HMSO, London.

Leach, S., and Davis, H. (1990) Impact of the abolition of the metropolitan county councils. *Local Government Studies*, **16**, No. 3, pp. 1-11.

Page, E. (1981) Grant consolidation and the development of inter-governmental relations in the United States and the United Kingdom. *Politics*, **1**, No. 1, pp. 19-24.

Rhodes, R.A.W. (1986) *The National World of Local Government.* Allen & Unwin, London.

Rhodes, R.A.W. (1988) *Beyond Westminster and Whitehall.* Unwin-Hyman, London.

Rhodes, R.A.W. (1991) How Nobody Understands the System: The Changing Face of Local Government. In Norton, P. (ed.) *New Directions in British Politics*, pp. 83–112. Edward Elgar, Aldershot.

Rose, R. (1982) *Understanding the United Kingdom.* Longman, London.

Urwin, D.W. (1982) Territorial structures and political developments in the United Kingdom. In Rokkan, S. and Urwin, D.W. (eds.) *The Politics of Territorial Identity*, pp. 19-73. Sage, London.

4

The Changing Local State

MARK GOODWIN

Introduction

In the previous chapter we saw the ways in which the institutions of local government, and their relationship with the centre, have undergone significant changes since the mid-1970s. This chapter will remain focused at the local level, but will broaden the perspective by looking at the changing nature of the local state. Immediately we shift our attention to the state, rather than just the institutions of government, our conceptual and theoretical framework must widen accordingly. In any consideration of the state, we need to give equal weight to both the "state form" and the "state apparatus". The latter refers to a set of physical institutions (such as health authorities or County Councils), the former to the social relations expressed through them (such as those between dominant and subordinate classes, or between men and women). If we manage to retain this balanced perspective it should then be possible to examine both the changing relations of the local state under Thatcherism and the changing policy arenas therein.

The chapter contains four main sections. The first outlines the key processes of change and restructuring undertaken by three successive Thatcher governments. The second looks at the effects that these changes have had on the institutions *and* relations of the local state, and the third examines differing explanations of the driving forces behind them. Finally, a concluding section will develop one of these explanations, based on the concepts of Fordism and post-Fordism, in order to account for changes in both local state policy and local state relations. However, before we begin any of this, a preliminary word is necessary concerning the chapter's contents. These will focus primarily on the local state at a general level, thus concentrating on the activities and relations surrounding local government, and individual policy changes for detailed consideration in chapters—although particular pieces of legislation will be dıs.ussed briefly where appropriate.

Restructuring the Local State

According to one of the most respected commentators on Mrs Thatcher's first decade in office, the *Financial Times* journalist Peter Riddell, "roughly 50 separate acts have been passed since 1979 aimed at reducing the independence of local authorities" (Riddell 1989: p. 177). When allied to the mass of legislation designed to restructure other aspects of the local state, such as the Health Service and transport provision, this represents a considerable amount of government time, effort and trouble. As we shall see, the changes have not remained uncontested, and have generated extensive political conflict and debate. The end result has been a system of local administration and policy making which is almost unrecognizable from that which existed in 1979. In order to simplify what at times has amounted to a bewildering array of changes, I have identified four key areas of restructuring, involving the control of local finance: the privatization and "marketization" of public services; the loss of local state autonomy over the remaining public services; and the expansion of non-elected agencies. Each area of change will be described briefly in turn (see Cochrane 1989, Duncan and Goodwin 1988, Goodwin and Duncan 1989, Stewart and Stoker 1989, Stoker 1988, 1990 for details).

The control of local finance has involved constraints on the amount of grant given by the central to the local state (including unelected agencies such as health and transport authorities), controls on the levels of current and capital spending undertaken by the local state and limits on the amount of money local government is able to raise via local taxation. It would be wrong to portray this process as completely new. The oil crisis of 1973, and subsequent economic depression, reinforced by the conditions of the 1976 IMF loan, had led the Labour government to tighten central control prior to 1979. However, this form of intervention remained at the very general level of local state expenditure as a whole, and in particular concerned total levels of public borrowing and central grant. If the political will and political support were there, local governments could still make and meet their own policy plans by raising rate revenue to finance expenditure.

This changed in 1979 when the Conservative Government introduced a legislative path which led to direct and overt expenditure controls over individual local authorities, beginning with one of Mrs Thatcher's very first major acts, the 1980 Local Government, Planning and Land Act, which replaced the Rate Support Grant as a mechanism for determining central grants to local authorities. Through their use of a complicated mixture of controls, targets, and penalties it became clear that the Conservatives were placing the stress not only on the control of total spending, but also on targeting individual authorities. Moreover, lost grant could only be made up by a further increase in rates, hence increasing the electoral pressure against high spending authorities, and shifting the "blame" for local expenditure crises from the central to the local state.

These initial manoeuvres set the tone for the next decade, and the only change was in the intensity with which local spending was controlled. The penalty systems became more and more finely targeted, and in 1984 legislation was introduced through the Rates Act, enabling central government to set a maximum rate level (or rate cap) for particular councils. In 1990 a community charge (or poll tax) replaced domestic rates in England and Wales, following initial testing in Scotland two years previously (as occurred with rate capping). Instead of a local taxation system based on property values, it is now based on a flat rate *per capita* charge levied on all adults. A "community charge cap" replaced rate capping in order to specify maximum spending levels for particular authorities. Theoretically the new charge is supposed to increase the "accountability" of local authorities and local elections. But the electors will not be able to choose to spend above a centrally prescribed limit, and the imposition of a uniform business rate lowers the amount of spending decided and voted upon locally to around 20 per cent. Central government will control the remaining 75-80 per cent of local expenditure, and thus any increase beyond that considered necessary by the centre will have to be financed disproportionately by local residents. The new system also replaces a slightly progressive tax with a generally regressive one (Travers 1989). When introducing the new charge, the centre took the opportunity of another comprehensive financial reform by restructuring its system of central grant, and increasing controls on local capital spending.

The second key area of local state restructuring has involved the privatization of previously public services, and the "marketization" of services as a whole. This has proceeded via three distinct mechanisms—the sale of locally owned public assets; a more direct involvement of the private sector in providing local services; and the introduction of market discipline into public service provision through competitive tendering and deregulation (Stoker 1988). The most important sales of public assets have been in the two areas of housing (see Chapter 7) and land, and again the gradual and constant intensification of the process has been a feature of Thatcher's first decade. In the decade since 1979, public spending on council housing in England has fallen by 80 per cent in real terms and around a million council houses have been transferred to private ownership since 1979, at a time when public housing starts fell from 107,000 in 1978 to only 30,000 in 1987. Land sales have not generated as much political controversy as have those of council housing, but they have been of vital importance in terms of the transfer not just of ownership but also of control, especially over key urban development sites.

The provision of local services under Mrs Thatcher's governments has been increasingly undertaken by commercial enterprises under contract to the local state agency concerned. The 1980 legislation made it compulsory for local authorities to engage in competitive tendering for the construction and maintenance of buildings and highways, and to make a return on capital of at least 5 per cent within their direct labour organizations. In 1983 the government extended the policy of compulsory competitive tendering to the catering, domestic and laundry services of the National Health Service, and in 1985 the Transport Act required public bus undertakings to operate commercially via tenders. Passenger transport executives were reduced to little more than administrative co-ordinators, no longer directly accountable to the local electorate and no longer responsible for overall transport planning. Tendering was also introduced for "socially necessary" services, which were placed in direct budget competition with more profitable routes following the cutting of route cross-subsidization. The Local Government Act 1988 requires authorities to place refuse collection, street cleaning, catering, grounds and vehicle maintenance and cleaning of buildings out to tender, and orders them not to "act in a manner having the effect or intended or likely to have the effect of restricting, distorting or preventing competition" (Walsh 1989: p. 39). This latter clause means that the private sector will be able to take action against any authority which they consider to be acting anti-competitively.

Although the indications are that local authorities will initially retain many of their service contracts because of their detailed experience and knowledge of the service area concerned, increasing transfers will take place as the private sector expands into new areas of work. Moreover, restrictions on local authority budgets have encouraged new forms of service provision, without tendering—private homes for the elderly, for instance growing at the expense of increasingly destitute public homes, and housing associations increasingly taking on the task of public sector housing provision from cash-starved local councils. In any case, the effect of this tendering process is considerable even when the local authority retains the contract. Pay, conditions of service, and level of employment are all likely to decline in the face of competition, and the indications are that in order to win tenders, public sector workforces are being cut by between 15 and 30 per cent (ibid. p. 5). This indirect effect has been called the "marketization" of the local state, where decisions concerning service delivery are now taken according to quasi-market principles and not with regard to professional or political judgements.

Those services which have remained in public sector hands have been increasingly subject to a standardized central control, or a fragmented and non-elected local control. This removal of local autonomy amounts to the third major facet of local state restructuring, and often the process is a complicated mixture of both these strands. (In addition to others, such as the restrictions placed by legislation on the political content of local authority publicity.) In education, for instance, the 1988 Education Reform Act allowed schools to opt out of local authority control by becoming grant maintained; gave parents greater flexibility in choosing schools; and devolved financial management from the local authority to the individual school. But it granted these "freedoms" against a background of a nationally governed curriculum, and a centrally determined system of "formula funding" (Ranson and Thomas 1989). Similarly under the 1988 Housing Act and the 1989 Local Government and Housing Act, tenants, both individually and collectively can now choose an alternative "social landlord" to the local authority, but the authority itself is constrained by a series of financial reforms which manage to increase both central control and local rent levels at the same time (Spencer 1989). And of course the abolition of the Metropolitan County Councils in 1986 transferred their functions to a bewildering array of joint boards, regional authorities, district councils, regional quangos and central government.

The byzantine structure of agencies levered into place to replace the Metropolitan Councils was but one stage in the continual increase in non-elected authorities since 1979, an increase which represents the fourth major theme of local state restructuring (Stoker 1988: ch. 3). But as with financial control, the growth of the non-elected local state had begun before the rise of Mrs Thatcher in 1979. In many policy arenas local electoral influence and accountability were reduced or removed by the creation of regional scale corporatist bodies of appointees and nominees, heavily subject to central direction, but often representing specific interest groups (Duncan and Goodwin 1988: ch. 7). Mrs Thatcher continued this trend. The 1982 health legislation reduced local government nomination to one-fifth of the members of the District Health Authorities (compared with one-third on the abolished Area Health Authorities), ruled out elections for any DHA member, took away common boundaries with local authorities and severely weakened the access, status and financing of Community Health Councils. Similarly, the 1983 Water Act abolished council membership entirely on Regional Water Authorities and removed the need to allow public audience at their meetings. In these particular policy areas the remaining significance of these regional agencies has been weakened considerably by privatization in the case of water, and by financial and management changes in the case of health. In other areas, however, regional bodies have increased under Mrs Thatcher—most notably the joint boards set up following the abolition of the Metropolitan Counties, to run activities such as strategic planning, fire and police services.

But the largest and most important proliferation of non-elected agencies over the past decade has occurred at the local level. Some have been set up as a direct result of central initiative—Urban Development Corporations, City Action Teams and Task Forces, for instance have taken over development control powers and urban renewal tasks from local authorities (see Chapter 10), and now spend some £300 million per year (Duncan and Goodwin 1988, Lawless 1989, Robson 1988). Housing Action Trusts were established under the 1988 Housing Act to take over run-down council estates and facilitate their transfer to the private sector, but local opposition has made this scheme all but unworkable (see Spencer 1989, Woodward 1991). Around 100 Training and Enterprise Councils are now responsible for the local provision of training and vocational education, and are controlled by boards, to which two-thirds of the appointments must be senior managers from the private sector. Each will have an annual budget of £20 million of public money. Other non-elected bodies have been instigated by the local authorities themselves, most notably Enterprise Boards and co-operative development agencies, in the field of local economic development, and still more have resulted from private sector initiative, such as local enterprise agencies designed to co-ordinate small business initiatives and advice. Whatever the source, the result has been a considerable increase over the past decade in both the variety and scope of non-elected local agencies.

The first Thatcher decade has thus increased central control, via financial and legislative means; shifted services from the public to the private sector, and introduced a range of non-elected agencies to run those services left in public hands. What have been the overall effects of this programme on the actions and relations of the local state?

The Effects of Local State Restructuring

In order to examine the effects of these changes we will turn to a framework put forward by Bob Jessop, when he claimed that there "is now a distinctive pattern to the shifts in the state system" under Mrs Thatcher (1989a: p. 29). Jessop backed up this claim by reviewing six different dimensions of the political system centred on the state. Three are largely concerned with the institutions of the state while three examine the surrounding social relations, and although he was concerned with the central state, we can also utilize these six dimensions to examine changes in the local state. Jessop labels them the *representational regime*; the *internal organization* of the state system; *patterns of intervention*; the *social basis* of the state; the *state project* purporting to give the state system some cohesion and unity; and the *hegemonic project* which defines the interests of the "illusory community" which government claims to represent. Although there have been significant changes along each of these dimensions over the past decade, as we have already noted it would be wrong to attribute all of these purely to Thatcherism. We can, however, agree with Jessop when he writes that "the overall trend in political reorganization has been strongly influenced by the ten-year dominance of the Thatcher government" (ibid). In order to show this, we will deal with each of the six dimensions in turn.

1. Restructuring the Representational Regime

The representational regime of the local state has been restructured in three main ways. First, as the only form of direct representative government in Britain apart from Parliament, local authorities play a crucial role in the representational process. Local interests are able to promote their preferred policies, often in opposition to those of the centre, which become legitimated through the ballot box (Duncan and Goodwin 1988). What has happened over the past ten years is that their ability to carry out this role has been severely curtailed, not least through changes in the representational regime itself. Business representation has substantially increased on non-elected local state agencies, and even those that are directly elected must now increasingly enter into partnership arrangements with the private sector. As Michael Heseltine said, when reorganizing the Urban Programme as early as 1979, the need was to "ensure that the balance of the programme is influenced by people employed other than in the public sector" (Duncan and Goodwin 1988: p. 141).

The representational regime has also changed in terms of party politics. There has been a move away from the broad bipartisan consensus on the role of local government which both main parties embraced during the period of postwar stability identified in the previous chapter. Instead, as Jessop puts it "the populist . . . party no longer functions primarily as a relay for relatively stable interests or clearcut programmes from below but as a means of mobilising popular votes" (1989a: p. 31). In terms of local government we have seen policies emerge at both the central and the local level that are electorally driven by short-term considerations of such mobilization for party advantage. With regard to the former, the clearest example is perhaps Mrs Thatcher's continued insistence on reforming what she saw as an electorally unpopular rating system, a gut instinctiveness which was to lead to an even more unpopular poll tax, against the advice of most of her close advisers. At the local level we witnessed the growth of "market research socialism", especially in London, where a bitter internal battle was fought within the Labour Party to remove the so-called "loony left" from control of several Borough Councils, because their activities through the local state seemed to be causing electoral unpopularity. Paradoxically, the stimulus for this unpopularity was a somewhat ridiculous, and often vicious, Conservative campaign which was intensified because of Labour's relative success in the May 1986 local government elections. Professor James Curran has estimated that between 1981 and 1987 there were some 3,000 "loony left" stories in the national tabloid press alone, a large proportion of which were partially or entirely fabricated, and all of which were aimed at swinging public opinion against a small number of Labour controlled urban authorities (Gyford *et al.* 1989: p. 312). The end result was the infamous attack in 1987 by the Labour leadership on its own London councils, orchestrated via a leaked letter written by Neil Kinnock's press secretary. The key reason for this was the belief that the actions of these left wing councils were preventing Labour from building up sufficient electoral support to defeat Mrs Thatcher in 1987. The local state has thus become a key area of political contention, and has itself played a leading role in shaping the new representational regimes of the leading parties, a shift from the rather quiet backwater it occupied over most of the postwar period (Goodwin 1989).

A third change in the representational regime was that on local government issues the government often decided to cut out intermediate representation and appeal directly to "the people". There was a failure to consult affected interests, or take into account their views when they were asked; a marked reluctance to set up any sort of review body (the plethora of commissions and enquiries which accompanied the reform of local government in the 1960s and 1970s were especially conspicuous by their absence); and an obvious inability to justify the reasons for several major pieces of legislation—even to Conservative MPs. As one senior Conservative back-bencher said of the very first piece of local government legislation, the 1980 Local Government, Planning and Land Act, "it is unique to have a Bill on which all local government associations of whatever complexion are sensibly united against the Government's measures. It is also unique that no one outside the Government has spoken up for the Bill . . . I have been years in local government and have not come to Parliament to turn a partnership into a dictatorship" (Duncan and Goodwin 1989: p. 111). Such feelings were voiced on almost every occasion a major Bill affecting local government came to Parliament in the course of the next decade, but all were paid a singular lack of attention by the Thatcher governments.

2. Restructuring the Internal Structures

The *internal structures* of the state have undergone what Jessop, quoting Harden, calls "a movement towards an 'undemocratic centralism' " (1989a: p. 32). We have already given several indications of this, and further details will be provided in subsequent chapters. The overall effect has been to concentrate power in Whitehall and Westminster at the expense of elected local government, through removing, reducing or curtailing the powers of the latter. However, although the role of the local state has been lessened in many policy arenas, it has still had to cope with implementing some of the most difficult and politically sensitive elements of the Thatcherite vision. Not only has there been a shift in the balance of power within the internal state structure, but there has also been a polarization in the functions carried out by each part. The local state now finds itself operating an emergency service for the less fortunate section of Mrs Thatcher's "two nations". Local government stands at the increasingly sharp end of a means tested society, and has to administer a residual maintenance system, housing benefit, rent and poll tax rebates, special needs payments, child care, domiciliary services, residential care charges. On the other hand, the central state continues to concentrate wealth through tax concessions, mortgage interest relief and private pension support. As Jessop says, "overall, 'two nation' effects will be marked not only in the polarisation of income but also in the provision of services" (1989a: p. 35).

3. Restructuring Patterns of Intervention

The *patterns of state intervention* have obviously changed at the local level, with the boundaries of state activity perhaps being redrawn here more than anywhere else in a relative sense. Privatization, "marketization" and deregulation have all shifted the accepted edge of local state activity. In addition, this activity has increased on the supply side with the development of new local agencies such as the Training and Enterprise Councils, the enterprise agencies, the task forces and city action teams and the Urban Development Corporations. Jessop states that "local authorities have become crucial agencies for supply-side intervention" (1989a: p. 39), but what has in fact occurred is the development of new local agencies to by-pass local authorities, coupled with the growth of partnership schemes which severely limit their influence.

4. Restructuring the Social Bases of the State

Jessop then discusses three less formal or less institutional aspects of the state, beginning with its changing *social bases*, which he defines as "the ensemble of social forces with a direct material and/or symbolic stake in the continuation of that particular regime relative to one or more feasible alternative(s)" (1989a: p. 40). At the national level we can chart a movement from a social democratic, Keynesian welfare state, with a one-nation social base, orientated towards full employment and high welfare provision, towards a two-nation social base, structured around the beneficiaries of the entrepreneurial society and popular capitalism. As we have seen, the local state's prime role has shifted accordingly and it no longer appeals to the whole community as the key provider and manager of an expanding range of collective services, but rather comes increasingly to be seen as the shepherd of the dispossessed. There are other consequences for the local state of this shifting social base. In geographical terms there is an increasing disparity within the nation, and the local state has to manage, and reflect, the consequences of an intensifying social and spatial diversity. This has led to the breakdown of the old bipartisan consensus that used to surround local government, and hence to the polarized policy outcomes that we have seen in the course of the past decade. The institutions of the local state have offered a site where a variety of social bases can demonstrate alternative values and practices. The local politics of centre versus local and Labour versus Conservative has been underscored by "wets" versus "drys", by "left" versus "right", by "rural traditionalism" versus "suburban Thatcherism" and by "working class militants" versus "the new urban left". Although dampened at the national level by the British electoral and political system, what we have witnessed at the local level is the emergence of a host of conflicting forms of local politics, centred around a number of competing social bases. It should be noted that many of these alternatives have been fuelled by central attempts to control this very diversity.

5. Restructuring the State Project

At a national level the *state project* purporting to give cohesion and unity has been based around conviction politics, resolute leadership and a strong state ideology. This has given the government the political space and legitimation to exercise control over the local state, and has given it the power to try out a number of competing models of its own at the local level—ranging from enterprise zones to local management of schools to complete privatization. In this way the central state uses local state agencies to "penetrate more effectively into local niches and micro-economic interstices" (Jessop 1989a: p. 43).

6. Restructuring the Hegemonic Project

In a similar manner, the social relations of the local state have been changed as Thatcherism has passed through three main phases in its attempt to construct a *hegemonic project* able to satisfactorily define the interests of the "illusory community" which the government claims to represent. Initially, the local state was used during an "oppositional phase", both as a central object of criticism under the old social democratic consensus, and as a key site to promote an alternative vision. Then in a second consolidating phase, initial state restructuring was heavily centred on controlling the actions of the local state, which has paved the way for a more recent and more positive third phase in which the institutions and relations of the local state have been used to facilitate "the entrepreneurial society" and "popular capitalism".

The actions and relations of the local state have thus been restructured, as the welfare state itself has been recomposed over the past decade. Indeed, the attack on the local state has been a crucial element in Mrs Thatcher's assault on the social democratic settlement and its supporting political coalition. This is because the local state is not just an innocent bystander as society changes around it, but itself plays a crucial role in promoting, facilitating, opposing and interpreting such change. Hence, the local state was not just the prime vehicle for the delivery of services under a Keynesian welfare state consensus imposed from outside via a stable external support system, but was perhaps the key site where this consensus was established and experienced on a day-to-day basis by people using a rising standard of universal welfare provision. And hence the restructuring that has occurred as this consensus has been replaced by a discretionary, means tested and minimalist neo-liberal state (Jessop 1989a,b, Jessop *et al.* 1988). How have these changes been interpreted?

Interpreting Local State Restructuring

Cochrane (1990) identifies four main interpretations of local state restructuring. The first two focus their attention fairly narrowly on the politics of Thatcherism, being centred respectively around the introduction of the market, and the moves towards an increased citizen involvement through the "enabling state". Rhodes's interpretation of changing intergovernmental relations (Chapter 3) as a move towards an "enabling authority" based on accountability, competition and consumerism, combines these two perspectives. However, our concern here with the local state means that we also have to consider the other two interpretations identified by Cochrane since these place the changes "in the context of wider moves in economy and society" (1990: p. 4). The first of these suggests that local state changes should be seen as part of broader moves towards neo-corporatist state arrangements, while the second locates the changing local state within a more general societal shift from Fordism to post-Fordism. We will briefly outline each of the four interpretations in turn, before moving on to develop the latter.

Those who interpret the driving force behind the changes as the desire to introduce market measures into the local state, point to the set of arguments developed by the "public choice" school of the new right as providing the legitimation for such a move (Green 1987, Mather 1989). Indeed, Pirie (1988) claims that public choice theory has underpinned the legislative strategy of the Thatcher governments on this issue. These theorists see the public provision of goods and services as inherently flawed by the self-interest of politicians and bureaucrats and the rigidity of the large-scale agencies that they manage. In contrast it is claimed that the market will increase efficiency by ensuring smaller scale organizations, accountable directly to the consumer and operating around the principle of value for money (Cochrane 1990, Stoker 1990). The logic is that local state institutions need to be broken up, deregulated, and opened up to the purifying winds of the market in order to permit true competition and choice for the consumer. Their role would then be a much more limited one "as specifier, purchaser and regulator of community services", a task which could "be despatched in one, two or three meetings a year" (Mather 1989: pp. 216 and 222). Obviously this position has not yet been reached, even after a decade of Mrs Thatcher, and indeed Cochrane argues convincingly that "the market model is not so much an assessment of what has happened but of what some people would still like to happen" (1990: p. 13). He shows how it lacks justification on both theoretical and empirical grounds, and the reality is that powerful and well-established interest groups simply reorganize themselves to maximize their own gains from the new system. Monopolies of service provision often still exist, sometimes through private companies run by former local authority personnel. It is difficult to disagree with Stoker, when he claims that such ideology "looks less like individual choice conquering bureaucratic red-tape and more like the intellectual underpinning to a system of increased inequality and unfairness" (1990: p. 32).

Those who see the aim of the Conservatives as increasing citizen involvement via an enabling state extend the "marketization" principle. They argue that the local state should be broken up into more fragmented single service agencies, but not just as a means of facilitating the market. The process also results, it is claimed, in the development of a more positive "enabling state" with an increasingly diverse range of service provision. Local government retains a core role within this vision as the site of a coherent central professional/political/managerial leadership and as the base for teams of entrepreneurial officers to manage and co-ordinate the diverse provision of services. The problem with this vision is that it seems to be most favoured by those senior officers who have managed to retain some semblance of power within the reformed system. The mass of service provision still takes place without any citizen involvement, and the majority of local state managers have no leeway at all to act as entrepreneurs of any kind (at least not within the law). It is also difficult to interpret the changes as giving a central strategic role to an elected local government, especially when the only example of strategic authorities were abolished in 1986. Like the previous interpretation, this one seems based more on wishful thinking than on empirical observation.

A problem with these interpretations which Cochrane identifies is that both "tend to discuss changes within local government as if they were the product of more or less rational political debate within identifiable policy communities" whilst playing down, minimizing or ignoring "the wider context within which the changes are taking place" (1990: p. 20). He goes on to discuss two broad frameworks within which the changes may be placed. The first, which he favours, emphasizes the changing balance between key political interests within the state system at the local level before interpreting these as part of a move from the welfare to the enterprise state, a move combining business and state interests at the local level "in ways which are rather more reminiscent of corporatist or neo-corporatist arrangements" (1990: p. 5). The second, which is based around the notions of Fordism and post-Fordism, is favoured here as the more complete interpretation, and as such will be discussed later.

Cochrane begins his own analysis of the move towards an enterprise state by crucially noting how any analysis must include non-elected as well as elected elements of local government. This broadens the definition—"perhaps closer to that of the local state" (1990: p. 32), and allows functional as well as electoral representation to be considered. He also stresses the ways in which the postwar settlement has changed under Thatcherism. The Keynesian welfare state, of which local government was a key part, must in fact be seen as "a continually contested element, within a basically political compromise" (1990: p. 33). So far, so good. But unfortunately Cochrane never provides us with an explanation of what kept this "basically political compromise" alive, and never really explores the reasons why it should have come under such strain over the past fifteen years. We do have references to the fact that it is helpful "to look more closely at the changing balance between key political interests within the state system at local level" (1990: p. 34), but are never given any analyses of why the balance changes, and in particular why it should have changed so much under Mrs Thatcher (aside from some pointers towards the new politics of growth machines in the field of local economic development).

Instead we are given a description of the increasing role of business in local politics, where as Cochrane notes "the extent and significance of change is difficult to exaggerate" (1990: p. 37). The only hint as to why changes of such a "significant extent" should have come about appears in the conclusion, which echoes the themes of the introduction. Cochrane writes that "if the post-war settlement was one which acknowledged the role of the working class and its organisations, the settlement of the 1980s, arising from the crisis of social democracy which characterised the 1970s, is one which starts from the needs of business and its organisations" (1990: p. 44). The stress on the political settlement is crucial, but overplayed—again we need to ask why did social democracy undergo a crisis throughout the 1970s, and what caused the new settlement to take a particular form?

Towards a Reinterpretation of Local State Restructuring

One way of approaching these questions, whose answers are central to an understanding of the local state under Thatcherism, is to use the concepts of Fordism and post-Fordism. These have recently begun to be applied to local government and the local state, and constitute the fourth main area of interpretation discussed by Cochrane (see, for example, Chouinard 1990, Geddes 1988, 1990; Goodwin *et al.* 1989, Hoggett 1987, Painter 1991, Stoker 1989, 1991.) Unfortunately, as the concepts have become increasingly popular, so a common usage has become more and more elusive. One reason for this is that Fordism, and hence the supposed transition away from it, can be analysed on a number of levels—as a distinctive *labour process*, involving mass production on moving assembly lines; as a *regime of accumulation*, involving the stabilization of relations between production and consumption via what Jessop terms the "virtuous circle"; and as a *mode of regulation*, involving the "ensemble of productive, institutional, social and political relations and practices that, in combination, regulate the accumulation process" (Schoenberger 1989: p. 101).

Those using the concepts to analyse changes in the local state do so at each of the above levels, and often use a mixture of two or three. This only spreads confusion, and lessens the utility of the terms for theoretical understanding. Hoggett (1987) concentrates largely on the switch from Fordist to post-Fordist labour processes within local government, while Geddes (1988) discusses the local state explicitly in relation to all three levels. Stoker (1989) also operates on all three levels, but does so more implicitly. Goodwin *et al.* (1989) and Chouinard (1990) favour an analysis which stresses the mode of regulation, and Painter (1991), perhaps most explicit in his use of terminology, situates the local state in a complex relationship to both mode of regulation and regime of accumulation. This diversity is one reason why Cochrane (1990) chooses to reject the concepts, in addition to his repudiation of Hoggett's arguments concerning the labour process and a general criticism that ideal type classification of local state activities as Fordist or post-Fordist (Stoker, 1990) ultimately becomes no more than a form of listing and labelling, "like cataloguing butterflies" (Cochrane 1990: p. 31).

These criticisms are important, but they can be overcome by modifying our analysis rather than rejecting the concepts totally. We can agree that the local state labour process was never classically Fordist, and also admit the dangers of slipping into mere typology, but still feel that it is "worthwhile to deploy the notion of Fordism as part of a broader conceptual system" (Jessop 1990: p. 41). If we limit the usage of the concept to Fordism as a mode of regulation, it enables us to theorize the processes which actually underpinned the postwar settlement, and offers a means of linking economic, social, political and ideological features within such a framework. As Jessop puts it, "the story of Britain since the war is often treated in terms of the rise and fall of the postwar settlement between capital and labour, embodied in the Keynesian welfare state. This typical view concentrates on how governments tried to stabilise the economy and redistribute income and wealth. It ignores how wealth came to be produced during these years. Yet it was the consolidation of 'Fordism', a new system of capitalist production, which made it possible for the Keynesian welfare state to survive as the political shell and organising myth of the postwar settlement" (1986a: pp. 11-12). It is, of course, also the case that it is the collapse of Fordism, as mediated through the Thatcher governments, which now threatens the survival of that very same welfare state. The myth has been laid bare, and the shell all but crushed over the last decade, as an attempt has been made to forge a new settlement. The restructuring of the local state described above is heavily implicated in this process.

The shape of such restructuring is, of course, not given in advance, nor technically determined by the demands, or needs, of the economy. As we have already seen, the policies of Mrs Thatcher's government have, especially in this area, been underpinned by a particular political ideology. Thus, although the general political and economic situation, which was partly responsible for Mrs Thatcher's initial election in 1979, did not leave an incoming government of whatever political persuasion much room for manoeuvre, and made the local state a likely target for any policy based around a reduction in public expenditure, the exact form of such a policy was open to political debate. Indeed, a simple desire to reduce public expenditure would, of its own accord, not necessitate the specific and detailed restrictions, described elsewhere in this volume, which the Thatcher governments have placed on local state activities. These centralized controls have been driven as much by a specific political desire to neutralize opposition and use the local state instead to promote the government's preferred ideological discourse, as they have by a broad macroeconomic desire to curb inflation.

To sum up, the postwar period in Britain thus saw an economic expansion which temporarily stabilized the contradictions of capitalist accumulation, based around mass production and mass consumption, providing full employment and an expanding welfare state. Fordism as a mode of regulation refers to the prevailing or dominant institutions and practices sustaining this; for instance, those of exploitation, authority and negotiation in the workplace, of exchange and contract in the market, and of the family in the home. It is important here to note that the Thatcher governments have deliberately helped to replace both the "structural" and the "strategic" moments of Fordism. "The former refer to the actual organisation(s), the latter to the strategic perspectives and discourses which are currently dominant" (Jessop 1990: p. 9). The local state played a vital role in helping to underpin both these "moments" of Fordism as a mode of regulation. On a structural level it provided the day-to-day means for managing an expanding range of welfare services, and offered the mechanism for the local planning and regulation of economic growth. On a strategic level it was perhaps *the* key site, given the inaccessibility of central level politics, where consensual social democratic politics could be constructed as well as experienced (Goodwin *et al.* 1989, Painter 1991). Each "moment", of course, reinforced the other, and led to a steady postwar increase in the scale, and acceptance, of publicly provided local services through the local state.

In a like manner, the recent "crisis" of Fordism contains elements from both these "moments", and thus "involves much more than the forces of production or profitability in any simple sense. Much more fundamental is capital's inability to create a new regime of accumulation with appropriate institutional forms, social relations and balance of social forces within the power bloc and among the people" (Jessop 1986b: p. 12). To overcome this inability involves the creation of a new "historic bloc", Gramsci's phrase describing the fragile correspondence achieved between state, economy and civil society via the "coupling of different institutions and practices as reinforced and mediated through specific economic, political and ideological practices" (Jessop *et al.* 1988: p. 162). The local state becomes a leading player in this process, and the governments of Mrs Thatcher have promoted changes in its activities, institutions and social relations in an effort to help create a new "historic bloc". In the words of Gramsci, "An appropriate political initiative is always necessary to liberate the economic thrust from the dead weight of traditional policies—i.e. to change the political direction of certain forces which have to be absorbed if a new homogeneous politico-economic historical bloc, without internal contradictions, is to be successfully formed" (1971: p. 168). What has happened in the first decade of Thatcher is that this political initiative has been carried through using the local state as both a structure and strategy. The institutions and policy arenas of the local state, together with the social relations which operate through and around them, have all been reformed as Thatcherism has attempted to forge this new historic bloc, as part and parcel of a new economic and political settlement. But such a shift is not predetermined or ordained and the process is one of conflict and struggle rather than an automatic technical change from one regime of accumulation to another. This is why the local state has had such a high political profile under Mrs Thatcher, and why it promises to remain a key area of contention in the immediate future.

References

Chouinard, V. (1990) the uneven development of capitalist states: 1. Theoretical proposals and an analysis of postwar changes in Canada's assisted housing programmes, *Environment and Planning A*, **22** (10): 1291-1308.

Cochrane, A. (1989) In Cochrane A. and Anderson J. (eds.) *Politics in Transition*, Sage, London.

Cochrane, A. (1990) The changing state of local government in the UK: restructuring for the 1990s. Unpublished paper given to the Urban Politics Group of the Political Studies Association, London, June 1990.

Duncan, S. and Goodwin, M. (1988) *The Local State and Uneven Development*, Polity Press, Cambridge.

Geddes, M. (1988) The capitalist state and the local economy: "Restructuring for labour" and beyond, *Capital and Class*, **35**: 85-120.

Geddes, M. (1990) Capital, class and the local state: Issues of structure and determinism. Unpublished paper given to the Urban Politics Group of the Political Studies Association, London, June 1990.

Goodwin, M. (1989) In Cochrane A. and Anderson J. (eds.) *Politics in Transition*, Sage, London.

Goodwin, M. and Duncan, S. (1989) In Mohan, J. (ed.) *The Political Geography of Contemporary Britain*, Macmillan London.

Goodwin, M., Duncan, S., and Halford, S. (1989) Urban politics in the post-Fordist economy. Unpublished paper given to the Urban Change and Conflict Conference, Bristol, September 1989.

Gramsci, A. (1971) *Selections from Prison Notebooks*, Lawrence & Wishart London.

Green, D. (1987) *The New Right* Wheatsheaf, Brighton.

Gyford, J., Leach, S., and Game, C. (1989) *The Changing Politics of Local Government*, Unwin Hyman, London.

Hoggett, P., (1987) In Hambleton R., and Hoggett, P. (eds.) *The Politics of Decentralization: Theory and Practice of a Radical Local Government Initiative*, University of Bristol, School of Advanced Urban Studies, Working Paper, No. 46.

Jessop, B. (1986a) Thatcherism's mid-life crisis, *New Socialist*, March, pp. 11-15.

Jessop, B. (1986b) The welfare state in the transition from Fordism to post-Fordism, *PROKLA*, **55**: 4-33 (page numbers refer to translated manuscript).

Jessop, B., Bonnett, K., Bromley, S., and Ling, T. (1988) *Thatcherism*, Polity Press, Cambridge.

Jessop, B. (1989a) *Thatcherism: The British Road to post-Fordism*, Essex Papers in Politics and Government, No. 68, University of Essex.

Jessop, B. (1989b) In Gottdiener, M. and Komninos, N. (eds.) *Capitalist Development and Crisis Theory; Accumulation, Regulation and Spatial Restructuring*, St. Martin's Press, New York.

Jessop, B. (1990) Fordism and post-Fordism: a critical reformulation Unpublished paper given to conference on "Pathways to Industrialisation and Regional Development", California, March 1990.

Lawless, P. (1989) *Britain's Inner Cities*, Chapman, London.

Mather, G. (1989) In Stewart, J. and Stoker, G. (eds.) *The Future of Local Government*, Macmillan, London.

Painter, J. (1991) Regulation theory and local government: insights and issues, *Transactions of the Institute of British Geographers* (forthcoming).

Pirie, M. (1988) *Micropolitics*, Wildwood House, London.

Ransom, S., and Thomas, H., (1989) In Stewart, J. and Stoker, G. (eds.) *The Future of Local Government*, Macmillan, London.

Riddell, P. (1989) *The Thatcher Decade*, Blackwell, Oxford.

Robson, B. (1988) *Those Inner Cities*, Clarendon Press, Oxford.

Schoenberger, E. (1989) Thinking about flexibility; a response to Gertler, *Transactions of the Institute of British Geographers*, **14**: 98-108.

Spencer, K. (1989) In Stewart, J. and Stoker, G. (eds.) *The Future of Local Government*, Macmillan, London.
Stewart, J. and Stoker, G. (eds.) (1989) *The Future of Local Government*, Macmillan, London.
Stoker, G. (1988) *The Politics of Local Government*, Macmillan, London.
Stoker, G. (1989) In Stewart, J. and Stoker, G. (eds.) *The Future of Local Government*, Macmillan, London.
Stoker, G., (1990) In Drucker, H. *et al. Developments in British Politics 3*, Macmillan, London.
Stoker, G., (1991) In King, D. and Pierre, J. (eds.) *Challenges to Local Government*, Sage, London.
Travers, T. (1989) In Stewart, J. and Stoker, G. (eds.) *The Future of Local Government*, Macmillan, London.
Walsh, K. (1989) In Stewart, J. and Stoker, G. (eds.) *The Future of Local Government*, Macmillan, London.
Woodward, R. (1991) Mobilising opposition; The campaign against Housing Action Trusts in Tower Hamlets, *Housing Studies*, **6**(1): 44-56.

5

Changing Planning Relations

PETER AMBROSE

"Planning" is a "catch-all" term that requires precise operational definition. In this chapter it is related exclusively to the processes that bring about the evolution of the Built Environment (the BE). There is no need to stress the significance of these processes since the BE forms the human habitat and therefore affects nearly all aspects of life. "Planning" implies premeditated action to alter this habitat. It is therefore nothing new. The construction of a mud hut requires some planning at the level of the individual household. To carry the potted history further forward, the pyramids, city walls, Roman road systems, drainage arrangements in the Netherlands and the large-scale reconstructions of central Paris and Birmingham in the 1870s onwards all required planning on a scale which few modern developments can match. Resources for such schemes had to be allocated, and the construction organized, on some collective rather than individual basis. At this point questions of power hierarchies and relationships become significant. Who owns and organizes the use of the construction resources, who has power to allocate the product and what part do the "consumers", the users of the BE, play in the process?

One potential danger when considering these questions is to confuse the issue of premeditation in development with that of scale. One historical tradition (characterized, for example, by Mumford 1961) tends to see the large-scale developments such as those of Baroque German princes as "planned" but the piecemeal, smaller scale developments of, say, medieval York as spontaneous in some way—the product of "natural forces". An appeal to "natural forces" is always politically disabling. Every development, whether a 1930s extravaganza such as the Nuremburg Stadium or a terraced house built in 1880s Brighton as an investment, shares certain characteristics. They all result from a promoter's initiative, reflect a specific political, social or economic purpose, involve the investment of funds and the transformation of materials and get allocated to users on some basis or another. They were therefore all planned and carried out in a specific power relations context. To see the big ones as "planned" and the small ones as the product of "natural forces" is to depoliticize the issue. This leaves one with little power to analyse the processes that in Thatcher's Britain drastically reduced the housing tenure choice in Berkshire or induced thousands of people to sleep rough in London—issues to which we return later.

While planning is not new, there were significant changes in the power relations context in which it occurs in Britain during and after the Second World War. Under the 1947 Town and Country Planning Act the right to carry out development, previously almost unchallenged as part of the "bundle of rights" of freehold ownership, was largely removed and vested with the newly set up "local planning authorities" (see, for example, Cullingworth 1985 or Ambrose 1986). This represented a considerable shift in the balance of power between state and market. By the preparation of land use plans, some sites were specified as developable and others not. Owners of the former could make enormous profits from land sale or development. Owners of the rest lost significant potential gain. The act of drawing a land use plan thus also redrew the map of land values. The issues of compensation for the loss of development rights and of taxation on the extra value conferred have never been solved (Parker 1985). They have, over the last forty-odd years, been the subject of a compromise that has swung backward and forward with changing administrations. Clearly, in view of the scale of the gains and losses involved, these statutory changes provided a new battleground on which power relations had to be renegotiated. The 1947 Act, and all the subsequent consolidating legislation, did not so much introduce "planning" as define a new power game about values and profits—one which is still being played for very large stakes.

The "New Right" and Land Use Planning

To return to the two situations referred to in Berkshire and London, to what extent can they be seen as a product of British national politics in the 1980s? At this point it may help briefly to identify some of the main strands of the ideology that underpin and pervade the political project known as Thatcherism. The "New Right", or neo-liberalism, has been usefully discussed in a number of recent books (for example, Green 1987, King 1987). Broadly speaking it is an amalgam of the free market and free trade principles of nineteenth-century liberalism, the social and economic beliefs of Hayek (see, for example, Hayek 1986) and the Mont Pelerin Society, the monetarist theories of Chicago economists including Friedman (see, for example, Friedmans 1980) plus in the British case a strong nationalistic, authoritarian and centralist streak. This latter component may have derived as much from Mrs Thatcher's own personality as anything else. Certainly the apparent incapacity to hear or accept conflicting views (exemplified by the "there is no alternative" position when politics is manifestly full of alternatives) seems more strongly marked in her case than in any other European politician since the early 1930s. Fortunately those with oppositional views within her party suffered nothing worse than a forced or voluntary retreat into the City, Brussels or the bosom of their families.

The espousal of neo-liberalism by the Conservative Party was publicly marked by a speech of Sir Keith Joseph in 1974. Mrs Thatcher, perhaps best described as a "mono-directional pragmatist" rather than a political theorist, became leader of the party in 1975. The mid-1970s under Labour were marked by increasing economic difficulties, financial and balance of payments crises and latterly by chaotic industrial relations. The Conservatives went to the country in 1979 with their intentions very explicitly stated and they swept to power. The new regime was clearly to be a break with what some have called the "post-war consensus". The enterprise of individuals and private corporations was to be "released" by the removal of the "burden of the state". The power of the unions was to be reduced. Public regulation, control and initiative, especially at the local level, was to be constrained. Taxation and public expenditure was to be reduced. "Market forces" were to come more into play in fields such as housing, transport, health and education to replace the "dead hand" of bureaucratic and wasteful local authority control (a line which, to be fair, had been partially adopted in the latter years of the Callaghan administration). The effects of all this have been discussed by a number of authors (for example, Brown and Sparks 1989 and Andrews and Jacobs 1990).

Socially there was to be a return to "Victorian standards" of respect for old-established values, authority and the family. This approach was underpinned by the notion that there is a "natural order" in any society and that while one may make some moves towards equality of opportunity it is pointless, even immoral, to seek equality of outcomes. In a memorable and much repeated phrase "if you make everyone equal at breakfast time there will be a pecking order by lunchtime". In addition, differential rewards provide incentive. People should be "free" to find their own level as consumers in a market-based system—and the prices in this market should not be "distorted" by state subsidy. Such "distortion" of price signals violates the freedom of the individual to make rational economic choices. State support should be available only for the residual category of the "socially inadequate" who could not, for some reason, stand on their own two feet. Finally, and memorably, Mrs Thatcher asserted that there is no such thing as society—there are only individuals and families seeking to maximize their own welfare.

How might an administration with such a set of beliefs be expected to approach the system of land use development planning established in 1946/47 and still, as at 1979, enjoying relatively consensual support? Various commentators over the years (including the present author—see Ambrose 1986) have advanced the argument that attempting to guide the land development process by seeking to make the output pattern of land uses conform to a land zoning "design" is quite different from taking positive control over the application and use of the resource inputs (finance, land and materials). The British postwar approach is better described as "regulation" than "planning". Some (for example, Pickvance 1982) have seen it as simply reflecting market tendencies. Others (Kirk 1980) have judged it to be weak in the face of capitalist forces. It has had its marked successes in terms of conserving the natural environment and protecting sensitive urban and rural areas. But no one would claim that this regulatory strategy could of itself rejuvenate a failing local economy such as Liverpool's or directly bring about a more equitable system of access to housing. The "long retreat" from the bold and socially directive intentions of the Uthwatt Committee in 1941, drawn up in the very special political circumstance of the time, has been discussed elsewhere (Ambrose 1986, Parker 1985, Rees and Lambert 1985).

Despite the relative blandness of the British "planning" regime it was too interventionist for the Thatcher administrations. Through the 1980s various natural allies of the right advanced their own prescriptions for the revision of the system (Adam Smith Institute 1983, Royal Institute of Chartered Surveyors 1986 and British Property Federation 1986, for example). There is no need here to rehearse the existing discussions (for example, Brindley, Rydin and Stoker 1989 and Thornley 1989, 1990) which cover the impact of new rightist ideology and politics on the land use planning system. These reviews identify the changing role of the central and local state and the sharp shift in power from the latter to the former (Duncan and Goodwin 1988). The overall effect is that the capacity of the local government system, at both county and district level, to make and implement plans has been undermined.

In particular the structure planning process was weakened by the 1980 Local Government, Planning and Land Act and there have even been subsequent proposals to abolish structure planning departments altogether. A string of circulars from the Department of the Environment (detailed in Thornley 1989) have aided industry, small businesses and the housebuilders in the undermining of local planning intentions. In Circular 13/87 the Use Classes Order simplified the categories of land use recognized by the system and in doing so weakened the sensitivity of the system. "Flexible planning permissions" have undermined the capacity of the system to regulate, in particular, office development. A greater dependence on decision making on appeal has shifted power from the formally democratic arena of the local planning department (whose plans must evolve through statutory public consultation procedures) to a more legalistic arena.

The metropolitan authorities, including the Greater London Council, all of which had a democratically accountable planning function, have been abolished (Duncan and Goodwin 1988). Enterprise Zones (Roger Tym and Partners 1984) and Simplified Planning Zones (Lloyd 1987) have sharply undermined the capacity of a number of local authorities to control the development process. Perhaps most strikingly democratic planning procedures have been bypassed altogether by the non-participatory Urban Development Corporations run by Boards appointed by the Secretary of State. Some of these corporations, notably the London Docklands Development Corporation, have produced a striking *rate* of new development in their areas but in at least the London case the mix of development, and especially the relationship between the pattern produced and the evident social needs of the area at the outset of the process of transformation, has been the subject of prolonged criticism (for example, Ambrose 1986, Docklands Consultative Committee 1985, 1990, Docklands Forum 1990, Brownill 1990).

The present intention is not, therefore, to reiterate the statutory and administrative changes that have been made in land use regulatory arrangements during the 1980s. Instead the analysis will be directed towards the changing behaviour of the interlinked system of organizations and agencies which bring about modifications in the BE. Which organizations and agencies are involved, how do they interact, how has the system responded to the radically new power relations that have evolved since 1979 and what changes have occurred in the pattern of development produced?

How is the Built Environment Modified?

The production or renewal and use of any element in the built environment, whether it is a building or a facility such as a road, airport or sewage works, requires five relatively discrete operations. These are;

1. *Promotion*—the making of the decision to produce the building or facility in the chosen location and the taking of the first steps to implement the intention.
2. *Investment*—the commitment of finance to the scheme in order to assemble the inputs.
3. *Construction*—the combination of the necessary inputs including the site, materials and labour (including professional skills) to make the building or facility.
4. *Allocation*—the allocation of the building or facility to the first user or users on one of a number of possible bases.
5. *Subsequent management*—the subsequent management, maintenance, repair, and possible convertion and reallocation of the building or facility until it reaches the end of its life.

The entire process may be sequentially integrated so that one agency organizes and carries out all the stages (as, for example, with a British local authority housing unit—although even here much of the funding and construction effort comes from other sources). Alternatively each stage may be carried out by separate organizations although the promoter may maintain an interest of some kind "downstream" to at least the allocation stage. These five stages, and the organizations that operate to carry them out, are shown in Fig. 5.1. The five stages are laid out horizontally. The movements back and forward between the last two stages indicate that reallocation or use convertion may occur several times during the lifetime of the building or facility. "End" in Stage 5 indicates its eventual demise. This will be because it has reached the end of its useful life. "Useful" may sometimes be defined in terms of social utility as when, for example, a house has reached an uninhabitable state. Or changes in technology may mean that some facilities no longer fulfil their original purpose (for example, the British canal network). Or the criterion may be

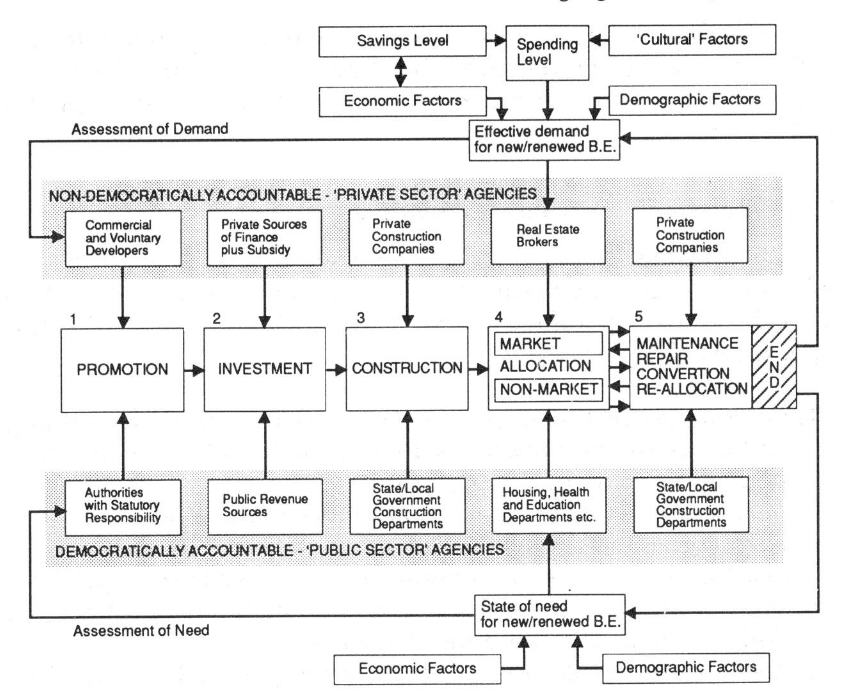

FIG. 5.1 The Built Environment provision system.

commercial in nature as when, for example, a perfectly serviceable filling station is bulldozed and replaced by another one of slightly different design to reflect the oil company's commercial image and to further its search for profits. The criterion, therefore, will be somewhere along a spectrum that has "use value" at one end and "exchange value" at the other.

Power Relations and Forms of Accountability

This leads directly to questions of power relations and control over the entire process. The last example poses an analytical question. Were urban processes under Thatcher characterized by the the even greater ascendancy of exchange values over use values (see especially Harvey 1989)? It also raises a normative issue. Is it justifiable that resources are used to reconstruct a building where most of us spend five minutes every few days filling our car with petrol when resources are not forthcoming to produce enough housing for people who cannot afford either cars or petrol? If the question were put in this form it does seem plausible that many would opt for the life-protecting form of development. So how *are* the preferences of people at large fed into the processes that bring about one or the other form of development? Who controls these processes and to what extent are they still subject to "democratic" accountability?

Returning to Fig 5.1, the organizations and agencies operating at each stage of the chain are shown in shaded boxes above and below the chain itself. Conventionally, the development process is divided into "private" and "public" sector operations—alternatively as operations by "the market" and "the state". Thus British council housing is often regarded as "public" or "state" and a new downtown shopping centre as "private" or "market". These two sets of terms do convey some meaning but they are imprecise—perhaps increasingly so. For example, most of the loans taken out to build council housing in recent years have come from "private sector" institutions. Similarly the freehold for the new shopping centre may be "public" in the sense that it is owned by the city and leased for a term to the developer. There is also the view, once heard expressed at a developers' conference, that there is no public money anyway—only private money that has been appropriated by the state. Without pursuing this one, the point can be made that the "private/public" distinction gets muddier the more one looks at it, and especially when one "unpacks" the sequence of activities in the chain of stages that produces new or renewed BE.

The present analysis therefore steps around the concepts of "public" and "private", "market" and "state", and distinguishes activities instead on the basis of power relations, especially as expressed in terms of *formal democratic accountability*. This notion too carries a multiplicity of meanings and partly concealed ideologies. Ironically the German Democratic Republic was, apparently, non-democratic but has now acquired democracy by a merger with the Federal Republic. Hungary and the other formerly socialist states of eastern and central Europe are striving towards "democracy" and "free market systems" at the same time. This important issue will be examined in more detail later.

For the moment, and in relation to the categorization used in the diagram, a simple definition of democracy is adopted—"government by all the people, direct or representative" (*Oxford Reference Dictionary*). In practice this means that the electorate as a whole are legally entitled to play a part in the vesting of power by the periodic use of a vote to choose those who will exercise this power. Thus organizations and agencies in the system whose managing members are *elected* either locally or nationally, and whose behaviour or participation in the process can therefore be changed via the ballot box, are termed "democratically accountable" (DA). Those which do not meet these conditions are termed "non-democratically accountable" (NDA).

NDA organizations can be subject to different forms of accountability and are driven by a range of motivations. Private developers, financial institutions, construction companies and estate agents obey accumulative imperatives and are accountable in their behaviour to a set of shareholders or depositors. Anyone can become a shareholder or depositor provided he or she has money to invest or deposit. So the capability to affect behaviour in these cases is accessed by the use of money. Other NDA organizations, for example the London Docklands Development Corporation (LDDC), are run by small groups of people appointed directly by a central or local government department to whom they are accountable. Individuals affected by the actions of these organizations have no direct power to affect their behaviour unless they themselves become members of the appointed group. A third set of NDA organizations are "voluntary"—they come into being simply because groups of people wish to form them. These include housing associations or co-operatives. Since they are typically managed by self-selected groups of people they are again not democratic under the definition adopted although they may take active steps to enlist user participation. NDA organizations (voluntary organizations to some extent excepted) generally respond to "feedback" signals concerning the *state of effective demand* for BE of various kinds. This in turn is affected by the kinds of factors shown on the diagram.

DA organizations, by contrast, normally have statutorily defined status and areas of responsibility. They include the central and local authorities responsible for housing, transport facilities and other "public" functions. In many cases they are formally responsible to a council made up of locally elected representatives who may hold *ex-officio* a proportion of the places on the management board so these authorities are only partly democratically accountable. Most DA organizations share the characteristic that they undertake land development primarily as part of the process of discharging a responsibility laid upon them by law. Thus housing, education and health authorities, as part of their function, need to arrange the production of housing, schools and hospitals. Their promotional activity depends upon assessments of the *state of need* for these kinds of publicly provided facilities.

This book is about the changing power relations in Thatcher's

Britain and the pattern of policies they produced. Policy about the evolution of the BE does not emerge fully formed from Westminster and Whitehall. It may be *written, enacted and administered* from there but it is actually shaped by the interplay of the organizations in the diagram as they are continually active in renewing the BE within the context of their own motivating strategy. Policy relating to the development process, for example that concerning taxation, subsidy support, development control or the legal framework for construction activity, is partly an *output* from the interplay of power relations and lobbying within the system. Specific measures such as the setting up of the LDDC reflect the preferences of its dominant actors. The power balance between NDA and DA organizations at any point in time is therefore obviously relevant to the future evolution of BE policy.

So how, and in which directions, has the system operated to affect both policy and development outcomes during Mrs Thatcher's period of office? How, at each stage, did the balance of NDA to DA influence and funding change? What has been the direction of the shifts in accountability? Did the entire process become more democratic (as previously defined) or less so? To answer these questions we need to identify some of the specific organizations in the system. Then by assessing the changing pattern of new BE produced we can deduce their changing position in the heirarchy of power relations between 1979 and 1990.

Organizations, Agencies and the Changing Pattern of Output

Specification of the particular organizations and agencies in the system depends on the type of BE under consideration. The promoting organizations for motorways and other roads are those government departments having statutory responsibility for road building. Investment finance is still largely from public revenue sources. Construction and subsequent maintenance and repair is by civil engineering firms. Allocation is by market forces (anyone that can afford a vehicle can use them) and in this case no specific allocating agencies are involved except perhaps those which issue discs to indicate that road fund taxation has been paid. One could work through the production of other forms of BE, for example hospitals and recreational facilities, in a similar way. But for present purposes most emphasis will be placed on those forms of development which occupy by far the largest proportion of the land area in most towns and cities—housing and commercial schemes such as offices and shopping centres.

Changes in the pattern of promotion over the last decade and changes in the "mix" of buildings produced, can be seen in Table 5.1. It can be seen that from 1978 to 1989 the value of all construction orders increased in real terms by over 29 per cent but that activity has been highly cyclical with a deep trough in the early 1980s. The very scale of these fluctuations illustrates some of the difficulties facing the construction industry and helps to explain its lack of confidence about future long-term investment in new plant and technology. For present purposes attention is focused on the balance between the sectors of activity and the types of work. The official statistics characterize orders as "Public" or "Private". Although the equivalence is not perfect, these sectors are taken for present purposes to be DA and NDA respectively (the latter differentiating criterion in not of course recognized in official statistics). In 1978 the DA proportion of all construction contracts was about 40 per cent—£6,188m in a total of £15,372m. In 1981, before neo-liberalism had had the chance fully to assert itself and in the depths of the construction recession, the proportion was still 40 per cent. As the recovery took place, private orders rose much more sharply than public

TABLE 5.1
New Orders Obtained by Contractors
(£ million at 1985 prices)

	New housing		Other new work			All
	Public	Private	Public	Private		
				Industrial	Commercial	
1978	2113	4108	4075	2389	2687	15,372
1979	1512	3805	3803	2389	2466	13,975
1980	882	2739	3410	1923	2553	11,507
1981	789	2648	4206	1718	3090	12,451
1982	1115	3647	3872	1455	3077	13,166
1983	1050	4686	4564	1723	3108	15,131
1984	911	4294	4386	2425	3772	15,788
1985	734	4555	3877	2149	4028	15,343
1986	746	4896	4240	2088	4624	16,594
1987	808	5202	4232	3463	6054	19,759
1988	712	5431	4264	2654	7499	20,560
1989	643	4046	4836	2630	7727	19,882

Source: *Housing and Construction Statistics*, HMSO, London.

so that the DA proportion fell to 34 per cent in 1984, 30 per cent in 1986 and around 27 per cent in 1989.

All housing work, as a proportion of total orders, has fallen sharply. In 1978 housing orders constituted about 40 per cent of all work—£6,221m of £15,372m. By 1984 this proportion had fallen to about 33 per cent and at the end of the period it was less than 24 per cent. In real terms the value of housing work fell by about 25 per cent over the period. Within the housing sector the balance has shifted sharply. In 1978 public orders were about 34 per cent of all housing work. By 1984 this had fallen to less than 18 per cent and by 1989 to less than 14 per cent. In other words over the decade as a whole two effects are clearly discernible. First, far less housing was being produced as a proportion of all construction effort and second, of this absolutely declining amount a rapidly diminishing proportion was obtained from democratically accountable organizations.

Turning to the "Other new work" category, a number of similar trends are evident. In 1978 "Public" work was about 45 per cent of all orders. By 1984 this had fallen to about 41 per cent and by 1989 to less than 32 per cent. Over the decade "Public Other new work" fluctuated considerably but showed some overall growth (notably in road construction projects). "Private" sector orders for "industrial" construction work (roughly, factories and warehouses) showed a deep trough in the early 1980s but recovered at the end of the decade to levels somewhat above those of the late 1970s. But the brightest "star" of the construction firmament has been the "Private" orders for "Commercial" construction (roughly, retail centres, offices and hotels, etc.). Orders for these forms of BE stood at £2,466m at the beginning of the Thatcher years (at 1985 prices), rose sharply in the early and mid-1980s, and stood at £7,727m in 1989—a real terms increase to 313 per cent of the 1979 figure. Over the period 1980-89 the value of construction work for private promoters in each of the main types of development rose in real terms as follows:

	%
Housing	+174
Industrial	+76
Offices	+333
Shops	+254
Entertainment	+212

Source: *Housing and Construction Statistics*, HMSO, London Various tables.

Regardless of any statements of intent to the electorate about regenerating Britain's industrial capacity or solving the housing problem, this pattern of work constitutes the actual new increment to the total stock of BE in Britain (the total usable stock at any given moment depends also, of course, on the pattern of buildings ceasing to be used or to exist). The commissioning of new BE has become strikingly less democratically accountable—less of it now comes from "public" agencies which we have regarded as "democratic" in this analysis. It follows inevitably that the pattern of orders and output has tended to follow the logic of the market. NDA investment has increasingly promoted those forms of development which appear to offer a better ratio of reward to risk. Industrial development, although providing on average a higher yield than other forms (Hillier, Parker, May and Rowden 1987) has not been attractive to NDA investors—partly because the dangers of obsolescence for a factory are greater than for a retail centre.

The inevitable conclusion is that no matter how much planning authorities may wish to encourage new housing and industrial development in the areas for which they are responsible, it is orders for new shopping centres, offices, hotels and leisure centres which have bounded ahead—especially towards the end of the decade. Given the commercial environment which has increasingly characterized the 1980s, an era of consumerism and easy (if expensive) credit for the better off, there is really no mystery here. Most NDA organizations have a clear and direct legal responsibility to their shareholders or they stand as trustees of other peoples' money. They are simply doing a job. It is the government, under lobbying pressure from within the NDA sector, who position the goalposts. DA organizations, with statutory responsibilities, may well have to rely increasingly on "planning gain" negotiations to derive some "community benefit" (see, for example, Brindley, Rydin and Stoker 1989).

Relating this changing pattern of activity shown in Table 5.1 to Fig 5.1, it is clear that the NDA/DA balance has increased sharply at the Promotion and Investment stages. What of the Construction and Maintenance stages? The construction industry in Britain has always been largely privately owned and managed (Ball 1988) except, to some extent, during the "command economy" periods during the two world wars. The main publicly owned construction organizations have been the Direct Labour Organizations—the building departments of local authorities and other public bodies. These have been resourced by, and directly responsible to, their local authority. Under the definition adopted in this chapter they are therefore Democratically Accountable.

The value of the work they have carried out, in £million at 1985 prices, for selected years during the 1980s is as follows;

1980	3,732
1982	3,298
1984	3,115
1986	2,972
1987	2,927

Source: *Housing and Construction Statistics* HMSO, London.

Given the 29 per cent real increase in the value of all construction work noted earlier (in fact it was nearly 72 per cent between 1980 and 1987), the proportion of total construction carried out by these DA agencies has decreased very sharply. In fact since new local authority house building is virtually at a standstill, their role is primarily to carry out repair and renovation contracts of the rapidly shrinking public stock.

At the Allocation stage of the provision chain it follows from what has already been established that there was a sharp swing in the 1980s from non-market to market bases of allocation. With the partial exception of the "command economy" wartime periods, certain types of BE have always been allocated on "free market" principles. For example, newly developed retail, office, hotel and leisure space is almost invariably rented or sold to the highest bidder. There was one period in 1973, under a "prices and incomes" policy implemented in "crisis" conditions by a Conservative administration under Edward Heath, when a shortlived attempt was made to control commercial rents. No doubt the facts of life relating to commercial property were quickly impressed upon the administration. As in privately rented housing, the control of rents equals the control of profits. But whereas private investment in rentable housing comes mainly from small entrepreneurs, investment in commercial rented property schemes is largely from massive financial institutions handling pensions and life insurance money (Ambrose and Colenutt 1975, Smyth 1985, Rose 1985). If their profitability is affected by rent control the consequences are massively more destabilizing than those following the gradual contraction of the private rented housing sector. The Heath attempt to control commercial rents survived only a few months.

By contrast the allocation of housing on "rent controlled" rather than "free market" principles has at least a hundred years of history in Britain but it has been seriously undermined in the 1980s. In 1979 the proportion of total housing stock owned and managed by housing authorities, including New Town corporations, stood at about 29 per cent of the total. Allocation methods for this housing can reasonably be claimed to be DA because policy about priorities and the granting of new lettings is made by elected members of local councils. As a result of the Right to Buy policy of the 1980s, the public stock has fallen by about 1 million units by the end of the decade (see, for example, Malpass 1990, Oldman 1990). Whereas there were 74,000 additions to this stock in 1979, the number in 1989 had fallen to 13,000 and over one-third of these were designed for "special needs" such as for the elderly or disabled. Inevitably the number of new lettings in this sector fell sharply (from 289,000 in 1978/79 to 235,000 in 1988/89). Since all private housing transactions are by definition NDA it can be seen that the NDA/DA ratio at the Allocation stage has also risen sharply.

Does Growing NDA Dominance Mean a More "Efficient" BE?

Changes in the ratio of NDA to DA activity at all stages of the BE Provision Chain have been accompanied, for easily understandable reasons, by a profound shift in the balance of BE types produced. This is because effective demand becomes relatively more important than need as a "trigger" of new promotion. One question which should at least be raised is whether the heavy concentration of construction effort on forms of BE which accommodate trading, administration, exchange and leisure activities of various kinds, as opposed to forms which accommodate "production" and life reproducing activities, is in the interests of overall economic development. Is it, in fact, the pattern which is likely in the long term to help maximize GDP and local economies? Given present inability to devise any satisfactory test, since the scenario cannot be wound back to 1979 and rerun with a different development pattern, the position taken may depend to some extent on one's politics.

To the neo-liberal, market-led output patterns *must* be economically optimal because the market is held to be the most efficient form of allocating investment in construction effort. While neo-liberals might regard this as indisputable, they may concede that whatever else has happened the promotion, financing, construction, allocation and maintenance of new and renovated built environment has become less democratically accountable. This means that the equity question "economic efficiency for whom?" cannot fairly be disregarded when contemplating the pattern of additions to the BE in the Thatcher decade. But that question is not pursued here because it was made evident in the earlier discussion that neo-liberals do not make a virtue of equality (although they sometimes claim—see Friedmans 1980—that egalitarian ideals are more nearly reached in capitalist than socialist societies).

So we come back to the New Right's more favoured ground—economic efficiency. Has the increasing domination of "free market" forces at all stages in the provision chain in fact produced a more *efficient* BE—one in which rates of accumulation can be maximized and in which Britain's economy can flourish demonstrably better than those of some of our major Western European competitors? The question is dogged with definitional difficulties. The very concept of "economic success" is open to multiple definitions. Even when one has decided that Economy A is doing "better" than Economy B there might be any number of reasons for that other than the appropriateness of the pattern of development and the availability of externalities such as reasonably priced housing.

Nevertheless, the claim is frequently made from the right that while the market-led 1980s pattern of development in, for example, London's Docklands may well have caused individual social hardship it is in the end justifiable because of the benefits to Britain's overall economic prosperity. The architect of the largest single development in London's Docklands was recently quoted (*Docklands Digest* 25, 1990) as saying "Canary Wharf Tower addresses itself to the proposition that Britain is going to play a leading role in the world of tomorrow". Similarly it was observed in *The Economist* of 31 January 1982 that "Berkshire was the last bit of Britain into the recession. Signs are it will be the first out . . . Britain needs more Berkshires" (quoted in Barlow and Savage 1987). Neither commentator referred to the extent to which these flagships of "free market" accumulation were in fact heavily dependent on externalities resulting at least partly from public sector initiative. The success of Berkshire's economy must depend to some extent on the provision of an appropriate array of housing. That of the Docklands depends partly on the light railway that connects it to the existing City. It is precisely these helpful externalities which often depend on mixed, rather than a market-led, development processes.

We can begin tentatively to evaluate the apparent efficiency of market-led patterns by considering some results of a comparative study of the degree to which housing supply responds to employment growth in selected "boom" regions in three Western European countries (Barlow, Ambrose and Duncan 1988, Barlow 1990). This particular development situation was selected because the capacity of housing provision systems to produce an amount and mix of new development appropriate to the needs of the local economy can perhaps best be assessed when they are confronted with the strains of sudden employment expansion and restructuring. The restructuring means that a high proportion of the new jobs may well be filled by in-migrants to the area rather than by those laid off from old jobs. This in turn means that the strains placed on the housing supply arrangements are disproportionately greater even than the rate of employment growth. It has been argued elsewhere (Ambrose 1991) that the issue is not simply one of increasing supply. A full evaluation of housing supply arrangements needs also to consider questions of choice, space and health standards, cost effectiveness of production, and the inflationary effects of price/rent levels. It is not possible to pursue all these issues here.

The countries chosen, on the basis of previous comparative research projects (Ambrose and Barlow 1986, 1987), were France, Sweden and the United Kingdom. In terms of three important parameters of housing organization—subsidy regimes, promotion patterns and landflow regulation characteristics—these three countries exhibit significant differences. On a rough spectrum of the degree of state intervention in the development process, Sweden is the most interventionist (Dickens *et al.* 1985, Duncan 1989). Nearly all development takes place on land that has been acquired by the local commune at something around existing use value. It is then either developed by the commune in accordance with the local plan or sold on to private constructors, co-operatives or self-promoters. The sale price is geared to the "cost yardstick" imposed by the state and a State Housing Loan at preferential rate is available to the constructors on condition that they enter into agreements about the number, type and cost of the housing provided. Permission for some commercial development may well be part of the agreement. The aim of these arrangements is to ensure that the pattern of development accords with local planning intentions.

By contrast, as Table 5.1 has shown, housing development in the 1980s in Britain swung sharply away from public initiative towards "free market", and largely speculative, production. Builders prospect for land using a variety of strategies—sometimes varying their route to work each morning to see what sites look available. They have to pay whatever price the local market requires. Finance, from either loans or capital issues, has to be obtained at market rates with no mechanisms to protect the constructor from the sharp interest rate fluctuations that have characterized the 1980s. The capacity of the purchasing public to take up the product is affected by the same financial instability, expressed in this case by fluctuations in the interest cost of house purchase loans. As we have seen the structure and local planning processes have been undermined and there is consequently a weaker relationship between planning intentions and housing output.

France is in an intermediate position (Barlow 1990, Duncan and Barlow 1991). Land use plans are legally binding and once areas have been zoned for residential development, permission to carry out individual housing schemes is virtually automatic. This means that typically a far higher proportion of applications receive consent than is the case in Britain. The HLMs (roughly, housing associations providing housing at relatively low rents) continue to produce a sizeable proportion of total output. Land supply arrangements exist to assist housing self-promoters although these have become less prevalent in recent years. In addition a proportion of housebuilding takes place on "ZAC" land assembled by local authorities or semi-public bodies. Various subsidy systems (PAP and PLA) are geared to encouraging lower income owner occupancy and renting. Finally fiscal concessions under the *Loi Mehaignerie* have encouraged housing investment and helped to underpin a boom in apartment development. The French arrangements, while not so regulatory as the Swedish, are marked by the range and variety of intervention strategies and by the well-developed pattern of co-operation between the state and development entrepreneurs.

The high-growth sub-regions selected for study were the Metropolitan Area of Toulouse, parts of the E4 corridor between Stockholm and Uppsala and the county of Berkshire. Some bare facts will establish the reasons for the choice of areas. The methodology used, the precise definition of areas (which are not always the same for the population and employment data) and the main body of empirical findings are available in the various references cited.

Population change

Toulouse	607,000	(1975)	700,000	(1987)
E4	327,000	(1980)	357,000	(1987)
Berkshire	655,000	(1976)	718,000	(1987)

Employment change

Toulouse	415,000	(1975)	482,000	(1985)
E4	26,000	(1980)	62,000	(1987)
Berkshire	284,000	(1976)	301,000	(1984)

Apart from the sheer weight of numerical increase in employment, there was a considerable qualitative change in the demand for labour. For example, during the period the percentage of workers in the E4 case who were employed in the high technology sector rose from 10 to 16 per cent. In Toulouse the proportion of senior managerial and technical workers almost doubled between 1975 and 1985. By 1987 nearly a fifth of the workforce were employed in high technology areas. In Berkshire the percentage of workers in this sector rose from 7 per cent in 1981 to 20 per cent in 1987.

The study identified a "Housing Impact Zone" (HIZ) in each case within which the housing supply response to this growth situation was analysed. A supply well matched to the growth and providing supportive externalities for the development of the local economy would have a number of characteristics. Housing should continue to be available at all price and rent levels so that employers experience no undue recruitment difficulties or pressure on wages stemming from high accommodation costs. There should also be adequate product diversity to maximize consumer choice. According to neo-liberal beliefs, the flexibility of "free market" processes should produce such a housing response more effectively than interventionist and bureaucratic arrangements.

What in fact do we find? This brief review will confine itself to four aspects of the supply response;

(1) the rate of output,
(2) tenure choice,
(3) house price/rent levels and inflation, and
(4) land price inflation.

Full discussions of all these, and other, aspects of the development situations in the three areas are available in the works cited.

The crude *output* of housing units per thousand population over the period 1980-89 in each area was as follows:

Toulouse	6.8	(France 6.0)
E4	7.3	(Sweden 5.0)
Berkshire	6.1	(Britain 3.5)

On the basis of this evidence alone there is little to choose between the three local cases. Britain nationally has a much weaker record than the other two countries, hardly evidence that the house production industry has prospered in the "free market" 1980s. But within the selected growth areas the British output is only marginally weaker than the French or Swedish cases.

In terms of the *tenure choice* available there are much sharper differences. This might well have implications for labour recruitment, especially for the lower paid workers needed by any local economy no matter how sophisticated the general profile of labour demand may be. In Toulouse, the HLMs continue to produce about 15 per cent of output. Since 1982 about one-third of total output has been financed under PAP loans to produce lower cost housing. Of all private sector production, between 30-40 per cent has been subsidized by cheap loans of some kind. In the nine Swedish communes the tenure pattern of all completions over the period 1980-89 was well balanced at 40 per cent commune, 27 per cent co-operative, 4 per cent for private renting and 29 per cent for owner-occupiers divided between 15 per cent self-promoted and 14 per cent built for sale. Virtually none of the production was speculative. Almost all, including the private output, was carried out under the "land condition" and State Housing Loan provisions (see Dickens *et al.* 1985 and Duncan 1989). In Berkshire the annual housing reports of the relevant housing authorities show that the stock of public plus housing association units fell from nearly 51,000 to about 45,000 in the period 1985-89 alone. Of the total output of 45,000 units between 1979 and 1988 over 86 per cent were built speculatively for sale (in fact the proportion was 91 per cent in 1988). Clearly the market-led system in Berkshire is providing far less choice of tenure than are the more interventionist systems in France and Sweden.

Turning to *house price, rents and inflation* there are also considerable differences when calculated at "purchasing power parity" (Barlow 1990). In 1989 a typical new house in Berkshire cost £80,000, a similar new house in suburban Toulouse was £52,000 and a much larger house in the E4 corridor £72,000. House price inflation over the decade had been virtually zero in real terms in the E4 area (despite some rapid rises towards the end of the decade), somewhat higher in Toulouse (an average rise of 4.3 per cent per year in the period 1984-88) and highest by far in Berkshire (average annual rises of 23 per cent over the same period).

In relation to rented housing, the Toulouse output was nearly all subsidized in one way or another and continued to be a significant addition to the stock between 1984 and 1988. In the E4 area the communes and co-operatives supplied a high proportion of new output at rent levels fixed under a variant of the pooled historic cost principle and in discussion with tenant associations. This ensures that public rents are related to net production costs and to a broad range of needs rather than to what the current market in the area will bear. Also, by law, the rent levels for the small amount of private lettings are set by comparison with similar properties in the public sector. In any area of high housing pressure these procedures are likely to moderate the effects of scarcity on rent levels. In Berkshire the stock of public housing has been decreasing and their rents have been increasing much faster than inflation as a result of central government subsidy withdrawal. Private sector rents have been rising steeply reflecting partly the availability of user subsidy (Housing Benefits), partly the weakening of rent control and partly sheer shortage.

Finally, in terms of *land price levels and inflation*, quite spectacular differences emerge. In Toulouse in 1987 building land cost about £275,000 per hectare. The E4 data show that communes currently buy land for the public land bank at around £50-60,000 per hectare. This land is then sold on to public or private builders for prices which are held down by the "cost yardsticks" applied under the State Housing Loan System. For the very small amount of housing developed outside this system land prices were many times higher. In Berkshire in 1987 housing land averaged £804,000 per hectare (in 1988 this rose to £1,242,000 per hectare). The land cost per square metre of built space was 2.5 times more than that of Toulouse for a luxury apartment and 3.5 times more for a suburban house. Over the period 1980-88, land prices in the E4 declined by an average of 0.5 per cent per annum, in Toulouse they rose by 2.2 per cent per annum and in Berkshire the average annual increase was 15 per cent with huge fluctuations year by year (the peak year land price increase was 63 per cent). The combination of possible reasons for these differences are discussed elsewhere (Barlow 1990, Duncan and Barlow 1991). The implications of very high land costs for the cost effectiveness of housing production are also discussed elsewhere (Ambrose and Barlow 1986, 1987).

Conclusions—What of Democracy?

What conclusions can be drawn from the analysis and evidence presented in this chapter? Clearly, after eleven years and three administrations locked into a neo-liberal philosophy, profound changes have occurred. In terms of power relations, Non-Democratically Accountable forces have gained much ground over those that are answerable to the electorate. Inevitably, given the dynamics of the market, the pattern of BE produced has reflected the relative reward/risk environments available to development entrepreneurs. The result has been a growth of development activity in shopping centres, offices and leisure complexes that has been much greater than the growth of activity in housing or industrial development. These shifts are now less amenable to democratic local influence because the mechanism by which this influence is fed in, the electorally sanctioned land use planning process, has lost significant degrees of power.

Does any of this matter? Should we worry about

> . . . the effects of handing over the control of space, once subject to publicly accountable local government, to the balance sheet driven values of private sector retailing (Fisher and Worpole 1988: p. 7).

Are we not all consumers and can we not exert our sovereignty by acting as selective purchasers of the goods on offer? Of course—if we can afford to. This model of power relations relates our capacity to influence the economy exactly to our strength as consumers and ultimately, give or take some "distortion" of prices, to our strength in the labour market. This seems to be a recipe for perpetuating the social order until it does indeed look like a "natural order".

Most of the rest of the world looks upon Britain as a mature democracy—a model for countries currently making the transition from "socialism" to "democracy". The democratic institutions of the central state have taken the best part of a thousand years to develop while local democracy now has a hundred years of history. Universal suffrage, having been fought for over many generations, was finally achieved only in 1929. A formal proposal progressively to abolish universal suffrage would presumably be received with some horror as an affront to human rights. But in one important area of activity—the production of the human habitat—the 1980s have seen a very significant weakening of democratic accountability. In this respect the vote has lost a proportion of its value. Privately controlled and financed activity, responding inevitably to the opportunities presented by the market, has become much more powerful. The capacity of ordinary people to shape their environment by democratic processes has been diminished. The trends are, if anything, accelerating as the 1990s unfold.

It will be argued that Mrs Thatcher was democratically elected—three times—and that no secret was made of her intentions in the Conservative Election Manifestos. The argument has force. It could be used to support the view that these increasingly non-democratic arrangements for producing the built environment are those that the British electorate voted for and therefore want. But maybe this is too hard a dictum and assumes too much about public understanding of the complex processes involved. Presumably few would have voted for escalating homelessness, steeply rising rents, a clogged up housing market and a rate of mortgage repossessions that is currently doubling every year.

Alternatively it may be held that all this, while regrettable, is part of the price paid by a small minority in the interests of producing a pattern of built environment that more nearly suits Britain's economic needs—that keeps her ahead of her main European competitors by facilitating a high rate of accumulation and providing valuable externalities in the all important growth regions. The evidence in this chapter, while limited, indicates that this assertion can be questioned. In the three key growth areas considered, the indications are that the housing supply arrangements in Berkshire are not serving the needs of the local economy as well as are those in Toulouse and Stockholm.

More intervention and regulation, especially in the Swedish case, have produced more housing, better housing, more choice, lower prices and rents, negative land price inflation and a more secure business environment for the construction industry. The local consequences, although we have not yet researched these systematically, may well be less hardship, less social division, better environmental health standards, less inflationary pressure stemming from high housing costs and fewer construction company bankruptcies. Against this the speculative, market-led "boom-bust" sequence of events in 1980s Berkshire has produced one unprecedented phenomenon—the £1 million hectare. There must be a lesson here for those countries in eastern and central Europe currently engaged in making the transition from "socialism" to "democracy".

References

Adam Smith Institute (1983) *Omega Report: Local Government Policy*. ASI, London.
Ambrose, P (1976) *The Land Market and the Housing System*. University of Sussex, Urban and Regional Studies Working Paper No. 3.

Ambrose, P. (1986) *Whatever Happened to Planning?* Methuen, London.
Ambrose, P. (1991) The performance of national housing systems—a three-nation compariosn, *Housing Studies* (forthcoming).
Ambrose, P., and Barlow, J. (1986) *Housing Provision and Housebuilding in Western Europe: Increasing Expenditure, Declining Output?* University of Sussex, Urban and Regional Studies Working Paper No. 50.
Ambrose, P., and Barlow, J. (1987). In van Vliet, W. (ed.) *Housing Markets and Policies under Fiscal Austerity*. Greenwood Press, Westport, Conn.
Ambrose, P., and Colenutt, R. (1975) *The Property Machine*. Penguin London.
Andrews, K., and Jacobs, J. (1990) *Punishing the Poor*. Macmillan, London.
Ball, M. (1988) *Rebuilding Construction*. Routledge, London.
Barlow, J. (1990) Owner occupier housing supply and the planning framework in the "boom" regions: examples from Britain, France and Sweden, *Planning Practice and Research*. **5**(2): 4-11.
Barlow, J., and Duncan, S. (1991) *Housing Provision in European Growth Regions*. Progress in Planning, London (forthcoming).
Barlow, J., Ambrose, P., and Duncan, S. (1988) Housing provision in high growth regions. A comparative study of four European sub-regions, *Scandinavian Housing and Planning Research*. **5**(1): 33-37.
Barlow, J., and Savage, M. (1987) The politics of growth: cleavage and conflict in a Tory heartland, *Capital and Class*, **30**: 156-182.
Brindley, T., Rydin, Y., and Stoker, G. (1989) *Remaking Planning*. Unwin Hyman, London.
British Property Federation (1986) *The Planning System—A Fresh Approach*. BPF, London.
Brown, P., and Sparks, R. (eds.) (1989) *Beyond Thatcherism*. Open University Press, Buckingham.
Brownill, S. (1990) *Developing London's Docklands*. Chapman, London.
Cullingworth, J. (1985) *Town and Country Planning in Britain*. 9th ed. Allen & Unwin, London.
Dickens, P. *et al.* (1985) *Housing, States and Localities*. Methuen, London.
Docklands Consultative Committee (1985) *A Memorandum on the London Docklands Development Corporation*. DCC, London.
Docklands Consultative Committee (1990) *The Docklands Experiment*. DCC, London.
Docklands Forum (1990) *How They Got It Wrong*. DF, London.
Duncan, S. (1989) Development gains and housing provision in Britain and Sweden, *Transactions of the Institute of British Geographers*. **14**: 157-172.
Duncan, S., and Barlow, J. (1991) Regulation or marketisation in housing provision? Sweden and the E4 growth region in European perspective, *Scandinavian Housing and Planning Research* (forthcoming).
Duncan, S. and Goodwin, M. (1988) *The Local State and Uneven Development*. Polity Press, London.
Fisher, M. and Worpole, K. (1988) *City Centres, City Cultures*. Centre for Local Economic Studies, Manchester.
Friedman, M., and R. (1980) *Free to Choose*. Secker & Warburg, London.
Green, D. (1987) *The New Right*. Wheatsheaf, Brighton.
Harvey, D. (1989) *The Urban Experience*. Blackwell, Oxford.
Hayek, F. (1986) *The Road to Serfdom*. Routledge & Kegan Paul, London.
Hillier, Parker, May, and Rowden (1987) *Average Yields*. HPMR, London.
King, D. (1987) *The New Right*. Macmillan, London.
Kirk, G. (1980) *Urban Planning in a Capitalist Society*. Croom Helm, Beckenham.

Lloyd, G. (1987) Simplified planning zones; the privatisation of land use controls in the U.K., *Land Use Policy*, January 1987.
Malpass, P. (1990) *Reshaping Housing Policy*. Routledge, London.
Mumford, L. (1961) *The City in History*. Penguin, London.
Oldman, J. (1990) *Who Says There's No Housing Problem?* Shelter, London.
Parker, H. (1985) from Uthwatt to DLT—the end of the road? *The Planner*, **71**(4).
Pickvance, C. (1982) in Paris, C. (ed.) *Critical Readings in Planning Theory*. Pergamon, Oxford.
Rees, G., and Lambert, J. (1985) *Cities in Crisis*. Arnold, London.
Roger Tym, and Partners (1984) *Monitoring Enterprise Zones*. RTP, London.
Rose, J. (1985) *The Dynamics of Urban Property Development*. Spon, London.
Royal Institute of Chartered Surveyors (1986) *A Strategy for Planning*. RICS, London.
Smyth, H. (1985) *Property Companies and the Construction Industry in Britain*. Cambridge University Press, Cambridge.
Thornley, A. (1989) Planning and the ideology of the New Right, *Planning Theory Newsletter*. **2**: 23-37.
Thornley, A. (1990) *Urban Planning and Thatcherism: the Challenge of the Market*. Routledge, London.

6

The Economy

Has the British Economy Been Transformed? Critical Reflections on the Policies of the Thatcher Era

RON MARTIN

> It is extraordinary that a programme based essentially upon common sense should constitute a revolution: but such it has been. . . . First, there had to be a quiet but real *political* revolution. This required that the boundaries of the State should be re-drawn in favour of freedom and enterprise. . . . Second, there had to be an *economic* revolution. Britain's economic performance in the post-war years had been risible. Much ground had to be made up—and this at a time of, in the early years at least, deep international recession. . . . Few would dispute that the British economy has now been transformed: although inflation is still too high, our economic performance as a whole is the envy of Europe (Peter Brook, The Conservative Revolution. In *The First Ten Years*, pp. 6-7. Conservative Party, London 1989).

Introduction

Political history is littered with claims of new dawns and new eras. Such claims are of course the very stuff of political rhetoric. Successive Labour and Conservative governments in postwar Britain have been elected on manifestos which promised a new beginning in the management and modernization of the economy. Staging a *Wirtschaftswunder* is what all serious postwar British political leaders have aimed at. By the late 1950s it seemed to contemporary observers that the "new Britain" planned for and promised during and immediately following World War II

(Barnett 1986) had been secured. And perhaps for good reason: there was near full employment, the economy was growing faster than at any other period in its modern history, *laissez faire* was dead, Keynesian demand management had transformed the market economy, the country at last enjoyed a comprehensive welfare state, and social and spatial inequalities were narrowing. What was true of policy practice was also true of political debate. This was the era of "the end of ideology": political philosophy had expired, replaced by a new cross-party commitment to social democracy.

Today that political and policy consensus seems to have been a mere interregnum. Even by the mid-1960s, as non-inflationary growth became progressively more difficult to maintain, the permanence of the "new Britain" began to be questioned. And during the course of the 1970s economic growth virtually stopped altogether, while double digit inflation, industrial unrest and declining competitiveness became the norm. None of the three main attempts to modernize the economy made over this period succeeded, either in reversing Britain's relative economic decline or the ailing efficacy of the postwar Keynesian welfare policy settlement. Although they differed in orientation, Wilson's technology-national planning (1964-70), Heath's pro-market "quiet revolution" (1970-74), and Labour's "new industrial strategy" (1974-79) shared one thing in common: all three modernization strategies suffered the same fate of never being fully carried through, and of being far less radical in practice than their protagonists had intended (Newton and Porter 1988).

In one sense, then, Mrs Thatcher's pledge back in 1979 to rebuild the economy and reverse the country's industrial stagnation was but the latest in a series of such promises. Where it did prove different from its predecessors, of course, was in both the marked change in political ideology and policy regime by which the goal of economic renewal was to be achieved, and in the determination with which this new regime was pursued. According to Mrs Thatcher, the election in 1979 was possibly the last chance the country had of reversing the process of economic decline and ineffective government (Conservative Party 1979). As the 1980s progressed so more and more of the basic economic goals, political values and social commitments that made up the postwar policy settlement came under attack from the Thatcher governments as they sought relentlessly to install a new radical politics of free market liberalism and self-reliant individualism. By the end of the decade, the Conservatives were hailing this new programme as having wrought an economic revolution. Their approach, they asserted, had succeeded where those before had failed.

There are three main issues involved in assessing this claim. The first concerns the policy revolution that the Conservatives allege they have forged. There can be no doubt that Thatcherism initiated a marked break from the form and pattern of previous state intervention in the economy, though not all of its policy changes have been as radical as is often portrayed. It is also important to distinguish between the rhetoric associated with what the government has said it intended to do or claims it is doing, and the reality of what it has actually done. The difference between political rhetoric and actual policy has often been significant. Second, there is the government's claim that it has also produced an "economic miracle", that after a decade of resolute application its policies have achieved the economic reconstruction promised back in 1979. This assertion has been the subject of intense controversy. Not only is there fierce debate over the empirical evidence for an "economic miracle", opinion is also deeply divided over whether the achievements highlighted by the government have been merely short-lived and superficial or whether they do indeed reflect a transformation of the underlying long-term growth prospects of the economy. And thirdly, there is the important question of whether the internecine overthrow of Mrs Thatcher in late 1990 effectively brought the Thatcher revolution to an end, or whether the changes to the political and economic landscape fashioned by the Conservative governments under her leadership have so recast the terms of the policy debate, not only for the Conservatives themselves but also for the Labour Party, that the legacy of Thatcherism will continue to influence state intervention and economic policy for some time to come. My aim in the remainder of the paper is to examine these three aspects of the Thatcher economic revolution in greater critical detail.

Thatcherism as an Economic Agenda: In What Sense a Policy Revolution?

In assessing the nature and extent of the economic policy revolution claimed by the Conservatives, it is necessary to recognize that Thatcherite political economy was not just a set of alternative policy nostrums for reviving British economic growth. It was also an attempt to redraw the boundaries of state involvement in the economy in favour of private enterprise: in other words, an attempt to change the way the economy works, to change the form and range of state–economy relations, and to instil a whole new economic ideology in society. In short, the policy agenda was to recast the mode of state intervention in the economy in the widest possible terms, and in so doing to render any return to the old policy nostrums difficult if not impossible to achieve.

To accomplish these aims, the Thatcher governments mounted an assault on all four main elements that make up and distinguish a given mode of economic intervention. Every mode of economic intervention is predicated on some sort of *accumulation model* or model of economic growth and organization (Jessop 1990: chap. 7); that is, a politically and ideologically grounded vision of the pattern of growth in the economy, of how that pattern can be sustained, of how the benefits from accumulation should be distributed across the social base, of the position and insertion of the nation in the international economic system, and of the role and scope of the state in promoting and regulating the accumulation process. There can be little disagreement about the radicalism of the accumulation model that underpinned Thatcherism. It marked a break in economic ideology as dramatic and emphatic as Labour's Keynesian welfare agenda back in 1945. The very basis of that postwar model, its goals of full employment and demand stabilization, its extensive state intervention in industry and markets, its expansive welfare system, and its social egalitarianism and collectivism, were attacked by Thatcher as inimical to individual enterprise and wealth creation, and as excessively statist and bureaucratic. What had once been politically accepted as a successful approach to organizing the economy and promoting growth was instead declared to be inherently inefficient and dysfunctional, in fact as one of the prime causes of the country's economic stagnation. In its place, Thatcherism promulgated a grandiose neo-liberal vision of the economy in which the control of inflation, the management of sound money, and the promotion of competition, efficiency and supply side flexibility were substituted as the legitimate economic goals of the state. In Mrs Thatcher's Britain free markets, possessive individualism and self-reliance were to replace state intervention and subsidy as the motive forces shaping economic growth and allocation. This move to enlarge the province and agency of free market capitalism was projected not merely as the only sure road to economic prosperity (there was "no alternative"), but also as a way of increasing the sum of human welfare by extending the scope for individual freedom and expanding consumer choice.

The novelty and radicalism of this project stemmed from two features. Almost all assessments of Thatcherism agree that the latter's enthusiastic acceptance of "New Right" political economy, with its commitment to free markets and hostility to state intervention, was what gave the Thatcher counter-offensive to Keynesian social democracy its most distinctive thrust (see Keegan 1984, Riddell 1985, Krieger 1986, Jenkins 1987, Gamble 1988, Hall 1988, Jessop *et al.* 1988, Jessop 1989, Skidelsky 1987, Smith 1988, Thompson 1986, 1990). But what also made Thatcherism radical was that it repudiated the whole postwar Conservative consensus. In effect, Thatcherism represented a radical new expression of traditional Conservativism. The economic creeds of New Right scriptual writers such as Friedman and Hayek were used by the Thatcherites to revive, in modern form, the twin pillars of "true Conservative" ideology—economic liberalism and social traditionalism—which, they argued, had been emasculated during the postwar years by the party's drift to the Keynesian welfare "middle ground". In this way the radicalism of Thatcher's focus on the "free economy and strong state", to use Gamble's (1988) descriptive epithet, was articulated politically as a "return to the mainstream" (Lawson 1980).

This accumulation strategy, like the one it was intended to replace, had to have social legitimacy, that is the support of an appropriate *social coalition*. It required the construction and maintenance by the state of some sort of national popular programme or hegemonic project of political, intellectual and ideological leadership which would advance the long-term interests of the leading sectors in Thatcherism's accumulation strategy while granting economic concessions to the masses of the social base. What was striking about Thatcherism was the aggressively ideological and populist style with which it prosecuted its programme of "reactionary commonsense" (Gunn 1989). It sought to shift social interests and values away from the inherited culture of state support and subsidy towards a new ethos of self-help, thrift, competition and individual initative. This conversion of society from the old welfare-based social democracy to a new market-based economic democracy was promoted rhetorically as well as materially. The concepts of "enterprise culture" and "popular capitalism", together with slogans about "rolling back the state" to increase individual choice, have been the principal means by which consent for the new free market, entrepreneurial economy has been constructed ideologically. These phrases have been used by Thatcherite Conservatives to cast a beneficent glow of universal economic opportunity over the divisive effects of free competition. At the same time, tax reductions, the public sale of state industries, the sale of council houses, the introduction of various tax-free savings schemes, and a host of incentives to encourage the small investor, were all intended to elicit that consent by material means. In these ways, the government hoped to forge a social coalition that fused the possessive interests of the private individual and the profit-orientated interests of the private business sector.

All this was accompanied by a radical restructuring of the style of state intervention or *statecraft strategy*, that is the system of governmental procedures and mechanisms by which policy is formulated and implemented. Thatcherism proved extremely adroit in circumventing, isolating and dismantling the social democratic apparatuses of intervention and representation built up over the postwar period. The pattern of interest representation has been altered in various ways. Former corporatist elements of the economic intervention process, such as the NEB, the MSC and the NEDO have either been abolished or recast into non-consultative, administrative organs of the central state. Similarly, private sector bodies that had previously had some influence on or input to economic policy formulation, such as the CBI, the primary representative of big business, have been largely ignored. The result has been an extraordinary level of state autonomy in policy formulation and implementation, and a regular resort to *raison d'état* (Jessop *et al.* 1988). A key factor in this recentralized approach to economic intervention, itself a return to traditional Tory statecraft, was Mrs Thatcher's own robust leadership style. Her combative attitude, her unshakeable faith in the infallibility of her views and opinions, and her disdain for compromise, qualities she described as "conviction politics", imparted an authoritarianism to the policy-making process unprecedented in the postwar era. It was an approach moulded by the experience of the Heath debacle back in the early 1970s, and defended by her supporters as an essential driving force behind the government's economic strategy. It was also an approach that ultimately proved to be her downfall.

But what of the actual *economic policies* which were meant to translate that strategy into practice? In most accounts, the Thatcher economic policy revolution is delineated in terms of four main sets of policy reforms (see, for example, Walters 1986). The first and overriding policy objective was, and remains, to secure financial stability, particularly the reduction of inflation. The Keynesian deficit financing approach to the maintenance of full employment was abandoned and replaced by a commitment to monetarism. The Medium Term Financial Strategy (MTFS), with its planned reductions in the growth of the money supply and public sector borrowing, was the centrepiece of the policy. But as the decade progressed high interest rates, the maintenance of a strong exchange rate, and most recently membership of the European Exchange Rate Mechanism, were added to the government's policy in its attempt to impose monetary discipline on the economy.

Second, in its quest to sponsor a market-generated industrial recovery the Thatcher governments introduced a range of policies designed to liberalize and improve the flexibility of the supply side of the economy. Taxes were cut not in order to fiscally stimulate aggregate demand—or that at least was the theory—but to alter the incentive structure in the economy in favour of more effort and to promote private and corporate wealth accumulation. Similarly, spending on industrial and regional support was cut by a third in real terms (Table 6.1 and Fig. 6.1), the map of assisted areas was dramatically "rolled back", and the system of aid made much more selective and discriminatory (Martin 1985, Thompson 1990). In fact by 1988 any vestiges of an industrial strategy in the conventional sense were finally swept away by the government's "Enterprise Initiative". This rejected the very notion of industrial policy altogether and replaced it by a new national "enterprise strategy" of promoting entrepreneurialism and innovation-based small firm development (HM Government 1988). At the same time, in its attempt to establish London as the centre for international finance capital and to secure an export role for Britain through its specialization in financial services, the government also acted to liberalize the movement of internationally mobile capital into and out of the British economy, first by abolishing exchange controls and then by deregulating money and security markets ("Big Bang").

TABLE 6.1

Government Spending on Trade, Industry and Employment 1979/80 to 1989/90

	Expenditure in £million				
	Nominal terms		*Real terms*		
	1979/80	1989/90	1979/80	1989/90	% change
Total	4643	6665	7738	5379	−30.5
Industry	1789	2071	2982	1672	−44.0
Employment	1211	3272	2018	2641	+30.8

Notes: (1) Nominal spending measured as actual out-turn figures.
(2) Real spending calculated by deflating out-turn figures by implicit GDP deflator (at 1985 market prices).

Source: HM Government's Expenditure Plans (various).

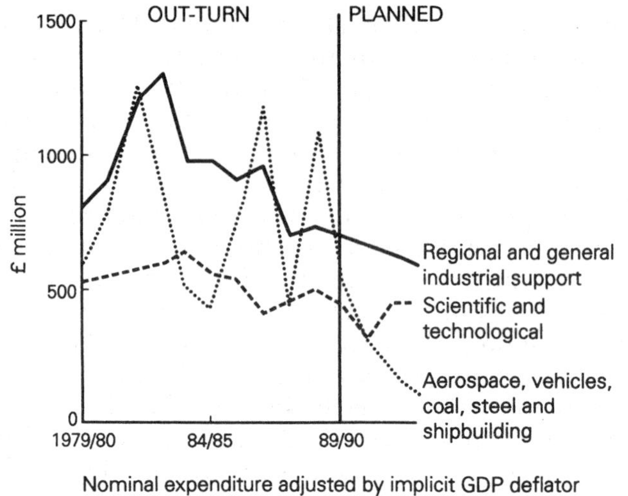

FIG. 6.1. Government spending on industrial support (in real terms, 1985 prices).

The third major policy shift, and in many ways the most radical, was its restructuring and privatization of state-owned industries (Veljanovski 1987). Although during Thatcher's first term of office the government channelled large sums of money into a number of unprofitable public businesses, including British Leyland, the British Steel Corporation and British Shipbuilders, it subsequently embarked upon a major rationalization programme led by specially appointed industrialists, renowned for their managerial ruthlessness. More than half a million jobs were cut in the nationalized industries over the 1980s (some 200,000 in coal alone). Many of those industries were then subsequently privatized. The privatization programme has played a central role in the government's strategy of reducing the size of the state, promoting popular share ownership and increasing consumer choice. By the time Mrs Thatcher resigned, the proceeds from privatization had reached more than £30 billion, with more to come from the latest sale involving the electricity industry. What were once acquired by the state as the "commanding heights" of the economy have been sold off at a considerable market discount, and in certain cases with the aid of "financial sweeteners" (as in the sale of Rolls Royce to British Aerospace, one of Lord Young's deals currently under scrutiny by the European Community Commissioners). This "selling off of the family silver", as the late Lord Stockton (Harold Macmillan) termed it, has dramatically redrawn the boundaries and landscape of the postwar mixed economy (Hudson 1989), and helped to reduce public spending and borrowing. As for the activities still remaining in state hands, the policy has been to impose ever more stringent commercial criteria, including internal markets and contracting out of functions wherever possible.

Fourthly, considerable policy attention was accorded to freeing up and increasing the flexibility of the labour market. The failure of the labour market was alleged to be the weakest link in the economy (HM Government 1985). The aim of the various employment policies introduced since 1979 has not been to promote jobs directly but to liberalize, decentralize and restructure employment and wage relations. This was to be the cure both for the unemployment problem and for the skills shortage that emerged from the mid-1980s onwards. It has been of the few areas of economic policy where state spending increased substantially during the 1980s, by more than 30 per cent in real terms over the decade (Table 6.1). Much of this has funded a plethora of training programmes, ranging from the early Youth Training Scheme (YTS) to the recent Training and Enterprise Councils (TECs). This is not to say, however, that the Thatcher governments had a coherent national training strategy (Ashton, Green and Hoskins 1990). Rather, the policy has been one of expanding the number of schemes while seeking to return training to the private business sector by paying it to implement the various programmes on the state's behalf. Alongside its various training measures, the Thatcher governments also reduced the role and significance of Wages Councils, and brought in legislation to curb and undermine the power of the unions in the workplace, particularly with respect to the right to strike, secondary picketing and closed shops, in an effort to promote the reassertion of managerial control.

Some observers, such as Walters (1986), consider these sets of reforms as having constituted nothing short of a revolution in economic policy. Other right wing commentators, though certainly welcoming the Thatcher reforms, have argued they were not radical enough. In contrast, left wing critics have attacked them as far too radical in their destruction of the postwar policy settlement. There has in fact been considerable debate over how best to characterize the mode of economic intervention fashioned by Thatcher. It is often labelled as monetarist. In practice, however, the Thatcher monetarist revolution proved to be more rhetorical than real. Although the Conservatives did begin with a firm commitment to monetarism, as embodied in the MTFS, and although this has been ritually reaffirmed each Budget time, actual policy has been somewhat different. While the Thatcher administrations managed to restrict the growth of money supply in the narrow sense, defined by notes and coins (M0), they singularly failed to contain the growth of money in the wider sense, that is including lending by banks and building societies (M3 and M4), and consumer credit in general. Partly as a result of the government's own deregulation of financial services, lending and credit grew dramatically during the second half of the 1980s (Figs. 6.2 and 6.3), with the result that the money supply similarly escalated, consistently exceeding official targets. Where the government did secure a more radical policy shift was in abandoning Keynesian deficit financing as a countercyclical instrument. Allowing for cyclical and inflation effects, the general government financial balance (GGFB), measured as a percentage of GDP, was actually moved into surplus during the recession of the early 1980s. As for public sector borrowing, the nominal PSBR was steadily reduced throughout the decade, and by 1989 had been turned into a public sector debt repayment (PSDR) of nearly £12 billion. According to monetarist theory, this should have helped reduce the growth of the money supply and keep interest rates down. It did neither. In practice, then, after 1983 there was a progressive retreat from strict monetarism, despite a continued rhetorical commitment to it. Instead Thatcherism relied primarily on high interest rates to pursue its monetarist goals.

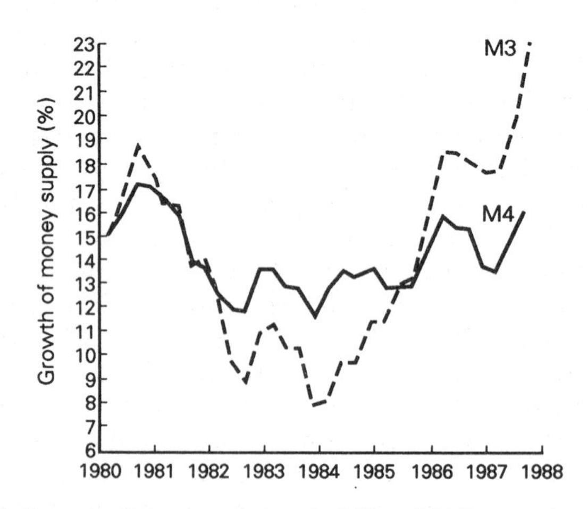

FIG. 6.2. Growth of the money supply (M3 and M4) annual percentage rates.

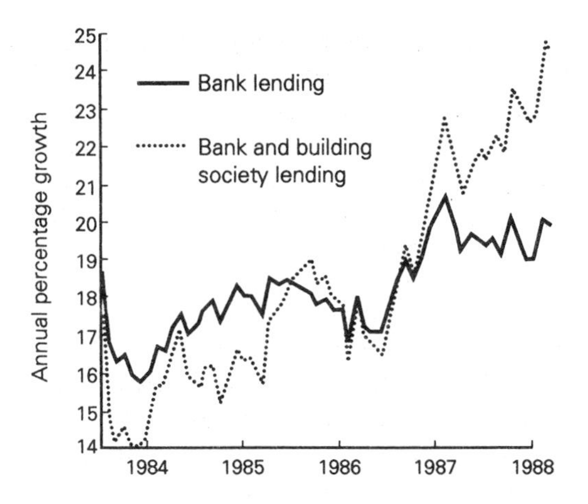

FIG. 6.3. Growth in lending by banks and building societies.

In other accounts, including that advanced by the government itself, Thatcherism is portrayed as having installed a new anti-interventionist mode of economic management, as having successfully rolled back the degree of state involvement in economy and industry. The reality, however, is that the Conservative governments since 1979 have not withdrawn from intervention to allow the market a freer hand: rather they have replaced the postwar *extensive* form of intervention with a new *relatively intensive* form. This new model has four features (Thompson 1990). The first is the narrowing of the field of operation of intervention, involving not just a reduction in financial support, as in the case of regional policy, but also a more specific definition of purpose. Second, economic intervention and regulation have been deepened, that is made much more selective, discriminatory, and value-for-money orientated. Third, intervention has been made more multilayered, in the sense that an increasing range of overlapping regulatory and legislative mechanisms have been introduced to facilitate the operation of market forces (as in the case of competition policy, the City, employment legislation, and new union laws). And fourth, intervention has become more discretionary. In fact, in an era supposedly typified by *de*regulation, there has instead been considerable *re*regulation of economic activity. For example, as the state industries have been privatized so the government has created an elaborate regulatory structure in order to protect consumer interests against the new private sector monopolies and duopolies. While prosecuting their ideology of liberalization and deregulation, then, the Thatcher governments actually presided over what can only be characterized as a renaissance of intervention.

Equally questionable is the view that Thatcherism represented a new *national* strategy of economic regeneration. Thatcherism deliberately rejected any economic programme based upon new alliances with either the business community or with labour. Above all, it made no commitments or concessions to British capital as such. Indeed, one of the most dramatic components of Thatcherism's economic agenda was its open recognition—even proclamation—that the interests of the British state are no longer synonymous with the interests of explicitly domestic capital, but with capital operating in Britain and the operations of British capital overseas. To some extent this posture reflected the process of multinationalization and internationalization of industrial, commercial and financial capital that has been underway for some time. In part it also reflected the fact that as a result of this process, there is no significant bloc of domestic UK capital that might provide the basis for a national strategy of economic modernization. But it also reflected the government's own desire to establish Britain as a leading actor in the multinationalization process, both as a source of and as a destination for foreign investment. In effect, despite its policies supporting domestic small and medium sized firms, the government's strategy was as much, if not more, directed at *internationalization*, building up an economic structure based on the export and import of multinational capital, a strategy that in many ways has made it more rather than less difficult for many small domestic firms to compete on an independent basis, even in the home market.

The most ambitious interpretations of the Thatcher economic project are those that see it as an attempt to construct a post-Fordist regime of accumulation and regulation (see Jessop 1989, Overbeek 1990). According to this perspective, just as the emergence of the Keynesian welfarist mode of state intervention in Britain during the 1930s and 1940s was instrumental in supporting and facilitating the postwar Fordist regime of accumulation based on mass production, mass consumption, welfarism and extensive intervention, so Thatcherism (and the new Conservatism) was brought to power by the subsequent crisis of that regime, and represented a specific political response to it, a neo-liberal strategy of flexible accumulation capable of breaking the Fordist impasse and promoting the passage to a new post-Fordist Britain. As described by its protagonists, the new post-Fordist economy is characterized by the flexible specialization of production and labour processes, the internationalization, deconcentration and fragmentation of capital, the disorganization of trade unions, the decentralization of wage-setting, and increasing differentiation of products and consumer demand (Harvey 1989, Hall and Jacques 1989, Murray 1989). Set in this context, Thatcherism's promotion of deregulated and flexible markets in capital and labour, its support of small firms and individual entrepreneurs, its offensive against the British trade union movement, its celebration of private property and consumerism, its alignment with the new service classes, and its favourable disposition towards international capital, are all deemed to be quintessentially post-Fordist in orientation.

However, in my view, tempting though these arguments are, identifying Thatcherism as a specifically post-Fordist accumulation strategy is problematic. On the one hand, regulationist theorists see the shift from Fordism to Post-Fordism as a series of deep-seated structural changes which they argue form the necessary shaping context, the determining material conditions, for any political strategy, whether of the right or left. Thatcherism is seen as an attempt to construct a new mode of intervention that "fits" this emerging post-Fordist regime of flexible production and consumption, in the same fashion that the Keynesian mode of intervention "fitted" the Fordist mass production—mass consumption regime of accumulation. Yet, on the other hand, regulationists like Jessop are concerned to stress that Post-Fordism does not necessarily have a neo-liberal policy agenda inscribed in it, and that considerable scope exists for other policy "fits". But this presumably implies the possibility of other versions of "Post-Fordism", and hence that the economic and social characteristics that supposedly define the latter are in fact far from firmly established or determinate. These ambiguities about what exactly Post-Fordism is and how extensive it is, render its precise connection with Thatcherism unclear. In fact, there are good grounds for disputing the ideas of Post-Fordism and flexible specialization altogether, and arguing that the restructuring and increasing emphasis on flexibility over the past decade do not signal the end of mass production, mass consumption or large capital, nor the advent of a decentralized and fragmented economy. Rather they represent a shift to a new phase of neo-Fordism (see Gertler 1988, Sayer 1989, Costello, Michie and Milne 1989). Under this alternative view, Thatcherism should be seen as a radical attempt to resolve the crisis of British "Fordism" by promoting the maximum scope of action for capital restructuring by reducing and redefining state regulation in order to allow a greater play of free market forces. In a sense Thatcherism was an explicitly capitalist strategy for resolving a capitalist crisis. The key question, of course, is whether and how far Thatcherism succeeded in this task.

An Economic Miracle: Myth or Reality?

By 1987, following their third election victory, and six years of economic recovery, the Conservatives were already convinced they were presiding over the arrival of the New Jerusalem:

> Remember the conventional wisdom of the day. The British people were "ungovernable". We were in the grip of an incurable "British disease". Britain was heading for "irreversible decline". Well, the people were *not* ungovernable, the disease was *not* incurable, the decline *has* been reversed (Conservative Election Manifesto 1987).

In 1988, the then Chancellor of the Exchequer, Nigel Lawson, was even more emphatic, arguing in his Budget Speech that the "country is now experiencing an economic miracle comparable to that previously enjoyed by West Germany and still enjoyed by Japan", a claim echoed in the government's Enterprise Initiative launched that same year:

> Since 1981 the economy has been transformed. Instead of being bottom of the league, the UK is now . . . top in terms of productivity growth. . . . And, alongside major improvements in profitability and productivity, there has been a significant growth in enterprise (HM Government 1988: pp. 1-2).

Only a few months later Mrs Thatcher herself boldly asserted that her Conservative governments had "rebuilt the nation's fortunes" (Scarborough Speech 1989). And alongside these declarations of a national economic miracle, another of the government's recurring assertions has been that its policies have also led to the economic turn-around of the nation's depressed regions and cities.

Evaluating the economic achievements of the Thatcher administrations is not, however, straightforward. For one thing, since ideological issues have been pushed to the forefront of policy formulation, not surprisingly debates over the impact of Thatcherism have often been as much about political ideology as about actual policy outcomes. But, in addition, there appears to be no general agreement over what is actually happening to the British economy in terms of the brute facts of the case: diagnoses and opinions differ according to the base year chosen to assess growth trends and the particular indicators used to measure economic performance. To compound this problem, there are, of course, no precise counterfactuals against which comparisons can be made: we simply do not know for certain how the economy would have performed in the absence of the Thatcher "revolution", or had different sorts of policies been pursued. And, in any event, there is the further difficulty that a decade may well be too short a time to be able to separate short-term effects from more fundamental structural changes, and thus to be able to determine whether and in what sense the British economy has been transformed (Senker 1989). It is not surprising, then, that different assessments of the economic impact of Thatcherism have come to quite different conclusions.

On the one side there are those who believe that Thatcherism has indeed reversed Britain's declining fortunes and set the country on a Japanese style growth path: most of these commentators point to a "breakthrough" or "miracle" in productivity, especially within the manufacturing sector (for example, Muellbauer 1986, Spencer 1987, Crafts 1988, Maynard 1988, Ball 1989), as the basis of what they see as an "economic renaissance" (Walters 1986). On the other side, however, are those who, whilst acknowledging the recovery of the economy from the deep recession of the early 1980s, dismiss the Thatcher economic miracle as a mirage (Courts and Godley 1989, Nolan 1989, Rowthorn 1989, Wells 1989). To the extent that there have been improvements, they say, these are merely temporary, arising from the economic respite provided by oil revenues and the current quiesence of the labour movement. According to these critics the economic and industrial policies since 1979 have done little to fundamentally resolve the "British disease" or redress the long-standing inferior performance of the country relative to its main competitors; if anything, they argue, those policies have intensified the nation's economic problems.

The government's economic claims can be grouped under four heads: a major reduction in inflation, though it acknowledges the problem is not fully resolved; a dramatic improvement in growth and productivity performance, reversing the stagnation and relative decline of the past; a fundamental recasting of the supply side resulting in a new incentive-based enterprise economy; and a major boom in employment. Let us examine each of these in turn.

On the inflation front, the government can claim to have achieved some success. Compared to the 1970-79 period, when Britain's inflation problem spiralled out of control, under Thatcher the average annual rate of inflation was almost halved (Table 6.2). However, it has still been more than twice

TABLE 6.2
Inflation and Unemployment

	1960–70	1970–79	1979–90
Retail prices (average annual % change)	4.8	19.7	11.7
Unemployment (average annual numbers, 000s)	362	640	1,943

Sources: Economic Trends, Historical Abstract of Labour Statistics.

the average for the 1960-70 decade and, more importantly, significantly above our main competitors, namely West Germany, France, the United States, and Japan. Furthermore, the cost of this disinflation has been record levels of unemployment (Fig. 6.4): during the Thatcher years annual unemployment averaged nearly 2 million, and would have been greater had large numbers not been removed from the count as a result of some thirty changes in definition made by the government. What is also clear is that the government's restrictive fiscal stance, and its raising of indirect taxes (VAT) and interest rates between late 1979 and 1982, contributed in no small way to the intensity of the UK's economic depression and doubling of unemployment between those years. The government in effect imposed a classic deflation when the economy was in any case moving into recession. The result was an unprecedented shakeout of labour and capacity from manufacturing: between 1979 and 1981 employment in manufacturing fell by nearly 16 per cent, output by 18 per cent and investment by 35 per cent. Although the severity of the downturn took the government by surprise, it did nothing to allay

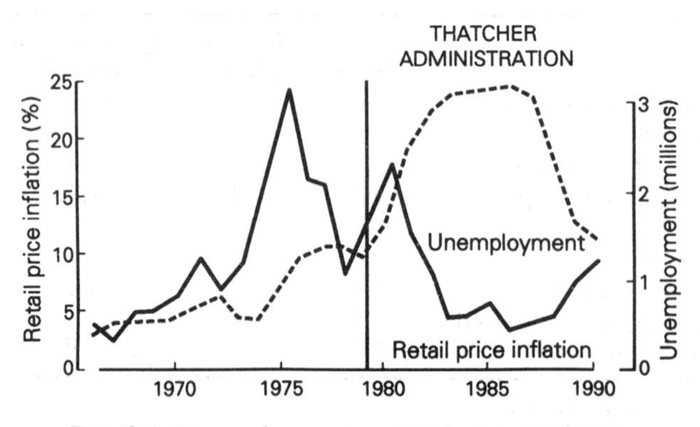

FIG. 6.4. Unemployment and inflation 1967-90.

its impact, and even turned it to political advantage. Thus the scale of the depression, the government argued, was due not to its own policies but to a much needed and long overdue rationalization of excess capacity and overmanning. The recession, though painful, was actually justified as being positively beneficial for the country: the result would be a leaner and fitter industrial base. And since then, the government has taken great care to measure all of the improvements in the economy relative to the bottom of that downturn, 1980 or 1981 in the case of output and 1983 in the case of employment, rather than from the pre-recession position that obtained when they first assumed office. The assumption was that restrictive monetary policies would bring down inflation, and this, together with the government's supply side policies, would soon reduce unemployment. In fact unemployment continued to rise until 1986, when it reached 3.3 million. Only then did it begin to fall, and then because of the consumer boom promoted by tax reductions and the relaxation in the government's fiscal stance—in other words as a result of a classic Keynesian demand stimulus—rather than because of low inflation, which in fact rose again as unemployment fell.

If the Conservatives acknowledge that the inflation problem has yet to be completely resolved, they are far more confident about the "growth and productivity miracle" they believe they have engineered. Table 6.3 compares the Thatcher record with that of the 1970s and 1960s. Real GDP output actually fell between 1979 and 1981 by some 1.8 per annum. For the remainder of the Thatcher era the annual growth rate averaged 3.4 per cent. This

TABLE 6.3
Output and Productivity Growth

	Growth rates (average annual %)			
	1960–70	1960–73	1970–79	1979–90
Whole Economy				
Total output (factor cost)	3.3	3.4	1.9	2.3
Output per person employed	2.7	3.0	1.7	1.8
Manufacturing				
Manufacturing output	3.4	3.7	0.6	1.3
Output per person employed	3.5	4.5	2.2	4.6
Employed labour force	−0.1	−0.8	−1.6	−3.3

Source: Economic Trends.
Note: All measured at 1985 market prices.

was certainly a marked improvement over the average of 1.9 for the 1970-79 period, but is virtually identical to that achieved during the 1960s decade. If the whole Thatcher period is considered, however, the average annual growth rate of real GDP was only 2.3 per cent, hardly better than the 1970s figure and well below the performance of the 1960s. And since 1989 the growth rate has been falling as the economy has returned to recession. Nor has the growth record of the Thatcher years been a nationwide phenomenon. Although all major geographical regions of the country experienced an upturn in output growth after 1981, the recovery has been predominantly a feature of the southern half of Britain. Indeed, since 1979 there has been a growing gap between the four southern regions (South East, South West, South East and the East Midlands) and the rest of the country in terms of GDP per head (Table 6.4). This increased regional imbalance in the pattern of economic growth and wealth generation has been one of the most distinctive features of the Thatcher era. It has also proved to be a major constraint on the overall growth process, for by the late 1980s the faster growth of the south and east strained the limits of supply there, leading to inflationary overheating that subsequently spread to the rest of the country and led to retaliatory deflationary action by the government (see Martin 1989a). The irony is that the uneven nature of Thatcher's "economic miracle" has also been a major reason for its instablity.

TABLE 6.4

The Growing Regional Gap in Output Per Head

	GDP per head relative to UK average			% change
	1970	1979	1989	1979-89
South East	113.7	116.1	120.6	3.9
Greater London	124.5	128.9	129.6	0.5
Rest of South East	105.5	107.4	114.9	6.9
East Anglia	93.6	94.0	99.3	5.6
South West	94.8	90.9	95.6	5.2
East Midlands	96.6	96.1	95.0	−1.1
West Midlands	102.8	96.0	91.7	−4.5
Yorkshire-Humberside	93.3	93.0	88.1	−5.3
North West	96.2	96.5	91.5	−5.2
North	86.9	91.1	86.9	−4.6
Wales	88.3	84.8	83.8	−1.2
Scotland	93.0	95.1	93.1	−2.1
Northern Ireland	74.3	78.1	76.1	−2.6

Source: Economic Trends.

Although much has been made of the growth of total output during the 1980s, it is the growth of productivity in manufacturing that has formed the core of the government's claims about economic transformation. According to the government manufacturing productivity growth in the UK was faster during the 1980s than in almost all other leading industrial nations, thus reversing the position that obtained during the 1960s and 1970s (Fig. 6.5). While output per person grew at an average of 2.2 per cent per annum in manufacturing over 1970-79, for the period 1979-90 the average annual growth rate was 4.6 per cent (Table 6.3). Although this has indeed been high by international standards, it is not so much a miracle or revolution as a reversion to pre-1973 trends (Coutts and Godley 1989, Muellbauer 1986). Whereas the growth rate during the Thatcher period compares favourably with that for the 1960-73 decade, when the average was 3.5 per cent per annum, it is less dramatic when compared against the average growth rate for the period 1960-73, which was 4.5 per cent. As argued earlier, much depends on the period over which trends are measured. It is also important to set the improvement against the far less impressive growth in manufacturing output, a mere 1.3 per cent per annum on average over 1979-90, which although an advance over the virtual

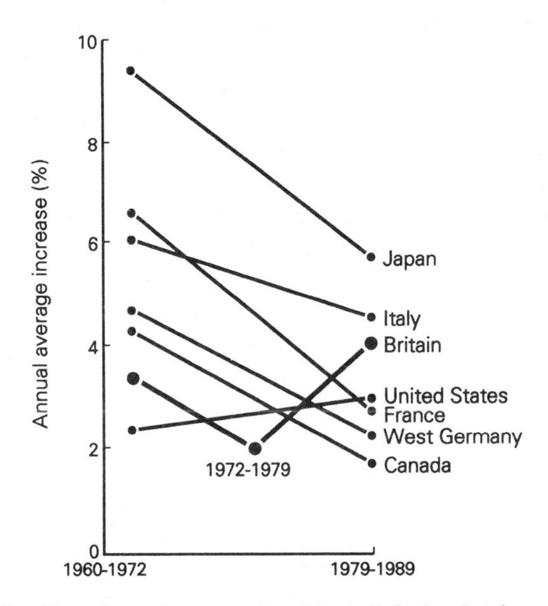

FIG. 6.5. Manufacturing productivity; Britain in international perspective.

stagnation of the previous decade, is barely more than a third of the growth rate achieved during 1960-73. Moreover, the UK's growth in manufacturing output over the 1979-90 period, 13.1 per cent overall, fell far behind that of other advanced industrial nations: 20.1 per cent in Italy, 22.1 per cent in Germany, 30.2 per cent in The Netherlands, 36.4 per cent in the US, and 56.9 per cent in Japan. This is hardly the stuff of which economic miracles are made.

The government believes that the marked surge in productivity growth in British manufacturing over the 1980s was the direct result of its various policies to promote a more efficient and less disruptive environment in which work and management could flourish. There can be no doubt that Thatcherism encouraged a significant "managerial offensive" throughout British industry. Its programme of industrial relations reform, its stand against organized labour in a number of key industrial disputes (in steel, coal, newspapers, shipping and the ambulance service), its deliberate isolation of the unions from national discussion and involvement in economic policy making, and its dilution and virtual non-enforcement of a whole range of factory regulations, all weakened union power in the workplace. This in turn has enabled management to reorganize the internal labour process so as to push through productivity gains. But the extent of such changes should not be exaggerated. Nor have they been peculiar to Britain. Although the average number of working days lost through industrial disputes was much lower in the 1980s than in previous decades, and although union membership dropped by a quarter between 1979-89, similar shifts occurred in a number of other countries (Fig. 6.6). The decline in militancy and unionization have had as much to do with the collapse of manufacturing employment, the growth of non-unionized jobs in service activities, and the overall threat of mass unemployment, as with the emergence of a "new realism" in management–labour relations of the sort that the government's policies were supposed to facilitate.

In the early 1980s at least, much of the improvement in productivity was probably due to shakeout and compositional effects associated with the depression. There is evidence to suggest that it was those industries that suffered particularly severe economic shocks as a result of the 1979-81 downturn that subsequently showed the largest productivity gains, more or less regardless of their unionized position (Layard and Nickell 1989). Gains were possible especially where there was inherent excess capacity and overmanning. For this reason, some of the

FIG. 6.6. Working days lost in industrial disputes.

higher productivity growth during the first half of the 1980s derived from the huge shakeout of labour that occurred in that period (Table 6.3). It is likely that these catch up effects were largely complete by about 1986, however, when the decline in manufacturing employment bottomed out and manufacturing output started to grow much more rapidly as the government began to stimulate demand. In the second half of the 1980s, then, it would seem that improvements in work effort did contribute to the continued improvement in productivity growth (Schor 1988).

Yet even if manufacturing productivity growth is a partial success story, the position of the manufacturing trade balance casts an altogether different light on the Thatcher "miracle" (Table 6.5). Thatcherism did nothing to halt the long-term deterioration in the balance of trade in manufactures, which by 1983 had moved into deficit for the first time in history (Fig. 6.7). By 1989 the deficit on visible trade had reached £23.8 billion. Although the surplus on invisible trade grew over the decade it was far from sufficient to offset the mounting deficit on visible trade, so that the current account also moved into increasing deficit, amounting to some £19.6 billion by 1989. Despite the improvement in productivity performance, the export competitiveness of British manufacturing actually declined under Thatcher, in part because labour costs far outstripped productivity growth and in part because of the government's maintenance of a strong exchange rate. Yet the Conservatives

TABLE 6.5
Balance of Payments

	Annual averages 1960–70	1970–79	1979–90
Visible balance (£million)	−291.4	−2282.2	−6994.4
Invisible balance (£million)	336.1	1850.0	4521.1
Current balance (£million)	44.7	−432.2	−2473.3
Relative export prices in manufacturing	83.1	87.7	102.0

Source: Economic Trends.
Note: In the case of relative export prices, a lower figure indicates greater competitiveness.

have seemed unconcerned by the visible trade deficit, and instead have pinned their hopes on the financial sector and the country's role in international money markets as sources of export earnings to compensate for the decline in manufacturing. However, services cannot be relied upon in this way as an automatic replacement for manufacturing output and export, for the signs are that Britain's competitiveness in international services is also declining. Over the past twenty years the country's share of world invisible exports has actually fallen more in percentage terms than its share of world trade in manufactures. And since 1986, the trade surplus in services, by which the Conservatives set so much store, has itself fallen. What cushioned the overall trade balance during the Thatcher years was North Sea Oil, but here too the positive benefits began to decline after 1985. There has been little indication, therefore, of an economic miracle as far as

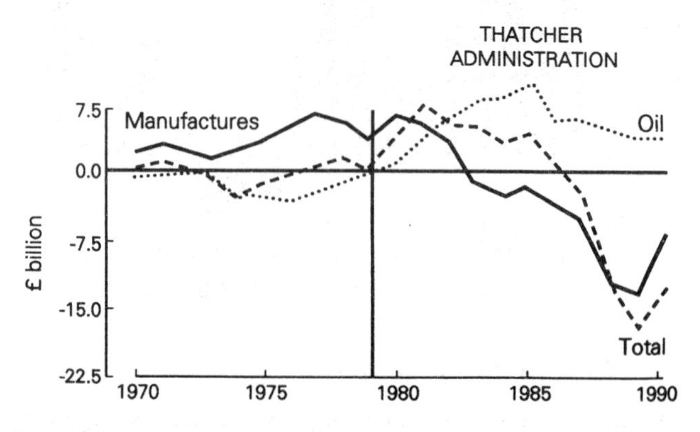

FIG. 6.7. Current account and its components (billion pounds).

Britain's underlying balance of payments weakness is concerned, and the long-term prospects are no better, if anything worse, than they were before the Conservatives came to power.

Some of the excessive growth in manufacturing imports relative to exports during the 1980s can be blamed on the government itself. First, by intensifying the scale of the 1979-81 recession the government contributed to what many now regard was an excessive loss of industrial capacity: between 1981 and 1983 there was net disinvestment of capital by the manufacturing sector (Fig. 6.8), most of this in the West Midlands and industrial north of Britain (Martin, 1986). Then, as the government fuelled the post-recession consumer boom, the domestic manufacturing sector was unable to respond fully to rising demand and so large volumes of imports were sucked in. The government has refuted this, arguing that many of the imports have consisted not of consumer products but of investment goods needed for the re-equipment of British industry. This interpretation does not, of course, refute the basic argument, for the fact that British manufacturing has had to look abroad for capital equipment is but another indication that too much domestic industrial capacity was slimmed down and rationalized during the first Thatcher administration.

In any case, many British firms have preferred to invest overseas rather than at home, often while simultaneously reducing their domestic operations (see Martin 1986, Cowling

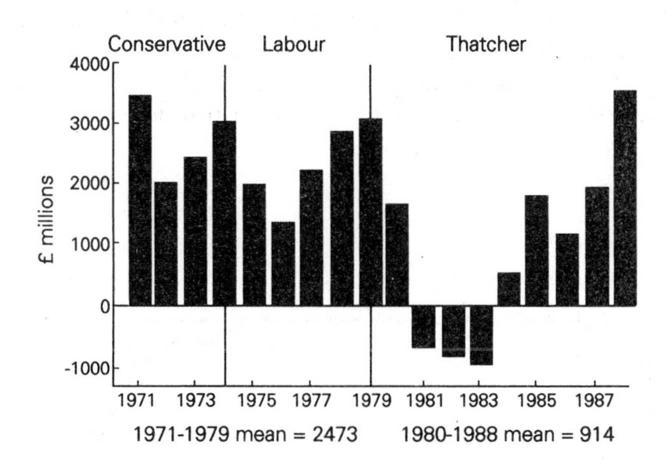

FIG. 6.8. Investment in manufacturing less capital consumption (plus leased assets).

1986). The abolition of exchange rate controls back in 1979 paved the way for a huge exodus of investment capital. Between 1980-88 more than £30 billion left the country as direct overseas investment. By the end of the decade the UK had the largest value of foreign direct investment outflow relative to exports of any of the OECD nations, and by far the largest stock of overseas direct investment relative to GNP (Julius 1990). While this is clearly a valuable source of profits and rentier earnings, it does little to regenerate the industrial base at home. Under Thatcher there was an increasing dependence on inflows of foreign investment to achieve that process. During the 1980s, inflows of foreign direct investment into Britain were higher than into any other European country, six times those into West Germany. Much of this inflow has been by Japanese multinationals: the UK attracted a third of all Japanese direct investment in Europe over the decade. In fact the government actively courted foreign capital as part of its approach to regional policy, even if in a rather confused way. While Peter Walker as Secretary of State for Wales emphasized the success of his interventionist policy in attracting foreign investment into that region, Lord Young, the then Secretary of State for Trade and Industry, played down the need for regional policy as such and emphasized instead the role of Thatcherism in creating the general business climate which he argued had made the regions successful in attracting foreign investment (for example, Nissan and Fujitsu in the North East, Toyota in Derbyshire and Bosch in South Wales). Yet at the same time that Lord Young celebrated the role of foreign capital regenerating the regions, Mrs Thatcher became intent on dismantling and recasting the activities of the Scottish Development Agency, a body generally considered to have been highly successful in attracting foreign investment into Scotland. Nothwithstanding all this, the inflows of direct investment capital reached only half the value of the outflows, so that Britain ranked second only to Japan as a net exporter of direct investment: but Japan, of course, also ran a huge balance of payments surplus over this period, in stark contrast to Britain.

Thus while in some respects, namely productivity growth and profitability, the performance of manufacturing did improve under Thatcher, in others, notably output, competitiveness, investment and trade, it has been anything but miraculous. Much of the manufacturing growth and investment that has occurred since 1983 has involved increased levels of company borrowing, which has made this key sector of the economy highly vulnerable to the government's high interest rate policies.

By 1987 the financial surplus in the industrial and commercial companies sector had been replaced by a deficit, which reached more than £22 billion in 1990. The British economy needs a dynamic and strong manufacturing base, for it cannot rely on financial services to fill the gap. But Britain's trade balance deteriorated in almost every sector of manufacturing during the 1980s, including key areas such as engineering and electronics. Considered in these terms, Thatcherism's claim to have reversed the country's industrial decline is wholly unconvincing.

The productivity improvement in manufacturing is only one aspect of what the government argues has been a transformation of the supply side of the economy. It claims to have created a new enterprise and incentive society. Thatcherism used the reform of the tax and benefit system to increase the incentive to work and to promote saving and wider share ownership. For much of the population, however, the low tax "incentive economy" has been a myth. The various cuts in income tax made during the 1980s were in fact outweighed by increases in other forms of taxation, especially VAT, personal national insurance contributions and domestic rates. Rather than falling, the overall tax burden for the average family increased under the Conservatives, at least up to the 1989 Budget. If anything can be said with certainty about the government's tax reforms, it is that the better off tax payers are the ones who have systematically gained, at the expense of the poor and non-working population (Johnson and Stark 1989): all measures of income inequality show a marked increase between 1979-89 (Layard and Nickell 1989). The rich, it seems, have needed incentives while the lower paid have not. What is also clear is that the savings ratio in the economy has not improved: personal savings relative to GDP fell from 11 per cent in 1979 to a mere 2.5 per cent in 1988 (HM Treasury 1989).

As for shareholding, it is certainly true that the privatization programme stimulated a sharp increase in share ownership of the sort hoped for by the government, from around 7 per cent of the adult population in 1979 to more than 20 per cent by 1990. But how far this has turned Britain into a nation of private capitalists is questionable. On average some 90 per cent of privatization shares are held by just the top 10 per cent of shareholders, and many purchasers only bought them in order to make a quick capital gain, which was practically guaranteed given the discount at which most issues were offered (Bishop and Kay 1988). And far from being nationally popular, the new "shareholder capitalism" has been overwhelmingly a phenomenon of the southern half of the country. In the South East the proportion of the adult population owning shares has now reached some 25 per cent, compared to about 15 per cent in the West Midlands and around 10-12 per cent in the North and in Scotland (HM Treasury 1986, 1988, Martin 1988).

The two most commonly used measures invoked by the Conservatives as evidence of their new enterprise Britain are self-employment and small firm creation. The numbers of self-employed rose by some 1.25 million or 57 per cent between 1981 and 1989 (Daly 1991), though estimates of this type of employment are subject to a considerable margin of error. Again there have been some marked differences between the regions, ranging from high rates of increase of 63 and 71 per cent respectively in the South East and East Anglia and much lower rates of only 31 and 45 per cent in the North and North West. To some extent this reflects the greater opportunities for self-employment in the more prosperous regions. How far this upsurge in self-employment is a result of government policies is difficult to assess. Certainly the government has made it easier to set up new small businesses through its various start-up allowances and grants. Some of the increase, however, is almost definitely a by-product of the mass redundancies and unemployment of the 1980s. It is also important to consider that the vast bulk of self-employment is in services, especially construction, distribution, catering and personal services, all of which are crucially dependent on rather than being themselves autonomous leading sources of national wealth creation. Arguably, what has been happening is a catching up of the self-employment rate to that typically found in Europe, although the highest rates there are found in the least rather than most prosperous countries (Greece, Spain, Portugal, the exception being Italy).

It is as the champion of the small firm that Thatcherism is frequently portrayed. The sharp rise in new business registrations since the early 1980s (Fig. 6.9) has caught the attention of politicians and academics alike, to a degree that an image has been created of a Britain in which a whole new industrial landscape of small innovative, flexible and dynamic enterprises is rapidly replacing the old landscape of large, mature and inflexible firms. It is an image that should be treated with scepticism. As with other aspects of the Thatcher economic miracle, it is a frequently exaggerated. For one thing, the small firm enterprise phenomenon is not a nationally uniform process. New firm creation rates, the take-up of the government's small business incentives (such as the Business Expansion Scheme and the Enterprise Allowance), and the allocation of venture capital to

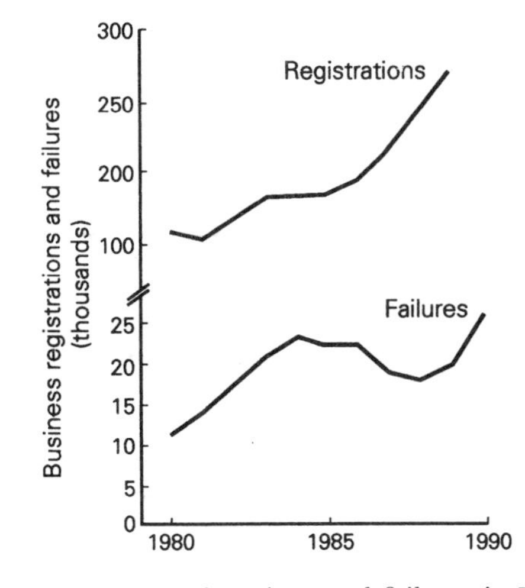

FIG. 6.9. Business registrations and failures in England.

fund new start-ups all have been distinctly higher in the south-east of Britain than in the north (Mason and Harrison 1989, Martin 1989b, Keeble 1990). Furthermore, as new firm formation rates have increased so too have failures (Fig. 6.9). Small firms are notorious for their high death rates, and the government's high interest policies have done little to improve the survival prospects of countless new small firms that supposedly symbolize the advent of the "enterprise culture". Moreover, although small firms (less than 100 employees) have increased their share of national output and employment, large multinational businesses still overwhelmingly dominate the economy and trade, and exert considerable leverage and influence over the small firm sector.

The final boast of the Thatcher economic miracle is the much quoted boom in employment, of nearly 2 million (8 per cent) between 1979–90. The expansion in self-employment accounted for some 1.54 million of this, and those on work related government training programmes for a further 0.4 million. The number of employees hardly changed at all. It is at the regional scale that the limited extent of the employment boom is really exposed (Table 6.6). In the four southern regions the loss of almost one million jobs in the production and construction sectors between 1979-90 was more than compensated by the growth of 1.8 million new jobs in services, so that the total number of employees in employment expanded by 0.8 million. By contrast, in the northern half of the country some 1.5 million jobs disappeared from industry whereas service employment expanded by only 0.8 million,

TABLE 6.6
The North-South Divide in the Employment Boom

	Absolute change 1979–90 (000s)			
	Employees			
	Production and construction	Services	Total	Self-employed
South East	−664	846	165	547
East Anglia	−29	150	111	77
South West	−78	256	173	160
East Midlands	−169	190	12	104
"South"	−940	1442	461	888
West Midlands	−336	198	−144	130
Yorkshire-Humberside	−279	209	−82	137
North West	−368	119	−250	112
North	−187	58	−133	37
Wales	−127	89	−40	75
Scotland	−240	129	−129	87
"North"	−1537	802	−778	578
Great Britain	−2477	2244	−317	1466

Source: Department of Employment.

with the result that for this part of Britain the total number of employees in employment fell by more than three-quarters of a million under Thatcher. The available data suggest that the growth of self-employment has not eliminated this huge disparity between the north and south of the country: up to 1989 more than 60 per cent of the increase in self employment had been concentrated in the four southern regions. For northern Britain, then, the supposed employment boom has yet to be witnessed.

It is, as Coutts and Godley (1989) state, somewhat difficult to write temperately about the Thatcher "economic miracle". Of course the economy has been changed, and in certain respects quite fundamentally, as with the privatization of the state owned industries. There are also the definite improvements in inflation and productivity. And the government has achieved some success in its aim of reducing state spending in relation to GDP (Fig. 6.10). The various costs and benefits of these changes have not, however, fallen evenly across the regions. Much of the apparent success of Thatcherism's neo-liberal strategy has been based on trends in the southern half of the country, and the South East region especially. The northern regions bore the brunt of the government's macroeconomic policies (such as high interest and exchange rates) and its specific microeconomic measures

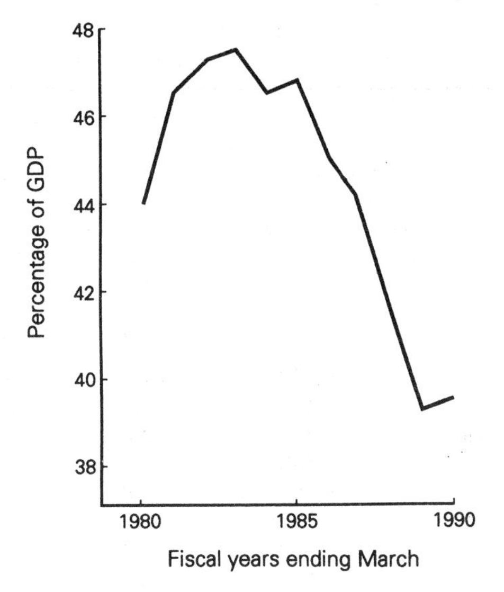

FIG. 6.10. Public spending as a percentage of GDP, excluding privatization proceeds.

to restructure and rationalize the nationalized industries. In contrast, the government's policies of internationalization, deregulation, liberalization, privatization and tax cuts were especially advantageous to the City, rentier and producer service interests located above all in London and the South East. It was in the north of Britain that the need for economic modernization was greatest, but Thatcherism made no positive attempt to assist the regeneration process there, preferring to rely on market forces while at the same time underwriting much of the growth in the south through various forms of public spending (defence procurement, research laboratories, airports, motorways, etc). By default if not by design, Thatcherism was a "divided Britain" project which produced the inevitable divided results.

Pulling all these different strands together we can say that the Thatcher years were quite distinctive, but not miraculous, in economic terms. Much of the growth success of the 1980s rested on an enormous, government-sponsored, credit and savings based consumer spending spree. This promoted an accelerated shift of the structure of the economy towards sectors which serviced the boom (retailing, distribution, personal financial services and credit) and away from those involved with producing tradeable commodities. The inflationary and balance of payments effects of that boom, themselves testimony to continuing economic weakness, eventually forced the government into another round of deflationary action, which in its turn brought the economy back into recession, back almost in fact to a situation not unlike that in the early-1980s. Perhaps worse of all, Britain alone in Europe had the bonus of North Sea Oil. The waste under Thatcher of some £100 billion of North Sea oil revenues, together with more than £30 billion of privatization proceeds, which ought to have been used to upgrade the country's industrial, technological and training capabilities, but which instead have been used to fund tax reductions, mass unemployment and reductions in government spending, is a huge missed opportunity verging on the scandalous.

Post-Thatcherism: Old Legacies or New Policies?

Nevertheless, in many ways the most significant aspect of the Thatcher revolution may prove to be its impact on the economic policy debate. Her resignation, not over the state of the economy but over her determination to preserve national economic sovereignty in the face of movements towards greater monetary intergration in the European Community, raises all sorts of questions about the post-Thatcher era. Some commentators believe that even before her resignation, the decomposition of Thatcherism had already in fact begun, due to a failure and collapse of the Thatcherite accumulation model, a failure to consolidate a stable social base, a steady erosion of her authority as unease spread at her leadership style, and a crisis of economic policy, especially over inflation and Europe (Jessop *et al.* 1990). By the end of the 1980s, they argue, the Conservatives' neo-liberal mode of economic intervention was in crisis on all four fronts. Others, however, contest this interpretation, and argue that the problems of her leadership style aside, the Conservatives' neo-liberal project is still hegemonic, in the sense that no viable alternative has yet emerged (Leys 1990). The one view tends to play down the longer-term impact of Thatcherism as an ideological and political force, while the other seems to accept the possibility that the legacy of Thatcherism may well prove to be more pervasive than its opponents are willing to admit.

One element of this debate relates to the response of the Conservatives themselves. Are there signs within the government of a substantial shift away from Thatcherism as a form of political economy? Certainly, under the new Prime Minister, Mr Major, there has been a definite change in leadership style, a move to a less strident and more conciliatory tone. This has been most notable in the emergence of a more positive and co-operative approach to Europe. There is also now an apparent readiness to reconsider particularly unpopular policies, especially the controversial poll tax, though this rethinking is due more to pressure arising from recent by-election defeats than to a genuine change of political philosophy regarding the financing and central control of local government. Some observers believe they have also detected a distinctly more pragmatic approach to economic policy since Mr Major assumed office. What is evident is that the post-Thatcher Conservatives have been quick to establish their own political rhetoric: the talk now is of a "classless society", an "opportunity economy", and even the "social market". In part this must be seen as an attempt by Mr Major to develop his own distinctive style and to minimize any impression of direct influence from or dependence on his predecessor. But in part it is also an attempt to maintain the party's electoral prospects, by changing policy on one or two politically sensitive issues and by seeking to impart a more social and caring image to their promotion of private market capitalism.

As for the underlying neo-liberal ideology established under Thatcherism, very little has changed. The commitment to the reduction of inflation through monetary discipline (now reinforced through membership of the European Exchange Rate Mechanism) remains the overriding priority. Similarly, the emphasis on the role of markets and enterprise continues. The privatization programme is to be extended further: plans are being drawn up for British Coal and British Rail. And the commercialization of remaining state activities is set to continue, especially in education and health. It is difficult to detect any substantial intention to change or roll back the accumulation strategy or model developed under Thatcher. Style may well have changed, but policy substance has remained largely intact. Indeed, Major has on more than one occasion affirmed his commitment to the general policy thrust inherited from Thatcher, and his intention to build on her achievements. What policy changes there have been to date (especially the review of the poll tax) have been directed at repairing the Tories' social and electoral base rather than forging a radically different post-Thatcher strategy.

If the ideology of "Thatcherism" is very much still at the centre of Conservative policy, it has been equally influential in shaping policy thinking within the Labour Party. One of the complaints of the New Right Conservative ideologues in the late 1970s was that Labour's construction of the postwar welfarist mode of economic development and organization had pulled the Conservatives increasingly leftwards towards the political centre. It was that consensus, ideological, political and economic, that Thatcher challenged and attempted to change. Labour has, naturally, vehemently contested the Thatcher project, both on the terrain of ideology and policies, and on the performance of the economy, particularly what it sees as Thatcherism's failure to stem the tide of industrial decline. But beneath this protest, Labour has steadily revised its own policies. Three successive election defeats have in part forced this process. In addition, however, in at least some sections of the party, the realization has dawned that the economic, social and political landscape of Britain has changed since the 1970s, in many respects irrevocably and in ways that are at variance with the traditional aims and policies of the party. Some of those changes, for example the shift away from manufacturing towards services, the decline of the industrial working class, the emergence of new social classes (especially within the service economy), and the decline of any simple correlation between socio-economic status and voting allegiance, were already established before Thatcher came to power. But they were unquestionably accelerated by Thatcherism, which also promoted other significant socioeconomic shifts that have profound implications for the Labour Party, among them lower taxes, the sale of council housing and privatization.

The latter, especially, strikes at the very centre of traditional Labour ideology. So much of the nationalized industries has been sold off and reorganized since 1979 that Labour has had little choice but to abandon its former policy with respect to state ownership. As one commentator put it, back in the late 1980s,

> Labour has moved a long way from its previous insistence on sweeping state control of the "commanding heights" of the economy . . . The Government's approach to privatisation may still be far from commanding universal approval. But Labour's change of attitude is eloquent testimony to the extent to which the policy has shifted not only the frontiers of the state, but also the terms of the political debate (de Jonquieres 1987).

Not only would large-scale renationalization be prohibitively expensive, it would meet resistance from the very interest groups whose support and co-operation a Labour government would need, namely the business and financial community, and the share-owning voter in southern England.

It is also unlikely, despite the very strong public desire for an extensive and modern welfare system—something that has remained impervious to the individualism promulgated by Thatcherism—that a Labour government would be willing to raise income taxes back to their pre-Thatcher rates. Labour might be prepared to increase public borrowing to finance such services, but here too its apparent conversion to sound money policies in order to control inflation may limit room for manoeuvre on this front, unless it introduced credit controls in order to restrict the growth of the money supply. In terms of managing the macro-economy, Labour's policies would probably not differ dramatically from those of the current government, save that they argue they would rely on a wider range of policy instruments to control inflation. Furthermore, although Labour would repeal some of Thatcher's employment legisation, the party's whole approach to the unions has become less supportive and more "arms-length".

As set out in its most recent policy statement, the major thrust of Labour economic policy would be directed to two principal issues: the regeneration of British manufacturing, mainly by encouraging industrial investment through a new system of tax and savings incentives, and the retraining and reskilling of the nation's workforce (Labour Party 1991). In effect these are the Labour Party's version of supply side economics, and here too there is evidence of a "Thatcher effect". For while in the past Labour emphasized the need to work with and exercise control over whole industrial sectors and big business, the emphasis, of the new policy has clearly shifted towards fostering small firms, innovation and enterprise. The main difference from the government's approach, apart from the promise to increase public spending on this area, is that Labour would decentralize much of its promotion of industrial investment to new regional development bodies. This new emphasis on the small and medium sized firm sector would seem to be a recognition that the accelerated internationalization of big business during the Thatcher era has made the task of constructing a regeneration strategy based on that segment of British industry increasingly difficult. It is also obviously a response to the rise in small business formation that has taken place since the early 1980s, and for which Thatcherism was possibly partly responsible, or at least rhetorically supportive. And it would seem to be a move closer to the views being expounded by a number of left wing academics who believe that the only viable industrial strategy is one which abandons the large, mass production, heavily unionized firms that were the hallmark of the Fordist era, for the small dynamic firms that they believe are leading the new post-Fordist regime of national and regional flexible specialization (Hirst 1989, Hirst and Zeitlin 1989).

All this is not meant to imply that Thatcherism so remoulded economic policy thinking and the policy-making machinery that there are now "no alternatives", or that Labour policy does not differ in significant respects from that of the Conservatives. It is a fact, however, that after more than a decade of Conservative economic neo-liberalism, the terms of the policy debate have changed in fundamental ways. The Labour Party has been outmanoeuvred by the Conservatives to a point where in order to improve its electoral prospects Labour has had no option but to bring its vision of the economy and its policies closer to those of the Tories. In this sense, the undoubted achievement of Thatcherism was not just that it succeeded in breaking from the policy "middle ground" of the postwar years, but that in so doing it constructed a new right wing "middle ground" to which Labour, albeit reluctantly, has been pulled. It is perhaps in this sense that it is most meaningful to talk of a Thatcherite transformation. The task of modernizing the British economy, however, remains as great and as urgent as ever.

References

Ashton, D., Green, F., and Hoskins, M. (1989) The training system of British capitalism: changes and prospects. In Green, F. (ed.) *The Restructuring of the UK Economy*, pp. 131-154. Harvester Wheatsheaf, Hemel Hempstead.

Ball, J. (1989) The United Kingdom economy: miracle or mirage? *National Westminster Bank Quarterly Review*. February, pp. 43-59.

Barnett, C. (1986) *The Audit of War: The Illusion and Reality of Britain as a Great Nation*. Macmillan, London.

Bishop, M., and Kay, J. (1988) *Does Privatisation Work? Lessons from the UK*. Centre for Business Strategy, London Business School, London.

Brook, P. (1989) The Conservative revolution. In *The First Ten Years: A Perspective on The Conservative Era That Began in 1979*, pp. 4-8. Conservative Central Office, London.

Conservative Party (1979) *Election Manifesto*. Conservative Central Office, London.

Costello, N., Michie, J., and Milne, S. (1989) *Beyond the Casino Economy*. Verso, London.

Coutts, K., and Godley, W. (1989) The British economy under Mrs Thatcher, *Political Quarterly*, **60**(2): 137-151.

Cowling, K. (1986) The internationalisation of production and deindustrialisation. In Amin, A. and Goddard, J.B. (eds.) *Technological Change, Industrial Restructuring and Regional Development*, pp. 23-40. Allen & Unwin, Hemel Hempstead.

Crafts, N. (1988) British economic growth before and after 1979: Has economic decline been reversed? Centre for Economic Policy Research, Discussion Paper 292.

Daly, M. (1991) The 1980s—A decade of growth in enterprise, *Employment Gazette*, March, pp. 109-134.

de Jonquieres, G. (1987) Privatisation: irreversible, warts and all, *Financial Times*, 25 March.

Gamble, A. (1988) *The Free Economy and Strong State: The Politics of Thatcherism.* Macmillan, London.
Gertler, M. (1988) The limits to flexibility: comments on the post-Fordist vision of production and its geography, *Transactions of the Institute of British Geographers*, **13**(4): 419-432.
Gunn, S. (1989) *Revolution of the Right.* Pluto Press, London.
HM Government (1985) *Employment: The Challenge for the Nation*, Cmnd 9474. HMSO, London.
HM Government (1988) *DTI—The Department for Enterprise*, Cmnd 278. HMSO, London.
HM Treasury (1986) *Economic Progress Report*, No. 183. HMSO, London.
HM Treasury (1988) *Economic Progress Report*, No. 195. HMSO, London.
HM Treasury (1989) *Economic Progress Report*, No. 200. HMSO, London.
Hall, S. (1988) *The Hard Road to Renewal: Thatcherism and the Crisis of the Left.* Verso, London.
Hall, S., and Jacques, M. (1989) *New Times: The Changing Face of Politics in the 1990s.* Pluto Press, London.
Harvey, D. (1989) *The Condition of Postmodernity.* Basil Blackwell, Oxford.
Hirst, P. (1989) *After Thatcher.* Collins, London.
Hirst, P., and Zeitlin, J. (1989) Flexible specialisation and the competitive failure of UK manufacturing, *Political Quarterly*, **60**(2): 164-178.
Hudson, R. (1989) Rewriting history and reshaping geography: the nationalized industries and the political economy of Thatcherism. In Mohan, J. (ed.) *The Political Geography of Contemporary Britain*, pp. 113-129. Macmillan, London.
Jenkins, P. (1987) *Mrs Thatcher's Revolution.* Jonathan Cape, London.
Jessop. B. (1989) Conservative regimes and the transition to post-Fordism: the cases of Great Britain and West Germany. In Gottdiener, M. and Komninos, N. (eds.) *Capitalist Development and Crisis Theory: Accumulation, Regulation and Spatial Restructuring*, pp. 261-299. Macmillan, London.
Jessop, B. (1990) *State Theory: Putting Capitalist States in their Place.* Polity Press, Cambridge.
Jessop, B. Bonnett, K., Bromley, S., and Ling, T. (1988) *Thatcherism: A Tale of Two Nations.* Polity Press, Cambridge.
Jessop, B., Bonnett, K., and Bromley, S. (1990) Farewell to Thatcherism? Neoliberalism and "New Times", *New Left Review*, **179**: 81-102.
Johnston, P., and Stark, G. (1989) Ten years of Thatcherism: the distributional consequences, *Fiscal Studies*, May, pp. 29-37.
Julius, D. (1990) *Global Companies and Public Policy; The Growing Challenge of Foreign Direct Investment.* Pinter Publishers, London.
Keeble, D.E. (1990) New firms and regional economic development: experience and impact in the 1980s. In Cameron, G.C. *et al.* (eds.) *Cambridge Regional Economic Review*, pp. 62-71. Department of Land Economy, Cambridge.
Keegan, W. (1984) *Mrs Thatcher's Economic Experiment.* Penguin, Harmondsworth.
Krieger, J. (1986) *Reagan, Thatcher and the Politics of Decline.* Polity Press, Cambridge.
Labour Party (1991) *Building a World Class Economy: Modern Manufacturing Strength.* Labour Party, London.
Lawson, N. (1980) *The New Conservatism.* Centre for Policy Studies, London.
Layard, R. and Nickell, S. (1989) The Thatcher miracle? Discussion Paper No. 343, Centre for Labour Economics, London School of Economics.
Leys, C. (1990) Still a question of hegemony, *New Left Review*, **181**: 119-128.
Martin, R.L. (1985) Monetarism masquerading as regional policy: the government's new system of regional aid, *Regional Studies*, **19**(4): 379-388.

Martin, R.L. (1986) Thatcherism and Britain's industrial landscape. In Martin, R.L. and Rowthorn, R.E. (eds.) *The Geography of De-industrialisation*, pp. 238-290. Macmillan, London.
Martin, R.L. (1988) The political economy of Britain's north–south divide, *Transactions of the Institute of British Geographers*, **13**: 389-418.
Martin, R.L. (1989) Regional imbalance as consequence and constraint in national economic renewal. In Green, F. (ed.) *The Restructuring of the UK Economy*, pp. 80-100. Harvester Wheatsheaf, Hemel Hempstead.
Martin, R.L. (1989) The growth and geographical anatomy of venture capitalism in the United Kingdom, *Regional Studies*, **23**(5): 389-403.
Mason, C. and Harrison, R. (1989) Small firm policy and the north–south divide in the United Kingdom: The case of the business expansion scheme, *Transactions of the Institute of British Geographers*, **14**: 37-58
Maynard, G. (1988) *The Economy Under Mrs Thatcher*. Basil Blackwell, Oxford.
Muelbauer, J. (1986) Productivity and competitiveness in British manufacturing, *Oxford Review of Economic Policy*, **2**(3): 1-25.
Murray, R. (1989) Fordism and post-Fordism. In Hall, S. and Jacques, M. (eds.) *New Times: The Changing Face of Politics in the 1990s*, pp. 38-53. Pluto Press, London.
Newton, S. and Porter, D. (1988) *Modernization Frustrated: The Politics of Industrial Decline in Britain Since 1900*. Unwin & Hyman, London.
Nolan, P. (1989) The productivity miracle? In Green, F. (ed.) *The Restructuring of the UK Economy*, pp. 101-121. Harvester Wheatsheaf, Hemel Hempstead.
Overbeek, H. (1990) *Global Capitalism and National Decline: The Thatcher Decade in Perspective*. Unwin & Hyman, London.
Riddell, P. (1985) *The Thatcher Government*. Martin Robertson, Oxford.
Rowthorn, R.E. (1989) The Thatcher revolution. In Green, F. (ed.) *The Restructuring of the UK Economy*, pp. 281-298. Harvester Wheatsheaf, Hemel Hempstead.
Sayer, A. (1989) Post-Fordism in question, *International Journal of Urban and Regional Research*, **13**: 666-695.
Schor, J.B. (1988) Does work intensity respond to macro-economic variables? Evidence from British manufacturing, 1970-86, Discussion Paper No. 1379, Department of Economics, Harvard University.
Senker, P. (1989) Ten years of Thatcherism: the triumph of ideology over economics, *Political Quarterly*, **60**(2): 179-189.
Skidelsky, R. (ed.) (1987) *Thatcherism*. Chatto & Windus, London.
Smith, D. (1988) *Mrs Thatcher's Economics*. Heinemann, London.
Spencer, P. (1987) Britain's productivity renaissance, *CSFB Economics*.
Thompson, G. (1986) *The Conservatives' Economic Policy*. Croom Helm, London.
Thompson, G. (1990) *The Political Economy of the New Right*. Pinter Publishers, London.
Veljanovski, C. (1987) *Selling the State: Privatisation in Britain*. Weidenfeld & Nicolson, London.
Walters, A. (1986) *Britain's Economic Renaissance: Margaret Thatcher's Reforms, 1979-1984*. Oxford University Press, Oxford.
Wells, J. (1989) Uneven development and de-industrialisation in the UK. In Green, F. (ed.) *The Restructuring of the UK Economy*, pp. 25-64. Harvester Wheatsheaf, Hemel Hempstead.

7

Housing

PETER WILLIAMS

1. Introduction

Over the last twelve years there have been major and some would say catastrophic changes in housing policy and housing provision in the UK. It is arguable as to whether these changes have been any greater than those experienced in other sectors of the economy, but there can be no doubt that changes of great significance have taken place. In looking back, perhaps the most notable piece of policy and certainly the one most Conservative politicians would point to is the Right to Buy (RTB). This was established in 1980 and allowed council tenants to buy their homes at discounted prices. It contributed to the twin objectives of promoting home ownership and reducing and changing the role of local authority housing. It was an electoral success and encouraged the government to grant rights to repairs, shared ownership and to a new landlord, though none of these subsequent developments have had the appeal of RTB and some have "failed".

Housing policies, and perhaps especially those that have been politically very contentious can be evaluated at different levels. For example, was the outcome consistent with the objectives set by government? What has been the final outcome in terms of housing provision and who has benefited/suffered? Has policy been consistent with and non-contradictory to overall policy objectives? In seeking to take stock and answer such questions we move into an arena of deeply polarized views as to what has been achieved. It is evident from existing evaluations of the 1980s that there are grounds for a substantial critique from a variety of perspectives (see, for example, Coleman 1989, Labour Party 1990, Malpass and Murie 1990, Murie 1989, 1990 and 1991, Reardon 1990) and some of this will be repeated here. But it will also be argued that some of the changes introduced have been positive, a reflection, perhaps, of the clarity of thinking which can come from the single minded pursuance of certain objectives. Whatever one's view, Chris Patten, the former Secretary of State for the Environment, was broadly correct when he suggested (1990) that "the government has implemented what is arguably the most radical reform of housing policy for a generation".

That some changes have been successful, challenges orthodox liberal thinking about how best to organize housing policy and housing provision. Much academic debate about housing has turned on traditional, perhaps even "statist", solutions, i.e. the solution is more direct provision by local authorities and more public expenditure. Despite any intrinsic merits such solutions may hold, the decade has shown that broader and bolder thinking is probably required if we are to really confront the housing problems faced by the population as a whole. In taking stock, therefore, it is important that we consider ideas as well as policies and programmes and that we look ahead to how these might develop up to the end of the century and beyond.

This chapter then will seek to describe the main changes in central government policies and the outcomes which have arisen over the period 1979-90. It will then analyse the main directions of policy and offer an evaluation of them. The chapter will conclude with a look ahead to the policy agenda for the 1990s and related impacts this will have on academic debate and analysis.

2. Context: The Labour Inheritance

Peter Malpass (1990) has argued (p. 186): "The changes imposed in the 1980s and those planned in the 1990s are rooted in trends that were well established before 1979". Looking back over the 1970s it is clear that the decline in housebuilding and capital investment had already begun and that these were visible reflections of both the International Monetary Fund (IMF), imposed cuts and a real uncertainty as to whether the public sector had reached its optimum size with housing needs largely met. Housebuilding, for example, had fallen through the decade (with fluctuations). Total completions for Great Britain stood at 313,017 in 1975 falling to 244,504 in 1979. Local authority completions were 129,883 in 1975 and 75,573 in 1979 and the equivalent figures for New Towns and Housing Associations were 15,758 and 14,693 in 1975 and 9,476 and 17,835 in 1979. The squeeze on public expenditure which began in the mid 1970s had resulted in a decline in local authority gross capital expenditure from £8,511 million in 1974/75 to £5,344 million in 1979/80 (Great Britain at 1987/88 prices; see Hill and Mullings 1990 for details).

The Housing Policy Review (Cmnd 6851, 1977) undertaken over the period 1975 to 1977 under a Labour government asserted the importance of home ownership and proposed no changes in mortgage interest tax relief. It noted the crude surplus in dwellings over households and suggested that although substantial housebuilding was still necessary to meet a predicted increase in households, "much can be done by the rehabilitation, conversion and repair of existing houses and by the better use of the existing stock" (p. 12). Overall, as Harloe (1977) argued, the outcome of the review was disappointing with little attempt to redress the balance between tenures. Indeed it suggested the need for much more carefully targeted subsidy to the public sector and for an altogether tougher regime for local authorities. The planned introduction of housing investment programmes and a tenants charter were welcomed, but in total the Green Paper was seen as a missed opportunity. According to the government there was no national housing problem, just a series of local difficulties, a view which sadly still seems to be held in 1991.

In 1978 the Labour government introduced its new Housing Bill. This included proposals for Management Priority Estates, a Tenants Charter, a new housing subsidy system (including for the purposes of subsidy calculation a central determination of rents) and measures to extend home ownership and improve the allocation of council housing. As will be evident now, much of this was taken up by the Conservatives when they returned to power in 1979 and introduced their own Housing Bill. Their key addition was the Right to Buy with Mr Heseltine, the new Secretary of State for the Environment, setting a target of 250,000 sales a year (a figure never achieved; the highest total of any year for Great Britain of sales of local authority, new town and housing association property was 202,558).

3. Housing under Mrs Thatcher

The incoming Conservative government of 1979 was thus confronted by declining level of housing investment and an existing policy agenda which had promised significant change in certain directions, most notably with respect to local authorities. However, over the next twelve years it was to develop a programme which reached far further than many could have imagined in 1979.

Objectives

Within the general rubric of a concern to ensure that a decent home should be within the reach of every family, the Conservative government's objectives throughout the decade and beyond have been very clear. They have also changed in important ways as new concerns have been identified. In the early years they emphasized their commitment to the growth of home ownership, the repair and improvement of the existing stock and a determination to focus public resources on those most in need. By 1987 a new emphasis on the private rented sector was evident and by 1990 housing policy was expressed as follows: to support the growth of home ownership; to encourage investment in the private rented sector; to ensure an adequate supply of publicly subsidized rented housing; and to ensure through housing benefit that poorer tenants can afford decent housing (Cm 1008, 1990). This last objective reflects the move away from subsidies on property to subsidies to people. Within these broad parameters has come a concern to promote choice within the rented sector, a wish to see housing associations become the main providers of new subsidized rented housing and the hope that local authorities will cease to be major landlords and instead focus their efforts on playing an enabling role. Finally, there has been a concern to ensure the effective targeting of expenditure where needs are greatest and that public expenditure in particular is focused and "concentrated on functions that cannot be carried out by the private sector without subsidy, and wherever possible with a view to attracting the maximum private sector contribution" (ibid. 4).

Although the general policy themes are clear, the precise instruments of policy have resulted in the emphasis shifting somewhat over the period in question. As Malpass and Murie (1990) and Hill and Mullings (1990) suggest, there have been two broad phases: the first phase (1980-84) related to the promotion of home ownership and the reorientation of subsidy, while the second phase (1986-90) resulted in a substantial reorientation towards the market and a fundamental restructuring of the arrangements for "publicly subsidized housing" (i.e. housing associations and local authorities).

For any government, policy is about what is possible politically and administratively. The clarity of the broad principles enunciated above might suggest that the government had proceeded through the decade with a clear "game plan" of what to do and when to do it. This is not so, however, tempting as it is to construct such an argument. The very division of labour within the Civil

Service, for example between Environment and Social Security, prevents an understanding of the totality and of all the levers and mechanisms which might be needed to produce certain specified outcomes. Moreover, as all of those engaged in research will know, there are simply huge gaps in our understanding of how the housing system actually works and what impacts policies have upon it. Furthermore, as is shown later, over the decade there have been a succession of Secretaries of State for the Environment and ministers with responsibilities for housing bringing different emphases to the process and adding to the uncertainties.

Alongside all of this it should be evident that policy is made in a context which is not entirely of central government's own making. Economic and social forces can force a change in or redirection of policy. Local government can resist or develop its own responses to the policy environment (and indeed one theme through the 1980s has been a cat and mouse game between central and local government with central government seeking to counter each new initiative local government has taken to get round the latest polices). Moreover, while the broad principles may attract general support, the detailed implementation can produce unintended results. Sometimes this is a consequence of legislative drafting whereby what began as a simple set of ideas becomes an almost unworkable policy in practice. Alternatively, by the time legislation emerges market forces may have moved against it with the result that take up is much reduced or entirely different than what was intended.

Throughout the last twelve years the government has often been accused of having no systematic and comprehensive housing policy. Instead, it has been seen as promoting a series of initiatives which relate to the broad objectives given earlier. In particular, the government has been criticized for having rejected taking a view on overall housing needs as a basis for policy formulation and the setting of expenditure guidelines. The absence of such a planning tool reflected a view shared by a number of ministers that estimates of needs were always likely to be inaccurate and a potential millstone around which all debate would focus. Reflecting this position early in the 1980s the government substantially reduced its own research capacity with respect to housing, cut its budget for externally commissioned housing research and terminated the funding for the DOE sponsored Centre for Environmental Studies which had a large in house research team covering housing. These actions significantly reinforced the view that policy was to be developed on the basis of ideology and political commitment rather than detailed analysis.

One consequence of this was that, with no explicit plan, it was difficult to predict in detail what the next steps would be and in that sense government retained an advantage. It forced local authorities and others to respond to its own agenda rather than the opposite and at times the pressure of new legislation coming forward was such that it became difficult to mount any effective opposition.

Outcomes: Legislation

The volume of housing related legislation in the last twelve years has been very considerable, even though housing as an electoral issue has not been particularly significant. In Table 7.1 the primary legislation introduced between 1979 and 1990 is given. However, it is important to add three important provisos which are critical to understanding the reality of policy over the last twelve years. First, legislation has often gone onto the statute book with only limited detail as to what it would mean. Often the Act would simply indicate that the Secretary of State had the power to determine and would do so when he saw fit. This meant that statutory instruments and circulars became very important. Second, the government's majority in the Commons was such that it meant that often the focus for debate and possible delay became the House of Lords (for example, the Lords prevented the Right to Buy being extended to tenants of charitable housing associations). Third, there can be no doubt that the complexity of housing legislation (notably housing benefit and housing finance generally) was such that errors did arise which were not easily picked up in the passage of legislation through Parliament. This problem was compounded by the volume of legislation generally and the scope of some Acts specifically (notably the Housing Act 1988 and the Local Government and Housing Act 1989).

As Table 7.1 shows, the scope of legislation has been wide. As well as major legislation affecting local authorities and housing associations there has been legislation in respect of the building societies, financial services generally and conveyancing. The private rented sector has been transformed in terms of its legal framework with a new system of assured tenancies and freedom to set rents at market levels and, via the 1988 Budget, the Business Expansion scheme was extended to private rented property. As will be argued later, not all of this legislation has met the objectives set and in some cases, notably with respect to homelessness legislation, the government has not proceeded with expected changes.

TABLE 7.1
Main Housing and Related Legislation 1979–90

Year	Title	Main focus
1980	Housing Act	Right to Buy, Tenants Charter, New Housing Subsidy System
1980	Local Government Planing and Land Act	Local Government Finance Competitive tendering
1982	Social Security and Housing Benefits Act	Housing Benefit introduced
1983	Mobile Homes Act	Gave tenants better protection from eviction
1984	Housing and Building Control Act	Extended Right to Buy via Shared Ownership
1984	Housing Defects Act	Assistance to purchasers of defective LA homes
1985	Housing Act	Consolidation of legislation
1985	Housing Associations Act	Consolidation of legislation
1985	Landlord and Tenant Act	Consolidation of legislation
1985	Local Government Act	Abolished the GLC and Met counties
1986	Building Societies Act	Liberalization of system
1986	Housing and Planning Act	Extended Right to Buy. LA power to dispose of estates
1986	Social Security Act	Modified Housing Benefit
1986	Financial Services Act	Changed the system re selling of financial products; impact on estate agency
1987	Landlord and Tenant Act	Gave new rights to tenants of privately owned blocks
1988	Housing Act	New private finance regime for Housing Associations; Deregulated private renting; Tenants Choice and HATS
1989	Local Government and Housing Act	New financial regime for local authorities (capital and revenue). New improvement grant regime

Adapted and extended from Malpass and Murie (1990), p. 96.

Outcomes: Trends in Housing Provision

The programme of legislation would imply an intention to fundamentally restructure housing provision in the United Kingdom and to some degree this has been achieved. Aside from the explicit concern to promote home ownership and private renting, the government's main concern has been to cut direct public expenditure and again one can point to certain budget items where major reductions have occurred. In the space of a short chapter it is not possible to discuss all of the outcomes of legislative and related change introduced in the twelve years under discussion. Moreover, there are different ways of examining the outcomes. There is a good case, however, for focusing first upon what might be seen as achievements in what are the core areas of policy, namely home ownership and private renting. The structuring of policy means that developments in these areas have direct implications for local authorities and housing associations and changes in these areas are also reviewed. Finally, any examination of outcomes must consider the extent to which housing conditions have improved, current housing needs and demands are being met and at what cost to the consumer.

Home Ownership

The promotion of home ownership has been the cornerstone of policy and this has risen from 54 per cent of dwellings in the UK in 1979 to 67 per cent in the first quarter of 1990. This figure obscures important national and regional variations. Thus while in England 68 per cent of dwellings were owner occupied, in Wales the level was 71 per cent and in Scotland 48 per cent (by the second quarter of 1990 Scotland had passed the 50 per cent mark). Approximately half of the 13 percentage point increase is accounted for by the Right to Buy (RTB) and other sales programmes. This is seen as a measure of the success of policy and an expression of personal preferences and choice. RTB was important, but so was the growth in real incomes and, between 1982 and 1988, a downward trend in the mortgage rate. As the home ownership market has grown, so it has become more differentiated and more exposed to problems related to changes in incomes, prices and interest rates (Hamnett 1989; Forrest *et al* 1990). Low interest rates and higher incomes drew in many who might have been considered marginal buyers in previous decades and as a consequence home ownership is now the most heterogenous tenure in terms of household types, class and income (ibid.).

The growth of home ownership has been achieved despite relatively little adjustment to mortgage interest tax relief (MITR). The limit for relief was increased from £25,000 to £30,000 in 1983. Although there have been rumours of increases in the limit at each subsequent budget, it has been maintained at this level and it has been assumed the plan was to let it wither away under the effects of wage and house price inflation. Had the limit been index linked since 1983, it would now be set at around £70,000. In that sense MITR is less significant than it was, with only 37 per cent of building society advances in the first quarter of 1990 being less than £30,000. The Halifax Building Society calculates that at current rates the basic rate taxpayer benefits by around £90 a month and the higher rate taxpayer by a further £55 a month. Most recently, it has been suggested that the government is planning to take away relief at higher rates of tax in the 1991 Budget.

Although MITR has not been increased since 1983, the growth of home ownership, the rise in house prices and the increase in the number of people holding a mortgage on their property has resulted in the cost of tax relief rising from £1.6 billion in 1979/80 to over £7 billion in 1990/91. Thus, despite the reduction in income tax, and therefore the rate at which relief is given, it has grown dramatically over the period. The absence of a capital gains tax on the selling of home owned property is another benefit enjoyed by home owners which has not been altered. It has been estimated to be worth £7 billion a year in 1990. Perhaps less well known are the changes in inheritance tax. It has been significantly reduced through a combination of ever higher exemption limits (now £128,000) and the reduction in tax rates (see Hamnett *et al.* 1990).

The level of home ownership has thus benefited from a combination of explicit policy (RTB) and the maintenance or enhancement of existing favourable tax treatments. House prices have risen from an average of around £20,000 in 1979 to about £67,000 in 1990 and mortgage debt has grown to £275 billion from £45 billion. Explanations for this rise in house prices vary, but in essence they were a product of the combination of personal preference and demand (which in turn reflect the tax treatments discussed above), demographic change, wage inflation and favourable interest rates (especially in the mid to late 1980s), the much improved supply of mortgage finance and short- and long-term movements in the supply of housing. The interactions between these different factors are considerable and have varied over time.

The current level of house prices, despite recent falls, and the substantial tax income foregone, are, of course, a major cause for concern. It is recognized that the most recent price boom was stimulated by lower interest rates and the 1988 Budget which phased out double tax relief for unmarried couples or others buying property together. The boom and the consequent slump has massively destabilized the market with serious effects for individuals, housebuilders and estate agents. Even if government accepted arguments about the inefficiencies of current tax treatment, they will naturally be reluctant to do anything more which could worsen the position. The number of households with a building society mortgage who were 6-12 months in arrears had risen to 58,380 in 1989 albeit that this was less than 1 per cent of total loans outstanding (*Housing Finance Quarterly* 1990) and as is shown later there has been a dramatic rise in 1990.

Private sector housebuilding completions in the United Kingdom in 1990 are likely to have been below 140,000, a significant decline from the peak in 1988 of 201,000 and marginally less than the 144,000 completed in 1979. There is little likelihood of a recovery before 1992 and a number of firms have gone out of business. The 1980s have seen major fluctuations in sales with the market swinging towards and then away from first-time buyers. Builders have sought to develop specific market niches, e.g. up-market, country homes, sheltered housing, marina and river developments, as a means of securing output and profit, but it has proven problematic not least because of high interest rates at the end of the 1980s and into 1990s.

Private Renting

Despite the government's concern to promote renting it has continued to decline throughout the 1980s. It is estimated it has been losing 50,000 to 60,000 units a year throughout the period. Although this is considerable, it is worth remembering until the 1980s the growth of home ownership was largely based upon new build and the decline of the private rented sector. While the latter continues in a limited way it has been supplanted as an important source of growth for home ownership by the sale of council housing under the Right to Buy. A range of policies have been introduced to regenerate the private rented sector and there is some evidence that a limited and specific revival is underway (Crook and Kemp 1991). The current downturn in the housing market has encouraged many would-be sellers to rent out their property and for buyers to hold off making a purchase and to rent instead. It is unlikely that this will be maintained in the long term. There have been suggestions that the era of home ownership as a good investment is over and private renting may grow again, but it is too early to make firm predictions about this (Forrest *et al.* 1990).

There are some signs of new energy in the private rented market partly in response to new legislation and partly as a consequence of the favourable tax treatment via the Business Expansion Scheme (BES). The latter was introduced in the 1988 budget and gives tax relief on investment in private rented property. It is estimated that around 10,000 units of accommodation have been produced as a consequence. The evidence does suggest that outside of London and Glasgow BES does provide for some of the traditional clients of the rented sector (the young and the old). However, it is an expensive housing option.

The liberalized market has given landlords new power and brought new pressures on tenants. Any expansion is likely to reflect the reweighting of this relationship. Under the Local Government Act 1988 local authorities are allowed to offer financial assistance to private landlords, although because expenditure will come within the authorities basic credit approval (the amount of capital it is allowed to borrow) take up is likely to remain limited. However, where an authority has disposed of its stock under the voluntary transfer process now in place there may be a greater attraction to follow this path. More common is the support given (but normally to housing associations) in the form of cheap land in return for nomination rights to the properties which are then built. Despite this it has been predicted that the private rented sector will continue to decline (falling from an estimated 1,449,000 in England in 1989 to 1,200,000 dwellings in 2001; see Wilcox 1990).

Housing Associations

The period 1979-90 has marked a remarkable transition in the role and responsibilites of housing associations. Although the numerical increase in housing association stock is not as dramatic as might be imagined (from around 450,000 to 650,000, a 44 per cent increase over 12 years) and there have been important fluctuations in their fortunes (e.g. the moratorium on spending in the early 1980s), the associations have been moved from a supporting to a primary role in the provision of new social housing. Of course, at present their stock and range of activity is much smaller than local authorities (except in specific localities, e.g. Kensington and Chelsea where associations have around 12,000 properties and the local authority approximately 6,000 and where local authorities have transferred their stock to existing or new associations) but the government clearly intends this to change through both new building and via further transfers. Government spending on associations has risen considerably. For example, in England, the gross capital expenditure for the Housing Corporation was £815 million in 1989/90. In 1979/80 it stood at £401 million. A similar pattern can be observed for Scotland and Wales.

The move to favoured status has not been without its costs, nor has it protected associations from being included in the Right to Buy. In taking on this new role associations have moved from a financial regime in which "fair" rents were set by the Rent Officer and an average of over 85 per cent of the costs of a scheme were paid for by Housing Association Grant (HAG) to one in which market rents apply and on average 25 per cent of the costs of a scheme are met by private finance to be repaid from the rent. HAG is still substantial, but there is now clear pressure to charge higher rents. This does mean that more homes will be produced for each pound of grant spent, but it could also influence who benefits directly from this expenditure. Moreover, it is apparent that despite the continuing need to improve the housing stock housing associations have rapidly reduced their role in rehabilitation, not least because it is more expensive and the risks of cost overruns are greater.

The new regime for associations introduced by the Housing Act 1988 has moved them much closer to the market. Indeed Kemp (1990b: p. 801) refers to the changes as the "reprivatization of housing associations" and it is already evident that the new system has unleashed substantial competitive pressures. The need to raise private finance has made associations more aware of their asset base and has resulted in mergers designed to increase their financial strength. New rent setting procedures, cross-subsidy between schemes and greater cost consciousness are all evidence of the new approach. However, associations are still subsidized to a considerable degree and subject to control and regulation. David Coleman, a special adviser to John Patten when he was at the DOE, has been a trenchant critic of the new regime. He has questioned the very ethos of the associations by suggesting

(Coleman 1989: p. 53): "In some ways they look more like an extension of council housing than a suitable replacement for it" as well as doubting their capacity to take on greater responsibilities. Should associations fail to deliver what government requires (whether in terms of new homes, or as approved landlords ready to take over council stock and/or the management of council housing) it is likely they would rapidly fall from favour.

Coleman's critique of the associations looked slightly misplaced in 1990 when, in England, the Housing Corporation had to cut back its approved development programme partly because of speed with which associations were bringing projects to fruition. This caused a cash "crisis" and a major disruption to the planned output of dwellings in 1990/91. The consequences of this for both associations and the authorities in whose areas they were to build have been considerable. The fluctuating fortunes of associations are also revealed in completion statistics. In 1979 they completed 17,835 new homes and renovated 20,097 properties in Great Britain. By 1989 this had fallen to 12,105 new homes and 13,100 renovations. As the expenditure plans would suggest, this is intended to increase significantly and this will be necessary if they are to become a real substitute for local authority new build.

Local Authorities: Capital Expenditure

The government's intentions for local authorities have become ever more severe and explicit as the decade has progressed. Concern with making authorities more accountable has over time been replaced by concern to break up their apparent monopoly of social housing and more recently to see the complete demise of the council landlord. While some of this may be dismissed as rhetoric, it is evident that over the period 1979-90 local authorities have had to face ever-increasing pressures on what they can do. The amount local authorities have been allowed to borrow for housing (Housing Investment Programme allocations) has fallen throughout the period.

As the National Audit Office (1989) shows in England they declined from £2,544 million in 1979/80 to £1,110 million in 1989/90 in cash terms (a 56 per cent fall) and to £560 million in constant 1979/80 prices (a 78 per cent fall). Under the new credit approval system the planned basic credit approval (BCA) allocation for England for 1990/91 was £1,428 million and £1,539 million for 1991/92. Roughly 30 per cent of these totals are set aside for specific initiatives which authorities have to apply to participate in (e.g. Estate Action projects for improving "run down estates"). The "unallocated" basic credit approval for 1990/91 stood at £1,026 million and £1,060 million in 1991/92. The reduction in HIP/BCA permission to spend has been facilitated by the growth in the volume of capital receipts local authorities receive from the RTB sales. Despite reductions in the proportion of the receipts that councils were allowed to spend, via the intricacies of the finance system, authorities were actually able to spend 100 per cent of the receipt from sales. The result was that the gross capital expenditure of local authorities has been at a significantly higher level than would have been possible simply via HIP/BCA.

In their detailed analysis of the United Kingdom, Hills and Mullings show capital receipts rising from £902 million in 1979/80 to £3,733 million in 1988/89 at 1987/88 prices (an increase of more than 300 per cent) while gross spending by local authorities declined from £5,344 million in 1979/80 to £4,018 million in 1988/89 (a 25 per cent reduction). The decline in net new expenditure via HIP/BCA and the reliance upon receipts is illustrated in Fig 7.1 for England for the period 1979/80 to 1990/91. While reliance on receipts may appear to be very sensible, it should be recognized these accrued to individual authorities. Typically sales are low in high need areas and high in low need areas, The "windfall" capital from sales supplemented the declining HIP/BCA allocations in all areas but has had a very variable impact on authorities.

Moreover, the decline overall masks a dramatic fall in spending on new building by local authorities. There has been a real fall of

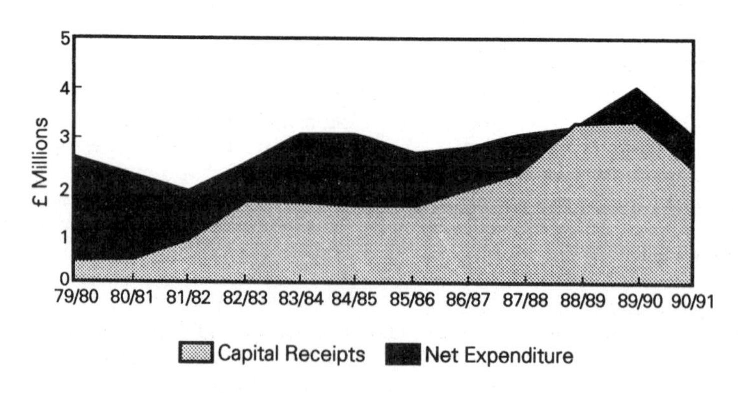

Source: Wilcox (1990)

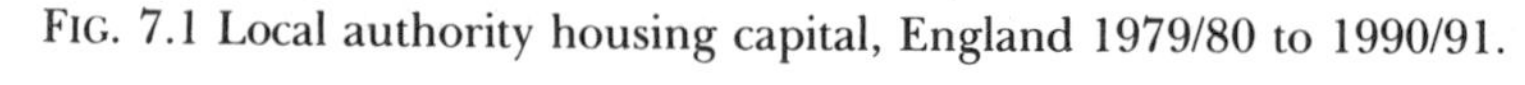
Fig. 7.1 Local authority housing capital, England 1979/80 to 1990/91.

86 per cent over the period 1976/77 and 1988/89. In output terms local authority new building fell from 79,009 completions in 1979 to 17,087 in 1989 (a reduction of 78 per cent) and it will continue to fall. Such a pattern is entirely consistent with stated policy objectives. However, the question remains as to whether overall housing needs can still be met. The evidence from homelessness figures and other data would suggest not.

In ceasing to be a major source of new building, local authorities have turned instead to major renovation of their existing property. This is partly a product of the rules related to the expenditure of capital receipts and the top slicing of HIP/BCA for special initiatives (e.g. Estate Action), but it also relates to the identified need to upgrade and improve a housing stock which had been built in the interwar and postwar years. Thus, in England in 1979, 75,967 dwellings were converted or improved. By 1989 the provisional figure was 194,905. Despite this considerable upsurge there is real concern that the number of properties being improved is far below what is necessary and that much higher levels of capital resources must be released to sustain the improvement process.

Local Authorities: Revenue Expenditure

Fundamental changes have taken place in the mechanisms for and the patterns of local authority revenue expenditure. As Malpass (1990) shows, there has been a fundamental shift in the sources of income which go to pay for the expenditure on providing the housing service [e.g. supervision and management (mainly staff, offices and related costs), repairs and maintenance, debt charges, etc.]. In 1979, all authorities received subsidy on their housing revenue accounts. By 1986/87 this had fallen to 130, though under the new regime introduced in England and Wales in 1989 probably all authorities are back in subsidy again (but by 1990/91 2 authorities were out of subsidy and more will follow). Thus in 1979/80 exchequer subsidies to local authority (and new town) revenue expenditure stood at £2,996 million in 1987/88 prices. In 1988/89 it was down to £679 million, a 78 per cent reduction. The movement in and out of subsidy reflects assumptions made by government as to the level of rent authorities should charge and the the costs of running their housing service. Where that model indicated assumed income was greater than assumed costs, subsidy was withdrawn. Although this should have meant that authorities most in need continued to get subsidy, in reality this was not always so (ibid., p. 147).

The rundown of new building over the decade along with rent increases has meant that many authorities had moved into surplus on their housing revenue accounts (and were in some cases transferring this to the Rate Fund). The reforms of 1989 in England and Wales were intended to give the government greater control of these surpluses (thus reducing central government expenditure) and to bring in tighter control on rents, management and maintenance expenditure. The complexities of the new arrangements are beyond the scope of this chapter, but in essence they are as follows: there is now one subsidy entitlement which covers "deficits" on the revenue account and expenditure on housing benefit for local authority tenants; rents will be related to market prices; management and maintenance allowances will be derived from a formula rather than actual expenditure; and finally the Housing Revenue Account (HRA) will be ring fenced, i.e. no payments can be made from it to the rate fund (or charge fund as it is at the time of writing) or vice versa.

The new system has resulted in increases in rents (in reality many authorities are putting rents up more than the official guideline to generate spare cash from which to fund capital expenditure) and the prospect that as these rise over time subsidy entitlement will fall. Given that housing benefit payments are covered by the same subsidy, there will be a growing number of authorities where rent increases effectively fund housing benefit.

One positive consequence of the ring fencing referred to above is that on close examination of their accounts, many authorities have finally stopped charging to the HRA costs which should be met by the community as a whole, e.g. expenditure on maintaining open spaces used by the community as a whole or the provision of aid and advice services. It has led to much closer financial management by housing departments themselves, in part as a way of ensuring maximum revenue at a time of reduced resources. Equally renewed attention has been given to rent fixing procedures and management and maintenance costs. If the new regime results in improved efficiency it will be a major step forward. However, cost reductions could lead to greater inefficiencies and a much lower level of service and there is a view which suggests that by not providing incentives to improve, the new system is really primarily directed to encouraging transfers from the public sector (Wilcox 1990).

Over the period 1979–90 there have been very significant developments in the whole area of housing management within local authorities (and housing associations). Some of this has come about via direct legislation, but much has derived from the authorities themselves and from the context in which they found themselves. There was a wide recognition amongst authorities that improvements had to be made if they were to survive as major landlords. Service delivery regarding repairs and maintenance had not improved in line with tenant expectations; consultation was often very limited; allocation systems were not responsive to new needs and there was a growing problem of empty property and rent arrears. However, while authorities increasingly recognized these weaknesses and were addressing them they were operating in a context of restricted finance. Initiatives had to be taken, but balanced against other pressing local needs it was often difficult to achieve all that was needed.

Decentralization is a case in point. Under local authority reorganization in the 1970s and the moves to corporate planning many authorities ended up with highly centralized structures for managing and delivering their housing service. This was recognized to be a major weakness and a process of decentralization began in some authorities (and others had been decentralized for a very long period of time). Creating local offices was only part of the process; equally important was the concern to improve repair and management services and to develop local accountability. Constraints on expenditure limited what some authorities could achieve and there was considerable reluctance to bid for the DOE Priority Estates programme money because it imposed specific requirements on the decentralization process. Over the decade many local authorities have decentralized, although there is now a tension between the devolved management achieved and the tight financial management required under the new regime.

Tenant participation has been slow to develop for a number of reasons (Institute of Housing and TPAS 1990), but some authorities have been active in the promotion of the tenants' role in the housing service. The introduction of "Tenants Choice" in the Housing Act 1988 gave added momentum to a process which had been underway since the early 1980s while the government funded and local authority supported Tenant Participation Advisory Service (TPAS) has helped tenants (and authorities) develop their own role. The problem many organizations now face is that the expectations of tenants have risen at a time when housing organizations are less able to respond to them. As the new regime bites, budgets and staff morale may fall while tenants rightly demand the service they are paying for. Higher rents are one response to this, but this will encourage some to exercise the

Right to Buy and others to move elsewhere. Those who stay are likely to be elderly and/or on full housing benefit.

The climate created has been one in which local authorities have sought to innovate, if only to survive. Thus we have seen guarantee schemes introduced on repairs, menu style improvement packages, enveloping, appointments systems, incentive schemes for tenants to buy in the private sector, partnerships with housing associations and new training schemes. While some authorities only react to change, others have quite clearly gone ahead to pursue their own objectives. The spirit of enterprise is perhaps most obviously captured in the voluntary transfer of stock. Voluntary transfer was initiated by authorities as a response to Tenants Choice. By the end of January 1991 12 English authorities had secured a yes vote from their tenants and were transferring their stock (or had done so). So far transfers have involved some 63,000 properties, about 1.5 per cent of the local authority stock in England. More significantly, many more authorities reviewed their options and in committing themselves to remain as major landlords they then engaged in a thorough renewal of the service they were offering. In that sense many authorities went into the 1990s stronger than they were in the 1980s.

This process has been reinforced by a new concern with performance and a recognition of the role training can play in enhancing the capacity of housing organizations both to respond to change and to manage their responsibilities more effectively. Until the late 1970s housing management and the organization of housing services had been neglected (see Kemp and Williams 1991, Provan and Williams forthcoming). In the 1980s a whole series of reports were produced aimed at assessing the current performance of housing authorities and associations and recommending better practice (see, for example, Audit Commission 1986). The studies also pointed towards the complexities of housing management practice and the need to find local solutions to problems. As part of the renewal process which has been underway, training has become an important ingredient. Housing training has been massively expanded in the 1980s through a combination of organizations expanding their budgets and commitment and via central government funding. Ironically perhaps given its overall stance, but the government has put considerable financial resources into training (notably bursaries for housing education courses, grant aid to the Institute of Housing, the Local Government Training Board and others). In reality such support is entirely consistent with a concern to ensure organizations operate more effectively. Recently the Department of the Environment has reviewed housing training and affirmed its concern to see further development (DOE 1990).

What has been evident is a real capacity by local government to innovate and develop. The stereotypes of the inefficient and unresponsive authority are now very inadequate and policy should recognize this by moving from a penalty to an incentive based system of financing. Over the decade central government policy on occasions negated or rendered ineffective initiatives which local government was taking, e.g. on private sector leasing or the right to repair. This reflected the fundamental mistrust which existed and a determination to assert the role of central government. One outcome of this has been greater inefficiency as local and central government manoeuvre against each other.

Housing Needs and Housing Conditions

Ultimately all initiatives should be directed towards ensuring change "on the ground". By one means or another, policy should ensure that housing needs and demands are better met both through new provision and the enhancement of the existing stock. The picture here is somewhat mixed. Need and demand can be defined in a variety of ways, but one of the most obvious expressions of it is homelessness.

Since 1979 the number of people in Britain "experiencing or threatened by homelessness" has doubled (Murie and Forrest 1988, Greve with Currie 1990). In 1979, local authorities in Great Britain accepted more than 67,000 households as homeless. In 1989, the figure stood at over 160,000 households (Oldman 1990). Probably as many were turned away, reflecting the restrictive definition of priority which is applied. Moreover, the public awareness of homelessness across the United Kingdom has grown sharply via the media and their own observations. There are many and competing explanations for the increase in homelessness and a series of studies were undertaken to assess the problem and its treatment (Greve with Currie 1990, Audit Commission 1989, Niner 1990). Local authorities have sought to respond to homelessness by making better use of their stock (void levels have fallen to below 2 per cent in many authorities) and through the use of property leased from the private sector. The latter has grown significantly in the last few years, not least as an alternative to expensive and unsatisfactory bed and breakfast accommodation (see Evans 1991, Hill and Mullings 1990: p. 169). The government has begun to target funds directly to homelessness initiatives through local authorities to housing associations, but this has been countered by recent changes which will make private leasing more difficult.

Debates about homelessness through the 1980s were made more problematic by an official reluctance to estimate and discuss housing need. This reflected the view that nationally there was a balance between supply and demand (and therefore it was partly a question of making better use of the existing stock) and the judgement that debate about need merely postponed action. Any estimation requires calculating the number of unfit and inadequate dwellings, the number of people without anywhere to live as well as those sharing housing when they would prefer separate accommodations (e.g. in overcrowded accommodation). The Inquiry into British Housing (1984) and the National Housing Forum (1989) both attempted to assess the position. In the latter report it was concluded that the "pent-up housing need in England and Wales stood at 500,000 households in 1989". Moreover, the Forum report suggested that by 2001 a further 2–3 million households would need to be housed. Hill and Mullings (1990) argue that there is evidence of a significant improvement in the household/dwelling balance over the period 1971 to 1981, but a marked slowing since then (see Table 7.2 below). Clearly the results of the 1991 Census will provide important evidence of change in the 1980s.

TABLE 7.2
Households and Dwellings in England and Wales

	1971	1981	1986
Households[a]	16,779	18,196	19,094
Dwellings	17,024	19,111	19,944
Crude surplus	245	915	850
Unfit dwellings	1,364	1,253	1,125
Deficit allowing for unfit dwellings	1,119	338	275
Concealed households	426	349	262
Deficit allowing for concealed households	1,545	687	537

[a] Definition change between 71 and 81 reducing the number of households in the later years.
Source: Hills and Mullings (1990: p.165).

House Condition

Part of the calculation of the household/dwelling balance rests on the assessment of the state of the housing stock. Dwellings unfit for use indicate a need either for improvement or replacement. The evidence does indicate a general improvement in the state of the housing stock since 1979, although any detailed assessment is made problematic by the absence of any house condition survey in Scotland, changing definitions and most recently the cancellation or postponement of the 1991 Welsh house condition survey.

The evidence from the English and Welsh house condition surveys of 1981 and 1986 suggests a reduction in the number of dwellings which are unfit or lacking in one or more amenities. The number of dwellings defined as unfit for habitation fell over the period, but still stood at around 1 million in 1986. Progress on tackling lack of amenities was greater, but even then over 500,000 dwellings were lacking one or more amenities in 1986. Proportionately, conditions continued to be worst in considerable concern to the extent of disrepair in the public sector with the DOE's own survey of English local authority stock in 1985 indicating that 84 per cent of dwellings needed work at a cost then of some £18 billion. In this sense the shift in local authority capital expenditure towards renovation of its own stock rather than new build was a matter of necessity. In 1979/80 28 per cent of gross capital expenditure by local authorities in England was on renovation of its own stock. By 1990/91 64 per cent of their spending was on renovation, though the evidence suggests more must be spent to overcome this problem.

Repair and improvement in the private sector has become ever more important with the decline in clearance and new building. In 1979 some 80,000 grants of all types were paid to private owners and tenants in Great Britain. By 1989 this had risen to 145,000, though it should be noted that in the intervening years changes in the grant regime pushed the number of grants to a peak of some 320,000 (in 1984). In total, grants have been paid to the owners and tenants of around 1.85 million dwellings over this period at an actual cost of about £5.5 billion. The poverty of many owners, especially elderly owners, is such that grants are a vital instrument of policy. The new means tested regime introduced in the Local Government and Housing Act 1989 could result in better targeting of resources, but there is a real fear that this will result in less grant based activity rather than more. The evidence from the English House Condition Survey that grants covered only about 3 per cent of the value of all repair and improvement undertaken in 1986 puts this into perspective, but we cannot ignore the real problems which exist with the condition of the housing stock.

Costs and Resources

Ultimately the efficacy of the housing system is expressed in what individuals, organizations and government must pay for housing. At an individual level the price of housing, whether in the form of rents or prices and mortgages, has to be at a level people can pay from their income, in other words there is a critical relationship between costs and prices and wages. Where housing costs are high and feed through into high prices or rents, government may choose to subsidize either the costs of production, "bricks and mortar subsidy" or the price to the user, "subsidy to people" or both. Clearly there are a range of options.

Over the period 1979-90 housing has "become significantly more expensive in relation to incomes" (Hills and Mullings 1990: p. 201). This reflects a number of factors. First with respect to local authorities, this is a product of the reduction in general subsidy through the withdrawal of spending permission via HIP/BCA, the increase in rents (via annual determinations for subsidy purposes, the new market related regime and local authorities own actions in pushing up rents to sustain expenditure levels) and the reduction in housing benefit. There have been important variations over the period, with rents rising rapidly in the early 1980s and then falling in relation to average incomes before increasing again at the end of the decade. Indeed local authority rents have begun to move closer to housing association rents. Although this reflects a policy objective, the rapid upward trend in both and its likely continuation in the 1990s has set in motion what is likely to be an ever-increasing demand on the housing benefit system.

Local authority rents have risen faster than inflation (Shelter calculates that had rents moved in line with inflation they would be £13 in 1989 as against an average of £21) and the balance has moved in favour of home ownership. Housing benefit has become a major central government expenditure item rising from £1,306 million in 1979/80 to £2,566 million in 1988/89 (in 1987/88 prices for UK local authority tenants; see Hills and Mullings 1990). While this assistance has helped many tenants (between 50 and 70 per cent in most authorities) to meet the higher rent bills, the structuring of it remains problematic with a substantial poverty trap.

The popular perception of housing costs is that it is the home owner who faces most difficulties. Nationally, house prices rose sharply in real terms from 1982 to 1989 though the picture subsequently is rather varied. The house price/earnings ratio also increased from 3.82 in 1979 to 4.43 in 1989 and there have been suggestions that this marks a long-term shift to a higher ratio (Costello 1990). Overall house prices have been able to rise because of the growth in earnings and this has cushioned many from the impact of higher house prices and higher mortgage costs. However, there have been a growing number of cases in mortgage arrears and repossessions. In 1979 there were 8,420 borrowers 6-12 months in arrears and 2,530 cases of repossession. In 1990 these had risen to 123,110 and 43,890 respectively. Repossessions had trebled since 1989, albeit that the numbers involved are still only a tiny proportion of total borrowers.

Affordability and Resources

The problems of increased housing costs have led directly to an intensifying debate on affordability and the resources committed to housing. Considerable attention has been focused upon what people should expect to pay for housing and given these assumptions how that converts into current access to housing. Bramley (1990) has argued that less than one quarter of new households can afford to buy a three-bed family house anywhere in England. From this he goes on to argue that the affordability gap can only be bridged by increased subsidy and, given certain assumptions, the production of around 100,000 units of social housing a year.

The reality, however, is that overall gross capital spending on housing has gone down. In the early 1980s cuts in housing expenditure were severe (Murie 1985 and 1987). By 1982/83 75 per cent of all public spending cuts had been borne by housing and its share of public expenditure had fallen from 5.8 to 2.3 per cent (Forrest and Murie 1988). While it subsequently stabilized, there were important national variations (England, Scotland and Wales) and a major shift to housing associations (Kearns and Maclennan 1989). This pattern has continued into the 1990s. Planned gross capital expenditure on associations will rise to £1,668 million in 1991/92 and £2,022 million in 1993/94 (from £818 million in 1989/90). By contrast, local authority gross capital expenditure in England is likely to fall from £3,749 million in 1990/91 to £2,955 million in 1991/92 (and the Basic Credit

Approvals from £1,445 million in 1990/91 to £1,395 million in 1993/94).

4. Successes and Failures

Set against its own policy objectives, the government has achieved modest success with its housing programmes. Clearly it has met its objective of expanding home ownership and in so doing has significantly limited the role of the public sector. It has not, as yet, revived the private rented sector and most commentators still feel it is unlikely to do so. It has redirected subsidy from bricks and mortar towards people, but has not targeted this as effectively as it could. As a consequence there remains a substantial band of households some of whom neither get full housing benefit nor mortgage interest tax relief and who cannot readily purchase or sustain (whether as renters or owners) an adequate standard of accommodation (see Maclennan *et al.* 1990). As Hills and Mullings comment (1990: p. 201):

> Whatever the bench-mark, the price of housing is clearly less within people's means than it was before. And around these increases in the average costs of housing, the rise has meant substantial increase since 1979 in the numbers so overstretched that they have defaulted on their mortgage payments or rents. For these people at least, the policy aim of housing within people's means has clearly failed.

Over the period the local authority (and housing association) sector has become more evidently the home for the least well off. All the evidence shows growing concentrations of people on the lowest incomes, without employment and reliance on state benefits in this sector (Forrest and Murie 1988). Certainly there remain poor owners and poor private tenants (especially the elderly), but this does not diminish the changes recorded in the local authority sector. The implications of this are considerable in terms of management and financing. While it can be argued that this concentration reflects an effective targeting of this stock, we should recall this has been achieved with significant shifts in the pattern of subsidy. Subsidy for council housing has diminished significantly (in part because it is now a smaller sector), though this has been balanced to some degree by housing benefit. Hills and Mullings (ibid., p. 200) conclude that in assessing the true costs and benefits of housing that tenants are no longer in a favoured position in economic terms and that "there may have been rough tenure neutrality in the period since 1979". The new system of financing for council housing has put in train changes which could significantly move any balance against tenants and this must remain a key concern for the 1990s.

Choice

Choice has been an important theme in government policy and the clear sentiment from ministers has been that local authorities denied choice. It has become an important watchword and housing organizations as a whole seem much more aware of offering alternatives than they were in the 1970s and in recognizing that at least some of their "customers" do have choices. The success of the RTB programme would be seen as most evident expression of choice at work and one can argue that the response by local authorities was a reflection of the power of choice now given to their tenants under "Tenants Choice" in the Housing Act 1988. However, choices are always exercised within a context, and with respect to the RTB, discounts have been a major influence on take up in conjuction with rising rents and booming house prices. We should therefore look closely at other choices introduced by the government which have not been taken up so enthusiastically.

In the 1980s the rights to repair, to shared ownership and to change landlords were introduced for local authority tenants. Introduced in 1984, the right to get repairs done by private contractors and charge the authority was seen as a means of helping tenants overcome delays in the local authority housing repairs service. Despite extensive promotion and training, take up has been very limited (and indeed in England data collection has now been discontinued). In England between 1986/87 and 1988/89 there were 81 claims for payment, of which 75 were accepted, resulting in a total payout of £7,300 (*Hansard*, 31 October 1990: p. 535). In total it is believed there have been less than 300 claims for the right to repair in England and Wales (it does not apply in Scotland). The take up on the right to shared ownership has been somewhat better and figures are reported for England and Wales in *Local Housing Statistics*. However, this initiative which was targeted at tenants who could not afford RTB, has resulted in less than 8,000 sales since it was introduced in 1984. Indeed it is worth noting that aside from the RTB all the other low cost home ownership initiatives (build for sale, build under licence, improvement for sale, homesteading and shared ownership) offered via local authorities had, over the period 1979-88 resulted in just over 40,000 sales in Great Britain (*Social Trends*,).

Tenants Choice

Tenants Choice was a major new initiative which was seen as leading to a mass exodus from the local authorities. "End of road for the council house" was the headline in *The Observer* (27 September 1987: p. 6). The consultation document on the new legislation commented (DOE 1987: p. 2).

> Many tenants may prefer smaller, less remote landlords who are more responsive to their needs and undistracted by non-housing activities. Many face a virtual monopoly of rented housing in their area. As tenants, such people are deprived of the opportunity to help themselves or obtain the landlord they want, offering the services they deserve.
>
> . . . Those tenants who are dissatisfied with their local authority landlord but who want to go on renting their existing home rather than to buy it will be able to bring in the new landlord of their choice to take over the ownership and management of their home. The effect of this will be to open up the closed world of local authority housing estates to competition and to the influence of the best housing management practices of other landlords.

In reality no group of tenants have moved from council ownership via Tenants Choice. Tenants in Westminster (Waterton and Elgin estate) and Taff Ely (Glyntaff Farm estate) have gone down this path, but have yet to complete the process. In practice the exercise of choice via this legislation is very difficult and demanding. It would appear to be a solution most tenants reject not least due to the time, energy and resources it takes but also because in the majority of cases they simply do not want it. The two estates concerned both have major physical defects and Tenants Choice has been exercised as the only way of getting the resources to deal with them. The estate is valued and the price of the transfer reflects its condition. If it is in poor condition and there is a negative valuation (price minus cost of putting it into good order) the authority must give a dowry to the purchasing landlord. Despite expectations, very few private landlords have come forward to be approved as landlords wishing to buy estates and all the evidence so far would suggest that few tenants will change landlords via this route. In part the initiative has been overtaken by "voluntary transfer" but it also represented a misreading of the relationship between authorities and their tenants. Whatever the authority's failings, many tenants do feel they have a degree of control over their landlord (if only via the councillor and local elections). They also feel very uncertain about making a once only one way choice to a landlord who none may know.

Housing Action Trusts

Not dissimilar to the above, the government also introduced in England the concept of Housing Action Trusts (HATs). These trusts were to take over specific local authority estates, improve them and sell them on to the new landlords (though the government changed its mind on this and agreed tenants could vote for the estate to go back to the council). Seven HATs were announced (in Lambeth, Leeds, Sandwell, Southwark, Sunderland, Tower Hamlets in 1988 and Waltham Forest in 1989). There was no consultation with the authorities in the process of selection and this resulted in non-co-operation in at least three authorities. Subsequently, following elaborate tenant consultation (which resulted in majority against HATS votes in four of the designated areas), the DOE abandoned six of them. Waltham Forest continues at present and Hull has come forward with its own voluntary HAT. The reasons for rejection are many and complex, but all the evidence seems to suggest that, despite dissatisfaction with their current landlord and a wish to see the investment a HAT could bring tenants were mistrustful of the outcome. As with Tenants Choice, HATs offered a leap into the unknown (Frew 1990, Dennis 1990).

Despite their "failure", the positive outcome from HATs and Tenants Choice has been the impact they have had on the balance of power between authorities and their tenants. At the end of the day it is possible for tenants to leave and it has made authorities and tenants more conscious of their positions *vis-à-vis* one another. If current momentum can be maintained, much could be achieved in terms of developing efficient and effective services which meet the needs of the residents. On the other hand, much energy has been channelled into defensive responses to these initiatives rather than into the underlying services. Government should accept that remaining a tenant of the local authority is a legitimate choice. There does appear to be a view that tenants who wish to do so are not properly aware of their options. This may be true in some cases, but tenants are much better informed than before and their views should be respected.

The Housing Market

There is not space to cover this in detail, but one of the important changes of 1979-90 has been the liberalization of the mortgage market and improvements in the operation of the private housing market (see Forrest, Murie and Williams 1990). In the 1970s mortgage rationing was common and it was often difficult to obtain a mortgage. The Building Societies Act of 1986 marked the final stages of a move away from what had been a sheltered market into a genuinely open market for the raising and selling of mortgage funds. The consequences of this have been considerable not least the ready supply of credit which, some would argue, fuelled the price boom of the mid to late 1980s, but the variety of mortgage products and the ease of access to a loan has made house purchase a lot easier. Alongside this important change have come developments in conveyancing (the seller has to provide better information about the property for sale), improvements in the Land Registry and more competition amongst the professionals involved in the transaction process. The Financial Services Act (as well as the Building Societies Act) helped to encourage major institutions take over estate agencies and build them into chains offering new levels of service and an integrated property shop approach. The recent slump has hit the estate agency sector very badly and with important consequences. The Prudential recently sold its estate agency business (acquired in the mid 1980s) at a loss calculated at £250 million.

Taking Stock

Unsurprisingly, the record of the last twelve years is mixed. At one level a number of achievements can be noted. However, the belief in the private rented sector's capacity to make up the shortfall between what local authorities and housing associations can provide and who can become and remain an owner is misplaced. Certainly it can contribute, but if the cost of developing an effective rented sector is high could this money be better spent? Moreover, how long do we wait for it to happen? While examples can be found of countries where there is a large private rented sector, this does not mean Britain should follow this path. In some senses it has been there already and it is that experience which makes a return very difficult. Government recognized this with its assured tenancies and the approved landlord system, but in reality the checks built into the latter process have frightened off most traditional private landlords.

The matters of greatest concern which then feed on into a number of issues concern the cost of housing and overall supply. Hill and Mullings (1990: p. 201) conclude that "housing has become significantly more expensive in relation to incomes in the period since 1979". Recession, continuing high interest rates and the now substantial upward pressure on rents in local authorities and housing associations means this pattern will continue and perhaps worsen. The consequences are borne by the individuals who lose their homes or who fail to find one they can afford in the first place. The imperfections of the housing market are such that even if supply was greater rents and prices would be unlikely to fall significantly.

Increasing homelessness, like the success of the right to buy, will be one of the milestones of the period. As already noted, it rose to over 160,000 households in 1989/90, up from around 70,000 in 1979. The London Research Centre estimates that the 160,000 households contained over 430,000 people and of course this is only the acceptances. Homelessness is now a national problem, although we must recognize its complexities. The figures describe people in very different circumstances (homeless at home as well as nowhere to live). The homelessness route has become a main way (and in some authorities almost the only way) into council housing.

An expansion of the supply of rented housing would certainly diminish the pressures, but in itself that will not be enough unless questions of access and affordability are resolved. The evidence does suggest that although there have been major changes in housing policy the increased reliance on the market has not borne fruit yet in terms of new housing units and reduced pressure on the existing stock. The coincidence of high interest rates and an economic downturn at the end of the 1980s and into the 1990s has meant that the market has been badly affected at the very moment when more was needed from it. At present it is unclear when there will be a recovery, leaving a considerable and growing "housing crisis".

Setting this aside for the moment, it is clear that the government has met some of the objectives it set itself. Public expenditure spent directly on housing has been reduced and redirected. Moreover, the new system in place will see this continues via private finance for housing associations and a rental driven subsidy system for local authorities. Against this housing benefit costs will rise, though government would seem to accept this. There remains serious doubt as to whether it can or will continue to carry this bill given the impact of higher rents under the assured tenancy regime are only now coming through and local authorities have clearly embarked on a new higher rent regime. The latter will be offset in some cases by the "surpluses" on the housing revenue account being offset against the housing benefit component of the subsidy bill for the authorities in question (though as more better off tenants exit via RTB this will diminish).

A freer private rented sector has been created, although in practice the pre-1988 market operated largely outside of Rent Act restrictions. This freedom has not resulted in an upsurge in new long-term lettings yet and restrictions are already in place as to what are acceptable housing benefit payments for private lettings. Here government finds itself in a continuing dilemma. It wants a free rented sector but it cannot afford to resurrect Rachmanism nor does it wish to be exploited itself via the housing benefit system. Regardless of ideology, therefore, controls are inevitably reimposed. The promotion of and subsidies to home ownership and the subsidy to the social rented sector make the private rented sector unattractive to potential tenants not least because landlords want a rate of return on a par with owners.

Earlier, reference was made to the successful promotion of home ownership, but the highly preferential subsidy system for this tenure cannot be ignored. For government it is a legitimate expenditure directed towards the achievement of a policy goal, but it is now very expensive and it remains poorly targeted. Moreover, in a high interest rate and high house price regime it will be evident that increases in either or both feed directly into the cost of mortgage interest relief. A refocusing of this subsidy might save money directly and through reduced income support going to owner occupiers.

Despite making local authority housing departments and housing associations more like separate companies, freedom of action for these sectors remains constrained. As the relative importance of subsidy declines, the case for allowing the creative capacities of these organizations to flow is increased, perhaps even aided by the stimulus of financial incentives. Certainly looking at the level of overall housing output achieved over the decade and continuing into the 1990s it is vital that more effective use is made of them. The move from producer subsidy to subsidies for the individual has not triggered the level of market response required while the downturn in housebuilding has done nothing to improve the efficiency of the housebuilding industry and prepare it for new responsibilities.

Whitehead (1989: pp. 21-22) in a valuable review of the UK housing system concludes:

> Overall if one compares the situation with that at the beginning of the decade the main changes have been in terms of the liberalization in the private sector, . . . together with cutbacks in net public expenditure. Some limited coherence has been achieved in the framework for the rented

> sector but even this is eroded by the need for additional direct controls. The problems of access at the bottom end of the market have clearly worsened.

A number of valuable changes have been introduced but the system is still failing to produce the quantity and quality of housing at the right cost which would ensure all have decent housing at a price they can afford. Moreover the government has created and maintained inefficiencies with respect to the money spent on housing. The government entered the decade with a single minded view of the weaknesses of the social rented sector. What it must do now is to recognize the limits of the market, find the balance which must be achieved between the sectors and make the most efficient use of subsidy/public expenditure. This is not an argument for a return to the past but rather a wish to see a new realism dawn.

In this process there can be little doubt that there would be benefits in allowing ministers more time in post thus allowing them to accumulate more experience and understanding of housing issues. There have been seven Secretaries of State for the Environment since 1979 and eight ministers with responsibility for housing (albeit that at least one was reluctant to include housing in his portfolio). As Table 3 shows the typical length of tenure has diminished over the period especially at ministerial level (this pattern is less true in Scotland and Wales). This has created considerable uncertainty for civil servants and housing organizations and creates a policy environment which lurches between initiatives and does not easily build policy by learning from past mistakes.

The same is also true with respect to the now vital link between the policies of the Department of Social Security (via housing benefit) and the Department of the Environment, Welsh Office and Scottish Office. From the DSS point of view housing benefit is part of poverty policy not housing policy. Yet as has been argued throughout this chapter it is now critical to the Government's efforts to restructure the housing market and housing policy. Changes in the benefit system will have considerable repercussions on housing. At present the benefit system imposes barriers to change as well as a major poverty trap. For tenants on 100 per cent benefit there are no market signals to respond too and its very existence probably stops the market developing. Little wonder that suggestions have been made to put housing benefit on the same basis as the community charge rebates where everyone has to pay 20 per cent. Ultimately

TABLE 7.3
Secretaries of State for the Environment and Ministers responsible for Housing, 1979–90

(a) Secretary of State for the Environment

Year	Holder of office	*Months in post
1979–83	Michael Heseltine	45
1983-83	Tom King	6
1983-85	Patrick Jenkin	27
1985-86	Kenneth Baker	10
1986-90	Nicholas Ridley	39
1989-	Michael Heseltine	–

(b) Minister of State with responsibility for Housing

Year	Holder of office	Title of office	*Months in post
1979–83	John Stanley	Housing & Construction	50
1983–85	Ian Gow	Housing & Construction	28
1985–86	John Patten	Housing & Local Government	10
1986–87	John Patten	Housing, Urban Affairs & Construction	18
1987–88	William Waldegrave	Housing & Planning	14
1988–89	Earl of Caitheness	Housing & Planning Protection & Countryside	14
1989–90	Michael Howard	Housing & Planning	7
1990–90	Michael Spicer	Housing & Planning	11
1990–	Sir George Young	Housing & Planning	–

* includes part and whole months.
Sources: DOE Library.

government will have to resolve whether it wants to move further towards a system of total reliance upon subsidies to individuals or whether it will move back towards greater use of producer subsidy. Whatever it decides, the reality is that subsidy will be needed.

5. Ideas for the 1990s

It might be suggested that the agenda for the 1990s has been set already by the "failures" of the 1980s. Thus a realignment of subsidy to ensure greater tenure neutrality, a relaxation of controls on associations and authorities and a recognition that a quantified assessment of need and output combined with a forecast could provide a basic planning tool for the decade might be on the agenda. In reality, little of this would appear to be under consideration by the government and it has already begun to signal what it might do assuming it retains power. What is evident is that the lessons learned from the 1980s would appear to be more about extending the market and ironically strengthening central control.

With respect to local authorities, the 1990s current thinking would suggest it promises more of the same. The imposition of competitive tendering with respect to direct labour organizations and the introduction of the local management of schools would suggest we might see housing management put out to tender with the power to contract services devolved to tenant management co-operatives at estate level. Housing associations and the newly hived off housing departments would be encouraged to bid for this work and the local authority would exercise supervisory control under its enabling responsibilities. In some areas associations and the former local authority housing departments might combine to offer this service and to bid for work in other areas.

Even more radically, local authorities might lose their statutory powers to review and meet housing need in their local areas and this responsibility would pass to new regional bodies which might also incorporate the DOE and Housing Corporation's regional offices. In Wales, Scotland and Northern Ireland a similar rationalization of functions could occur. These new regional bodies might then take responsibility for the planning and funding of new housing with contracts going direct to builders or specialist development agencies which would form from the existing development functions of associations.

Under such a model, central control would be reinforced and housing would be seen to be removed from local political control. Mr Heseltine is already reported to have suggested that where housing authorities fail to meet specified standards they should be put under central control. With local government reorganization firmly on the agenda the possibilities of change are considerable and this might bring with it the long discussed housing inspectorate.

More immediately the government has already established pilot rents to mortgages schemes (RTM) by which it hopes more tenants will become home owners. There are considerable difficulties with RTM, but it moves the government closer to fulfilling its wish of permanently reducing reliance on council housing (see Wilcox and Williams (1991) for a detailed review of RTM). Recently Sir George Young, the Housing Minister, talked of home ownership rising to 75 per cent and 80 per cent is now seen as a realistic target. A decade or more ago 70 per cent was seen as the absolute maximum. As home ownership expanded so it has become ever more difficult to sustain by those at the margins. This will require management, but so far this has not been given the attention it deserves

In their review of the 1990s the National Federation of Housing Associations (NFHA 1990) also pinpoint a number of possibilities which should be mentioned here. They note that market rents will generally spread through the social rented sector and suggest that by the mid 1990s a genuinely competitive market may have emerged between private and social housing landlords. They also draw attention to the competition amongst associations which will result in large numbers of mergers with the subsequent risk that they would monopolize development. This process has already begun and one might go further to suggest there will be a major rationalization along the lines of the building societies. The NFHA also suggest we might see housing vouchers introduced which could be used in any tenure.

The NFHA's look ahead is a valuable examination of the possibilities and one which local authorities could sensibly replicate. Both sectors will face difficult challenges in the 1990s, the former concerned with the management of growth, the latter with the management of decline or at best stability. There seems little possibility of a return to the mass building of the 1950s and 1960s with governments of all persuasions promoting choice and diversity. This does not mean there is no future for local authorities. Indeed it is argued that they have vital continuing roles to play both as direct providers and as manager/co-ordinator of their local housing markets. More local authorities will withdraw from their role as direct providers, but this should only be done after careful consideration and evaluation and in full consultation with tenants. At present there is a real danger that transfers will arise solely as a way of cashing in an asset, the receipts from which can then be used to keep the community charge down.

The enabling role envisaged for authorities has been treated with considerable disdain. However, this should be adopted with vigour regardless of decisions about direct housing provision. The evidence at present suggests many authorities have not given any serious consideration to this role and are failing even to meet minimum requirements such as liaising with associations, making good use of nomination rights and promoting low cost and shared ownership alternatives. Moreover, it raises a key question about the links between planning and housing. In many areas it is the planning department that looks at forward strategy, yet under the enabling role, the housing department should exercise much more influence on this process. Local government reorganization may assist this. As it stands, many authorities are going into the 1990s with reorganization on the agenda not least as a cost saving device. Despite housing being one of the major functions of local authorities it is often sidelined in the process. This often reflects internal pressures and there is a real risk that this will weaken the housing function of local authorities at a critical time.

The pressures associations face are equally complex. Growth and the development of private finance pose fundamental challenges to the whole ethos of the "movement" and it is hard to see how the traditional community based association can survive alone in the new era. Federated structures offer one alternative to merger, retaining local control, but possibly offering the economies of scale associated with size. The pressures to produce housing at minimum cost also set up real tensions about quality and quantity and again here a careful balance has to be struck, bearing in mind that the housebuilding industry has advanced its own case to be recipients of HAG development finance. Associations should not understate (or overstate) the skill and expertise they have developed in responding to specific needs in ways which the majority of builders would be unlikely to replicate. Equally serious will be the issue of their relationship with local authorities. Associations have to respond to policy, but they must also operate in local markets where the authorities continue to play the key role. As the decade progresses, this will become increasingly demanding if the pressures on authorities are maintained.

The market as a whole will become more complex and differentiated, requiring better co-ordination and more sophisticated monitoring and management. Building societies are likely to continue merging with each other and with banks and other financial institutions. This raises the prospect of market domination by a very small number of conglomerates (see Ball 1990). This is a path estate agency has gone down and now seems to have stopped. Currently a resurgence of the small independents is taking place, though it can be argued this is only a temporary respite. Housebuilders too are facing a difficult time, but there is little sign of innovation in terms of the organization and structuring of the industry. At the end of the day the continuing weaknesses of the mechanisms through which supply is generated remain the achilles heel of the British housing system.

Speculations about the future are always likely to be wrong, but there would now seem to be a greater capacity on the part of the current government to consider what might have been thought of in the early 1980s as unthinkable. There may even be changes to mortgage interest tax relief! For analysts this poses particular problems because their starting assumptions could be ill founded. It is to directions in academic work that the chapter now briefly and finally turns.

New Academic Agendas?

Over the last twenty years the UK has developed a significant capacity with respect to the analysis and understanding of housing markets and housing policy. Despite that, very substantial gaps remain, not least because of the fundamental reshaping of housing which has taken place over the last twelve years. The recasting of the agenda has moved debate towards issues of affordability, the incidence of subsidy and the efficiency and effectiveness of housing organizations and away from concerns with need, demand and strategy. These issues are now re-entering the agenda, but any policy outcome is likely to be very different than in the 1970s.

Within the overall scope of debate about housing there has been a concern to break through what might be seen as the stereotypes of tenure and to examine the issues from a perspective of different class income and age groups. Within this process we have remained relatively insensitive to gender and race despite all the evidence which points towards great disparities along these dimensions (see, for example, Munro and Smith 1989). We have also until recently been somewhat blind to the geography and history of housing. On close inspection our understanding of many housing problems is an understanding of England and probably more specifically the South East. The locality based studies of the recent Rowntree Foundation Housing Finance programme provide some rebalancing here, though their overwhelmingly economic focus imposes important limitations. There is a real need to resurrect the city, neighbourhood and community dimensions of housing which flourished in the pre- and postwar years and focused on the social reality of housing. These would provide a real counterweight to the economy and efficiency driven arguments of recent years. We cannot afford to ignore issues of residualization and polarization and the outcomes and consequences of housing policy and practice for individuals and groups.

In recognizing the need to give a local and specific focus to housing analysis (because in the end local circumstances are very different) we also discover a neglected local housing history. This reveals much about housing tenure patterns, the role of local protest and local politics and the varied development of local housing organizations. Oddly perhaps, given the 1980s, there has also been a noticeble neglect of the study of the politics of housing except perhaps at the level of the effect of tenure on voting. The academic division of labour has once again done a disservice to the development of our understanding of housing as a complexly interconnected arena.

Theoretically the debate has shifted abruptly away from concerns with a Marxian political economy towards a more empirically based and less explicitly theoretical focus. Ball (1986) has argued strongly for a structures of provision focus while Kemeny has stressed the need to connect housing into mainstream academic arguments (Kemeny 1987). Both have their place, though the very pressure via funding and the concern for relevance will ensure that the main output of work continues to focus on shorter term policy related issues. This remains a very real weakness and one which is aided by a failure to take regular stock of what we now know and do not know. The very momentum of government initiatives can carry academic debate forward in an opportunistic and fragmented manner. The need for longer term and more reflective research remains very acute. Alongside this must also come the capacity to take our current understanding and forecast it forward to see what will happen if we continue along particular paths.

To conclude, the period 1979-90 has seen a fundamental recasting of many of relationships and the emergence of a renewed focus upon the market. By altering the focus many of the assumptions which guided research and analysis in the 1970s have to be reassessed. At the same time it must be recognized that the market has always been central to housing provision in the UK and that in essence most housing has been provided by the private housing market. In reorientating housing analysis it is important not to lose sight of the body of understanding built up over the years and which can offer valuable guidance as to possible future outcomes. Housing analysis, like housing policy, should be built upon a firm grasp of reality.

Acknowledgements

In writing this chapter I have had considerable help from Alan Murie (Heriot Watt University and Edinburgh College of

Art) and Bob Smith (University of Wales, Cardiff). Neither are responsible for any errors of fact or interpretation. I would also wish to indicate that I am writing in a purely personal capacity.

References

Audit Commission (1986) *Managing the Crisis of Council Housing.* Audit Commission, London.

Audit Commission (1989) *Housing the Homeless: The Local Authority Role.* Audit Commission, London.

Ball, M. (1986) Housing analysis: time for a theoretical refocus? *Housing Studies,* **1** (3): 147-165.

Ball, M. (1990) *Under One Roof.* Harvester/Wheatsheaf, London.

Bramley, G. (1990) *Bridging the Affordability Gap.* ADC and HBF, London.

Cm 1008 (1990) *The Government's Expenditure Plans 1990-91 to 1992-93,* chapter 8, Environment. HM Treasury, HMSO, London.

Cmnd 6851 (1977) *Housing Policy; A Consultative Document.* HMSO, London.

Coleman, D. (1989) The new housing policy—a critique. *Housing Studies* **4** (1): 44-58.

Costello, J. (1990) House prices and earnings, *Housing Finance Quarterly,* **7**: 8-15.

Council of Mortgage Lenders (1990) Housing under Mrs Thatcher, *Mortgage Finance Monthly,* **10** (12): 1.

Crook, T., and Kemp, P. (1991) *The Business Expansion Scheme* Rowntree Foundation, York.

Dennis, F. (1990) HATS—Who needs them? *Housing,* **26** (9): 14-15.

Department of the Environment (1989) *The Nature and Effectiveness of Housing Management in England.* HMSO, London.

Department of Environment (1990) *Training, Education and Performance in Housing Management; Efficiency Report and Action Plan.* DOE, London.

Evans, A. (1991) *Alternatives to Bed and Breakfast; The Use of Temporary Accommodation by Local Authorities.* Rowntree Foundation, York.

Forrest, R., and Murie, A. (1988) *Selling the Welfare State: The Privatisation of Public Housing.* Routledge, London.

Forrest, R. Murrie, A., and Williams, P. (1990) *Home Ownership; Differentiation and Fragmentation.* Unwin Hyman, London.

Frew, R. (1990) A HAT's last stand, *Roof,* November December, pp. 12-13

Greve, J. with Currie, E. (1990) *Homelessness in Britain.* Rowntree Memorial Trust, York.

Hamnett, C. (1989) The political geography of housing in contemporary Britain. In Mohan, J. (ed.) *The Political Geography of Contemporary Britain.* Macmillan, London.

Harloe, M. (1977) Will the Green Paper mean better housing? *Roof,* September, pp. 143-148.

Hills, J., and Mulling, B. (1990) Housing; A decent home for all at a price within their means? In Hills, J. (ed.) *The State of Welfare; The Welfare State in Britain since 1974.* Clarendon Press, Oxford.

Institute of Housing/TPAS (1990) *Tenant Participation in Housing Management.* IOH, London.

Inquiry into British Housing (1985) *Report,* NFHA, London.

Kearns, A., and Maclennan, D. (1989) *Public Finance for Housing in Britain,* Discussion Paper 22, Centre for Housing Research, University of Glasgow.

Kemeny, J. (1987) Towards theorised housing studies: a counter critique of the provision thesis, *Housing Studies*, **2** (4): 249-260.
Kemp, P. (1990) Deregulation, markets and the 1988 Housing Act, *Social Policy and Administration*, **24** (2): 145-155.
Kemp, P. (1990) Shifting the balance between state and market: the reprivatisation of rental housing provision in Britain, *Environment and Planning A*, **22**: 793-810.
Kemp, P. and Williams, P. (1991) Housing management; a contested history? In Lowe, S. and Hughes, D. (eds.) A *New Century of Social Housing*. Leicester University Press.
Kleinman M., and Whitehead, C. (1988) British housing since 1979: Has the system changed? *Housing Studies*, **3** (1): 3-19.
Kleinman, M., and Roberts, M. (1989) *Local Authority Housing Expenditure since 1980*, Housing Research Findings No. 1, Joseph Rowntree Memorial Trust.
Labour Party (1990) *A Test of Competence*. Labour Party, London.
London Research Centre (1990) Housing update, *Roof*, November/December.
Malpass, P. (1990) *Reshaping Housing Policy*. Routledge, London.
Malpass, P., and Murie, A. (1990) *Housing Policy and Practice*, 3rd edition. Macmillan, London.
Maclennan, D. *et al.* (1990) *Paying for Britain's Housing*. Rowntree Foundation, York.
Munro, M., and Smith, S. (1989) Gender and housing: broadening the debate, *Housing Studies*, **4** (1): 3-17.
Murie, A. (1985) What can the country afford? Housing under the Conservatives 1979-83. In Jackson, P. (ed.) *Implementing Government Policy Initiatives; The Thatcher Administration 1979-1983*. Royal Institute of Public Administration, London.
Murie, A. (1987) Housing. In Parkinson, M. (ed.) *Reshaping Local Government*. Policy Journals, London.
Murie, A. (1989) Housing and the environment. In Kavanagh, D., and Seldon, A. (eds.) *The Thatcher Effect*. Oxford University Press, Oxford.
Murie, A. (1990) Rehabilitating housing strategies, *Samizdat*, No. 11, July-August.
Murie, A. (1991) Housing. In Catterall, P. (ed.) *Comtemporary Britain, A Review*. Blackwell, Oxford.
Murie, A. and Forrest, R. (1988) The new homeless in Britain. In Friedrichs, J. (ed.) *Affordable Housing and the Homeless*, de Gruyter and Company, Berlin.
National Housing Forum (1989) *Housing Needs in the 1990s; An Interim Assessment*. NFHA, London.
Niner, P. (1989) *Homelessness in Nine Local Authorities: Case Studies of Policy and Practice*. Department of the Environment, London.
Oldman, J. (1990) Who says there's no housing problem? *Facts and Figures on Housing and Homelessness, Shelter Briefing*. Shelter, London.
Patten, C. (1990) A place to live, *The House Magazine*, 29 October pp. 13-14.
Provan, B., and Williams, P. (forthcoming) The future of the housing service; joining the professionals? In Donnison, D., and Maclennan, D. (eds) *The Future of the Housing Service*. Longman, Harlow.
Reardon, M. (1990) Change of face for housing, *Municipal Review and AMA News*, October, p. 155.
Roberts, E., and Kleinman, M. (1989) *The Evolution of Local Authorities' Housing Spending in the 1980s*. Research Memorandum, Department of Land Economy, Cambridge.

Wilcox, S. (1990) *The Need for Social Rented Housing in England in the 1990s*. Institute of Housing, Coventry.
Wilcox, S., and Williams, P. (1991) *Rents into Mortgages*. Council for Mortgage Lenders, London.
Whitehead, C. (1989) *Housing Finance in the UK in the 1980s*. Welfare State Programme Research Note 20, STICERD, LSE.

8

Transport

DAVID BANISTER

1. The Underlying Philosophy of Change

Until about 1980, governments have always played a major interventionist role in transport decisions. The underlying philosophy was that transport should be made available to meet the needs of the population and that everyone could expect a minimum level of mobility, almost as a right. To this end, once the basic motorway and trunk road networks had been established, investment was switched to public transport in the form of capital and revenue expenditure. Considerable importance was attached to integration and co-ordination of services.

Since 1980 the role of government has been significantly reduced and market forces have been allowed to determine both the quantity and to a great extent the quality of public transport services. All transport should, wherever possible, be provided by the private sector, services should be determined competitively not in a co-ordinated fashion, and fares should be market priced. Coupled with these changes is a move towards greater precision in defining the objectives of public transport enterprises, particularly financial performance objectives and quality of service standards. In practice the reduced role of government is more apparent than real as it could be argued that central government has become more powerful. It is at the local level that the impacts have really been felt with the abolition of the Greater London Council and the Metropolitan County Councils, the protected expenditure levels and the deregulation legislation. Similarly, where intervention has taken place, it has been targeted towards individual initiatives (e.g. Urban Development Corporations) to correct perceived market distortions.

In transport terms the 1980s has been the decade of the motorist with the costs of driving being significantly reduced and the growth in company financing of motoring becoming one of the major private subsidies. In addition to the phenomenal growth in car traffic of some 40 per cent over the decade, there has been a parallel increase in overseas travel, principally by air on business and holidays. Over 25 per cent of the population take two or more holidays and expenditure on leisure now accounts for 17 per cent of all household expenditure. The numbers of overseas holidays taken by UK residents has trebled from 7 million to 21 million (1976-88). Society is now in transition from one based on work and industry to one in which leisure pursuits dominate—the post-industrial society. This society will be highly mobile and depend increasingly on the car and technology.

The decade has been one of optimism, at least until the events of "Black Monday" in October 1987, with unprecedented growth in house prices, incomes and quality of life for those in employment and not on fixed incomes. It is difficult to conclude whether this wealth was policy induced or whether it was a longer term cycle of growth in the world economy. Nevertheless, it was a decade of almost continuous activity which has brought about the most fundamental changes in transport policy seen in Britain this century.

- The planning framework within which transport policy has been structured has been dismantled with the intermediate tier of local government being abolished. The government now deals directly with the districts (and Boroughs in London) and the statutory transport undertakings (e.g. British Railways and London Transport).
- The provision of bus services is now deregulated, with services being provided, wherever possible, by the market at the appropriate price. Subsidy is specific to routes where need has been identified and where services cannot be provided by the market.
- Transport enterprises have been sold to employees, to management, to other companies and to the general public. Most tranport related enterprises have been denationalized.
- A series of measures have been introduced to improve safety, such as compulsory seat belt wearing, changes in the motorcycle test, and changes in the drink–drive regulations.
- Traffic in towns and congestion have been identified as key problems and some remedial measures have been introduced, such as wheel clamps and the towing away of illegally parked vehicles, "Red Routes" in London, and increases in parking fines.

— The environment is now seen as the next major political issue, but direct action in the transport sector has been restricted to a reduction in tax levels on unleaded petrol. Some action has been taken in the new Environmental Protection Act (1990).

The main actions of the Conservative governments of the 1980s are summarized in Table 8.1. Underlying all these changes has been one consistent objective, namely to reduce the levels of public expenditure in transport, particularly on the revenue side. Although many of the policies have been justified on other criteria, such as ideology (e.g. deregulation), democracy (e.g. widening share ownership), efficiency (e.g. private enterprises are more cost effective than public ones) and accountability (e.g. to shareholders), it is the Treasury which has been the prime mover behind the radical transport policies.

Even capital expenditure on renewal and new transport infrastructure has been severely constrained by Treasury imposed limits. Over the last ten years replacement expenditure has been delayed, and this in turn has led to increasing unreliability in the system and may have contributed to recent accidents on the public transport. As can be seen in Table 8.2, capital expenditure on transport infrastructure has declined in real terms by 9 per cent over the eight-year period, despite an increase from 1981-82 to 1984-85 of 9 per cent. The decrease in expenditure over the last five years has been 17 per cent and this cutback has exactly coincided with record growth in the demand for travel by public and private transport since 1984, and an annual growth rate in the numbers of new cars peaking at 6 per cent in 1989. The second feature of the changing pattern of capital expenditure has been the switch from public transport investment to investment in roads. In 1981-82 public transport accounted for 16 per cent of total capital expenditure, but by 1988-89 this figure had declined to 2 per cent; in real terms the 1988-89 figure is only 13 per cent of the 1981-82 figure. This picture has changed with the recent relaxation of public expenditure constraints and new capital schemes for roads, railways and London Transport (Department of Transport 1989a and House of Commons 1990), but much of the present increase in capital expenditure could be seen as merely catching up on previous underinvestment in capital renewal.

Increasingly the government is looking to the private sector for capital. The scope for the private sector in urban areas may be limited as construction costs are high, development lead times are

TABLE 8.1
The Thatcher Years 1979–91

1979 – 83	May: Conservatives elected majority 43
	Crude oil $18–24 per barrel
	Increase in public transport fares 15–25%
	Fares Fair campaign in London and other cities
	Armitage Report on Lorries, People and the Environment
	Transport Act 1980—Deregulation Part I
	Transport Act 1981
Falklands War	Transport Act 1982
1982	Collapse of Laker 1982
	Seat belt wearing mandatory—January 1983
	Wheel clamps and travel cards in London—May 1983
1983 – 87	June: Conservatives re-elected
	Transport Act 1983—Protected Expenditure Levels
Miners' Strike	London Regional Transport Act 1984
March 1984	Local Government Act 1985—Abolition of GLC and MCCs
National Docks	Capital cards in London—January 1985
Strike	Transport Act 1985—Deregulation Part II
End of Miners'	Anglo-French Channel fixed link—February 1986
Strike	Terminal 4 opened at Heathrow and Piccadilly extension
March 1985	Crude oil $10 per barrel
	Completion of M25—October 1986
	British Airways privatized—January 1987
	Rolls Royce privatized—May 1987
	British Airports Authority privatized—June 1987
1987 – 91	June: Conservatives re-elected
	Docklands Light Railway opened—July 1987
Collapse of	City Airport opened—October 1987
Stock Exchange	Merger BA/British Caledonian—November 1987
and Gales	National Bus Company privatization—April 1988
October 1987	Central London Rail Study—January 1989
	Roads Programme expanded—May 1989
	New Roads by New Means—May 1989
	Autoguide Electronic Route Guidance piloted—July 1989
	London Assessement Study proposals axed—March 1990
Iraqi Invasion	Crude oil rises to $26 per barrel
of Kuwait	Roads for the Future—February 1990
August 1990	New terminal at Stansted Airport—Spring 1991

lengthy, risks are high, and returns are likely to be low unless the investment puts the developer in an effective monopoly position. Development rights along the proposed route may make private investment more attractive as would joint ventures with the government underwriting the risk (Section 2.3).

It is on the current expenditure side that the government has been most active. In the early 1980s there was a concern over the increasing levels of public support for both bus and rail services with subsidy levels for each amounting to about £1,000 million. The market philosophy is to ensure that all services are provided at a level and at a price which is determined competitively. Intervention should only take place when the market is seen to fail, for example for social need, but even then the intervention should be specific and clearly identified. This means that subsidy levels should be minimized and that there should be no cross subsidization between services. Protected expenditure levels were set for each conurbation and these were effectively the maximum permitted subsidy levels. A balance had to be established between the interests of travellers and those ratepayers/poll tax payers and taxpayers who contribute to the subsidy. The net result has been significant increases in fares on all bus and rail services, both prior to and after deregulation. Subsidy levels have been reduced by about 50 per cent (Table 8.2) as have other forms of assistance to public transport operators (e.g. new bus grant). Ten years ago there was an approximate balance between government expenditure on capital and current accounts (Table 8.2): the present figure is 2 to 1 in favour of capital expenditure on a total budget that has been cut by 24 per cent in real terms.

One continued area of concern for government is the increase in levels of concessionary fares (Table 8.2). At present eligibility is based on fairly broad social groups (e.g. the elderly, school children or disabled), but it is realized that not all individuals within each concessionary group need the same level of concession. More sensitive methods are being identified to allocate concessionary fares to those in need. The net effect would be a reduction in the total level of subsidy.

If the government is consistent in this policy then the subsidy to company cars should also be reduced or eliminated. Over 50 per cent of all new car registrations are in a company name and many organizations also pay for insurance, tax and petrol for their employees. Motorists who do not have to pay the true costs of their travel will use the car more frequently and make more trips. About a third of all vehicles on the road receive some form of company assistance. Tax liability has been increased over the last four years (1987-90) by 200 per cent, but the benefit is still over £2,000 for a 1200cc car and over £5,000 for a 2000cc car for an individual paying tax at 25 per cent (Reward Group 1990). Apart from the inconsistencies in subsidy policy between the reduction in subsidy for public transport and the increase

TABLE 8.2
Levels of Public Capital Expenditure on Transport Infrastructure. Great Britain (£million)

Year	National roads	Local roads	Public transport	Ports	Airports	Deflator	Real 1988–89 prices
1981–82	720	541	257	16	36	1.446	2270
1982–83	874	661	260	14	45	1.350	2503
1983–84	864	703	284	13	42	1.290	2459
1984–85	908	730	318	13	30	1.230	2459
1985–86	920	764	114	12	46	1.165	2162
1986–87	958	805	89	11	8	1.129	2112
1987–88	1110	795	118	14	15	1.072	2200
1988–89	1180	815	47	9	23	1.000	2074

Deflator is the Gross Domestic Product market price deflator.
Source: Based on Transport Statistics 1978–1988, Table 1.18.

Levels of Current Expenditure on Transport, Great Britain (£million)

Year	Revenue support for road public transport	Concessionary fares all modes	Public service obligation For British Rail	Real 1988–89 prices
1981–82	395	193	800	2007
1982–83	510	241	831	2136
1983–84	523	260	855	2125
1984–85	555	274	827	2037
1985–86	465	290	832	1849
1986–87	406	296	737	1624
1987–88	332	324	775	1534
1988–89	364	350	473	1187

Source: Based on Transport Statistics 1978–1988, Table 1.19.

in subsidy for the company car, the effectiveness of any policy designed to reduce the non-essential use of the private car (e.g. road pricing) is diminished if the user is shielded from paying those additional costs. For the market economy to work effectively, competition in both the public and private transport sectors must be fair.

Transport policy over the last decade has been driven by the desire to reduce levels of public expenditure on transport, particularly on the revenue side, and to reduce the role of government in determining policy. Overall, the government has been successful, at least in reducing levels of public expenditure by some 24 per cent in real terms. Demand for travel, principally by the private car but also by rail (since 1985), has continued to increase at an unprecedented rate and road user expenditure on transport now contributes over 12 per cent of all Exchequer revenues, some £17 billion in 1989. Over the decade this figure has risen by 184 per cent in actual terms (62 per cent in real terms), and this has been one factor in the ability of the government to reduce levels of direct taxation.

2. Radical Policy Innovation

Apart from the increased contribution of transport to Exchequer revenues and the decreases in public expenditure on transport, this sector has been the testbed for the three main policy innovations of the last ten years

— to transfer industries from public sector to private sector ownership: privatization or denationalization;
— to introduce competition into public transport services and reduce levels of public subsidy: deregulation;
— to encourage more private capital in major transport investment projects, particularly in infrastructure.

This section of the chapter takes these three issues and discusses the principal theoretical and practical arguments for and against each.

2.1 Privatization

After 1945 there was an extensive programme of nationalization which formed part of Herbert Morrison's plans for the reconstruction of British industry. Almost all the transport enterprises were placed in public ownership. Since 1979 the Conservative government has returned most of these nationalized industries to the private sector, either in their entirety or through partial sales. The reasoning behind this policy is partly ideological and partly financial. The ideological argument is that organizations are more efficient in the private sector with the normal pressures that competition brings. Public bureaucracies are inefficient suppliers of services because there are no measures of productive efficiency. In the private sector there is a simple measure of performance, namely profitability.

The financial argument is that the exchequer can gain through the sale of companies, and it can save through reductions in the levels of public support paid through subsidy or through lending to service capital debts.

Giving more freedom to management is crucial as it allows capital to be raised in a variety of ways on the financial markets, and releases the enterprise from the external financing limits imposed by government in the early 1980s. Deficits sustained by public transport operations have had an unwelcome effect on the government's public sector borrowing requirement. Privatization also contributes directly to exchequer revenue and reduces the public sector borrowing requirement as the ratio of government expenditure to national income is reduced. Supply side economics would also suggest that inflationary pressures are reduced, tax cuts can be introduced and this in turn would allow more private investment to take place so that productivity, output and profitability can all increase. This powerful logic is countered by the argument that these gains are short term. The longer term impacts of selling national assets may result in higher taxation as the government is foregoing revenue from these nationalized industries. In effect the government is borrowing against future income streams (Rees 1986).

From Table 8.3 it can be seen that there have been two distinct phases of transport privatizations which have coincided approximately with the first two Thatcher administrations. During the first phase, the privatizations were small in scale often involving management buyouts (e.g. the National Freight Corporation), or a single buyer (e.g. for Sealink), or a limited stock exchange flotation (e.g. Associated British Ports). The second phase has been much larger in scale and reflects the strong ideological commitment to privatization. It is here that the government has, through extensive publicity, encouraged wider share ownership and has made provision for the smaller investor to "buy" part of the newly privatized company, often at an advantageous price. The four transport privatizations in Phase I (1982-84) realized about £500 million and the four sales in Phase II (1987-88) have realized nearly £4,000 million. It is likely that if there is a fourth Conservative election victory further transport privatizations would include British Railways and London Transport. These are the last two major transport enterprises still in public ownership. At that time the thirty-year cycle, during which all major transport enterprises were in the public sector, will have been reversed and all "public" transport assets will now be in the private sector (Banister 1990).

TABLE 8.3
Privatization in Transport in the United Kingdom

National Freight Corporation:	road haulage operator.
February 1982	Sold for £53m to a consortium of managers, employees and company pensioners. The government paid back £47m to the company's pension fund to cover previous underfunding.
Associated British Ports:	ports and property development.
February 1983	Part of equity sold.
April 1984	Remainder sold by tender offer. £34m raised.
British Rail	
	Some non-essential assets sold. British Rail Hotels sold in 1983 for £30m.
July 1984	Sealink Ferries sold to Sea Containers Ltd for £66m. Proceeds retained by BR with subseqent adjustments to the borrowing limits.
Jaguar:	luxury car manufacturer which had become a subsidiary of British Leyland.
July 1984	Sold for £294m.
British Airways:	one of the leading international airlines.
January 1987	Sold for £892m.
Rolls Royce:	aeroengine business bought by the government in 1971.
May 1987	Sold for £1,360m.
British Airports Authority:	operates seven of the principal airports in Britain including Heathrow and Gatwick.
July 1987	Sold for £1280m.
National Bus Company:	consists of 72 subsidiaries which run most bus services outside the main metropolitan and other urban centres.
December 1988	Sale completed with gross proceeds of £323m. Net surplus to government after all debts paid of £89m.

2.2 Regulatory Reform

Deregulation of the bus industry has been the most important policy switch since regulation was first introduced in the 1930s to protect a vibrant growth industry against predatory practices. Deregulation as it affects all urban and non urban areas outside London has been introduced in two stages. The 1980 Transport Act deregulated long distance bus services (those with a minimum journey length of 48 kilometres), excluded small vehicles (less than eight seats) from licensing requirements provided that they were not being run as a business, and introduced the idea of trial areas where there would be no requirement for road service licences. The 1985 Transport Act has effectively created a trial area for the whole country. The commercial network only has to be registered, and the local authority has no control over the operator provided that he or she runs the services as registered. The subsidized network complements the commercial network with each service being put out to tender by the local authority who has to specify the route, levels of service and fares (in most cases). London has been given an intermediate position under the terms of the London Regional Transport Act (1984) with only limited competition through competitive regulation (Banister 1985 and Glaister 1990).

This two-tier system treats each route on its own merits and there is no commitment to a network of services. The government argues that competition will bring greater efficiency into the public transport industry and an end to the extensive practice of cross-subsidization. The main impetus to change has been the concern over the escalating costs of grants and subsidies to the bus industry which totalled over £1,000 million in 1983.

The net effect of deregulation in the Metropolitan areas has been significant increases in fares (+27.5 per cent in real terms 1985-87) and a decline of 16 per cent in passenger journeys. Undoubtedly some radical change was necessary, but competitive regulation or franchising may have been more appropriate than full deregulation (Banister and Pickup 1990). The British experiment has been keenly observed by our European partners, but it seems unlikely that they will adopt the same model of full deregulation.

2.3 Infrastructure

Britain completed its first generation of motorway construction with the opening of the last section of the M25 around London in October 1986. Progress has been steady since the building of the Preston bypass in 1958, and there are now some 2,800 kilometres of motorways. However, it seems that the 1990s may signal a significant period of new investment, not just in the motorway network. Much of the urban infrastructure is Victorian in construction and needs extensive renovation. In the transport sector several large new projects have been planned or approved—the Channel Tunnel, London's Third Airport and the electrification of the East Coast main railway.

Construction of new infrastructure has raised two important dilemmas. The first is the contradiction between the desire for greater mobility and meeting the ever increasing demand for travel, and the concern over the environment. Apart from needing land for new roads (6 hectares of land required for each kilometre of motorway), there are also development pressures, conflicts between conservation and landscape objectives and employment and economic objectives, and a wide range of pollution and resource implications as well as the direct impact on noise, vibration and severance. The relevant factors are complex, and although considerable debate has taken place over environmental concerns, they often only appear as an addition to the evaluation process and are rarely seen as being influential in decision making. The high mobility car oriented society is incompatible with reductions in levels of pollution, less consumption of energy and protection of the environment.

The second dilemma concerns the financing of major new infrastructure investments. In the past infrastructure has been seen as a public good and funded from the Exchequer. With the reductions in public expenditure, the private sector has been seen as taking more risk, putting together the finance and receiving payment in the form of tolls for the use of the facility. Implementation can be expedited through the use of parliamentary procedures which avoid the necessity for large, costly and lengthy public inquiries. Examples include the proposal for a second bridge across the Severn and the new bridge to supplement the two Dartford Tunnels on the M25. The Dartford River Crossing Company (Trafalgar House, Kleinwort Benson, Bank of America and Prudential Assurance) is building a suspension bridge to provide four new lanes for southbound traffic on the M25. As part of the deal they will also take over both existing tunnels which will be used for northbound traffic and receive all the toll revenue. The new bridge will open in 1991. The problem public of finance and public inquiry have not arisen and the government has taken no risk. Although there are controls on the levels of tolls which will be charged, the company has a maximum of twenty years to recoup costs and make a return on investment. As there is no other river crossing within 20 kilometres this return is almost guaranteed.

The most prestigious project is the Channel Tunnel which epitomizes the new optimism with large-scale infrastructure projects and the use of private capital. The Channel Tunnel Group—France Manche (CTG-FM)—receives no public funds or financial guarantees, and so takes the risk itself. The governments have given assurances to investors that there will be no political interference or cancellation, and that the promoter has full commercial freedom to determine policy including fares levels. The Channel Link Treaty was signed in February 1986 and a

Private Bill was introduced in Parliament. No public inquiry has been held, only Select Committee hearings where a tight schedule has allowed only limited discussion of many local concerns, in particular about the site of the tunnel entrance and facilities at Cheriton just north of Folkestone. Construction started on both sides of the Channel in 1987 and the tunnel should open in 1993. Capital has been raised in the City and through a public share flotation, and even though costs have escalated by nearly 50 per cent to nearly £8 billion, the scheme will be completed approximately on time. It has yet to be seen whether it will make a return for its investors.

The Channel Tunnel provides the procedural model for the future. Consultation procedures, which have often delayed road proposals for up to ten years, and the decision on London's third airport for nearly twenty years, have now been short circuited through the use of parliamentary procedures. The government now takes only limited risks as the capital has to be raised privately. The general public may feel that they have been ignored as they have no direct input to decisions that often affect them directly. Private companies are looking for investment opportunities which can guarantee a return or minimize any risk. Projects initiated in this way are unlikely to fit into any overall strategy and it does not reduce the need for public expenditure in infrastructure. Similarly, private sector projects are very much more dependent upon market conditions and assumptions of continued growth in the demand for travel. Consequently, private sector investment should be seen as an addition to the public sector programme, not as a replacement for it.

Through radical changes in policy, the government has succeeded in reducing the levels of public expenditure on transport (Table 8.4), and this has been offset by proceeds from the

TABLE 8.4
Public Expenditure in Transport in Real Terms

£billion

	1981–82	1983–84	1985–1986	1987–88	1988–89 (estimate)
Transport	6.9	6.4	6.1	5.7	5.6
Privatization	−0.7	−1.4	−2.9	−5.1	−5.7

Notes: 1987–88 price levels
Privatization proceeds are from all sectors not just transport.
Source: HM Treasury (1989).

privatizations. The growth in demand for travel and the increase in car ownership have also resulted in record revenues for government from the transport sector. However, even after ten years of unprecedented activity in the transport sector there has been no statement of transport policy, except that the tenets of a market approach, efficiency and value for money seem dominant; this dominance is implicit rather than explicit. The question now addressed is whether that non policy position is tenable and whether it can be maintained over the next decade.

3. The Decade of the Car

The 1980s has been the decade of the car with traffic increasing by 40 per cent and the numbers of cars and taxis by about 30 per cent. In real terms the costs of motoring have never been cheaper and some two-thirds of households now have a car. To the user the car offers real advantages which alternative forms of transport can never match except in congested urban areas and over long distances. The car has unique flexibility in that it is always available, it offers door-to-door transport, and it effectively acts as a detachable extension to the home. This freedom is entirely consistent with the emergence of the ideologies of the new right in the 1980s.

After a decade of consistent growth in the demand for transport certain major weaknesses and inconsistencies in the market approach can be identified. The private sector cannot replace the public sector for capital investment in the infrastructure, and at best there must be some form of partnership. The responses to the government's Green Paper on New Roads by New Means (1989c) were very clear on this. The only projects that the private sector were interested in undertaking were those that gave them effective monopoly control (e.g. the Dartford Bridge and Tunnels) or were necessary to attract tenants to major office developments (e.g. the Canary Wharf development funding the Docklands Light Railway extension to Bank). Even then contributions were tightly linked to the state of the property market and so the time scale for completion would be variable as are the completion targets for all major property developments. The government has now recognized the major role that the public sector should play. Consequently, a second generation of major road construction and upgrading is planned. The National Roads Plan's current investment levels are some 60 per cent higher in real terms than in 1979 (Department of Transport 1989b) and the total Roads Vote for the next three years (1989-92) is 22 per cent higher in real terms than over the last three years (£4,000 million).

This investment in roads will in turn alleviate congestion, but in the longer term may help to generate more traffic and continue the dominance of the car for personal mobility. Intervention is required. Despite the heroic efforts of traffic management schemes and more recent technological developments the transport system is operating close to capacity for considerable parts of the day. The dilemma for the government is to decide whether a strategic view conflicts with the free market. Although business has clear commercial objectives concerning its own profitability, it may prefer to operate within a publicly planned environment with a longer term horizon that reduces uncertainty.

Even though there is no strategy one is emerging by default. Road building in urban areas does not seem to be strongly supported except to ease particular bottlenecks. Road investment will take place on orbitals and intercity roads including the widening of motorways and the construction of new toll roads with some private sector involvement. New rail investment is likely to update existing lines through the introduction of new rolling stock and electrification. New underground lines may be constructed in Central London and there are some twenty proposals for light rail transit in other cities, some of which have already been started (e.g. in Manchester and Birmingham). Again, the private sector may make some contribution. Ironically, many of these capital schemes are similar to those promoted in the 1960s when there was a similar period of economic growth.

It is on the issues of demand management and subsidy that greater uncertainty is apparent. Road pricing seems to have been rejected, but no one has effectively tackled the problems of car parking, of interchange between car and public transport, and the effective provision of city transport. After five years of bus deregulation and a much greater involvement of the private sector in the provision of transport services it is unclear whether these services are provided more efficiently or more competitively. Subsidy levels have been significantly reduced for both bus and rail services, but concessionary fares have increased to almost cancel out the savings (Table 8.2). The user certainly pays a greater proportion of the full costs of public transport.

After a decade of the free market experiment in transport, it is now time for an evaluation and reassessment of priorities. The decade of high mobility is not sustainable. Redirection should be towards a policy of high accessibility which must include positive action on the links between land use and transport, investment in public transport and an equitable means to limit the use of the car in congested urban areas.

The environmental concerns of the 1990s will be the key to change. The question is whether the government actually wishes to make such a radical switch in policy as it would involve imposing "green taxes" on car users, incentives to use more environmentally benign forms of transport (e.g. increase subsidies for public transport), the co-ordination of land use and development policies, reductions in the use of resources, and the elimination of subsidies to company cars and the freight distribution industry. Perhaps the choice is not really with the government but with the attitudes of the electorate. If the government uses all the fiscal and regulatory levers available to correct anomalies and to ensure the polluter pays, will this actually change the transport decisions made by individuals and firms? The consequences of such a radical policy might be to raise government revenues from transport to even greater levels and it may increase inflation. But equally it may increase the inequities which already exist between individuals in their access to different forms of transport. Unless public attitudes to the car change, policy will continue to favour those who can use the car and its dominance will become even more complete.

References

Banister, D. (1985) Deregulating the bus industry in Britain—the proposals, *Transport Reviews* **5**(2): 99-103.

Banister, D. (1990) Privatisation in transport: From the company state to the contract state. In Simmie, J., and King, R. (eds.) *The State in Action: Public Policy and Politics*, pp. 95-116. Pinter, London.

Banister, D., and Pickup, L. (1990) Bus transport in the Metropolitan Areas and London. In Cloke, P., and Bell, P. (eds.) *Deregulation and Transport*, pp. 67–83, Fulton, London.

Department of Transport (1989a) *Transport Statistics Great Britain 1978-1988*. HMSO, London.

Department of Transport (1989b) *Roads for Prosperity*, Cm 693. HMSO, London.

Department of Transport (1989c) *New Roads by New Means*, Cm 698. HMSO, London.

Glaister, S. (1990) Bus deregulation in the UK. Draft paper presented to the World Bank, May, p. 36.

House of Commons (1990) *Roads for the Future*, Transport Committee Report, Session 1989-90, HC 198, Vols. I, II and III. HMSO, London.

HM Treasury (1989) *Government Plans*, Cm 621. HMSO, London.

Rees, R. (1986) Is there an economic case for privatisation?, *Public Money* **5**(4): 19-26.

Reward Group (1990) *Annual Survey of Employee Benefits*, Mimeo, June.

9

Health

Health Policy Under Thatcher: Pushing the Market to the Limits?

MAGGIE PEARSON

Introduction

The one "untouchable" which has thwarted the Thatcher governments' mission to roll back the frontiers of the state has been the National Health Service. Every successive election campaign has seen continual reassurances that the NHS is "safe in our hands". Arguably the only restraint on Thatcherism's demolition of the welfare state has been the strong public consensus about, and affection for, the NHS and the right to health care irrespective of ability to pay (Bosanquet 1988).

The ideological hallmark of the Thatcher years—the commitment to roll back the frontiers of the state in the economy and in personal welfare—was of specific relevance for the health sector. Thatcher's agenda for the health service was to reduce the welfare "burden" on the state by reducing both the unit costs of, and the demand for, state services. "Self-help", private care and the voluntary sector were officially encouraged by a government which echoed right wing critiques from the USA (Illich 1974) that "nanny" state welfare services induce dependency and erode self reliance. Thatcher's principal economic ideology—that unbridled market forces allocate resources most efficiently—underpinned the introduction of market mechanisms into the NHS, in an attempt to reduce unit costs perceived to be unnecessarily high. Market forces were also unleashed to promote cheaper sources of care and the private sector in health care and in residential care of the elderly. In short, the concerns of economic policy with cost reduction have usurped social policy concerns with meeting needs equitably.

Thatcher's Wider Impact on the Public Health

To see Thatcher's sphere of influence in health matters as restricted only to the organization of *care* would be to underestimate her impact. Economic policies have profoundly affected the public health over the last ten years. Unemployment, which was directly attributable to government economic policy in the first term, has been shown to affect the physical and mental health of unemployed people and their families (Fagin and Little 1984). Death rates are significantly raised in families touched by unemployment (Moser *et al* 1986a; b), as are general practitioner consultations and referrals to hospital (Beale and Nethercott 1985, Yuen and Balarajan 1989). Inequalities in income have increased, with doubling of the number of people living in poverty, from 5 million in 1979 to over 10 million in 1987, of whom over 1 million have seen their real income fall by 6 per cent. Poverty, which is arguably the biggest single health risk of all, is strongly associated with childhood illness and deaths (DHSS 1980a, Whitehead 1988), and with specific behaviours known to affect health, such as smoking amongst adults (Graham 1987).

The enormity of Thatcher's impact on health and health services was such that it is impossible to address all these issues in detail here. Without minimizing the importance of the impact of Conservative economic policies on health and the need for health care, this chapter focuses on principal changes in policy and the organization of health care. To set these changes in context, we first address the state of the NHS when Thatcher came to power in 1979.

The NHS In 1979

The NHS was in crisis when Thatcher was elected in 1979. A major reorganization in 1974 had introduced a new managerialist ethos which explicitly excluded the concerns of patients, and cost more financially and in staff morale than ever envisaged (Ham 1985). 1975 saw unprecedented industrial action by ancillary staff and consultants over the question of private medical practice within NHS hospitals. Hospital admissions were restricted to emergencies. Cash limits for health authorities (which account for 60 per cent of total NHS funding) were introduced for the first time in 1976, by the beleaguered Callaghan government. As a result, services were rationalized, some hospital wards and units were closed and waiting lists grew even longer (Thunhurst 1982). In 1978-79, ancillary staff had been involved in the "dirty jobs" dispute of the winter of discontent, with wide media coverage of cancelled operations, piles of hospital rubbish and dirty laundry.

There was a wider context to the specific crisis of 1978-79. Long-term, apparently intractable, problems in the NHS had been acknowledged by the Wilson–Callaghan Labour administration. A Royal Commission on the NHS was established in 1976, to consider how financial and manpower resources in the NHS could best be managed in the interests both of patients and of staff. But it wasn't just the organization of the service which exercised the minds of the Labour government. There was a far more fundamental problem: that health inequalities (as indicated by death rates) between social classes were persisting, *despite* thirty years of the NHS and rising expenditure. How could the "jewel in the crown" of the welfare state so manifestly have failed? A Research Working Group on inequalities in health was appointed in 1977, chaired by Sir Douglas Black, President of the Royal College of Physicians. Reports of both groups were submitted to the new Conservative administration within its first year of office (Royal Commission 1979, DHSS 1980a).

The findings of the Royal Commission, running to 17 volumes, were officially published, widely disseminated and underpinned the Thatcher government's first proposals for NHS reform, in 1979 (Royal Commission 1979, DHSS 1979a). Some of the Royal Commission's recommendations, that there were unnecessary tiers of bureaucracy, and that precise information on the costs of clinical care should be made available to clinicians and other managers, were in line with the new Conservative government's thinking. Indeed, the Royal Commission's recommendation that one tier of the administrative hierarchy be removed enabled the first Thatcher government to respond decisively to problems of NHS organization and morale, proposing within weeks of coming into office to remove Area Health Authorities and increase local power and accountability in health care (DHSS 1979a).

The report of Sir Douglas Black's Working Party, submitted in April 1980, had a very different reception (DHSS 1980a). The evidence presented was a damning indictment of social divisions in Britain. Two-fold differences between Social Classes I and V in death rates among children and adults under the age of 65 were attributed principally to social inequalities in material resources. Whilst accepting that health services could play a significant part in reducing inequalities in health, the Working Group argued that

> measures to reduce differences in material standards of living at work, in the home and in everyday social and community life are of even greater importance (DHSS 1980a).

In a bold strategy, the Working Group challenged the very basis of Conservative economic and social policy by advocating a massive increase in state spending and benefits to abolish child poverty and achieve a relative improvement in the living standards of the poorest people. Such a radical document, recommending a total, and not merely service-oriented approach to ill-health, with an *increase* in state spending was anathema to the new Conservative government which saw public spending as the *cause* of economic ills. The Group's recommendations, costed at upwards of £2bn *per year*, were dismissed by Patrick Jenkin, Secretary of State for Social Services, as "quite unrealistic in present or any foreseeable economic circumstances" (DHSS 1980a). He could not, therefore, endorse the Group's recommendations. The report was finally "published" by the Department of Health and Social Security on the August Bank Holiday weekend. Just 260 copies were photocopied, some of which were sent out to a few journalists with minimum publicity.

This distinction has characterized health policy under Thatcher: a concern with the low cost delivery of health services, and scant regard for the state of the public health. The former, being funded by the state is seen as a legitimate concern of government, whereas the latter is increasingly seen as a matter of individual responsibility: an appropriate arena for government pronouncements, but not for social or state *action*.

Health Service Costs: An Endless Spiral?

From the outset, the Conservatives have assumed apparently infinite scope for more efficient management of NHS resources. Deficiencies in the service could be rectified by "more sensible" spending rather than by an injection of more cash. Since health service costs and funding have been so central an issue during Thatcher's terms of office, it is important to set that debate in its specific and international context. Health service costs have increased rapidly, and way beyond all predictions, since the NHS was established in 1948. In 1965, NHS costs amounted to 4.1 per cent of GNP, rising to 5.9 per cent in 1988 (OHE

1989). Such costs, which at £23,627 million comprised 14.7 per cent of public expenditure in 1988, are clearly of interest to any central government. They are all the more significant, therefore, to a Conservative government committed to reducing public expenditure. Nevertheless, it is sobering to note amidst the outcry that the NHS is inefficient and expensive, that in 1987, Japan was the only industrialized nation which spent less GNP *per capita* (5.2 per cent on health care than the UK) (OHE 1989).

Three principal factors underpin the spiralling costs of health care in the industrialized world, together requiring an estimated annual increase of between 0.65-1.0 per cent in the total NHS budget. First, an annual increase of between 0.5 and 1 per cent in health authorities' expenditure on hospital and community health services (HCHS) is needed just to keep pace with demographic change (Maynard and Bosanquet 1986). Needing more frequent and longer periods of treatment, *per capita* spending on HCHS is nine times greater for very elderly people (over 75 years) than for people aged 16-64. Spending on general practitioner, pharmacy and other primary health care for the very elderly is twice the national average. In 1986, people over the age of 65 accounted for over 40 per cent of NHS expenditure, whereas they comprised 15.3 per cent of the total population (OHE 1989).

Second, advances in medical technology and procedures incur an estimated 0.5 per cent increase in HCHS spending, over and above the costs of demographic change. Third, the demand for services increases because public expectations of health care continually rise. The treatment of degenerative health problems, such as coronary heart disease with bypass operations, osteoarthritis with hip replacements and organ dysfunction with transplants are symptomatic of the increasing expectation that medicine can cure all ills. They have been estimated to imply a 2 per cent increase in real spending (Maynard and Bosanquet 1986). These rising expectations are not limited solely to traditionally "legitimate" physical health problems. Other problems of daily life such as dependency on alcohol and other drugs or child abuse have been "medicalized" (Zola 1972, Illich 1974, 1976), such that medical expertise and health care are seen as the appropriate response, whether or not the skills required were already available elsewhere. The concern to reduce costs had an added political edge for the Conservative government in a labour intensive industry in which salaries and wages comprised 52 per cent of total NHS costs in 1978 (OHE 1989). The NHS trade unions gained strength and confidence with the first national strike of NHS staff in 1979. The dispute was portrayed by the Conservatives as a classic example of the inherent selfishness of trade unionists, prepared to pursue disputes for their own ends despite the effects on patients. Pay demands were similarly "selfish" in diverting resources away from the "direct" patient care. If labour costs could be controlled, resources would be "released" for patient care.

Restructuring the Health Sector

Together, the economic and ideological agendas to reduce costs and open up the market in health care have shaped and underpinned changes in the health sector since 1979. A cascade of reforms and initiatives have comprised the government's drive to reduce unit costs, but no measures have yet been introduced to assess health care outcomes, by which to measure the *efficiency* (as opposed to the scale) of the reduced costs. In Thatcher's first term, the principal drive was to promote the private health care sector (largely *outside* the NHS) and to attack what were seen as costly, unnecessary tiers of bureaucracy. The maintenance of strict cash limits forced authorities to rationalize services in an attempt to reduce unit costs and look for other sources of funding. It was in her second term of office, after 1983, that there were more overt central initiatives to contain costs and restructure the delivery of care within the NHS. This was the era of general (as opposed to the pre-existing "consensus") management, cost improvement programmes and competitive tendering for ancillary services. In her third term, Thatcher went on to introduce market mechanisms and metaphors into the very heart of the NHS itself, not just to elements of the health care process, but to institutional arrangements for the provision of care.

Promoting Private Care

The National Health Service has never been the sole provider of health care in the UK. After 1948, private medicine continued within and outside the NHS, albeit on a much smaller scale than previously. For thirty years after the NHS was established, three provident associations (BUPA, PPP and WPA) dominated the private health care market, accounting for about 98 per cent of the business. BUPA was the largest, commanding almost 75 per cent of subscriptions.

TABLE 9.1
Private Medical Insurance Subscriptions, UK

Year	Subscribers	Persons Insured	
	'000	'000	% UK pop
1950	56	120	
1955	274	585	1.1
1965	680	1445	2.7
1975	1087	2334	4.2
1980	1647	3577	6.4
1985	2107	4506	8.0
1988	2386	5022	8.8

Source: OHE 1989.

Private medical insurance subscriptions rose steadily to 1,096,000 in 1974, after which there was a slight decline to 1,057,000 in 1977 (Table 9.1). The majority of subscriptions were employers' group schemes. These were essentially fringe benefits for key employees, who could be hospitalized quickly when necessary, to the mutual convenience of employer and employee (Higgins 1988).

There was relatively little debate about private acute care outside the NHS until the late 1970s (Higgins 1988), but private practice and fee-for-service medicine *within* the NHS gave rise to controversy and dispute in the mid-1970s. Although successive governments from Bevan onwards had allowed consultants to treat private patients within NHS hospitals, the number of beds used had declined, and occupancy rates were rarely above 50 per cent (Higgins 1988). In the mid 1970s, the question of NHS pay beds was raised by junior doctors' allegations that some unscrupulous consultants were abusing NHS facilities. Subsequent strike action by ancillary staff against private patients, and a work-to-rule by consultants in protest at proposals to curb their private practice, severely disrupted the NHS. The question of private medicine was given a public profile of which any public relations firm would have been proud. After 1978, subscriptions rose at an accelerating pace, as hospital care in the NHS with its chronic industrial relations problems became increasingly unreliable (Lee 1980).

It was in this context that the private health care sector was actively encouraged by Thatcher's first government, immediately on coming to power. The Health Services Act 1980 abolished the Health Services Board and restored to the Secretary of State powers to regulate the supply of private beds within and outside the NHS. The DHSS issued guidance to health authorities advocating partnership between the private and public sectors "in service of the sick", for example by using spare capacity in the private sector to reduce waiting lists (DHSS 1981). Between 1979 and 1985, the number of beds in private hospitals in the UK increased by 54 per cent to 10,155 (Higgins 1988). Private spending on health care increased by 456 per cent between 1978 and 1988, compared with an increase of 195 per cent in NHS expenditure (OHE 1989).

In January 1980, consultants' contracts were revised, entitling all consultants to take private patients. As a result, the number of consultants taking maximum part-time NHS contracts (thereby releasing sessions for private practice without losing NHS income) increased from 47.6 per cent in 1979 to 54.3 per cent in 1984 (Laing 1985). Private practice in NHS hospitals would be subject to a voluntary code of conduct (DHSS 1980b). Arguing that the new arrangements would work "most satisfactorily" if based on trust, consultants' contractual obligations to the NHS were not closely monitored, and detailed accounts were not required (DHSS 1979b).

Other measures promoting small business during Thatcher's first term encouraged the growth of the private sector. The Business Start-Up Scheme and Business Expansion Scheme, introduced in the 1981 budget, offered tax concessions against expenses incurred in creating or expanding small business. Consultants used these provisions to set up their own private hospitals.

Whilst the "supply" of private medicine was encouraged by deregulation of the market, the 1981 Budget introduced fiscal incentives to extend demand for private medical insurance into new sections of the population. With effect from April 1982, medical insurance premiums paid for workers earning less than £8,500 were exempt from tax, and companies could set premiums paid for their employees against Corporation Tax: a concession worth £30m to the companies involved (Higgins 1988).

The government's measures stimulated an increase in group scheme subscriptions. Several companies offered private medical insurance to all their staff, including manual workers. Individual subscriptions fell from 44 per cent of total in 1977 to 32.3 per cent in 1983. Divisions within the trade union movement were explicit when several powerful unions negotiated private insurance for their members. However, the extension of schemes to blue collar workers resulted in a rapid rise in claims, particularly among their dependents. Premiums escalated, rising by 31 per cent in 1981 and by 39.8 per cent in 1982 (Higgins 1988). As a result, the rapid annual growth in subscriptions fell from 25.9 per cent in 1980 to 1.9 per cent in 1983. In 1988, 2.39 million subscribers held insurance cover for just over 5 million people, comprising 8.8 per cent of the UK population (Table 9.1) (OHE 1989). This was a far cry from early predictions of the Thatcher government that 25 per cent of the population would have private insurance by 1990 (Higgins 1988). Acknowledging that insurance premiums were high, and mindful of demographic pressures on NHS funding, tax relief on private medical insurance premiums for retired people (whether paid by themselves or their families) was introduced from April 1990.

The majority of people who seek private medicine do so in order to avoid NHS waiting lists, which are themselves partly lengthened by the reduced availability of NHS consultants with some private practice. Indeed, the ability to "jump the queue" was a marketing message used by several financial companies entering the private medical insurance market for the first time in 1990. Government assertions that

> people who choose to buy health care outside the Health Service benefit the community by taking pressure off the Service (Secretary of State 1989: pp. 8-9)

fly in the face of the evidence. Whilst waiting lists may be shorter, waiting *times* for appointments have increased. Until the early 1970s, the number of NHS patients awaiting hospital treatment remained constant at approximately 500,000. However, this rose as a result of industrial action to 750,000 by 1980. After a directive in 1984 from the Secretary of State that patients should be "weeded out" of the list if no longer requiring surgery, the numbers waiting fell to 680,000 in 1985 (Higgins 1988).

Private Care: A Multinational Business?

The private health care sector has not simply increased in size since 1979. Its nature has changed significantly since the entry into the British "cottage industry" in 1983 of commercial organizations providing care for profit. American companies have increased their share of the market from three hospitals with 366 beds in Britain in 1979, to 31 hospitals with 2,239 beds (over 20 per cent of total) in 1986 (Higgins 1988). These multinational companies are aggressive and self-avowedly bullish, commanding considerable resources. For them, private care is big business. The

UK subsidiary of American Medical International (AMI) has 13 acute hospitals and 1,203 beds, rivalling the Nuffield Hospital Trust as the largest single provider of private care in the UK. It has a diversified "product", providing psychiatric care, alcohol and drug dependency clinics, the latter in association with the charity ACCEPT. In an entirely new departure for the private sector, AMI has established a head injury rehabilitation centre which offers medical and legal assistance to victims wishing to sue for damages. In 1984, to complete the commodification of health care, AMI introduced its own credit card (Higgins 1988).

Private Residential Care

It is not just in medical care that the private sector received a boost during the Thatcher years. Like private medicine, private residential care was not initiated by Thatcher, but received a shot in the arm under her policies, accounting totally for the expansion in services to keep pace with the increasing numbers of very elderly people. Despite government commitment to the policy of Care in the Community, formal sources of domiciliary support for elderly people have declined since 1980, the number of places in day centres and day hospitals has not increased (NAO 1987a). The demand for residential accommodation providing basic (but not skilled nursing) care has therefore grown.

Between 1975 and 1985, the total number of places for elderly people in residential or hospital care just kept pace with the increase in the very elderly population (Table 9.2). Whilst the number of hospital and local authority beds for elderly people declined slightly between 1980 and 1985, the number of places in private care increased by 129 per cent. In 1980, a third of elderly people in residential care in the UK were in private or voluntary homes. By 1987, they accounted for over half (CSO, 1990). Accounting for less than a tenth of institutional (hospital and residential) care for the elderly in 1975, private residential homes accounted for over a fifth in 1985 (NAO 1987a) (Table 9.2). For a government arguing that active promotion of the private sector would reduce public spending, it is the height of irony that the social security budget has financed exponential growth in private residential care. Until 1980, the charges of eligible elderly residents in private or voluntary homes could be met in full or in part by supplementary benefit, subject to local limits. The Social Security Act 1980 gave local DHSS offices the discretion to meet in full higher charges in residential and nursing homes in the private sector. There was no assessment of

TABLE 9.2
*Institutional Care for the Elderly in England, 1975–80**

Type of care	1975		1980		1985	
	No.	per '000 popn 75+	No.	per '000 popn 75+	No.	per '000 popn 75+
NHS Geriatric	51,100	21.4	50,500	18.7	50,000	16.4
LA Part III	95,113	40.0	102,890	38.2	101,526	33.3
Private homes	18,759	7.9	28,854	10.7	66,143	21.7
Voluntary homes	22,454	9.4	25,449	9.5	25,818	8.4
Total places	187,428	78.7	207,693	77.1	243,487	79.8

Source: NAO 1987b.
* Does not include places in registered nursing homes, as no statistics were available before 1982.
In 1982, 18,197 places were available, compared with 33,869 in 1985.

need for care. Demand constituted need, and the only assessment was of financial circumstances. In effect, the DHSS wrote a blank cheque for the private residential and nursing home market.

Between 1980 and 1983, the number of elderly supplementary benefits claimants in private and voluntary residential and nursing homes more than doubled from 11,558 to 23,577. By contrast, the number of elderly residents sponsored by local authorities fell by 22 per cent. Working within tight budgets, local and health authorities introduced "social security efficient" schemes for care of elderly people, which favoured expensive residential care rather than community services (Wistow 1988). Supplementary benefit paid for all such claimants increased by 483 per cent from an estimated £18 million in December 1980 to £105 million in December 1983 (NAO 1987a). In 1986, supplementary benefit support for residents in private homes was estimated at "£500 million a year and growing rapidly". Cheaper, more appropriate care could have been provided for many in their own or a group home, preventing their institutionalization, but local and health authority funds would have been implicated (Audit Commission 1986).

The DHSS was not initially aware of the scale of growth in supplementary benefits payments for private care. Local discretionary powers to meet residential charges in full were withdrawn in November 1983, and different limits were introduced for ordinary board and lodging (such as that paid for homeless people); private and voluntary residential care homes; and nursing homes (NAO 1987a). In April 1985, a new structure of national limits was introduced, with 12 categories. Continuing government concern about the shift in financial responsibility from cash-limited local authorities to the unlimited demand-led social security budget led to the Griffiths report on Care in the Community, which recommended that local authorities should be responsible for Community Care, with the appropriate transfer of funds (Griffiths 1988). This was a politically unacceptable policy for government, coinciding as it did with the first poll tax bills. Worried about the implications of the Griffiths recommendations for poll tax bills prior to a general election, the Secretary of State for Health announced in 1990 that the proposed transfer of responsibility would be deferred until 1992. Inadequate community support would therefore continue in the political interests of a fourth Thatcher government.

Containing (and Shifting) Costs

In its drive to reduce NHS costs, in 1982 the DHSS sought a reduction in manpower of 0.75-1 per cent. Health authorities were asked to submit to the DHSS manpower targets for March 1984 (DHSS 1982, 1983a) but when progress fell short of what was "desired and expected", individual authorities were given specific, quantified targets (DHSS 1983b). The latter circular reminded health authorities that their first obligation was to comply with their statutory duty not to exceed their cash limits. The health of the population was not mentioned. At the time, health authority budgets were particularly uncertain (Small 1989). Having been allocated an additional 1.2 per cent revenue in January 1983, a 1 per cent *cut* in NHS spending was announced in July. Savings were to be retrieved from health authorities' HCHS budgets, since FPC services were not then cash-limited. In direct contradiction of the government's rhetoric of local autonomy, authorities openly refusing to implement the manpower reductions, or to adhere to cash limits "requested", were threatened with dismissal (Mohan and Woods 1985).

Criticism by the House of Commons Public Accounts Committee of ineffective DHSS control over regional budgets (House of Commons 1981) led to the introduction of performance indicators in 1983, as a means of comparing authorities' costs and workloads. Indicating inputs and throughputs rather than outcomes or quality of care, they could not measure *performance* (Birch and Maynard 1988). Nevertheless, high unit costs were interpreted as poor value for money. The Secretary of State was in no doubt about who was to blame:

> Differences in performance such as these should raise questions for management, who should ask how these differences exist and how they can be reduced (Norman Fowler, *Hansard*, 27 October 1983, p. 459).

The Introduction of General Management

The concern to reduce costs prompted an inquiry (led by Roy Griffiths, Deputy Chairman and Managing Director of Sainsbury's) into the use and management of NHS manpower and related resources. Griffiths' principal criticism was that consensus management (introduced into the NHS in 1974 on the advice of private management consultants) resulted in weak leadership, with "lowest common denominator decisions" and long delays in the management process. Without a clearly defined general management function or "driving force", there were few precise management objectives, little measurement of health output, little clinical or economic evaluation of health care, and great difficulties in achieving change (DHSS 1983c). Interestingly, given subsequent events, Griffiths also indicated that continuous and unco-ordinated DHSS interference hampered the day-to-day operation of unit and district management teams (Parston 1988). General management would provide the necessary leadership and dynamism to motivate staff and maintain the search for change and cost improvement. One identifiable person would have overall responsibility for cost improvements and quality of care. An annual review process was implemented, in which district and regional health authority general managers and chairmen were held accountable to regions and the DHSS respectively.

Griffiths also proposed a new NHS management structure. A Health Services Supervisory Board, chaired by the Secretary of State, would determine policy and strategy, approve resource allocations and review performance. A full-time NHS Management Board, chaired by an experienced general manager, would implement policy, give leadership and control performance. Regional and district general managers would be managerially responsible for the achievement of their respective authorities' objectives, whereas unit general managers would be responsible for budgetary control, actively involving clinicians in unit management (Parston 1988). The distinction between political control of policy and managerial accountability for its implementation did not last long, however. In 1986, after only 18 months, the first Chairman of the NHS Management Board resigned after a dispute with ministers about his right to manage. Since then, the Minister of Health has chaired the Board, making political control of NHS management explicit.

Despite announcing a ten-week consultation period when the Griffiths report was released in November 1983, its recommendations were implemented immediately. The first District General Managers were appointed in January 1984, and regional and district authorities were directed in June 1984 to implement the Griffiths recommendations in full and as quickly as possible (DHSS 1984). Hospital and unit managers were to be in place by the end of 1985. In a direct challenge to the local autonomy of health authorities, all proposed management systems and appointments were subject to DHSS scrutiny at first. In several cases, local decisions were overruled. It had been anticipated that external management expertise would be drawn upon, but by December 1987 less than 12 per cent of general managers were new to the NHS (Leathard 1990).

Clinical Budgets

The Griffiths Report also recommended the introduction of clinical management budgets at hospital and unit level, whereby consultants would be allocated a set budget within which to provide care for their patients. The concept of clinical management budgets did not stem from the rapid introduction of general management *per se*. The need for better information on health service activity and finance had been identified in the Royal Commission's report in 1979, and the Korner Steering Group on Health Services Information had been established in 1980 to take the issue further. However, the rapidity and dictatorial style of its proposed introduction in 1984 did stem from Griffiths and its overarching emphasis on financial control, generating a hostile reception among medical and nursing staff (Coles 1988). Clinicians were concerned that their clinical autonomy and freedom would disappear, raising the spectre of accountants deciding who should receive health care. Nurses were incensed that they had no specific place in the new proposals: there was no acknowledgement of their independence as a profession, or of the financial implications of their decisions (Harrison 1988). Whereas other reforms such as competitive tendering were pursued relentlessly, despite concerns about standards of care, a more gradual, kid glove approach was adopted to the clinicians. Clinical budgeting was not introduced wholesale. Damage limitation measures included negotiation with the medical profession and piloting in four demonstration districts. The discredited clinical budgeting was relaunched in 1986, sanitized as the "Resource Management Initiative" (DHSS

1986), in which the critical importance of doctors' and nurses' involvement was emphasized.

Cost Improvement Programmes

The need to pursue value for money featured prominently in the Griffiths report (DHSS 1983c). In 1984, continuing its drive to contain NHS costs, the DHSS required health authorities to draw up cost improvement programmes to save a set per cent of their cash allocations (RSHG 1987). It was expected that general management would sustain and improve these programmes. Again, this development was intensified, but not introduced, by Thatcher. Cost reductions had begun under the last Labour government, when cash limits were imposed in 1976. Impetus was added by stricter cash limits since 1979.

In 1981-82, cash releasing cost improvement programmes amounted to £15.2m in England, rising to £42.0m in 1983-84 and over £150m in 1986-87 and subsequent years. Costs were reduced principally by rationalization of services, competitive tendering and "other" reductions in labour costs, such as the increased use of agency nurses (Table 9.3) (NAO 1985, 1986, House of Commons Social Services Committee 1987, 1990).

Rationalization of Health Authority Services

Services have been rationalized since the late 1950s by the closure of small hospital units, and the opening or extension of others to achieve economies of scale, particularly in the provision of support services and the use of operating theatres. Thus, the number of hospitals and beds available has decreased since the late 1950s (see Fig. 9.1), but there has been a particularly sharp fall in the number of hospitals since 1977, and an accelerated decrease in the number of beds since 1983. Whereas there were 8.7 beds per 1,000 population in the UK in 1976, there were 7.9 in 1983 and 6.5 in 1988: decreases of 9.2 and 17.7 per cent respectively (OHE 1989). Hospital and bed closures involve a shift in costs to the service user. Where units are closed, some people will have to travel longer distances for out-patient and in-patient care, or to visit hospital patients (Whitelegg 1982). For those reliant on public transport, such service rationalizations will be felt keenly (Pearson and Spencer 1989, Pearson 1990, Pearson *et al.* 1990). It is principally women who undertake emotional and caring work, visiting friends or relatives of patients amidst other household commitments (Graham 1985, Hamilton

TABLE 9.3
Cost Improvement Programme: Source of Saving

Category	1985–86 £m	(%)	1986–87 £m	(%)	1987–88 £m	(%)	1988–89 £m	(%)
Rationalization of patient services	29.8	(21.5)	37.3	(23.5)	35.4	(23.2)	55.3	(36.4)
Competitive tendering	16.3	(11.8)	48.4	(30.5)	30.6	(20.0)	9.7	(6.4)
Other reductions in labour costs	38.3	(27.7)	23.6	(14.9)	35.4	(23.2)	31.8	(20.9)
Rayner Scrutiny	7.3	(5.3)	7.6	(4.8)	3.6	(2.4)	3.5	(2.3)
Supply costs	9.5	(6.9)	7.8	(4.9)	10.2	(6.7)	8.8	(5.8)
Energy costs	6.8	(4.9)	8.7	(5.5)	8.5	(5.6)	8.0	(5.3)
Other sources	30.2	(21.8)	25.0	(15.8)	29.1	(19.0)	34.8	(22.9)
Total	138.4	(100.0)	158.4	(100.0)	152.8	(100.0)	151.9	(100.0)

Source: House of Commons Social Services Committee (1990).

and Jenkins 1989, Pearson and Grieco 1991). Since many women are dependent on public transport, the organizing skills required to accommodate even longer journeys are considerable (Hosking 1989, Pearson 1990, Pearson *et al.* 1990, Pearson and Grieco 1991).

Besides the reduction and spatial concentration of hospital beds, services have also been rationalized by their more intensive use. In the UK, the annual number of discharges and deaths per bed increased from 14.5 in 1979 to 16.7 in 1983 and 21.9 in 1988-89: increases in "throughput" of 15.2 and 31.1 per cent respectively. In acute hospital services (excluding mental illness, mental handicap and geriatrics), the number of discharges and deaths per available bed in Great Britain increased by 18 per cent from 28.9 in 1979 to 34.1 in 1983, and by a further 16.7 per cent to 40.9 in 1987-88. In the UK as a whole, the average length of stay (ALOS) in hospital fell by 30 per cent from 20 days in 1979 to 14 days in 1988-89 (OHE 1989). Between 1983 and 1988, the rate of day cases treated in the NHS acute sector in England increased by 28.4 per cent from 167.9 per 10,000 resident population to 215.6 (House of Commons 1990).

The published statistics do not easily enable one to distinguish deaths from discharges, but assuming that the proportion of deaths has not risen significantly (and may well have fallen), these increases in throughput of hospital patients also represent a shift in costs to the public. Whilst medical advances may mean that patients recover more quickly from acute episodes such as coronaries, strokes or major surgery, it is unlikely that such advances account totally for the increased rate of discharge. It is more likely that patients are discharged earlier in their stage of recovery, placing greater demands for support and care on health professionals in the community, and certainly on their family and friends, particularly female kin. It is also likely, but hitherto unquantified, that there has been an increase in readmissions of patients discharged early, particularly where people are living in poverty. Such increased "throughput" figures could therefore mask several indicators of poorer quality of care stemming from the reduced costs.

The most dramatic fall in ALOS was in geriatric hospitals, where it fell by 41.6 per cent in England between 1979 and 1986, from 76.7 days to 44.8 days (OHE 1989). However, there was no accompanying increase in domiciliary support services. Whilst some elderly people discharged from hospital would have gone into private residential care, they will only have constituted a small proportion of the 401,000 deaths and discharges from geriatric hospitals in England in 1987-88. Whether as a labour or love or of duty, an increasing number of sick elderly people are cared for by spouses or female kin (Finch and Groves 1983, Ungerson 1987, Finch 1989).

Competitive Tendering

In 1978, salaries and wages accounted for 52 per cent of total NHS costs (OHE 1989). By 1983 the salary bill had crept up to 55 per cent of total costs, principally as a result of an increase in the number of nurses after the length of their working week was reduced in 1980, and the improvement of staffing levels in geriatric and mental illness units (NAO 1985). Nurses are the largest single staff group, representing almost half of the work force, 44.8 per cent of the salary bill and accounting for 34 per cent of the NHS revenue budget and 3 per cent of all public expenditure in 1983-84 (DHSS 1990, NAO 1985). Since it would be political suicide for any government to explicitly reduce spending on medical and nursing staff in the NHS, (indeed, one of Thatcher's proudest claims is the increase in medical and nursing staff since 1979) NHS cost containment required a compensatory reduction in other staff.

In 1982-83, the largest single item of revenue expenditure

after nursing staff was ancillary workers, who accounted for 15.5 per cent of all HCHS wages and salaries and 11.6 per cent of total HCHS revenue expenditure in England (DHSS 1985). The search for cost containment measures focused therefore on ancillary services, despite NHS ancillary staff being amongst the lowest paid in the UK. Arguably, however, there was little room for cuts in ancillary staff. Whilst the number of staff employed in other areas of the NHS had increased dramatically between 1974 and 1983 (medical staff by 30.7 per cent, nursing staff by 27.5 per cent, there had been a negligible increase of 1.9 per cent in ancillary staff (OHE 1989).

Government statements about the need for greater efficiency savings within NHS ancillary services indicated fertile ground for private contractors who had been involved on a small scale well before 1979. However, their share of the market declined sharply between 1980-83. It has been suggested that this decline in market share resulted in a campaign by private contractors to re-open the NHS market for these three support services (Ascher 1987).

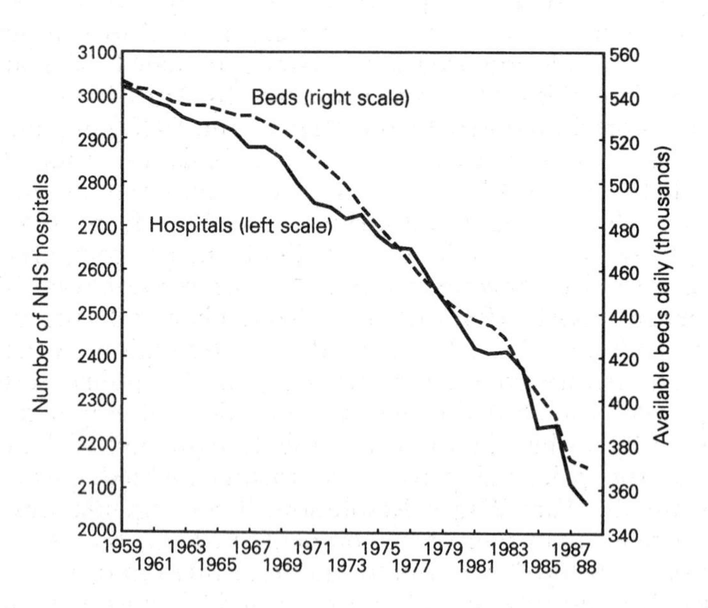

Source: OHE (1989)

FIG. 9.1. Number of NHS hospitals* and daily average available beds, Great Britain.

At the same time, Thatcher had a score to settle with the NHS unions. Encouraged by their industrial action in 1978-79, the ancillary staff unions again took action in 1982. This was the first strike in which the majority of blue collar and ancillary staff unions in the NHS were united, and was thus important to "break" in Thatcher's campaign to tackle trade union power. Moreover, the 1982 strike demonstrated just how vital ancillary staff were to the smooth running of the health service. Cast in the role of being "selfish" by taking action in 1982, the political climate was ripe for the notion that ancillary workers took resources "away" from direct patient care. Although their wages were still pitifully low, it was argued that the same service could be provided more cheaply by private contractors.

In September 1983, the Department of Health and Social Security issued a circular giving "guidance" to all health authorities that they should "test the cost effectiveness" of their ancillary services by putting them out to competitive tender (DHSS 1983d). The tendering programme focused on three services: domestic services, laundry and catering, which together cost £877 million in England and Wales in 1983-84, and in which labour costs comprised 90, 40 and 60 per cent respectively (Ascher 1987).

In December 1983, authorities were *directed* to complete all competitive tendering programmes by September 1986. Plans and detailed timetables were to be submitted by April 1984. Progress was monitored quarterly by the DHSS. The DHSS implemented two measures to ensure that "a fair basis for competition" prevailed. First, VAT levied on private contracts in the NHS was refunded to health authorities with effect from September 1983, to remove the relative cost disadvantage, compared with in-house services. Second, the basis for competition was "further sharpened" (NAO 1987) when in September 1983 the government rescinded the 1946 Fair Wages Resolution, which had required private contractors working in the public sector to comply with established terms and conditions of employment.

Ironically, rather than welcome the deregulation of the labour market, the principal private contractors lobbied government to retain the Fair Wages Resolution. Their agenda was more sophisticated than mere free competition. First, they wanted to keep out "cowboys" who would undercut them in order to enter the market and take quick profits. Second, they were anxious to minimize opposition from the trades unions. In May 1984, the Contract Cleaning and Maintenance Association Health Service Section agreed among themselves to pay rates agreed by the NHS negotiating body, the Whitley Council (Ascher 1987).

Health authorities varied widely in their enthusiasm for competitive tendering. In early 1985 "a significant number" of DHAs had not sought any tenders (NAO 1987). Between January 1984 and March 1985, only 120 contracts had been awarded (there are 192 DHAs in England), of which 55 per cent had been awarded to private contractors. The slow progress was attributed to the amount of work involved, and concerns by local managers about the impact on industrial relations. In some areas contractors were not interested in NHS work, particularly in catering where efficiency had improved between 1974 and 1982, with a reduction in real costs by 12 per cent (Ascher 1987, NAO 1987).

Having maintained their oligopoly, the cleaning, catering and laundry trade associations lobbied the DHSS anew, complaining that some authorities were stipulating Whitley Council pay and conditions in contracts; that capital used by in-house teams was subject to less than commercial rates of interest; and expressing concern that the slow start would lead to a later rush of activity to which contractors may not be able to respond. The DHSS responded by overruling local health authority decisions, preventing their stipulation of "Fair Wages" clauses or their unilateral cancellation of contracts on the grounds of unsatisfactory performance. Pressure on health authorities increased as the Parliamentary Secretary wrote to all RHA Chairmen; the NHS Management Board wrote to regional general managers; and DHSS officers maintained "close and detailed contact" with district and regional health authorities (NAO 1987).

Since catering contracts proved particularly difficult for the private sector to win, specific DHSS "guidance" was given on the need to introduce cook-chill and cook-freeze methods; to aggregate small catering units into larger units viable for contracting purposes and the amendment of fixed price contracts to "accommodate reasonable changes in food costs" (NAO 1987). Health authorities were required to give contractors the opportunity to tender for services provided from premises leased from the NHS, and were "reminded" that linen could be rented.

Although the tendering process accelerated, only 57 per cent of the potential number of contracts were awarded by the September 1986 target date. Private firms won only 8 per cent of contracts awarded in September 1986, and only 18 per cent of all contracts awarded since 1983. Savings generated by private contracts fell from 34 per cent in 1984-85 to 21 per cent in 1986 (Table 9.4). The exclusion of private contractors did not necessarily augur well for NHS staff, however. In-house tenders were successful only by using reducing staff, introducing bonus schemes, and increasing

TABLE 9.4
Progress in Competitive Tendering to September 1986

	Contracts let		Contractors		Ann Savgs	
	By no.	Value	No.	Value	£m	%
Domestic	68%	77%	24%	32%	56.5	26%
Catering	41%	55%	20%	20%	6.2	14%
Laundry	59%	73%	4%	7%	9.9%	10%
Total	57%	68%	18%	24%	72.7	20%

the number of part-time staff. Between 1983 and 1988 there was a fall of 31 per cent in the number of ancillary staff employed in England, representing a 35.3 per cent reduction in whole-time equivalent posts (DH 1990). By September 1986, savings of almost £73 million per annum (20 per cent of previous costs) had been achieved by the award of 946 contracts, representing 8 per cent of the total cost of support services in England in 1985-86 (NAO 1987), and 0.76 per cent of health authorities' revenue expenditure in 1985-86 (DH 1989). Potential annual savings were estimated at £120–£140m (NAO 1987).

Cost Containment in Primary Care

Because hospital and community health services provided by district health authorities account for more than 60 per cent of NHS spending, it is not surprising that the greatest weight of the government's drive to reduce costs was borne by health authorities, and hospitals in particular. Without any cash limits or other effort to control costs, Family Practitioner Services (FPS) provided by general medical practitioners, dentists, pharmacists and ophthalmic practitioners declined in *relative* financial importance, from a third of total NHS spending in 1950 to a fifth in 1980 (OHE 1989). However, since 1980, the actual and relative cost of FPS has increased. Whereas the real growth in total NHS expenditure increased by 21 per cent between 1980 and 1987, the respective increase for FPS was 38 per cent, such that in 1989 FPs accounted for 25 per cent of total NHS costs (OHE 1989).

This increase in FPS spending (which was not cash-limited or allocated by Regional Health Authorities until 1990) has been the result of two principal factors: demographic change and reductions in average length of stay (ALOS) in hospital. Elderly people make greater demands on FPS than any other group, particularly for general medical and pharmaceutical services which together comprise over 75 per cent of FPS costs (31.5 and 43.8 per cent respectively) (OHE 1989). Prescription costs have risen as a direct consequence of the demographic ageing of the population, the medicalization of ageing, and the sharp reduction in geriatric hospital ALOS. Between 1978 and 1988, the number of prescriptions dispensed by pharmacists to people of pensionable age increased by 44.3 per cent. The pharmaceutical budget will also have increased as a result of earlier hospital discharge.

Because of the independent contractor status of the professional groups (general practitioners, dentists and ophthalmic practitioners) providing primary care, cost reduction measures have principally comprised increased charges to the public and central control of prescribing costs. Prescription charges increased five-fold in cash terms, and trebled in "real" terms between 1979 and 1988. Since a prescription charge of £0.20 per item was introduced on 1 April 1971, there was no increase until 16 July 1979, when it was set at £0.45. Thereafter, there have been virtually annual increases, to £2.80 per item in 1989. Increased charges have not effectively reduced demand, although they constitute an important source of income for the government (OHE 1989). In 1988, prescriptions dispensed cost £2,527m, of which £192m approximately came from patient charges, and the remainder from public funds. The average cost per prescription dispensed was £5.97.

Pharmaceutical services constitute the greatest single component of FPs spending, amounting to 43.9 per cent of total in 1989 (OHE 1989). In an attempt to control FPS pharmaceutical expenditure, a limited list of medicines which could be prescribed under the NHS was announced in November 1984. The list, principally of tranquillizers and medicines used in minor illness, was intended to save £160m per annum in prescribing costs (Small 1989). This was the government's first shot across the bows of GPs, who were not subject to any cash limits. After an outcry from the medical profession (and the pharmaceutical industry) that the list eroded clinical autonomy and excluded some patients' treatments, the proposed list was modified. By May 1987, the limited list had saved £75m per annum, mainly from reduced spending on cough and cold remedies and on mild pain-killers: products which could be bought from chemists over the counter (Taylor 1988). Here, the principal cost shift would be borne by those on low incomes eligible for free prescriptions, who now have to pay for the medicine, and may therefore not buy it at all.

Charges for dental treatment have increased sharply since 1979, such that a non-exempt patient now pays approximately 70 per cent of the basic cost of a course of treatment, compared with a third in 1952. The contribution of patient charges to the cost of General Dental Services (GDS) grew more than two-fold in "real terms" between 1977 and 1987, compared with an increase of only 40 per cent in public spending in the same period. Whereas patient payments accounted for 22 per cent of all GDS expenditure in 1977, they comprised 31 per cent in 1987 (OHE 1989).

In a measure which further reduced the costs to the Exchequer of primary care, universal eligibility for NHS spectacles was abolished in April 1985. It has since been restricted to children, people on supplementary benefit and those needing particularly powerful lenses. Non-exempt groups have since had to pay the full cost of spectacles. The restriction of eligibility for NHS spectacles has had a striking impact. The number of pairs of spectacles funded by the NHS fell sharply from 6 million per annum in 1981-84 to 4 million in 1985 (OHE 1989). Sight tests were universally free until April 1989, since when only those exempt from ophthalmic charges were eligible.

Raising Income

Besides encouraging greater use of the private sector in health care, the generation of income from private sources has also been actively encouraged by stealth and by statute under Thatcher. Crippling cash limits forced health authorities to look for alternative ways of raising funds. The Health Services Act 1980 had permitted health authorities to raise funds from charitable sources. Since then, public appeals for expensive capital equipment (and, in some cases, revenue) have mushroomed. Children's hospitals, most likely to generate public generosity, rose to the challenge, and in one case became a private charity because cash limits were so severe. In some cases, professional fund raisers were employed for the purpose, amidst outcries that prestigious national hospitals, such as Great Ormond Street Children's in London, were tapping potential, but limited, sources of public donations in the regions.

Despite government aspirations to generate a charitable welfare economy in the UK, funds raised by public appeal have remained minimal. Other sources of raising revenue were explored by health authorities during the 1980s. The commercial potential to establish mini shopping malls in large hospitals' reception areas was exploited, but the work involved arguably diverted general managers away from alternatives with potentially greater cost savings (Ham and Robinson 1988). Income generation from the public as consumers has been negligible. The principal sources have been from the sale of services and care to the private sector (Willetts and Goldsmith 1988). No national data are published, but between 1979 and 1989, NHS finance raised from "miscellaneous" sources increased from 0.3 per cent to 1.5 per cent of total. The majority was from capital receipts from the sale of land and buildings (House of Commons, 1990). In 1979-80, £9.9 million was raised from the sale of NHS land and buildings in England, compared with £81.7 million in 1985-86 and £269.1 million in 1988-89, prior to the slump in property values. For many health authorities in 1989, sale of assets was critical to the funding of new capital projects.

Deregulating the Market in Health Care: NHS PLC?

Testing the Water for the Internal Market?: Vouchers for Spectacles

With little public attention, the first most significant changes in the delivery of health care occurred in general ophthalmic services (GOS) provided for Family Practitioner Committees, during Thatcher's second term of office. An internal market was introduced in several stages, reflecting right wing welfare (and education) policies, that the state's involvement in welfare should be reduced merely to funding: providing vouchers to be "cashed in" on the private market.

The gross cost of GOS had risen since 1976, rising particularly sharply to almost £200 million in 1983, when it comprised 1.6 per cent of NHS gross spending (OHE 1989). In December 1984, the government unilaterally ended the opticians' professional monopoly. Other retail outlets were allowed to sell spectacles on prescription. The reforms went further in July 1986, when the NHS stopped supplying spectacles. Contracts with dispensing opticians were abolished, opticians being the first professional group to be forced to survive solely in the private market. Vouchers were introduced for those eligible for free spectacles, to be used at any supplier who would accept them. In July 1988, the voucher scheme was extended to contact lenses. High street retailers, including one major pharmaceutical chain with specialist optician shops, now dispense spectacles, the more flamboyant of which advertise on television, emphasizing the speed of their dispensing service. This pilot commodification of health care is all but complete.

The 1987 Health Service Review

The 1987 Conservative manifesto heralded none of the imminent NHS reforms. The Conservatives won the election despite growing public concern about underfunding of the NHS. Indeed, the NHS was so central to the 1987 election campaign, that hospital consultants who supported Conservative party policy appeared on their hustings (in one notable case, retracting his support a few months later). Hardly had Thatcher begun her third term, however, when the storm brooding over the NHS broke. Cases hit the headlines of children being denied heart surgery for lack of beds and specialist nursing staff. In December, the Presidents of the three medical Royal Colleges published a "statement of unprecedented and blistering criticism" of the government's handling of the NHS (Leathard 1990: p. 129). Nurses were increasingly militant and vociferous in their campaign for improved pay and conditions, instituting a strict work to rule in some hospitals.

Despite the damaging organizational legacy of recent reorganizations, the government announced a review of the NHS. There was no indication as to who would be involved. Consultation and consensus had been consigned to the dustbin. The White Paper *Working for Patients* was published in January 1989 (Secretaries of State 1989). In characteristic political style, the government's Achilles heel had been turned to political advantage. Sidestepping the question of adequacy of funding, far-reaching changes in the organization and management of health services were proposed. Notably thin on detail, the White Paper proposed an internal market in the NHS. By implication, culpability for the crisis in NHS was placed firmly at the door of state monopoly of provision.

The rhetoric of the proposed reforms was of putting patients first, increased consumer choice and decentralization (Secretaries of State 1989). In reality, the government was proposing changes which would, at a stroke, increase its political control. Seven key measures were proposed, for the implementation of which £69 million was allocated in 1989-90, and a further £110 million in 1990-91 (House of Commons, 1990). First, as much power and responsibility as possible would be delegated to the local level. Regional Health Authorities would be maintained "to ensure that Government policies are properly carried out within their Regions" (Secretaries of State 1989: p. 13). General management was to be introduced into the Family Practitioner Services, with local FPCs accountable to Regions (arguably to ensure tighter control), rather than direct to the Department of Health.

Second, self-governing NHS Hospital Trusts would be established, which would sell their services to health authorities who placed contracts with them. Reflecting the government's general policy of abolishing national agreements on pay and conditions of employment, local flexibility would be encouraged. NHS Trusts would employ their own staff and would not be bound by national pay review bodies. Unlike health authorities which were required to stay within cash limits, Trusts would be free to manage temporary deficits. In April 1991, 57 hospitals and health service units opted out of local health authority control in the first wave of NHS Trusts.

Third, appropriate finance would "follow" patients crossing administrative boundaries for treatment, so that one health authority would charge another for the provision of care. Fourth, perhaps as a ploy to minimize medical resistance to the proposals, 100 new consultant posts were to be created, thereby reducing waiting times and junior doctors' long working hours. Fifth, large general practices (over 11,500 patients) would hold their own budgets and purchase a defined range of services direct from hospitals. General practitioners not holding their own budgets would "be encouraged" to refer patients to hospitals with which the health authority had placed contracts.

Sixth, smaller NHS management bodies would replace health authorities. Executive and non-executive directors appointed by the Secretary of State would be selected for their personal skills and experience. The faint concession to local accountability, in the shape of health authority members appointed directly by local authorities, was removed.* No other constituencies, such as professional groups or voluntary bodies had rights of representation. Seventh, quality of service and value for money would be "more rigorously" audited by the Audit Commission. Quality of care in general practice was to be more closely monitored by peer review medical audits, and the introduction of targets for immunization and cervical screening rates, below which payment would not be made. Indicative drug budgets would be set for each general practitioner. Those who "persistently refuse to curb excessive prescribing" would be subject to financial penalties.

Several other changes were proposed in general practice. Market mechanisms and greater competition would promote quality of care. In a significant challenge to professional traditions and etiquette, GPs were to be encouraged to advertise, and patients would find it easier to change doctors. The capitation fee paid for each patient registered on a doctor's list would increase in significance from 46 to 60 per cent of a GP's budget, so that GP's finances were more directly affected by consumers exercising choice. In effect, an invisible voucher system was proposed, in which patients would be encouraged to shop around with their capitation fee in hand, seeking the best quality of care.

The role of the private sector was again emphasized. More services would be contracted out to the private sector. Echoing measures taken in tendering for ancillary services, DHAs would be charged depreciation and interest for the use of existing capital assets and any future capital investment, since the private sector had to raise finance on "normal, commercial" markets. The revenue and capital potential of surplus property was also highlighted, and NHS Trusts would be able to dispose of assets transferred to them from the NHS.

Conclusion

Thatcher's programme for the health service achieved some of its stated aims. Unit costs were reduced to the extent that the proportion of GNP spent on health care (public and private) is all but the lowest in the industrialized world. More health care incidents are being "processed" each day, with significant yet invisible cost shifting on to the community, and people's families, particularly their female kin. The direct cost of the NHS to the state has therefore been reduced in the short term, but the longer term implications for the health of the population of unmet need and increased throughput yet to be identified, just as the health consequences of other social and economic policies have yet to emerge.

The programme to reduce the role of the state in the funding and provision of health care has not, however, been without its contradictions. The rhetoric has been of local autonomy, accountability to the people and reduction of state involvement, but the reality has been very different. The principal ideological and practical reforms: general management in 1983 and the internal market in 1989 were introduced without legitimation from the electorate. Consultation has been short-circuited, with reforms introduced wholesale, without piloting or validation. Although consumerism has been actively promoted by central government, health service users' collective rights of representation have been eroded. The only power which service users may now exercise will be as individuals, with token purchasing power which will be strictly circumscribed by health authorities' contracts for the provision of care. Guidance from the DHSS to district health authorities has, where the introduction of market mechanisms have been involved, been replaced by directives and requirements. General management and the annual review process have served to concentrate and increase central political control of the public health care sector.

Nor has the Conservatives' agenda been without its ironies. Private contractors showed tempered interest in tendering for domestic, catering and laundry services, and argued against the erosion of established deregulation of pay and conditions. The market has not only apparently reached its limits in the provision of support services: private medical insurance has not been embraced by the numbers of people anticipated. New subscribers have not been individuals "taking responsibility" for their own health care: an increasing proportion have been offered insurance by their employers. In its haste to reduce local and national state involvement in the direct *provision* of institutional and community care for elderly people and others needing care, the government generated an exponential growth in social security spending on the expensive option of residential and nursing homes. Attempts to generate income from the commercialization of hospital premises and the provision of support (now "hotel") services have largely foundered.

The political restructuring of the health service has, however, challenged paternalism and exclusive professionalism in the NHS which Aneurin Bevan chose not to confront in 1944, lest he should lose vital medical co-operation. The introduction of the market processes and terminology constitutes a fundamental challenge to the culture of health care in the UK, "cheapening" and "debasing" a myth of the honourable interaction between professional and client. Clinicians are now called to account for the expenditure, in a way which was previously unthinkable. The rationing of health care in Britain is, therefore, now much more explicit, rather than masked in professional mystique. As waiting lists grow, and budgets are increasingly constrained, health care will be rationed on the basis of ability to pay for extras and to travel for treatment.

Thatcher will have "rolled back the state" in welfare provision, but she will also have turned back the clock to the prewar era of two-tier services, in which social divisions and fragmentations within the working class were reflected in health and access to health care. Within constrained budgets, health authority spending will be allocated first to the purchase of "glamorous" high-technology acute services. Those considered key to economic production will have care purchased for them by employers' group insurance schemes. However, when budgets are tight, those seen as formally unproductive who need continuing care rather than acute treatment may well be left with inadequate care or no care at all.

References

Ascher, K. (1987) *The Politics of Privatisation.* Macmillan, London.

Audit Commission (1986) *Making a Reality of Community Care.* HMSO, London.

Beale, N. and Nethercott, S. (1985) Job-loss and family morbidity: a study of a factory closure, *Jnl Royal Coll. Gen. Prac.* **35**: 510-514.

Birch, S. and Maynard, A. (1988) Performance indicators. In Maxwell, R. (ed.) *Reshaping the National Health Service*, pp. 51-64. Policy Journals, Hermitage, Berks.

Bosanquet, N. (1988) An ailing state of national health. In Jowell, R. Witherspoon, S. and Brook, *British Social Attitudes. The 5th Report*, pp. 93-108. Social and Community Planning Research and Gower Press, Aldershot.

Central Statistical Office (CSO) (1990) *Social Trends 1990.* HMSO, London.

Coles, J. (1988) Clinical budgeting as a management tool. In Maxwell, R. (ed.) *Reshaping the National Health Service*, pp. 126-137. Policy Journals, Hermitage, Berks.

Department of Health and Social Security (DHSS) (1979a) *Patients First. Consultative Paper on the NHS in England and Wales.* HMSO, London.

Department of Health and Social Security (DHSS) (1979b) *Pay and Conditions of Service Contracts of Consultants and Other Senior Hospital Medical and Dental Staff* (PM(79)11). Department of Health and Social Security, London.

Department of Health and Social Security (DHSS) (1980a) *Inequalities in Health. Report of a Research Working Group.* (The Black Report). Department of Health and Social Security, London.

Department of Health and Social Security (DHSS) (1980b) *Health Services Development. Health Services Act 1980: Private Practice in Health Service Hospitals and Control of Private Hospital Developments. Amenity Beds.* (HC(80)10). Department of Health and Social Security, London.

Department of Health and Social Security (DHSS) (1981) *Health Services Management: Contractual Arrangements with Independent Hospitals and Nursing Homes.* (HC(81)1). Department of Health and Social Security, London.

Department of Health and Social Security (DHSS) (1982) *Health Services Development. Resources Assumptions and Planning Guidelines.* HC(82)14. Department of Health and Social Security, London.

Department of Health and Social Security (DHSS) (1983a) *Health Services Development. Resources Allocations for 1983-84.* Department of Health and Social Security, London.

Department of Health and Social Security (DHSS) (1983b) *Health Services Development. Cash Limits and Manpower Targets for 1983-84.* HC(83)16. Department of Health and Social Security, London.

Department of Health and Social Security (DHSS) (1983c) *NHS Management Inquiry.* (Griffiths Report). Department of Health and Social Security, London.

Department of Health and Social Security (DHSS) (1983d) *Health Services Management: Competitive Tendering in the Provision of Domestic. Catering and Laundry Services* HC(83)18. Department of Health and Social Security, London.

Department of Health and Social Security (DHSS) (1984) *Implementation of the NHS Management Inquiry Report* HC(84)13. Department of Health and Social Security, London.

Department of Health and Social Security (DHSS) (1985) *Health and Personal Social Services Statistics for England.* Department of Health and Social Security, London.

Department of Health and Social Security (DHSS) (1986) *Implementation of the Resource Management Initiative* HN(86)34. Department of Health and Social Security, London.

Department of Health (DH) (1989) *Health and Personal Social Services Statistics for England.* Department of Health, London.

Department of Health (DH) (1990) *Health and Personal Social Services Statistics for England.* Department of Health, London.

Department of Health (DH) (1989) *Working for Patients.* Cmd 555.

Fagin, L. and Little, M. (1984) *The Forgotten Families: The Effects of Unemployment on Family Life.* Penguin, Harmondsworth.

Finch, J. (1989) *Family Obligations and Social Change.* Polity Press.

Finch, J., and Groves, D. (eds.) (1983) *Labour of Love: Women, Work and Caring.* Routledge & Kegan Paul.

Goffman, E. (1961) *Asylum: Essays on the Social Situation of Mental Patients and Other Inmates.* Doubleday, New York.

Graham, H. (1985) *Women, Health and the Family.* Wheatsheaf, Brighton.

Graham, H. (1987) Women's smoking and family health, *Soc. Sci. Med.* **25**: 47-56.

Grieco, M., Pickup, L., and Whipp, R. (eds.) *Gender, Transport and Employment.* Avebury Press, Aldershot.

Griffiths, R. (1988) *Community Care. An Agenda for Action.* HMSO, London.

Ham, C. (1985) *Health Policy in Britain,* 2nd edition. Macmillan, London.

Ham, C., and Robinson, R. (1988) National Health Service plc, *New Society,* 19 February, pp. 11-12.

Hamilton, K., and Jenkins, L. (1989) Why women and travel? In Grieco, M., Pickup, L. and Whipp, R. (eds.) *Gender. Transport and Employment,* pp. 17-45 Avebury Press, Aldershot.

Harrison, S. (1988) The workforce and the new managerialism. In Maxwell, R. (ed.) *Reshaping the National Health Service,* pp. 141-152. Policy Journals, Hermitage, Berks.

Higgins, J. (1988) *The Business of Medicine: Private Health Care in Britain.* Macmillan.

Hosking, D. (1989) Organising the domestic portfolio: gender and skill. In Grieco, M., Pickup, L. and Whipp, R. (eds.) *Gender. Transport and Employment,* pp. 115-126. Avebury Press, Aldershot.

House of Commons Public Accounts Committee (1981) *17th Report. Financial Control and Accountability in the National Health Service.* HCP 255, Session 1980-81.

House of Commons Social Services Committee (1987) *Public Expenditure on the*

Social Services. Memorandum Received from the Department of Health and Social Security. HCP 413, Session 1986-87.

House of Commons Social Services Committee (1990) *Public Expenditure on Health Matters. Memorandum Received from the Department of Health and Social Security*. HCP 484, Session 1989-90.

Illich, I. (1974) *Medical Nemesis: the Expropriation of Health*. Calders and Boyers, London.

Illich, I. (1976) *Limits to Medicine*. Calders and Boyers, London.

Jowell, R., Witherspoon, S., and Brook, L. (1988) *British Social Attitudes. The 5th Report*. Social and Community Planning Research and Gower Press, Aldershot.

Laing, W. (1985) *Private Health Care 1985*. Office of Health Economics, London.

Leathard, A. (1990) *Health Care Provision. Past, Present and Future*. Chapman & Hall, London.

Lee, M. (1980) Charting the growth of the private health provident associations, *Medeconomics*, 11 April 1980.

Maxwell, R. (ed.) (1988) *Reshaping the National Health Service*. Policy Journals, Hermitage, Berks.

Maynard, A., and Bosanquet, N. (1986) *Public Expenditure on the NHS: Recent Trends and Future Problems*. Institute of Health Services Management, London.

Mohan, J., and Woods, K. (1985) Restructuring health care: the social geography of public and private health care under the British Conservative government, *Intl Jnl Health Serv.* **15** (2): 197-215.

Moser, K., Fox, A.J., Jones, D.R., and Goldblatt, P.O. (1986a) Unemployment and mortality: further evidence from the OPCS longitudinal study 1971-81, *Lancet*, (**i**): 365-367.

Moser, K., Goldblatt, P. Q., Fox, A.J., and Jones, D.R. (1986b) Unemployment and mortality: comparison of the 1971 and 1981 longitudinal study census samples, *BMJ*, **294**: 86-90.

National Audit Office (NAO) (1985) *National Health Service: Control of Nursing Manpower*. HCP 558, Session 1984-85.

National Audit Office (NAO) (1986) *Value for Money Developments in the National Health Service*. HCP 212, Session 1985-86.

National Audit Office (NAO) (1987a) *Community Care Development*. HCP 108, Session 1978-88.

National Audit Office (NAO) (1987b) *Competitive Tendering for Support Services in the National Health Service*. HCP 318, Session 1986-87.

Parston, G. (1988) General management. In Maxwell, R. (ed.) *Reshaping the National Health Service*, pp. 15-34. Policy Journals, Hermitage, Berks.

Pearson, M. (1990) Will the primary care reforms work? Paper presented to Annual Conference of the BSA Medical Sociology Group, Edinburgh, September.

Pearson, M., and Spencer, S. (1989) *Awareness and Use of Well Woman Services in Liverpool*. Occasional Paper No. 1, Department of General Practice, University of Liverpool.

Pearson, M., Dawson, C., Brown, P., and Dodgson, J., (1990) *Transport and Access to Health Services*. Transport and Urban Deprivation Working Paper 3, University of Liverpool.

Pearson, M., and Grieco, M. (1991) Spatial mobility begins at home? Re-thinking inter-household organisation (forthcoming).

Perrin, J. (1988) *Resource Management in the NHS* Van Nostrand Reinhold, Wokingham.

Radical Statistics Health Group (RSHG) (1987) *Facing the Figures. What is Really Happening to the National Health Service*? Radical Statistics, London.

Royal Commission on the National Health Service (1979) *Report*. Cmnd 7615, HMSO, London.

Office of Health Economics (OHE) (1989) *Compendium of Health Statistics*, 7th edition. OHE, London.

Secretaries of State for Health, Wales, Northern Ireland and Scotland (1989) *Working for Patients*. Cmnd 555. HMSO, London.

Small, N. (1989) *Politics and Planning in the National Health Service*. Open University Press, Milton Keynes.

Taylor, D. (1988) Primary care services. In Maxwell, R. (ed.) *Reshaping the National Health Service*, pp. 35-47. Policy Journals, Hermitage, Berks.

Thunhurst, C. (1982) *It Makes You Sick. The Politics of the NHS*. Pluto Press.

Ungerson, C. (1987) *Policy is Personal: Sex, Gender and Informal Care*. Tavistock.

Whitehead, M. (1988) *The Health Divide*. Health Education Council, London.

Whitelegg, J. (1982) *Inequalities in Health. Problems of Access and Provision*. Straw Barnes Press, Retford.

Willetts, D., and Goldsmith, M. (1988) *A Mixed Economy in Health Care—More Spending, Save Taxes*. Centre for Policy Studies, London.

Wistow, G. (1988) Off-loading responsibilities for care. In Maxwell, R. (ed.) *Reshaping the National Health Service*, pp. 153-170. Policy Journals, Hermitage, Berks.

Yuen, P., and Balarajan, R. (1989) Unemployment and patterns of consultation with the general practitioner, *BMJ*, **298**: 1212-1214.

Zola, I.K. (1972) Medicine as an institution of social control, *Sociological Review* (new series) **20**: 487-504.

10

The City

David Byrne

Introduction

Immediately after her election victory in 1987 Mrs Thatcher announced: "Now we must do something about the inner cities." This chapter deals with the policy response to that statement, with the set of programmes drawn together as *Action for Cities* in 1988. There is actually little new in those programmes. One element dates back to the Labour White Paper on *Policy for the Inner Cities* of 1978 and the most important and significant innovation of the Thatcher years, Urban Development Corporations, were introduced by that early catch-all piece of Thatcherite (and Heseltineite) legislation, the Local Government, Planning and Land Act of 1980. *Action for Cities* was a consolidating statement which drew together policies in a formal way. These policies had already had a profound effect in combination in practice, literally on the ground. Something was being done "about" the inner cities. The question is, was it being done "for" them or "to" them? The answer to that revolves around the distinction, and possible confrontation, between policies for inner city people and policies for inner city land.

Other chapters in this book deal with local government (as the local state), planning, transport and housing. All these intersect in "the city". However, since the late 1960s government has been involved with a particular set of problems having to do with the perceived decline of cities in general and their "inner cities" in particular. This latter, qualified, term "inner city" has only limited value as a way of specifying the location of "city" problems. Some of the worst urban conditions are located on "outer estates" which are on or beyond the boundaries of cities. However, it has considerable historical value because wherever the people affected by "inner city" policies actually live today, they or their parents came from the areas of working class housing which were in the centre of cities and worked in the factories, shipyards, docks and railways which surrounded them. These people may not now be in the inner city, but they are of the inner city. Indeed, to a considerable degree, they have been sent from the inner city by policies in that earlier era which Cooke (1987) has described as one of "modernization". To continue with Cooke's terminology, this chapter deals with urban conditions and policies in the era of "post-modernization".

Of course the situation of city people and of the land on which they lived and worked is not just a consequence of policy. Developments in the world capitalist system have had profound effects for "localities" (see Cooke *et al.* 1989), which have been transformed by the impact of a restructuring of the internal content and spatial arrangements of production. Policies have operated in a context set by these changes and, to some extent, are responses to them. A central argument of this chapter will be that policies, both the "post-modernization" policies of the Thatcher era and the earlier policies of modernization, have been rather more important than most recent theoretical discussions of these issues have allowed. The condition of our cities and of the people who live in them derives in large part from specific macroeconomic policies which affected the general condition of British manufacturing industry in the early 1980s.

The argument can be taken further. It is not just a matter of policy having an independent effect. The mesoeconomic spatial policies of the modernization era have to be understood as permitting the impact "global restructuring" has had on British cities. They had creative force and the post-modernization policies of the Thatcher era have equal creative potential. These policies make things happen. They shape what is to come. They do not do so independently of the world capitalist system but within the wide boundaries determined (see Williams 1980) by the nature of that system, they have specific impacts and set a frame for other developments. Other policies might have very different results. It is not all written!

This chapter will proceed by defining "cities", giving a brief account of changes in the economic and social structure of cities since 1971, and, simultaneously, reviewing some concepts which help in understanding those changes. It will then turn to the urban policies of the Thatcher government, not in terms of descriptive detail, for which see Lawless (1989), but taken together as an active programme of social change.

Change in the Cities

The United Kingdom is not a rural society. By any international definition the overwhelming majority of its population lives in urban settings and this has been the case longer than for any other nation state. However, not all urban contexts are cities. The most general of the policies which form part of *Action for Cities* operates in 57 selected urban areas in England. The first specification is that this chapter is about the urban policies of the Thatcher era as they have operated in England. The Northern Ireland, Scottish and Welsh Offices have been outposts of wet "one-nation" Toryism in exile. Belfast and Glasgow are cities by any criteria, but they have not been subject to the same intensity of Thatcherite pressure as have the English cities. It is simply not true to say:

> . . . major British Cities are unique in Western Europe (perhaps in the world) in having no city-wide governing bodies or elected councils (Fielding and Haltend 1990: p. 52)

although the statement would be perfectly accurate if the word "British" were replaced by "English". When Healey *et al.* assert that:

> It is in the older industrial city areas that the challenge and contradiction of the ideology of the Thatcher administration is at its most acute, since it demands both a reduction in state spending, and a return to private investment to achieve urban regeneration (1988: p. 8)

the statement is less true for Glasgow than it is for Newcastle. So this chapter is about England, a distinction made as much to remind readers that there are other parts of the United Kingdom, and they deserve at least the recognition of explicit exclusion, as for any other reason. The peripheral cities have a different recent history.

What is a city? In England one criterion is administrative form. There is a distinction between the areas covered by the six Metropolitan countries and the GLC on the one hand and the shire counties on the other. Clearly the people who live in Manchester, Leeds, Gateshead, Knowsley, Sandwell, Lambeth, etc., do live in cities, but what about Middlesbrough, Plymouth, Nottingham, Bristol? Are they not cities? For one purpose they may be. Of the 57 selected urban areas covered by the "Urban Programme" 16 are not in the areas of Metropolitan counties or the GLC. Four of these are in Cleveland County in which every district is a programme authority and has an essentially urban core. Likewise, Avon centred on the city of Bristol is really a single city plus suburbs shire county. For the purposes of this chapter these two shire counties will be included with the cities, whereas Nottingham, Leicester, Southampton and so on will not be. Both Cleveland and Avon have UDCs and are the only non-Metropolitan county's so favoured, so their inclusion is further justified. However, any distinction is arbitrary and involves a cut on a continuum rather than the specification of a precise typology.

What has happened to English cities in the recent past? The first evident trend is the loss of industrial employment (which includes manufacturing, mining, construction, water and energy supply). In the Metropolitan counties (Tyne and Wear, Greater Manchester, West and South Yorkshire, Merseyside and West Midlands) and in Cleveland there has been a large absolute decline in employment and the proportionate share of this smaller total represented by industrial employment was much less in 1987. These "industrial cities" lost nearly 1.2 million industrial jobs over the 16 years or over 40 per cent of the original total. There was some compensation by increased service employment but this was associated with a shift from full time to part time and from male to female employment, both of which are associated with much lower total and hourly wage remuneration.

The GLC area and Avon also deindustrialized, although from a smaller original proportion who were industrially employed. However, London is so big that it lost more industrial jobs than any other city, despite the proportionately lesser significance of industrial employment for it. It is worth noting that in 1971 London was about as industrial a city as Cleveland is today. Avon is unique in that it increased its overall volume of employment over the period.

All English cities, except Avon, lost population over the period. This was in part due to the adoption in the 1974 reform of English local government of the majority report of the Redcliffe Maude Commission (1969) instead of Senior's minority report which argued for city regions. Much of the population was located in new suburban development over the Metropolitan and GLC boundaries. This is particularly true of the relationship between London and the Outer Metropolitan Area but it applies more generally. For example, Chester-le-Street District in County Durham, which is immediately adjacent to Tyne and Wear, has had a population increase of more than 20 per cent over the period despite an almost absolute disappearance of any industrial base. If England had city regions on the Scottish model this would not pose the major problems it does for service provision and planning.

The cities have deindustrialized and simultaneously become residualized. This latter term has Victorian origins in the use of the word "residuum" to describe what contemporary theorists (see Bauman 1987, Dahrendorf 1987) usually call the "underclass". The implications of these terms will be returned to in the next section, but the idea of people and places having been left behind is an important one and that is what the notion of the residualization of the cities conveys.

To understand the process of residualization and the policies which contributed to it and have responded to it, it is necessary to reflect on the role of cities in society. Before the industrial/urban revolution cities were locations of trade, government and consumption. Well before the industrial era some, including London, had enormous populations employed in relation to these functions. Proponents of the "world cities" account, derived from Wallerstein's discussion of a world system of capitalism as a set of trading relations which precede the establishment of industrial capitalism, point to the continuing significance of these functions to which has been added the control function of transnational corporations (see King 1989). They identify a set of "world cities" which are . . . the cotter pins holding the capitalist world economy together" (Feagin 1987: p.4). Friedmann and Wolff define world cities as:

> . . . the principal urban regions in this (global) network (of production and markets) in which most of the world's active capital comes to be concentrated, regions which play a vital part in the great capitalist undertaking to organize the world for the efficient extraction of surplus . . . the world economy is defined by a linked set of markets and production units, organized and controlled by transnational capital; world cities are the material manifestation of this control, occurring exclusively in core and semi-peripheral regions where they serve as banking and financial centres, administrative headquarters, centres of ideological control and so forth (1982: p.313).

By this criterion London is a world city. The other English cities which were part of the world trade system before large-scale industrialization, Liverpool and Bristol, have responded very differently to the changes in that system which have reduced the significance of trans-Atlantic trade. Liverpool has lost its "world" status in shipping, insurance and banking. Bristol has developed a substitute industrial base underpinned by UK state defence expenditures (see Boddy 1989).

The remaining English cities were never world cities in a trading sense. They were primarily industrial. The archetype of the industrial city was early nineteenth-century Manchester. This was the city as location of production with an enormous resident industrial proletariat. Cities were integrated locations of production and reproduction. This was not just a matter of the integration of production with the reproduction of labour power through consumption, but also involved detailed integration of the processes of production themselves. This was characterized by "city speciality" in production, sustaining complexes of mutually related industrial enterprises which were generally locally developed and controlled. Tyne and Wear built ships (a derivative of the requirements of coal shipping) and had a marine manufacturing complex, which later spun off a power generation manufacturing complex. Leeds had an integrated clothing industry. Birmingham bashed metal for the world. Of course there was diversity within such industrial cities, but they represented specific and specialized nodes of organization for capitalist production.

A working definition of an "industrial city" is that it was such a node (in practice in the nineteenth and early twentieth centuries often taking the form of a set of linked industrial towns rather than a city in terms of a continuous built-up area) with all the organs of circulation and administration necessary for the maintenance of its workforce. Urry has identified the present situation of cities as involving ". . . not so much and interlocking economy of producing and consuming enterprises but a *community of subjects* (original emphasis) who produce and consume in order to produce" (1985: p. 35). In this view cities are now merely labour pools which connect with a capitalism which is integrated on a world basis and do so in a differentiated and fragmented way.

In understanding the origins of this change it is useful to employ a modified version of Cooke's (1987) distinction between the era from 1945 to 1975 which he describes as an era of "modernization" and the period since 1975 which is one of "post-modernization". In essence Cooke is looking at modernization as the implementation of a general set of social and economic policies which derived from the Keynes–Beveridge consensus. He refers to a "new kind of mechanical solidarity" involving a commitment to full employment, regional development and welfare state provision.

This seems a very reasonable summary of the immediate

postwar mood, but it might be preferable to associate the term "modernization" with departures from this model in the early 1960s. These began under the Macmillan–Home administration, especially in relation to the intervention of the then Quintin Hogg as Minister for the North East with a brief to handle the consequences of the run down of mining. However, the real "modernizing" administration was that of Wilson elected in 1964, looking to the "white hot heat of the technological revolution". It was this administration which abandoned the absolute commitment to full employment in order to facilitate an economic restructuring of a Britain which was falling behind Europe and Japan. The tool of modernization was to be indicative planning. The combination of planning objectives of modernization with housing objectives dating from the postwar era of social solidarity transformed the spatial and tenurial relations of England's industrial cities. Much of the inner city working class was moved to the periphery, to outer estates (see CES 1985).

At the same time, and particularly in London where outer estate development was prevented by the hostility of Outer London boroughs to overspill development from inner areas, new forms of "modernist" housing, Dunleavy's "mass housing" of "large flatted estates of a kind never built for the market" (1982: p. 1), were constructed on cleared sites. These "technical fix" solutions to housing problems were justified in terms of high land costs on inner city sites, although mass housing was frequently built on peripheral green field locations, e.g. Killingworth in Tyne and Wear (see Byrne and Parson 1983). The spatial change was considerable. The slum cleared, because after 1957 social housing was not for general needs, were moved in space and from a private renting system to the public sector. At the same time "the disappearing waiting lists" of those seeking general needs housing for new household formation and movement gained access to the new cheap and usually peripheral housing built by the new breed of developer builders.

The inner city working class housing which remained, typically, the best of artisan by-law housing from the late nineteenth and early twentieth century, was retained by the shift from clearance to improvement from early 1960s onwards. It is often asserted that much of this stock was gentrified. This is certainly true in particular places, e.g. Islington, but it would be better to say that the filtration process was to some degree reversed, and this older housing became the location particularly of the state employees who play a similar social, if not economic, function to skilled workers (whose children and grandchildren they largely are) in earlier periods.

The best co-ordinated aspects of this modernization were in the second generation of new towns where industrial and service development was integrated with both private and public sector housing construction. However, most of the urban outer estates were built just as labour pool reservoirs with little planned associated industrial development. The late 1960s and early 1970s were a period of enormous change in England's cities as these plans were implemented. Vast areas of housing were cleared. Urban motorways were constructed. Major population movements occurred. This was not a particularly democratic period. The plans were typically corporatist both in terms of development and in content. Planners (in the wider sense which includes politicians as well as professionals) were powerful and seemed to reign supreme.

This period produced a critical literature which emphasized the negative distributional effects of planning decisions (see Dennis 1972). The UK literature emphasized the role of planners themselves, the "evangelistic bureaucrats". Similar US literature also recognized the role of real estate—finance capital coalitions in "urban renewal" and coined the term "manipulated city" to describe the process. One difference between the UK and the US was the combination in peripheral regions of the UK of regional and urban development policies. City plans were parts of a programme of economic restructuring. This was happening simultaneously with changes in production processes. Cooke (1987) identifies the significance of the expansion of the "semi-skilled" occupational roles for both men and women in industrial production. In general the period was one of growth and change.

There is a developed and already cited literature in the "geography of production" which deals with the impact of global restructuring on particular places. The general line of argument is well summarized by Hill and Feagin:

> . . . answers to questions about a city's political-economic future are to be found as much beyond as within its local boundaries. Cities are spatial locations in a globally dependent system of production and exchange. That global system is in crisis and transition. So the path that a city follows in the future will depend upon the niche that it comes to occupy in a changing international division of labour (1987: p. 148).

This can be described as the internationalist position. It deals with changes at the level of the world space economy and the general line of argument is summarized in Massey (1984).

These processes have been of enormous significance for UK cities. Changes in the global division of labour have resulted in the wholesale loss of industrial sectors from UK cities to other production locations, particularly in the "newly industrializing countries". These processes were well underway in the 1970s. In addition, the general tendency towards increased productivity in manufacturing industry, the maturation factor (see Rowthorn and Martin 1986), was also reducing the volume of industrial jobs.

Thus the scene is almost set for the impact of Thatcherism. The only missing element is the policy context. That, however, is very important. Cooke's picking of 1975 as the date for the termination of the era of modernization is exactly right. The "cuts" introduced in 1975 in response to IMF demands marked the end of an era of growth in social and economic intervention. From then onwards local government was not to be again a change agent transforming cities through major planning programmes. In the more general economic context, mesoeconomic planning, in which control over a large part of production in the form of nationalized industries was to play a major part, was no longer a policy option or commitment. 1975 saw the end of a period when the political culture was one claiming an effective capacity to intervene. Callaghan marked this with his explicit abandonment of Keynsian macroeconomic policies as the key mechanism for government activity. There was a vacuum to be filled.

It was in the era of modernization that "cities" were recognized as a specific policy problem. Concern is usually dated from the establishment of Community Development Projects in the late 1960s in response to Enoch Powell's visions of "the river foaming with blood". This raises an issue of change in some, but not all, English cities. In West Yorkshire, the West Midlands, Avon and Greater London, labour shortages led to massive 1950s immigration of black people from the new commonwealth. This ethnic issue was seen as crucial to problems of urban disintegration and unrest and was to be the background to major disturbances of the early 1980s (see Scarman 1982). However, other English cities received minimal immigration, although Liverpool had an existing and very disadvantaged black minority. For the purposes of discussion here the position of black people will be understood as being that of a particularly disadvantaged part of the city working class. This is a simplification, but in relation to city change and city policy, it is not an over-simplification.

The CDPs were an imitation of US programmes under the Ford Foundation grey areas and Johnson administration anti-poverty projects (see Marris and Rein 1967). Such projects had been underpinned by the concept of a separate "culture of poverty" which offered an explanation of the exclusion of the poor from the increasing affluence of wider society in terms of the cultural incapacity to participate in that society. It was a subtle way of blaming poverty on the poor. Lawless summarizes the experience of CDPs and the subsequent Inner Area Studies:

> In essence the Inner Area Studies and CDPs concluded that the residents in the areas they were examining were not on the whole inadequate or deficient. There was nothing unique about the areas they were studying. They suffered from the same kind of problems as other inner urban localities, and these problems essentially revolved around issues of economic decline, a contraction in employment opportunities and diminishing individual and community wealth (1988: p. 532).

This is not quite the whole story. Another theme of this period was that of the failure of urban government in terms of administrative integration. This was a UK variant of US Federal attempts to interfere in municipal affairs, and "co-ordination" centred programmes, although dismissed as irrelevant by most CDPs, were an important part of 1970s Labour urban policy in the form of CCPs (Co-ordinated Community Programmes which came to little) and Inner City Partnerships which survive as part of the Urban Programme.

A common interpretation of developments in the early 1970s is that the CDPs in a strident and Marxist way sought to give central government a message which more diplomatically presented by Inner Area Studies was to be the basis of the 1977 White Paper on the Inner Cities and of the subsequent 1978 Act. This message was that of the absolute significance of industrial decline. As a CDP worker in this period, I remember things rather differently. The CDP publication with that message *The Costs of Industrial Change* (1976) was received without much fuss. What caused all the bother was *Cutting the Welfare State* (1976) which documented the effects of cuts in public expenditure on the localities in which the CDPs were located. It was all right to blame the anonymous forces of the capitalist system. Blaming governments for policies was quite another matter!

Be this as it may, the 1978 *Inner Urban Areas Act*, which still forms the basis of the Urban Programme, was really little more than a device through which some of the cuts in general social public expenditure might be restored in specific high priority places. It paid lip service to the need for economic regeneration and allowed the allocation of fairly minimal resources to it, but that was about all.

Thus the situation in 1979 was one of vacuum. There was a vacuum in policy and there was a developing vacuum in space. The cities were in a situation of suspended change. Planning had run out of steam. Land was vacant and much more was to become vacant as manufacturing industry reeled under the impact of exchange rate policies in the early Thatcher years. The cities were ripe for something. What were they to get?

Thatcher's Cities

The first thing they got was massive unemployment. There was indeed a world recession, but as Therborn pointed out in *Why some peoples are more unemployed than others* (1985) the relatively high unemployment in the UK as compared with other industrial countries owed a great deal to a specific economic experiment. J. K. Galbraith remarked that it was as well that these new rightist nostrums were being tried on the British because no other people would put up with them without a revolution. The effect was the generation of 3 million unemployed in the UK economy. Much of the discussion of localities (Cooke 1989, Harloe *et al.* 1990) and regions (Hudson 1989) has emphasized the impact of these developments on local economies taken as a whole. However, cities now relate to the world system in a fragmented rather than unitary fashion. Hill and Feagin say: "In the era of regional competition there is no longer one Detroit or two Detroits. There are many Detroits" (1987: p. 167). This is a description of the process of social differentiation, the post-modernization move from the more equal society of the era of modernization.

The theme is often expressed in terms of social polarization. One vivid account is that of the "fourth world" (see Harrison 1984) in which the conditions of the urban poor in British cities are compared with those of the stagnant reserve armies of the third world. This fourth world is described by CES in their report on "outer estates":

> These communities are sinking to a kind of subsistence level, where there is little cash circulating, no effective land market, little demand for consumer goods and little competition between shops (1985: p. 1).

Harrison compared the social distance between Hackney and Hampstead (non-gentrified Hackney) to a spatial distance of halfway round the world. This theme is now more generally expressed through discussions of the nature of an "underclass". As with the idea of "culture of poverty" in the 1960s, this is an American import. To a considerable degree it is simply a revival of that earlier concept, although some contributors (see Wilson 1989), whilst specifically rejecting simple culturalist conceptions of cause and firmly assigning primacy in explaining the contemporary condition of the urban poor to the effects of capitalist restructuring, nonetheless recognize the new extremely segregated condition of the contemporary urban (and in the US, particularly black urban) poor. Bauman has produced the most pessimistic account of these non-citizens:

> . . . the poor are less and less important to the reproduction of capital in their traditional role as the "reserve army of labour". They are no longer the object of concern for the twofold task of recommodification of labour and limitation of working class militancy. The previously taken-for-granted principle of social responsibility for the well being—and indeed, the survival—of that part of society not directly engaged by capital as producers has suddenly come under attack (1987: p. 21).

Bauman is wrong about the disappearance of the role of the poor as a reserve army of labour (see Byrne 1989), but his description of exclusion from political concern and potential for political action is accurate.

Thatcher's Urban Programme

The Thatcher government has addressed the city through policies derived from the same basic principles throughout the eighties. These principles are:

(1) Elected local government should have as little control as possible.
(2) Planning is bad and markets are good.
(3) The revival of the cities is the business of the private sector. Government may stimulate and subsidize, but it should not direct.

The hostility to elected local government reflects the increasing inability of the Tories to win control of any level of city government. This hostility was exacerbated by the efforts of some Labour controlled authorities, notably the GLC, Sheffield and some of the Metropolitan counties, to promote "alternative economic strategies" to that of central government. Generally these were meso-economic attempts at indicative planning using resources available under Section 137 of the 1972 Local Government Act. Authorities established "Enterprise Boards" which were local imitations of the venture capital activities of the National Enterprise Board of the previous Labour government. Land development and other activities were supposed to be co-ordinated with this general endeavour, although it is generally true that new initiatives were much more additional and bolt on, rather than involving transformation of the form and objective of existing activities (see Boddy and Fudge 1986).

The hostility to planning reflects the clear and explicit commitment of Thatcher to new right analyses and consequent policies. This commitment has not always been unequivocally supported by ministers. Heseltine, as Secretary of State for the Environment, was very hostile to elected local government but still retained interventionist leanings. However, this internal cabinet dissidence has now been eliminated.

The adherence to the private sector is in part a derivative of the belief in market forces. It is also, to be unfashionable, instrumental, a reflection of the relationship between finance and development capital and the Conservative Party apparatus. There are (or rather in 1990 it would be better to say "were") rich pickings in the cities and they are to go to friends.

Here the focus will be on the aspects of urban policy which clearly reflect this approach and these political commitments. This means that there will be minimal discussion of the Urban Programme, the special resource allocation process which the Tories inherited from their Labour predecessors. This is small in relation to total expenditure by the 57 programme authorities, but it is very important as marginal money which can be used for new developments, whereas most mainstream resources are precommitted to core services. However, the need to renew existing programmes has led to a reduction in this flexibility and Urban Programme as a whole has been redirected towards support for the general programme of urban restructuring represented by the composition of Enterprise Zones and Urban Development Corporations with a set of more detailed grant measures.

Enterprise Zones originated in concept with a proposal made by the prominent planning historian and critic, Peter Hall. In a 1977 speech to the Royal Town Planning Institute he asserted that the successful economies of the 1970s in the pacific rim had achieved that success in no small part due to the absence of planning constraints in them. This was a specific planning orientated version of Milton Friedman's general line on the superiority of free markets and absence of government intervention. The idea was an interesting one because it did in origin seem to be about the revival of manufacturing capitalism by restoring the conditions under which nineteenth-century capitalism had been able to innovate and develop in the UK. The early history of the concept and its translation into operation is given in Anderson (1983) who emphasizes the ideological content of the proposal as anti-planning and locates the idea in a specific intellectual context. Essentially this was one of crude comparative research. There was admiration for the successes of the pacific rim economies which were supposed, erroneously in most cases, to be shining examples of non-interventionism. There was also an obsession with the potential of small firms as the big employing enterprises of the future. Particular attention was paid to some of the companies operating in California's Silicon Valley where a whole new industrial structure seemed to have developed from small enterprises operating free of constraints.

Enterprise Zones were sold to participating (overwhelmingly Labour controlled) city authorities in terms of the claims made for employment creation. Although the key theme of the "experiment" was the reduction in planning controls, a principle continued into the successor "Simplified Planning Zones", there was a reasonably strong implicit suggestion that the zones were intended to provide a basis for the revival of the manufacturing sector. In practice the combination of elimination of planning restrictions and generous tax remission incentives (both through exemption from rates and 100 per cent capital allowances on investment in industrial and commercial buildings) have had varied effects. PA Cambridge Economic Consultants, in an evaluation of the experiment conducted in 1987, concluded that it had led to the creation of 12,680 additional jobs at an average cost of between £23,000 and £30,000 per job, depending on the inclusion or exclusion of construction jobs. As the National Audit Office commented (1989), this was a very high figure compared with other job creation schemes. Of the net additional jobs 18 per cent were in manufacturing.

PA had identified two yardsticks for the evaluation of Enterprise Zones. The first was that of job maintenance and creation as dealt with in the preceding paragraph. The second was:

> The extent to which the zones have contributed to the physical regeneration of their local areas through the provision of infra-structure, environmental improvement and the stimulation of the local property market (1987: p. 1).

If job creation and retention is about people, then this second objective is about land. The distinction between policies concerned with inner area people and policies concerned with inner area land is crucial to understanding recent developments. Enterprise Zones were, in intention, about both. That is by no means true of Urban Development Corporations.

The original urban development corporations were established in London Docklands and Merseyside in 1981 and subsequently, between 1986 and 1988, other UDCs have been designated in the Black Country (West Midlands), Tyne and Wear, Teeside, Manchester (two), Bristol, Leeds and Sheffield. Most attention has been given to the London Docklands Development Corporation (LDDC) for a general account of which see Ambrose (1986) and Stoker (1989). The objectives of UDCs have been clearly demonstrated by a fascinating confrontation between the House of Commons Select Committee on Employment and Ministers and senior civil servants from the Department of the Environment (1989). The then Secretary of State for the Environment, Nicholas Ridley, in his verbal rejoinder to the committee (12 May 1989) asserted:

> In the United States . . . on their list of objectives, employment comes first and the need to regenerate communities. The remit in our legislation does not mention employment at all, hinges on physical regeneration and talks of bringing land and buildings into effective use (1989: p. 1).

This was a reiteration of the earlier evidence of Butler, the DOE Under Secretary:

> . . . we do not see the UDCs as being primarily about and immediately concerned with employment; they are about regeneration and indeed about physical regeneration of their areas (1988: p. 21).

The Employment Committee had been very critical of the effects of UDCs arguing of LDDC that:

> When we looked at employment, we did not come to the conclusion that if you regenerate the land automatically it will solve the problems of unemployment. It has not had that effect at all (1989: p. 2).

Government did not like this line at all, asserting in its written rejoinder that:

> . . . the government does not consider that the report, taken overall, gives an accurate and balanced account of the role and position of UDCs, or of the achievement of UDCs (1989: p. 3).

Government was not pleased by the explicit identification of the prioritizing of land development over job creation in the UDCs, but that was clearly what had happened. Enterprise Zones are now a fading policy. The only recently designated example, Sunderland, has a very fishy background and can be considered to have served as a sweetener to distract attention from the enormous damage done to industrial potential by the land value prioritizing of the Tyne Wear (urban) Development Corporation. A fourth principle of Tory policy for the inner cities can be added to those delineated earlier:

(4) The objective of policy is to maximize market returns on land development. Inner city populations and existing inner city manufacturing are irrelevant to this and may be an obstacle to it. If so they are to be sacrificed.

This is a hard statement. Demonstrating its accuracy requires a brief case study which will be provided in the form of a review of recent developments in Tyne and Wear county.

The Deindustrialization of a County

In 1971 Tyne and Wear had nearly 250,000 industrial jobs from a total of 508,000. Nearly 200,000 of the jobs were full time male industrial and over 50,000 were full time female industrial. In 1987 there were 430,000 jobs in the conurbation. Of these just 132,000 were industrial, of which 98,000 were male full time and 25,000 were female full time. Overall the female part time proportion of the workforce increased from 12 per cent in 1971 to 22 per cent in 1987. Part of this change was the consequence of a specific city policy, the designation of an Enterprise Zone, and it seems as if the operation of the more recently designated Urban Development Corporation will push deindustrialization even further along.

The Tyneside Enterprise Zone was designated in 1981 in several locations in Newcastle and Gateshead. As of 1984 the Zone had a total workforce of 9,300. Of these 8,500 were in manufacturing and the great bulk of these had been in employment when the zone was designated. By 1988 the total employment had increased to 16,500 of which 9,600 were in manufacturing. Thus the greatest increase had been in services and also in part time employment which increased from 400 to 2,500 over the period. The Tyneside Zone has been second in public subsidy only to the Isle of Dogs and is the largest in terms of hectarage. The largest element in development has been the out of town shopping in *Metrocentre*. The content of and background to this development is described in Byrne (forthcoming), but in summary very large amounts of public money have been devoted without any tests for displacement or deadweighting to purely service development which is largely competitive with existing local facilities. *Metrocentre* and *Retail World*, on the Team Valley Trading estate pioneered in the 1930s as a base of manufacturing diversification, have taken up a substantial part of the available industrial land in Gateshead MBC area. However, this land was at least vacant. The operations of the UDC have been more offensive yet.

The Tyne Wear (Urban) Development Corporation was designated in 1986 and took over control of some 4,500 hectares of riverfronting land on both the Tyne and the Wear. The UDC is a government nominated body which replaces the Metropolitan districts as local planning authority and has wide ranging land development powers. It was expected that the UDC would receive some £150 million of public subsidy over the first five years of its existence. UDCs are the jewel in the *Action for Cities* crown. That document describes them as " . . . the most important attack ever made on urban decay". The Tyne Wear UDC illustrates the form of that attack in an industrial city.

The general approach of this body is best summed up by evidence given by its chief executive (a former DOE regional director) to the House of Commons Select Committee on Employment:

> . . . industry within the river corridors is characterized by heavy marine-based manufacturing. Due to world market conditions causing decline in these sectors, there are also a growing number of derelict factories, warehouses, shipyards, slipways and dry docks along both rivers, with river or rail access primarily, many of which are unlikely ever to be used again for their original purpose (1989: p. 309).

This was an image of dereliction and redundancy. The two rivers were no longer to be centres of marine manufacturing or ports, the reasons why there were industrial cities along them in the first place. Some new use was to be found.

The character of that new use was indicated by the original consultant's report prepared in advance of the establishment of the UDC and adhered to in broad outline by that body in subsequent activities. In broad outline (for details see Byrne 1987) the emphasis was on subsidized developments which were, at least in "flagship" projects, to be primarily non-industrial. The underlining principle, outlined by the UDC in its evidence to a public enquiry into compulsory purchase orders in the Newcastle quayside area, was that of catalytic planning. Hall has referred to the contemporary period as one involving the "City of Enterprise" in which the role of planning is as:

> ... property development. The task of planning in this view was to facilitate the most rapid feasible recycling of derelict urban industrial or commercial land to higher or better uses (1988: p. 354).

Here "higher or better uses" means higher immediate gains for developers. We need to look at what is meant by facilitate. The problem has been that the private sector, even at the height of the property boom, was reluctant to get into inner city development. It had to be bribed and shown the way. That is the idea of catalytic development—that state subsidized developments will create a property market in inner city areas which will develop autonomously, without, it is asserted, the requirement for further subsidy in subsequent phases. The catalytic developments clearly indicate intentions for the future. Thus to facilitate means not just to subsidize but also to determine general direction. This is not responding to markets but attempting to impose a particular variant of market result.

The TWDC has started and stopped a number of developments in its area of operation. The starts have largely involved the substitution, or intended substitution, of leisure retail housing uses for industrial uses (with the exception of the substitution of a business park for heavy industry on a derelict site in West Newcastle). The thing stopped has been the prospect of continued marine manufacturing on the Wear which would have preserved the most modern shipbuilding facilities in Europe.

The best example of active deindustrialization is provided by the proposal which the TWDC has currently put to itself as planning authority for some 1,200 dwellings, 470,000 square feet of retail development, 345,00 square feet of leisure development and a business park on land purchased from the Port of Tyne Authority at Whitehill Point in North Shields. This 250 hectare site is immediately adjacent to one of the poorest council estates in the North East and was designated in the County Structure Plan as a strategic site to be reserved for industrial uses requiring deep water access. Instead, under the TWDC's proposals (which come from their selected developer) the area will be used for an exclusive residential development, out of town shopping, expensive private leisure facilities, a business park and a marina.

London Docklands comes (perhaps) to North Shields. There are number of other similar proposals including the developed St. Peter's basin in the poor working class area of Walker in Newcastle and developments on the North Sands in Sunderland.

The latter site is closely connected with the TWDC's collaboration in the destruction of Sunderland's shipbuilding capacity. The full story of the murky deals between the UK government and the European Commission, which led to the closure of this facility, has been documented before the House of Commons Select Committee on Industry. The UDC's specific role was in relation to some 5 acres which it had taken over from the local authority. This land was essential for a ship repair, marine manufacturing proposal made for one of the Sunderland yards by a Greek consortium. TWDC insisted on a housing land valuation of £450,000 (reduced from an original price of £888,000). This was massively greater than industrial land values and priced out the proposal. The likely result is the elimination of marine manufacturing on the River Wear. The local Chamber of Commerce's magazine has referred to:

> . . . the TWDC's strategy of turning the traditional uses of the river inside out (1990: p. 25).

The Audit Commission in its review of *Urban Regeneration* and *Economic Development—The Local Government Dimension*—had the impertinence to assert of elected local authorities' opposition to UDCs:

> It is hard to see how this policy can be defended as in any way contributing to the welfare of local inhabitants (1989: p. 27).

Stoker's summary of the London Dockland's LAs objections suggests why the local authorities think differently.

> Their case is that the LDDC has failed to provide jobs and homes to meet local people's needs. Moreover it has usurped the only land available to LAs to meet those needs. Further, it has created a whole package of long-term costs to LAs in servicing and maintaining the development it has sponsored and now this has distorted the spending priorities of the LAs across the whole range of their activities (1989: p. 161).

At least in London Docklands the land was derelict before it was seized for consumption by the well off. In Tyne and Wear the operations of the UDC have actually created industrial dereliction as well as pre-empting the possibility of new industrial and job creating uses for strategic sites which were not in current use.

Conclusion

Fred Robinson has recently concluded that: "Either current policy (for inner cities) is ... something of an irrelevant sideshow or, more disturbing, an intervention aimed at further marginalizing and displacing the poor" (1989: p. 41). I think it is even worse. The programmes are directed against the industrial nature of English cities because that industrial base is the centre of potential opposition to the finance capital related interests served by Thatcherite market ideology. That is a real claim for conspiracy theory, but it has to be made. However, there is a saving grace. All the serious programmes, especially UDCs, depend on a buoyant property market for success in terms of real developments on site. In 1989 (and the article must have been written earlier) Stoker commented: "Plainly, if the property bubble bursts, many of the UDCs may find themselves in difficulties" (1989: p. 163). It has and they have. TWDC have lost the builder for their flagship East Quayside development through bankruptcy and given that house prices have now started to fall in real terms in the North East, it is difficult to see how many of their other schemes will go ahead. They are being demoted by market forces from disasters to nuisances. They are in the way, but will not necessarily happen, and if they don't happen, irreplaceable resources required for any urban reindustrialization will not be sterilized.

What will happen in our cities is what will be made to happen. The cities are grounds of conflict, not a simple conflict between labour and capital, but one between a vision of them as industrial centres and one which sees them as consumption possibilities. Industrial capital and the urban working class have a common (and beginning to be recognized) mutual interest against "consumption" development. Indeed consumption development is consumption in an old medical sense for our cities. They are open to being consumed by a disease process which will destroy their potential for long—term growth and development. Things are very bad. Local government has been stripped of power and resources. Cities are ruled by a new colonialism. However, the forces of the market are against this which means that the fight, especially outside London, is by no means over. Action will decide the course of events in the early 1990s and fix the frame well into the next century.

In terms of theory it is a time for history rather than structuralism. Indeed geographically derived structuralism has served action very poorly. It is inherently pessimistic and anti-organizational. Policies come, in part, from intentions. That is the way forward. This paper has summarized, but the message for critical social science is clear. If critical social science is to be a guide to emancipation (see Sayer 1984) then it needs to recognize the importance of strategic surveys intended to inform action by specific social groups. The battle for the industrial future of English cities is still going on. It is by no means a matter of vaguely constituted social movements organized around consumption issues. These planning battles are matters for class fractions. To a very considerable degree they are cultural battles, battles of those involved in the production of commodities who take meaning from that (and that category includes a lot of industrial managers as well as workers) against an active anti-industrialism which at its worst uses the artefacts of an industrial past as motifs for play. The result is not determined by the structural organization of capitalism, although that is not irrelevant to the way things are done. Policies matter, so politics matters.

References

Official Publications

DOE (1978) *Policy for the Inner Cities* HMSO, London.
DOE (1988) *Action for Cities*. HMSO, London.
Report of the Royal Commission on the Reorganisation of Local Government (1969) HMSO, London.
Audit Commission (1989) *Urban Regeneration and Economic Development—The Local Government Dimension*. HMSO, London.
PA Cambridge Economic Consultants (1989) *An Evalulation of the Enterprise Zone Experiment* (for DOE Inner Cities Research Programme). HMSO, London.
House of Commons Select Committee on Employment (1988) *Third Report—The Employment Effects of Urban Development Corporations*. HC 327 I and II London.
Fielding, T., and Haltend, S. (1990) *Patterns and Processes of Urban Change in the UK* (for DOE Inner Cities Research Programme). HMSO, London.

General References

Ambrose, P. (1986) *Whatever Happened to Planning?* Methuen, London.
Anderson, J. (1983) In Anderson J., *et al.* (eds) *Redundant Spaces in Cities and Regions*. Academic Press, London.
Bauman, Z. (1987) From here to modernity, *New Statesman*, 25 September 1987.
Boddy, M. (1989) Cooke P., (ed.) *Localities*. Unwin Hyman, London.
Byrne, D.S. (1989) *Beyond the Inner City*. Open University Press, Milton Keynes.
Byrne, D.S., and Parsons, D. (1983) Anderson, *et al.* J. (eds) op. cit.
CDP (Community Development Project) (1975) *The Costs of Industrial Change London.*
CDP (1976) *Cutting the Welfare State*. London

CES (Centre for Environmental Studies) (1985) *National Project—Outer Estates in Britain*. London.

Cooke, P. (1987) Britain's new spatial paradigm, *Environment and Planning A*, **19**: 1289-1301.

Cooke, P. (ed) (1989) op. cit.

Dahrendorf, R. (1987) The erosion of citizenship, *New Statesman*, 12 June 1987.

Dennis, N. (1972) *Public Participation and Planners' Blight*. Faber, London.

Dunleavy, P. (1981) *The Politics of Mass Housing in Britain*. Clarendon Press, Oxford.

Feagin, J.R. (1987) In Smith, M.P. and Feagin J.R., (eds) *The Capitalist City*. Blackwell, Oxford.

Friedmann, J. and Wolff, G. (1982) World city formation: an agenda for research and action, *International Journal of Urban and Regional Research*, **6**: 306-329.

Hall, P. (1988) *Cities of Tomorrow*. London.

Harloe, M. *et al.* (eds) (1990) *Place, Policy and Politics*. Unwin, London.

Harrison, R. (1984) *Inside the Inner City*. Penguin, London.

Healey, P. *et al.* (1988) *Land Use Planning and the Mediation of Urban Change*. Cambridge University Press, Cambridge.

Hill, R.C., and Feagin, J.R. (1987) In Smith M.P., and Feagin J.R., (eds) op. cit.

Hudson, R. (1989) *Wrecking a Region*. Pion, Oxford.

King, A.D. (1989) *Global Cities*. Routledge, London.

Lawless, P. (1988) British inner city policy: a review, *Regional Studies*, **22**: 531-542.

Lawless, P. (1989) *Britain's Inner Cities*. Paul Chapman, London.

Martin, R., and Rowthorne, B. (1986) *The Geography of Deindustrialization*. Macmillan, London.

Marris, P., and Rein, M. (1967) *Dilemmas of Social Reform*. Routledge, London.

Robinson, F. (1989) Urban regeneration policies in Britain in the late 80s—Who benefits? *CURDS Discussion Paper 94*. Newcastle.

Sayer, A. (1984) *Method in Social Science: A Realist Approach*. Hutchinson, London.

Stoker (1989) UDCs: a review, *Regional Studies*, **23**: 159-167.

Tyne Wear Chamber of Commerce (1990) *Contact*, August 1990.

Urry, J. (1985) In Gregory D., and Urry J., (eds.) *Social Relations and Spatial Structures*. Macmillan, London.

Wilson, W.J. (ed.) (1989) *Annals of the American Academy of Political and Social Science*. January 1989.

Williams, R. (1980) *Problems in Materialism and Culture*. Verso, London.

11

The Countryside

Development, Conservation and an Increasingly Marketable Commodity

PAUL CLOKE

1. Rural Areas and a New Political Order

Countryside Images and Interests

There is no one rural Britain. Just as it would be foolish to suggest that urban policies during the 1980s can be contained within a neat single category, so it should be stressed from the outset that there are both many rural geographies in Britain and many different changes to those geographies which took place during the Thatcher era. This emphasis on the seemingly obvious is a very necessary precursor to any account of "Thatcher's countryside" because at one fundamental level, rural areas have been used as a repository of ideological virtue in counterpoint to other more problematic locales. Thus the rural landscape has been characterized as offering natural beauty, health, fulfilment of life and freedom from problems. Equally rural communities have been viewed as friendly, desirable and secure living environments where traditional values are upheld. Such characterizations are at once *assumptions* which underlie any discourse over the necessity for policies requiring state intervention, *examples* for more problematic policy arenas, and *commodities* ripe for exploitation in the new politics of the marketplace.

Figure 11.1 presents a fascinating outsider's view of Thatcher's

FIG. 11.1 A cartoonist's-eye-view of depression in Thatcher's Britain.

Britain from the New Zealand cartoonist Hodgson. Many points of detail are suggested by this cartoon, but of particular interest in this context is the representation of "depression" in Britain which is entirely non-rural in character. This highlights the impression given by both government and media that the problems raised by Thatcherite government have certainly not been manifest in the countryside. It has only been with the rise of green concerns in the latter 1980s, and the pragmatic perceived need to "greenwash" policies, that the spotlight has been turned on to rural environments and even here, the blame for problems has been successfully shifted from the British state to other targets such as the European Commission, "foreign" financial institutions and companies, and "inevitable" (and timeless?) stresses between the need for development and the protection of the countryside.

This chapter attempts to show that rural areas have been neither problem-free nor unscathed from the direct impacts of policy changes wrought by the Thatcher administrations. It also stresses that different countrysides—with varying landscape quality, agricultural regimes, pressure on housing, suitability for competitive provision of services and so on—will have fared differently during the 1980s. These countrysides also represent arenas where important Conservative interests have met and clashed during the Thatcher era. Established land-based Conservatism focusing on agriculture and traditional middle class village residents has been increasingly paired with new middle class in-migrants whose business and professional connections are often external to the immediate locality and who have no particular time-honoured sympathy with agricultural processes. Housebuilding and construction interests, often major financial contributors to and supporters of the Conservative Party, have renewed their interest in rural locations as profitable and desirable sites for capital accumulation in the form of large, expensive and profitable new houses. New residents have often appropriated local political control in pursuit of protecting their interests against the "pollution" of farming and the threat of development. Local Conservatism is therefore potentially at odds with a central Conservatism which emphasizes the importance of market forces, reduced public expenditure, and green policies for agricultural landscapes. Rural Britain in the 1980s has thus seen a juggling of these interests by the Thatcher administrations. Indeed the busy juggling of Conservative interests has meant a disregard for the needs of other, minority, interests such as those of the rural deprived; this is a theme which is returned to at the end of this chapter.

Legacy and Ideology

In retrospect, the first Thatcher administration in 1979 can be seen to have inherited a legacy of problems and policies which inevitably shaped some of its initial activities. Economic recession and industrial restructuring on an international scale had led to high inflation and rising unemployment. Public expenditure restrictions were already being implemented, yet welfare payments were increasing with the rising number of benefit-dependent. More specifically in the rural context the Common Agricultural Policy was in place, and the problems of high expenditure and overproduction were already being felt, as was the impact of a highly mechanized, high technology CAP-directed agricultural industry on the landscapes of rural Britain.

Views vary whether the Thatcher response to this legacy was ideological or pragmatic. Potter and Adams (1989) suggest that

> Despite the many reshuffles and political repackaging the 1980's have seen a remarkable consistency of ideology and action in the countryside (p. 1)

whereas Blowers (1987) advances a different perspective:

> . . . conservation policy illustrates a mixture of ideology and pragmatism. Compromises had to be achieved between the potentially competing interests of farmers and those concerned with the protection of the rural environment, both regarded as naturally part of the Conservatives' constituency (p. 279).

To form any kind of judgement on these matters, however, it is important to place the Thatcher response as seen in rural areas into the wider context of new right ideology and policy. As Dunleavy and O'Leary (1987) suggest, groups associating themselves with the "new right" vary from libertarian philosophers to highly reactionary politicians, and as a consequence new right policies can range from stark reductions in the welfare state to moral crusades over individual rights. Thus our analysis of the new right policies introduced during the Thatcher administrations needs to take account of three important facets of this wider context (see Bell and Cloke 1989, Green, 1987, and King 1987):

(i) the political and economic theories associated with the new right are not new, but rather have been grasped during a period of economic difficulty;

(ii) the new right combines liberal and conservative notions which may lead to contradictory political objectives;
(iii) the new right is as much to do with dismantling previous structures of collectivism as it is with promoting individual rights and the efficacy of the marketplace.

The translation of these wider ideological guidelines into political strategies during the 1980s can be illustrated in terms of privatization policies in which reductions have been sought by the state's role in the provision of welfare services and a shift has been engineered in order to redirect various responsibilities for production and consumption into the private sector. The 1979 manifesto with which Margaret Thatcher swept into power gave little indication of the sweeping tide of privatization that has followed. Subsequently the drive towards a portfolio of privatization policies was justified on the grounds of both liberal philosophy (enhancing freedom and increasing efficiency) and practical expediency (controlling public sector pay rates and reducing the public sector borrowing requirement). Although the privatization programme was clearly conceived in the new right context, it was raised in a muddle of different political parameters. Shackleton (1986), for example, ascribes the surge in privatization to a range of non-ideological factors including: the weakness of the nationalized industries; regulatory failures in a stagnant monopolistic industrial environment; the funding crisis in the welfare state; the weakness of the trade union movement; and the stake that interested parties have in the privatization process once it is underway. For these and other reasons, the privatization policies pursued by the Thatcher administrations met with little successful resistance, and a retrospective look at the 1980s reveals four overlapping strands of policy (see Bell and Cloke 1989):

(i) *User-pays*: policies in which services are charged for rather than funded from general taxation, thus increasing the pressures on the least affluent social groups.
(ii) *Contracting-out*: policies which put out to tender in the private sector those services which previously had been provided directly by public sector agencies.
(iii) *Denationalization*: policies which sell industries previously in either total or partial public ownership to the private sector.
(iv) *Deregulation/competition*: policies designed to relax pre-existing controls on particular markets (from financial markets to public transport) so as to enhance competition.

These policies have had their greatest impact on particular *social* groups, particularly the least affluent, but it is possible to interpret the effects of these and other policies in particular types of area and so in this context the question of what mix of ideology and pragmatics has been displayed in Thatcher's countryside is an important and appropriate one. Bell and Cloke (1989) have suggested four important themes which can form the basis of such an evaluation. First, we need to look at rural areas as *arenas of competition*. If because of their low population densities and spaced-out pattern of settlement (although we need to guard against homogeneous views of "rural" here) rural areas are less healthy arenas for competition than elsewhere, then new right policies which emphasize competition will be less effective in these areas. Secondly, rural areas are *arenas of production and consumption*. If state subsidy and regulation of production in these areas is withdrawn or reduced, then specific policy impacts will accrue. Equally, if a deregulated business environment spawns commercial interest in the countryside as a commodity, we can expect rural effects to occur. Changing forms of consumption of the countryside, by both residents and visitors, will also raise important policy questions in a context of privatizing responsibilities previously lodged with the public sector. Thirdly, rural interests may be protected during an era of privatization as *arenas of continued regulation*, either through the offices of the watchdog agencies set up to oversee newly privatized industries, or more generally through other policies designed to regulate countryside land uses for the purposes of public consumption. Lastly, rural areas can be viewed as *arenas of planning* so that any deregulation of planning itself may be monitored.

It is these four themes that are used in the remainder of this chapter to assess the impacts of the policies of the Thatcher administrations on rural areas. For convenience of discussion, the assessment separates the interrelated matters of rural landscapes and land use, rural development, and rural service provision.

2. Rural Land: Where Production, Consumption and Management Meet

Forestry and Conservation

In some ways, the management of rural land during the Thatcher era represents very different and sometimes contradictory policy decisions. Take forestry, for example, where many commentators accuse the Thatcher governments of being responsible for the blanketing of huge areas of Britain's hills and moors with conifer plantations (see, for example, Tomkins 1989). Here, the public sector agency concerned—the Forestry Commission—has been gradually dispossessed of its strategic planning and planting roles and has been instructed to dispose of some 16 per cent of its holdings by the end of the century. It is perhaps remarkable that the Commission has not been fully privatized given the surrounding political climate, but this may, at least in part, be due to the influence of the private sector forestry lobby who wish to retain the Commission in some form as an agency for protecting wider forestry interests at the central government level.

By rolling back the activities of the Forestry Commission, and by setting new high targets for the establishment of new plantations, the Thatcher governments presided over a boom period for private sector forestry. Market forces were let loose on new planting with the result that conifer plantations spread northwards onto poor quality remote land. Up to 1988, this process was also fuelled by tax concessions and by a doubling of the rate of grants under the Forestry Grant Scheme for the mass planting of conifers. Public celebrities—Terry Wogan, Cliff Richard, Steve Davis and the like—represented the highly publicized tip of the iceberg of investors participating in this forestry boom. The popularity of investment was heightened by the closing of other tax avoidance loopholes. Even the 1988 Budget decision to sweep away the forestry tax loophole has not steemed the tide, as in its wake came a new grant scheme which increased the rate of grant aid for bulk planting by 256 per cent.

Thus, the Thatcher "policy" for forestry appears to have been one which bears little regard to wider conservation interests, although clearly the fact that more than 90 per cent of new planting has taken place in northern Scotland represents something of an appeasement to conservationists opposing such planting in England and Wales. By deregulating the planting activities of the Forestry Commission and sponsoring competitive investment by the private sector in a geographical area where public opposition was politically relatively unimportant, and in a land use sector which is not subject to planning restrictions, the ideologies which underpin the Thatcher administrations have in this case been able to drive policy decisions in a reasonably direct manner.

Agriculture and Conservation

The same cannot be said of the Thatcher record on policy for agriculture and conservation. Her political juggling act of implementing ideological leanings while accommodating the varying interests of different fractions of Conservative Party support has proved a difficult and often pragmatic task. As Potter and Adams (1989) suggest in the context of conservation policy:

> In place of strong but discriminating countryside planning, we are offered countryside management—a weaker concept which attempts not to plan change but to accommodate and ameliorate it. There is no rural policy, except that which emerges from the outworking of decisions made centrally.

There is insufficient space here to record the entire policy story for agriculture and conservation (see, for example, Britton 1990, Cox *et al.* 1986, Lowe *et al.* 1986, and MacEwen and MacEwen 1987 for very full accounts). It is important, however, to stress two main areas of constraint on the untrammelled adoption of new right policies in the agricultural and landscape conservation policy sectors. First, and most obvious, is Britain's place in the European state and consequent enmeshing in the Common Agricultural Policy (CAP) of the European Community. Margaret Thatcher's now famous "Iron Lady" posturing in Europe contributed to the isolated stance which tended to be adopted by the British government when participating in the decision-making processes of the Commission. The practical inability to force changes to the CAP masks any certain answer to the question of the extent to which the Thatcher administrations would have subjected agriculture to the deregulated cold winds of market forces had the power to do so been vested solely in the British state. Certainly the early indications of the first Thatcher government were that they favoured policies which would reduce any oversensitivity to environmental interests. Hence, the Wildlife and Countryside Act of 1981 settled the previous discourse over whether to pursue conservation goals by extending planning to cover agricultural land use change by using agricultural grants to support environmentally friendly farming rather than production, or by some voluntary mechanism between conservationists and farmers, in favour of the voluntary option desired by the farming lobby.

Within a few years, however, the political power of the farming lobby was having to compete much more strongly against politically sensitive demands from environmental and conservation interests (Hodge 1990). These interests were very different from the remote geography and politics of upland afforestation in Scotland, for they focused on issues which were located squarely in the Tory heartland constituencies of rural England. Accordingly, the Conservatives began the process of "greening" their policies. Two influential pamphlets were published in 1984 by Kenneth Carlisle (MP for Lincoln) and Tony Paterson (parliamentary liaison officer of the Bow Group). Each detailed the loss of landscape and habitat which was continuing despite the Wildlife and Countryside Act, and suggested reforms to this Act. The significance of these changes is neatly summarized by Blunden and Curry (1988):

> The Conservative Party, it seemed, was re-adjusting its historic attitude towards the land in a way that balanced the old Tory paternalism and the new monetarism: preparing on the one hand to give greater priority to countryside conservation and on the other, to subject agriculture to the rigours of greater competition and less state aid (p. x).

The juggling act was, however, becoming more difficult. It seems that there *was* an ideological urge to turn a new right economic spotlight onto rural production in the agricultural sector. In New Zealand, for example, David Lange's *Labour* government was to demonstrate what was possible by implementing a radical programme of scrapping agricultural subsidies in 1986 (Cloke 1989, Willis 1988) and influential opinion in Britain was pointing in the same direction. For example, the Institute of Economic Affairs fuelled a public discussion on deregulating the agricultural sector in 1985 (Howarth 1985) arguing that a free agricultural market would be a successful and low cost way of providing food for Britain. Howarth concluded that the objective of the Thatcher government should be to achieve a freely competitive agricultural industry and that this could only be reached, pragmatically, by working towards the demise of the CAP. With hindsight we can see that the CAP has proved remarkably resilient to such reform, so that the contradictions between both Liberal and Conservative concepts and the pragmatics of the European state have yet to be worked out.

Despite the underlying wish to expose farming to market forces, the Thatcher regime continued to support farmers' rights during the "greening" of countryside policies. In particular the interests of landowning capital were served in the Wildlife and Countryside Act by the transgression of two previously well established principles: that compensation should not be paid when development is refused; and that the cost of avoiding environmental damage should be paid by the pollutors themselves (Blowers 1987). Thus the Act was pro-farming in these respects even after its amendment in 1985 when the loophole of giving farmers three months' notice of designating an SSSI on their land was closed. In the major test case for implementing the Act, focusing on the threat by landowners to drain the Halvergate Marshes in Norfolk, the "voluntary agreement" mechanism enshrined in the legislation patently failed to cope with a major confrontation between agriculture and conservation (Lowe *et al.* 1986, O'Riordan 1986). Although one outcome of Halvergate was the development of Environmentally Sensitive Areas (ESAs) in which financial assistance may be given to farmers who agree to undertake farming practices which maintain or improve the landscape, the inescapable conclusion to be drawn from this round of "policy-making" is that there has been a pragmatic focus on a small number of elite areas, to the detriment of the remainder of rural landscapes.

The ALURE Proposals

The imposition of milk quotas by the EC in 1984 heralded a new mood in government and farming circles which represented a recognition that some reforms to the CAP were required to cut the cost and waste of overproduction. A new perception of the land budget required for agriculture was becoming common currency, with Richard North (1986; see also 1990) suggesting that up to one-third of agricultural land in Britain could be surplus to agricultural requirements by the year 2015 if no extensification was to occur and no overproduction was to be tolerated. Mrs Thatcher's suggestion that such land might be used for "golfcourses" clearly pinpoints her desire to see this issue settled in what *she* saw as a "please everybody" way. Other commentators have seen this potential availability of land as either a significant opportunity to promote an environment-friendly form of farming or a frightening context for a free-for-all in rural development. Once again the juggling of ideology, pragmatism and various Conservative interests was required.

In February 1987 the Thatcher administration issued two sets of proposals which emanated from a group established to look at alternative land use and rural economy (ALURE) in Britain. The immediate context of these proposals was a short-term concern over gaining middle class votes from those who were interested in green issues, although the longer-term issues of the CAP were also important here. One package of proposals came from the Ministry of Agriculture, Fisheries and Food (MAFF) and proposed some £25 million per annum of new expenditure on farm diversification made up of:

(i) £10 million to encourage the development of farm woodlands;
(ii) £3 million to expand the traditional forestry programme of the private sector;
(iii) £7 million to double the number of ESA designations; and
(iv) £5 million to grant aid for farm diversification.

The other proposals came from the Department of the Environment (DoE) and consisted of removing the presumption that agricultural use of rural land should be paramount for the purposes of town and country planning, and promoting three equal concerns for rural land use planning—agriculture, the environment and rural economic revival. Land in national parks, areas of outstanding natural beauty and SSSIs were to be exempt from this measure, as were plots of 50 acres or more of Grade 1 or 2 agricultural land.

The notion of this dual ALURE package was to present an integrated and coherent policy intiative which would appeal to farmers, conservationists, middle-class rural residents and even house building interests—the Thatcher juggling act personified. However, rivalry between MAFF and DoE, and unprecedented criticism of the then Agriculture Minister, Michael Jopling, by the NFU led to suggestions from the MAFF side that the DoE proposals would permit farmers wide scope for diversification, even to the extent of permitting widespread new development on farmland. As Cloke and McLaughlin (1989) have pointed out, such suggestions were hardly likely to appeal to middle class voters in the Tory South East and Midlands of England, and the action of MAFF only served to highlight rather than smooth over the inherent contradictions in the ALURE proposals.

Despite the predictable attempts to minimize the damage from this affair (Mrs Thatcher was said to be furious and embarrassed by the public disagreement between her two ministries) two fundamental fears for the future of the countryside were exacerbated by the ALURE proposals. First, to what extent was the way being left open for developers to move into previously protected areas of the countryside? Secondly, was ALURE part of a wider Thatcher programme of attacking the town and country planning process on ideological grounds? The proposed new expenditure associated with the ALURE package, then, was welcomed by some as a small (token?) step in the right direction, but others interpreted the policies as meaning that the juggling of Conservative ideologies and interests was no longer possible for the whole countryside, so elite areas were being protected but elsewhere development interests were beginning to be favoured.

The ALURE policies could only ever play a minor supporting role in the matter of agricultural policy reform, as any major changes and initiatives will stem from the wider decision-making of the EC. Recent meetings of GATT (General Agreement on Tariff and Trade) have suggested that in turn it is likely to be international pressures, particularly from the USA, which will ultimately force the hand of EC states to reform the CAP. Thus against all of the stated judgements of Margaret Thatcher, national sovereignty over agricultural policy has effectively been lost, not just into Brussels decision-making but even further away into the international capitalist state. Her only consolation was to press on with privatization ideologies in areas which remained under the jurisdiction of the national state—including the transformation of nature conservation into a private sector activity, finding ways of introducing "user pays" directives in national parks, and reorganizing countryside agencies in the public sector who are left with the prospect of what O'Riordan (1989: p. 6) calls "designer conservation", this being the inevitable consequence of corporatism with private sector partnership agencies. These changes appear to be of a type which will be difficult to reverse even if the successor regime of John Major so wishes. The Thatcher legacy is therefore partly one of gung ho ideological programmes of privatization in policy arenas which are accessible to the national state and can be juggled so as not to conflict too heavily with other interests, and partly one of a publicly "greened" but ultimately grin-and-bear-it inability to apply the same programmes to policy sectors where real power has shifted elsewhere, or where social relations at national and local levels cannot be juggled into submission.

3. Rural Development: Production, Consumption and Planning Meet Again

The Ideology and Pragmatics of "Anti-Planning"

A similar juggling act between ideology and pragmatics can be seen in the changing use of planning apparatus to regulate development in different rural localities during the 1980s. On the one hand, ideology has been seen to be strongly influential in this sector. For example, Blowers (1978: p. 281) suggests that "the Thatcher government has suffered few inhibitions about the application of ideology to development policy" and Brindley *et al.* (1989: p. 176) assert that "the Thatcher governments have consistently promoted market-led styles and attempted to undermine market-critical styles of planning". On the other hand, the battleground on which the release of market-led development forces has been fought out has tended to be those very commuter-land and green belt areas where Conservative voters and their representatives reside. Centralized ideology has thus had to be tempered somewhat by a pragmatic need to heed localized resistance to development.

Nowhere is this dilemma more starkly illustrated than in the career of Michael Heseltine. In 1981, as Secretary of State for the Environment, he signified the ideological need to deregulate the planning system:

> I do not look to the planning profession to recreate an economic base. But I would ask you to think and act with resolve as you create some of the necessary preconditions, *and remove some of the contraints* (author's italics) (quoted in Blowers 1987: p. 281).

By 1988, as MP for an Oxfordshire constituency, he was writing to the then Secretary of State for the Environment thus:

> . . . we now face a new threat posed by the rash of urban villages which developers seek to impose on green-field sites against the planning policies of national and local government—and against the wishes of local communities—with you forced to fight a field by field rearguard action through the appeal system at taxpayers' and ratepayers' expense. . . . Have you not the powers under planning legislation to indicate by circular that you will not countenance such large scale intrusive development? And can you not insure . . . that when developers indulge in these extravagant endeavours then the cost of resisting them will be met by the developers and not the ratepayers? (quoted in Blunden and Curry 1988: p. 190).

Some commentators will wish to account for this change of heart in terms of first the constraints of cabinet responsibility, and then the release from them. However, as Michael Heseltine has once again taken on the Environment portfolio, this time in John Major's "post-Thatcher" administration, it is important to recognize the incompatibility of supporting *both* market-led production by fractions of development capital *and* the consumer-environmentalism of middle class rural residents with their demands for protective planning (at least in their locality) and relief from the financial costs of fighting their own anti-development battles.

It is against this background that changing patterns of rural development during the 1980s should be viewed. These patterns have elsewhere been labelled the rise of *anti-planning* (see Cloke 1989a) and may be seen as part of the wider Thatcherite project of setting about the creation of a political economic environment for new rounds of economic restructuring. Accordingly a series of deregulatory devices have been introduced which have served to reduce the authority and scope of development planning (Cloke 1990):

(i) The *deregulation of planning*, including a reduced role for strategic planning, and thus greater opportunity for developers to bring direct pressure on district councils, particularly by offering them planning gain in return for granting permission for development; a diluting of development control powers on some agricultural land (as mentioned earlier in this chapter); the broad concept of "simplified planning zones", where a general permission for development, serves to hand over responsibility for securing the "public interest" to developers themselves; and the greatly diminished role of major planning inquiries which are increasingly being by-passed by the seeking of permission to develop major projects via private members' bills in Parliament.

(ii) The *deregulation of housing development*, by removing the theoretical limits on the scale of housing development in particular places (but note the important locational variations exist here between the South East of England and elsewhere in Britain); the imposition of an obligation on local planners to find a constant supply of suitable building land in their areas; and the success with which developers have been able to appeal against local authority refusal to develop.

(iii) The *deregulation of commercial and industrial development*, by allowing increasing freedom to those developers seeking to exploit sites in prime out-of-town and motorway corridor locations; and by responding to the need to be seen to be aiding the "creation" of new employment by giving very sympathetic consideration to any industrial development (particularly outside of the immediate London fringe).

This premeditated move towards deregulating the planning process is enshrined within policy statements such as *Lifting the Burden* (DoE 1985) which speaks of the need to "simplify" planning, and to make it "more efficient" by engendering a "presumption in favour of development". Inevitably, however, the unevenness of capitalist development has led to particular pressures on particular rural localities, and these have tended to be the focus of attention on rural development conflicts over this period.

Developing the Golden Horn?

It was Peter Hall who celebrated the terms "golden horn" and "golden belt" to describe that swathe of rural Britain from Cornwall to Norfolk in which population growth and increasing commercial activity have come together during the 1980s. It is in these areas that the most publicized configurations of production, consumption and planning in rural areas have occurred over the last decade. The locational advantages of rural areas in the "golden horn" are at least in part due to the availability of environmentally attractive landscapes and settlements which the new entrepreneurial and service classes can colonize, thus recreating their rural idylls and displaying their cultural capital at one and the same time. Housebuilders have therefore argued that they require a steady supply of *appropriate* rural sites, on which to develop *appropriate* homes to satisfy the consumption demands associated with these new forms of commodification of the countryside. The deregulation of various aspects of the planning apparatus presented above paved the way for a potential housebuilding boom in the rural golden horn.

Not unnaturally, the prospect of such a boom threatened the consumption norms of existing residents in these places, including those who had themselves only recently moved in. The much publicized "not in my back yard" (NIMBY) campaigns reflected a myriad of local struggles which demonstrated the unsustainability of granting *carte blanche* to development capital by the Thatcher governments. Production turned in on itself, first helping to create new consumption standards, then threatening to destroy those very standards through what was quickly viewed by local residents as an overexploitation of the countryside commodity of "village" or "small town" environments.

This tricky requirement of satisfying the demand for rural housebuilding sites in prime locations whilst seeming to protect the countryside from intrusive development has led to further juggling acts with the planning system. For example, as Elson (1986) has shown, a series of circulars from the Department of the Environment encouraged local authorities to relax some aspects of their green belt policies so as to accommodate the long-term needs for development, and to release some detached areas of land in amongst existing development for housebuilding purposes. These suggestions have been strongly resisted by many of the local authorities concerned, and the ensuing conflict between the retention of green belt restrictions and the allocation of sufficient housing land has led to mutually appeasing compromises such as the identification of existing institutional land within green belts (for instance, old hospital buildings) which might be made available for redevelopment.

The potential keystone of deregulatory planning in these areas has, however, involved the idea of *new settlements*, which represent a really interesting example of commodifying housing production to meet particular consumptive and political needs. Several of the major housebuilding companies established a collaborative body in 1983 with the idea of first marketing the idea of new small rural towns, and then reaping the profits of developing them. Sophisticated lobbying in local and national political arenas was enhanced by the increasing trend of "poaching" experienced local authority planners to work for the private sector and it included the specific strategy of persuading the planning profession of the aesthetic and strategic merits of developing new settlements as opposed to the norm of expanding existing ones. They drew upon the "traditions" of the self-contained and socially mixed rural community and were able to provide a platform for the social idealism which, although repressed, still existed in large measure within the planning profession. Perhaps most persuasively of all, given a sufficient scale of development, housebuilders could pay for the infrastructure required in the settlement and indulge in partial cross-subsidy to provide affordable housing for low income households and community and environment benefits as part of the overall package—and still not put too great a dent in their own profit margins. It is little wonder, in the age of increasing legitimacy for planning gain, that the new settlement idea received considerable professional and public support. Even the CPRE has not been totally opposed to new settlements:

> In areas of substantial growth, CPRE recognises a possible role for new settlements as the most environmentally and socially attractive way of providing new housing development (Burton 1990: p. 7).

The commodification of new rural housebuilding into new settlements received government encouragement in 1984 in the Department of Environment circular *Land for Housing*, and although the flagship schemes at Tillingham Hall, Foxley Wood and Stone Bassett (Fig. 11.2) have encountered extensive local opposition and have been rejected, it seems ever more likely that new settlement proposals will be included by beleaguered local authorities in their development plans over the next decade. As yet then, the deregulation of planning has not been permitted to run rampant over the opposition of local (Conservative-voting) residents in these areas, but it does appear that the seeds have been sown for a slightly more subtle, but equally

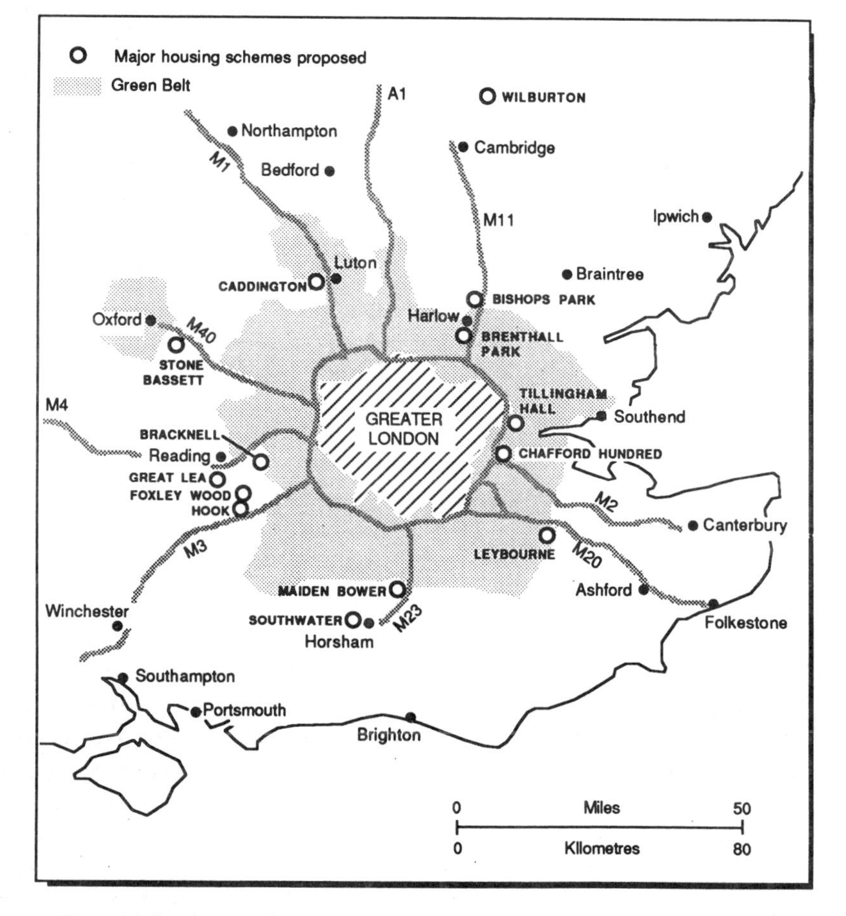

FIG. 11.2 New settlements in South East England (Blunden and Curry 1988: p. 93).

effective, mechanism for achieving the same end of supporting the market-led ambitions of housebuilding capital.

Development and the Other Countrysides

It was stressed at the beginning of this chapter that the Thatcher years will have had very different impacts on different rural areas—there is no *one* Thatcher's countryside. The emphasis given to development in the "golden horn" can overshadow the importance of these differences. Not only is the "horn" itself far from homogeneous, but it also has to be recognized that other areas of Britain have by no means been untouched by the ideology and pragmatics of the Thatcher administrations.

Thornley (1981, 1986) has suggested that the deregulatory devices employed during the 1980s have effectively resulted in three different planning systems:

(i) areas of elite landscape and settlementscape designation, such as National Parks, areas of outstanding natural beauty and conservation areas, where planning restrictions have been strengthened rather than relaxed;
(ii) areas given the status of enterprise zones, simplified planning zones and urban development corporation zones, where planning restrictions have been lifted and responsibility for the shape of development has been handed over to the private sector;
(iii) the rest of the country where the previous system remains in place, but has become more market-driven.

The demands of the market, however, vary considerably in rural Britain. Many of the commuter belts around the cities in the North and Midlands of England and the conurbations of Wales and Scotland display some of the traits of commodified consumption as described in the South and East of England. Some locations (such as the Peak District and parts of Dartmoor and Exmoor) combine these pressures with an elite landscape designation. Elsewhere, more remote areas have witnessed a weakened and partially deregulated planning system providing succour for fractions of capital connected with tourism and other forms of development. In parts of rural Dyfed, for example, there has been an explosion of new bungalow developments in open countryside, the legacy of the willingness of local councillors to ignore the basic tenets of town and country planning regulations and the unwillingness of central government to impose regulation on these activities.

Ultimately, then, the specific outcome of production, consumption and planning in local rural areas will depend upon the particular configuration of local social relations as well as the tempering of ideology with pragmatism in centralized decision-making derived from dominant social relations at a national scale.

4. Servicing Rural Communities: Competition and Continued Regulation

The Changing Relations of Government and the Private Sector

One further characteristic that has begun to emerge about different types of rural areas is that they often represent the least rewarding environments for policies which seek to allow competitive efficiency in the provision of services. During the postwar period, the establishment of a welfare state which incorporated the idea of direct provision by the state of services such as health, education and welfare to everybody, everywhere, an expectation has arisen that the problems of servicing rural communities would be tackled using public sector resources. In effect, public sector provision for rural areas has meant a direct subsidy to overcome the problems and costs associated with a "spaced-out" geography and a relatively low density of population. The Thatcher administration has initiated two main policy programmes which might, if unregulated, have served to dismantle this hidden subsidy given to rural services. However, there are clear signs that some continued regulation *on behalf of* rural areas and rural people has been considered a necessary policy accompaniment to the broader regimes of deregulation and privatization.

The first policy programme has been to engineer significant shifts in the relations between central and local governments. Here, central government has assumed increasing levels of power over local government (see Goldsmith 1986) invoking legislation, advice, and (most importantly) financial control to curtail the activities of local councils and to restrict their ability to intervene in local affairs such as the provision of services. As a result, local level planners and policy-makers now operate with greatly reduced discretion (Cloke and Little 1990) and central direction of policy has become commensurately more important. One particular outcome of these shifting relations is the likely future demise of local authorities at the county level as agencies of rural community development. The representative democracy and public sector bureaucracy inherent in these agencies are antithetical to the market mechanism of allocating goods and services. As Stoker (1987) has suggested:

> Party competition builds up public expectations, about what the state can provide as self-interested politicians seek to maximise their vote. Once in office it is possible for them to disguise the consequences of decisions with the true economic and fiscal situation being hidden from voters. . . . Vocal and highly organized interest groups are formed which constantly push for more and better provision to meet their special interests. The losers are the disorganized and silent majority who finance this expenditure (p. 226).

Accordingly, local government can be (and has been) criticized for being wasteful, inefficient and profligate, thus rendering it susceptible to reforming policies from the centre, including forms of privatization, deregulation and the fragmentation of administrative units. County councils have thus been threatened with being dismantled on ideological grounds: starting with policies for the opting out of schools, continuing with the breakdown of their integrating and co-ordinating transport planning role as part of the 1985 Transport Act; and further threatened by proposals both for changing town and country planning procedures (so as to emasculate the county council function) and indeed for radical reform of local government organization. All of these measures have reduced the effectiveness of county councils which have previously been regarded as one of the major agents of rural community development in Britain.

The second policy programme has brought about shifts in the relations between public sector and private sector responsibilities. Between 1979 and 1990, major components of the provision of services to rural areas have passed out of the public sector and into private hands. Privatization has included water, gas, electricity, telecommunications, public bus services, and local authority housing. In the case of the basic infrastructural services there had been previously a clear cross-subsidy to rural consumers under public ownership. Unitary charging for water, electricity, gas, and local telephone calls, for example, has ignored the wide variations in the cost of supplying a service to different people in different places—a cost which is usually higher in spaced-out and low-density rural areas. There is obviously a danger, then, that under new private sector ownership, conforming to market-led and profit-oriented maxims such as charging the consumer, the full cost of supplying a service, the previous cross-subsidies in favour of rural areas, will be abandoned, leading to significantly increased servicing costs for rural people.

In the virtual absence of nationwide competition in the supply of these newly privatized services, the Thatcher governments have found it politically necessary to build in "safeguards" for rural areas in the form of continued regulation of privatized service provision. As Veljanovski (1987) has suggested in the context of privatizing industry:

> privatization and liberalization have not meant the removal of the state from industrial activity. They have removed the state from its role as producer, and are transforming it into the "protective state" whose main function is to ensure that businesses play by the agreed rules of the game (p. 170).

Thus the privatization of gas, telecommunications, electricity and water have been accompanied by the establishment of "watchdog" regulatory agencies whose ostensible task is to ensure that consumers get a fair deal. This includes a *rural* dimension, for example in OFTEL's role of watching over the decisions made by British Telecom in order to prevent the drive for profit from overruling the requirements of providing a generally accessible service (such as the removal of uneconomic rural call boxes). It seems likely that these regulatory agencies will find it increasingly difficult to regulate private sector service providers in such a way as to maintain the "social" servicing function which was an integral part of public sector service provision. With their responsibilities to markets and shareholders, the neo-private service providers may retain "social" functions in the short term as part of initial public image building, but these functions are vulnerable to the profit motive in the longer term.

Another example of the way in which privatization has been linked with a continued form of regulation for rural areas is the aftermath of the deregulation of bus services under the 1985 Transport Act. Here the privatization of National Bus Company subsidiaries and the deregulation of previously non-competitive route structures were designed to release public transport from stifling regulatory shackles and to open up public bus services to the efficiencies of market competition. However, in further tacit acknowledgement that rural areas are often very poor arenas of competition, the measure was accompanied by continuing provision for the subsidy of "socially necessary services", and rural areas were especially eligible for transitional and innovatory grants.

The impacts of these policies in remoter rural areas have been the subject of a study in rural Wales (Bell and Cloke 1990, 1991). The main findings of the study were as follows:

— there was no on-the-road competition except in more urbanised areas (such as Wrexham and Colwyn Bay);
— some 60 per cent of route mileage was not commercial and had to be "bought back" as socially necessary services by the county councils;
— no new operators emerged as major forces in running tendered or commercial services in the more rural zones;
— the local authorities did not make significant net savings on putting out to tender their subsidized services;
— the phasing out of the transitional Rural Bus Grant and the uneconomic nature of some of the initial tenders for socially necessary services will mean that the upkeep of present levels of services will become increasingly expensive in the future, and may lead to a decline in the rural service network if additional finance is not available.

The conclusions from this study are clear:

> The use of subsidies to fund socially necessary routes in these areas represents a form of continued regulation and planning in the transport sector even though the 1985 Transport Act was born in an ideological context favouring privatization, deregulation and anti-planning. The designation of what is "necessary" is therefore a delicate political judgement, which can easily change. Although these studies suggest that the status quo has been maintained in the short term, there would seem to be real dangers ahead for the financing of rural transport services (Bell and Cloke 1991a; p. 120).

As with rural transport, so with rural services more widely. There does seem to be a case for arguing that rural areas are often poor arenas for market competition and that rural people will become increasingly disadvantaged by any continued drive to pursue nationwide policies of privatization and deregulation in the service sector. As privatization is matched with a reduction in the effectiveness of public sector servicing agencies, rural people will increasingly be forced to rely on their own resources in the development of their communities.

Self-Help: The Future of Rural Service?

The changes discussed above identify a significant reduction in the power and scope of external intervention in the provision of services as a social function of rural policy and planning. Part of the Thatcher package has therefore been to promote and appeal to sets of values which exalt community self-help as the appropriate and fulfilling mechanism for coping with any service deficiencies in rural areas. By now it is almost received wisdom that self-help is an acceptable planning "mechanism" to be harnessed by hard-pressed planners who have few other resources to plan with. Put another way, however, direct action in rural communities can itself be seen to have been "privatized" into the form of self-help.

The debate over the pros and cons of rural self-help has been vigorous in the latter years of the Thatcher governments. Lowe and Buller (1985), for example, point to the limitations of self-help as a "paternalistic" exercise occurring in a limiting "apolitical" context, while Rogers (1987) by contrast sees self-help as "responsive to people's needs". Within their own terms of reference each of these assessments is correct, but in the context of the changing social and political relations of the Thatcher era it is the class relations of self-help which perhaps allow us to appreciate more fully the changing nature of the role of voluntary action. Increasingly it is the newer middle class fractions which are dominating the leadership of self-help groups in some rural areas, and accordingly it is these groups, for whom the absence of state sector services and support often *adds* to the attraction and uniqueness of rural life, who will increasingly set the agenda for the community issues to be fought for. Voluntary action here, then, will sometimes represent a "paternalistic" or "responsive" regard for others in the locality, but it will also mean maintaining the local environment and ensuring the dominance of local social relations. It will also be connected with a reinforcing of rural gender relations, with self-help "values" placing women not only firmly in the home but also firmly in the centre of a household's community commitment. In this way, self-help can often become colonized by local elite class fractions, and is used to legitimize the necessary "community" action to maintain or enhance the cultural capital which they have invested in the locality. Certainly self-help cannot be regarded as a substitute for public policy, as McLaughlin has argued:

> self-help can never be regarded as the most appropriate policy vehicle for tackling the problems of the rural deprived. At best it can provide a short term immediate fire-fighting solution to deal with the physical expression of a more deep-seated malaise (p. 364).

It is rather an essential element of the ensemble of relations which are shaping and being shaped by the needs for different commodifications of the countryside during the 1980s.

5. Thatcher's Countryside: Some Conclusions

It was noted at the beginning of this chapter that the new right philosophies, from which most of the policies of the Thatcher era have been drawn, include what are sometimes contradictory strands of Liberal and Conservative theory. The notion of the single-minded ideologue relentlessly pressing forward with a preset and unchanging policy agenda founders both on these internal policy contradictions, and on the juggling act which Margaret Thatcher has had to perform in order to "balance conflicting interests in the Tory heartlands" (Blowers 1987: p. 291). Equally, we must beware of regarding some of the outcomes of policies in rural areas as having much to do with any political appreciation of "rural" problems. The grander policy ambitions associated with the privatization programme have inevitably been unevenly developed across the space of Britain, and rural areas have often been the places where some market mechanisms have to be shored up with continued government regulation so that "successes" elsewhere are not undermined politically by high-profile "failures" in Conservative constituencies.

Despite these caveats, however, the Thatcher era has ushered in new "structured coherences" (Cloke and Goodwin 1991) in some rural localities. The changes in governmental relations have led to significant limitations on the ability of planning authorities and other state agencies to intervene in the development of infrastructure and facilities in rural localities. The deregulation of planning has begun to offer new opportunities for private sector development in rural places, and the signs are that there will be strong incentives for interested capital fractions to find new ways to exploit the resources vested in the countryside. Privatization and deregulation have greased the wheels of these processes and the way has been opened up for a range of new countryside commodities to be developed by the private sector. The political adroitness with which the Thatcher administrations were able to juggle with the needs of capital and class interests during this period has been emphasized throughout this chapter. Building and development interests have benefited from policies associated with rural planning. *Large-scale* farming interests have benefited from agricultural policy, and may have enjoyed further deregulation were it not for the constraints which membership of the European state placed on the reforming zeal of the British government. Certainly there has been more direct encouragement given to large-scale forestry interests provided that they focus their energies on areas such as Scotland which, in relative political terms, has been regarded as out of sight and out of mind. The increasingly important conservation interests of middle class voters have also received attention in terms of strong rhetoric about the need to preserve areas of elite landscape value.

These policy directions have given rise to new markets for countryside commodities: the countryside as an exclusive place to be lived in; rural communities as a context to be bought and sold; rural lifestyles which can be colonized; icons of rural culture which can be crafted, packed and marketed; rural landscapes with a new range of potential, from "pay-as-you-enter" national parks, to sites for the theme park explosion; rural production ranging from newly commodified food to the output of industrial plants whose potential or actual pollutive externalities have driven them from more urban localities; and so on. With the race to commodify has come a set of increasingly significant contradictions between production and consumption in the countryside; agriculture and conservation; development and the NIMBY-style local opposition to development; new middle class opposition to the sights and smells of farming; deregulation and the maintainence of farming interests; development and landscape, and so on. As illustrated earlier in the chapter with reference to the seemingly contradictory views expressed by Michael Heseltine, pragmatic policy statements have had to be found which appear to appease these sometimes conflicting interests.

In all this juggling of Conservative interests within the new marketplace countryside, there has been little thought for those rural people who by dint of income or circumstance are unable to cope with the changing nature of rural life. The increasing exclusivity of commodified rural housing markets and the privatization of public sector housing have combined to produce a critical shortage of affordable housing in many rural areas (Shucksmith 1990). "Policy" responses to this policy-induced crisis have been at such a small scale as to be derisory. Even if a tenuous grip can be maintained or established in the housing market, the shrinkage of rural services delivery and the likelihood that the least affluent rural people will be most disadvantaged by the excesses of nationwide policies of privatization, are placing additional constraints on the opportunities available to low-income and low-mobility rural residents. Moreover, the influence of current processes of commodification on local labour markets in rural areas is often tied to the selling of rural places as non-unionized and low pay locales in which any new jobs will be unlikely to break out of the syndrome of low income employment and underemployment. These concerns have not been part of the Thatcher juggling trick; indeed the juggling of other interests has induced a significant detrimental impact on the rural disadvantaged. They are the real victims of countryside policy during the Thatcher era.

References

Bell, P., and Cloke, P. (1989) The changing relationship between the private and public sectors: privatization and rural Britain. *Journal of Rural Studies*, **5**: 1-15.

Bell, P., and Cloke, P. (1990) Deregulation and rural bus services: a study in rural Wales. *Environment and Planning A*, **23**: 107-126.

Bell, P., and Cloke, P. (1991) Public transport in the countryside: the effect of bus deregulation in rural Wales. In Champion, A. and Watkins, C. (eds.) *People in the Countryside*. Paul Chapman, London.

Bell, P., and Cloke P. (1991a) Bus deregulation in rural localities. In Bell, P., and Cloke, P. (eds.) *Deregulation and Transport: Market Forces in the Modern World*. David Fulton, London.

Blowers, A. (1987) Transition or transformation?—Environmental policy under Thatcher. *Public Administration* **65**: 277-294.

Blunden, J., and Curry, N. (1988) *A Future for Our Countryside*. Blackwell, Oxford.

Brindley, T., Rydin, Y., and Stoker, G. (1989) *Remaking Planning. The Politics of Urban Change in the Thatcher Years*. Unwin Hyman, London.

Britton, D. (ed.) (1990) *Agriculture in Britain: Changing Pressures and Policies*. CAB International, Wallingford.

Burton, T. (1990) The solution? Arguments for and against new villages. *Rural Viewpoint*, **38**: 6-7.

Carlisle, K. (1984) *Conserving the Countryside: A Tory View*. Conservative Central Office, London.

Cloke, P. (1989) Deregulation and New Zealand's agricultural sector. *Sociologia Ruralis*, **29**: 34-48.

Cloke, P. (1989a) Land use planning in rural Britain. In Cloke, P. (ed.) *Rural Land Use Planning in Developed Nations*. Unwin Hyman, London.

Cloke, P. (1990) Community development and political leadership in rural Britain. *Sociologia Ruralis*, **30**: 305-322.

Cloke, P., and Goodwin, M. (1991) Conceptualising countryside change: from post-Fordism to rural structured coherence. Paper presented to the Annual Conference of the AAG, Miami, Florida.

Cloke, P., and Little, J. (1990) *The Rural State*? Oxford University Press, Oxford.

Cloke, P., and McLaughlin, B. (1989) Politics of the alternative land use and rural economy (ALURE) proposals in the UK. *Land Use Policy*, **6**: 235-248.

Cox, G., Lowe, P., and Winter, M. (eds.) *Agriculture: People and Policies*. Allen & Unwin, London.

DoE (1985) *Lifting the Burden*. Cmnd 9571. HMSO, London.

Dunleavy, P., and O'Leary, B. (1987) *Theories of the State: The Politics of Liberal Democracy*. Macmillan, London.
Elson, M. (1986) *Green Belts: Conflict Mediation in the Urban Fringe*. Heinemann, London.
Goldsmith, M. (ed.) (1986) *New Research in Central Local Relations*. Gower, Farnborough.
Green, D.G. (1987) *The New Right: The Counter Revolution in Political Economic and Social Thought*. Wheatsheaf, Brighton.
Hodge, I. (1990) The future public pressures on farming. In Britton, D. (ed.) *Agriculture in Britain. Changing Pressures and Policies*. CAB International, Wallingford.
Howarth, R.W. (1985) *Farming for Farmers*? Institute of Economic Affairs, London.
King, D.S. (1987) *The New Right: Politics, Markets and Citzenship*. Macmillan, London.
Lowe, P., and Buller, H. (1985) Rural community councils from 1920. In Rogers, A., Blunden, J., and Curry, N. (eds.) *The Countryside Handbook*. Croom Helm, London.
Lowe, P., Cox, G.M., MacEwen, M., O'Riordan, T., and Winter, M. (1986) *Countryside Conflicts* Temple Smith/Gower, Aldershot.
MacEwen, A., and MacEwen, M. (1987) *Greenprints for the Countryside*. Allen & Unwin, London.
O'Riordan, T. (1986) Halvergate: anatomy of a decision. In Coppock, J.T., and Kivell, P. (eds.) *Geography, Planning and Policy Making*. Geobooks, Norwich.
O'Riodan, T. (1989) Nature conservation under Thatcherism: the legacy and the prospect. *Ecos*, **10**(4): 4-8.
Paterson, T. (1984) *Conservation and the Conservatives*. Bow Group, London.
Potter, C., and Adams, B. (1989) Thatcher's countryside: planning for survival. *Ecos*, **10**(4): 1-3.
Reade, E. (1987) *British Town and Country Planning*. Open University Press, Milton Keynes.
Rogers, A. (1987) Voluntarism, self-help and rural community development: some current approaches. *Journal of Rural Studies*, **3**: 353-361.
Shackleton, J.R. (1986) Back to the market. *Public Policy and Administration*, **1**: 20-39.
Shucksmith, M. (1990) *Housebuilding in Britain's Countryside*. Routledge, London.
Stoker, G. (1987) *The Politics of Local Government*. Macmillan, London.
Thornley, A. (1981) *Thatcherism and Town Planning*. Planning Studies No. 12, Polytechnic of Central London, London.
Thornley, A. (1986A) Planning in a cool climate: the effects of Thatcherism. *The Planner*, **74** (July): 17-19.
Tomkins, S. (1989) *Forestry in Crisis*. Christopher Helm, London.
Veljanovski, C. (1987) *Selling the State: Privatization in Britain*. Weidenfeld & Nicholson, London.
Willis, R. (1988) New Zealand. In Cloke, P. (ed.) *Policies and Plans for Rural People*. Unwin Hyman, London.

12

The Environment

TIMOTHY O'RIORDAN

A Perspective

Thatcherism and environmentalism don't mix. Which will prevail? A variant of environmentalism should do so, eventually, but the outcome will always contain an important legacy of Thatcherism. The new environmentalism is ideologically more powerful and politically more pervasive than the will even of the most authoritarian and presidential prime minister this country has so far known. It is in the ascendant because both the British economy and its society are ready for the opportunities and the strictures it provides. It will prevail also because it is locked into other social movements, notably those pertaining to rights to health, rights to know, consumer protection, feminism, pacifism and animal welfare. These social movements transcend national politics, they open up avenues for political critique regarding the role of political power and earthy well-being in a modern society, and they fill pressure group coffers and electoral opinion polls.

Thatcherism in its pure form has already waned, though it is arguable that it never overwhelmed deep seated values favouring social justice, a charitable approach to the less fortunate, and support for a strong public interest role by the state. As Thatcherism metamorphoses into a more social democratic version of late twentieth-century liberalism, allied to momentous political and economic changes on the European continent, so the new environmentalism will become ever more international and intergenerational. The ultimate challenge is to set correctly the related roles of the state, the economy, and the individual within the community for this forthcoming social democratic era.

Thatcherism has sought to alter the character of the state, by moulding it into a more ideological controlling force over society and the economy. The function of the state as a constructive guide for promoting the common good requires reinforcement. As a result, the state has attempted to argue the cause of individual social conscience via a neo-liberal form of Adam Smith's invisible hand. Self regulation, private expenditure to promote the public good, an aversion to public investment and public enterprise almost for their own sake, together with a determination to spend public money only when the benefits can be shown to be justified—these are some of the hallmarks of Thatcherism. They grate against the demands of the new environmentalism. These demands call for frank openness regarding trends in environmental and public health, arms-length regulation that is based on precautionary science and international standard setting, economic valuations that transcend the market place to include ethical and social justice considerations, and changes in the law to emphasize strict liability, collective insurance funds, and environmental rights.

These demands are beginning to triumph over the far narrower concepts of negligence, nuisance, retrospective awards for damage caused, secretive and cosy regulatory procedures and human centred interpretations of environmental values. In short, social change is occurring in post-modern Britain. Part of that change is creating a new moral mood for environment and the interests of our descendants. That new moral mood favours the incorporation of environmental protection in all affairs of the state, the workplace, and the home. The new environmentalism is part of a social revolution that is, in part, prompted by visions of catastrophe and global disorder.

Prior to 1988, environmentalism had never been a high profile component of British politics. In the mid 1980s there was a flurry of interest as Britain was painfully pulling itself out of a recession. The Labour Party (1986) called for social investment in environmental repair and restoration, and technological advance. David Clark, Labour's then environmental spokesman, asserted that for an expenditure of some £200 million, some 200–350,000 jobs could be created in cleaning up degraded and polluted areas, and in retraining the workforce into environmentally more benign occupations so as to prepare Britain for a more environmentally sustainable 1990s. Here was Labour seeking to use the resources of the state to help cure a social ailment, the benefits of which would be shared generally, though more particularly by private enterprise entering areas newly refurbished at the public expense. The Conservative Party never gave environment any pride of place in its 1987 manifesto. The party was getting on with its self proclaimed job of liberating Britain from the grip of the state and creating environmental policy in its wake (Blowers 1987).

The 1987 general election campaign removed an environmental motif that has been misleadingly regarded as a key voting influence, in favour of the economy and defence. For almost eight out of ten years of her administration, the Prime Minister never gave a speech on environmental matters, nor visited an environmental project. Environmental considerations simply were not on the Downing Street agenda, and successive environmental secretaries busied themselves far more with the reform of local government than with environmental protection in its broadest sense. Yet as Blowers (1987: pp. 292-293) concluded in a useful mid-term survey, "the Thatcher government's approach has been to nurture debate to the point where the environment is now a significant issue in national politics" because "the very stridency of market ideology has contributed to a reaction in favour of constraining market forces".

In mid 1986, Jonathon Porritt, a former director of Friends of the Earth and one of the most influential commentators on green politics, was more despondent. There may be changes of emphasis, he noted, even the odd policy shift with benign implications. "But the political limits to such changes are made quite clear, and unhesitatingly called upon whenever the adoption of green ideas threatens to dilute or contradict the fundamental consumer-orientated growth driven principles that still hold sway as the heart of our industrial society" (Porritt 1986: p. 342).

Two years later he had changed his tune:

> Sooner or later the realisation will dawn on more people that solving the planet's problems is going to require breathtaking radical action and international cooperation on a scale not seen since the Second World War. [The green movement] represents an awakening, a refusal to aid and abet humankind in its onward rush towards the abyss. Its influence has only just begun to be felt, but the fact that so much progress has been made in such a short space of time is enough to light a spark of optimism in even the weariest cynic (Porritt and Winner 1988: pp. 263, 268).

What has contributed to the recent ascendancy of environmental issues in British politics is the overwhelming influence of scientific prognoses on global change with improved estimates of the cost of environmental repair to national and international economies, the rise of media attention almost to the point of saturation, the growing political power of the major international and national "cause" groups (such as World Wide Fund for Nature, Greenpeace, Friends of the Earth), and the domination of the European Community over almost all aspects of British environmental policy. For a summary of the major global issues see the introduction to *World Resources 1990-91*, published by the World Resources Institute (1990). For a review of media attention see the valuable analysis by Porritt and Winner (1988) and by Dobson (1990). For an appraisal of pressure group activity, Porritt and Winner provide helpful coverage, and for a study of the role of the European Community and its influence on British environmental policies, read Haigh (1987) and Rose (1990).

Environmentalism is beginning to have a will of its own. Though Thatcherism will probably lose some of its influence in the process, one should be wary of the resulting triumph. There is a real danger that environmentalism is getting a little too big for its boots, that strident demands for huge investments to rid the world of climate change and toxic chemicals may induce expenditures way out of proportion to benefits, and that international protocols to which nation states may feel obliged to sign create more environmental aggravation than they solve. The legacy of Thatcherism is caution and proper perspective, ensuring all the while that the polluter pays, the consumer contributes and the victim is compensated. In the post-Thatcher enthusiasm of liberated social spending, the circle of history may begin to turn yet another revolution, opening the way for a twenty-first-century amalgam of reformed Thatcherism and revised social democracy to weld a new political ideology of environmental change.

Critical Theory and the New Environmentalism

There will always be many interpretations of critical theory. The one developed here follows that outlined by Kemp (1986) based on a thorough review of the relevant literature, particularly by Habermas (1976) and Thompson and Held (1982).

Kemp argues that critical theory contains three features, namely

(i) to *enlighten* as to the real nature of our relations with power in our social and political affairs so as to *clarify* what are the true interests which dominate our lives;
(ii) to *emancipate* our thinking so that we are enabled to become more aware of the forces that shape our lives and influence our views on the world; and
(iii) to *seek to achieve* a form of social democracy that is free of all forms of domination, especially the hidden biases of interests that distort language and forms of analysis through which our political ideology is developed.

Seen in this light, critical theory has both an educative and a radical role in social change. It provides a basis for opening up minds and raising the level of critical awareness generally, with a view to creating political structures that are more openly accountable and responsive.

Habermas (1976), widely regarded as the father of critical theory, was particularly concerned that the state, or the public sphere as he termed it, was too readily able to legitimize its actions. It did so by virtue of controlling information, exerting authority over the media, and manipulating events to gain acquiescence to its activities by a body politic that was increasingly becoming depoliticized as people concentrated more and more upon their material pleasures and commodified leisure.

Habermas introduced the concept of *legitimation crisis* to indicate how the state sought to parry the onset of political or economic embarrassment by driving inconsistencies into other realms of policy. In other chapters in this book, for example, reference is made to the attempt to offset public sector borrowing deficits by selling public assets in order to help fund taxation reductions for the primarily better off. The early privatization proceeds, mostly of utility monopolies (telecommunications, gas, oil), were certainly geared to this objective. As we shall see in this chapter, the selling of water utility services and of nuclear power could not be achieved without creating a financial and environmental crisis on their own account. In the case of water investment, especially for sewage treatment and drinking water quality, the "environment" and "Brussels" (in the form of European Commission directives sanctioned by UK environment ministers through collective bargaining (see Johnson and Corcelle 1989)) have been used as legitimating scapegoats to allow the private water utilities to raise prices well above the average level of inflation for at least ten years, while expensive investments are duly made via customer charging that were not made by the Thatcher-dominated state throughout the 1980s (see Environment Committee 1987, Kinnersley 1988).

In a similar vein, in the previous chapter Cloke itemizes the changing economics of modern agriculture where taxpayer-boosted subsidies on a vast scale encouraged excessive investment in crop, livestock and land productivity—all at the expense of the consumer, the natural environment and, it now appears, the marginal farmer (see Bowers and Cheshire 1984, Lowe *et al.* 1986, Marsden 1990). True, the Thatcher government had not wished to be party to this since 1984, but prior to that it actively encouraged the promotion of agricultural accumulation.

Now that the crisis of excessive capitalization, falling subsidies and environmental destruction is fully apparent (see Nature Conservancy Council 1984, Royal Society for the Conservation of Nature 1990) the government is busily trying to legitimate the continued expenditure of public money on a dispossessed agriculture via various programmes of production control and environmental conservation. None of these is sufficient to offset the crisis of capital deficit facing agriculture, yet in the process of adjustment, the task of environmental conservation has been transferred from an act of voluntary conscience to a salvaging operation of mercenary commodification (Marsden *et al.* 1986). This is not the case for all farmers, by any means (Country Landowners Association 1989), but the act of making a commodity out of environmental conservation has not only become enshrined in advisory institutions and the law. It is also presented as an article of faith in the government's White Paper on the environment (HM Government 1990). Here is the relevant passage at para 7.32 of the White Paper.

> Farmers need advice to help them adjust to changing circumstances. The Agricultural Development and Advisory Service will be mounting an intensive campaign in 1991 to encourage greater conservation awareness among farmers, and to demonstrate how they can make the most of opportunities for using and marketing the environmental assets of their farms.

Environmental restoration and maintenance of protected landscapes and habitats, very much after the event of widespread alteration and physical abuse of ecosystems, are now becoming the objects of private enterprise and public income support. It is precisely this duality of objectives, of the uneasy compromise between the public and private spheres, that Blowers was alluding to, and which heralds the tension between neo liberal Thatcherism and the realities of a caring state for the longer term public good.

This is a classic case of a legitimation crisis. British farmers followed the signals that collective governmental action, backed by commercial exploitation by the agribusiness industries, provided for them. In the process the farmer damaged the land, ran into debt, and lost room for manoeuvre in income diversification. Figure 12.1 illustrates the outcome. The big boys, known as accumulators in the Marsden *et al.* (1986) jargon, will not only survive. They will be the prime recipients of any state-directed cash to restore degraded land into a healthier or more scenic condition. The marginalized farmers, on the other hand, lack the skills and the financial flexibility to make the necessary

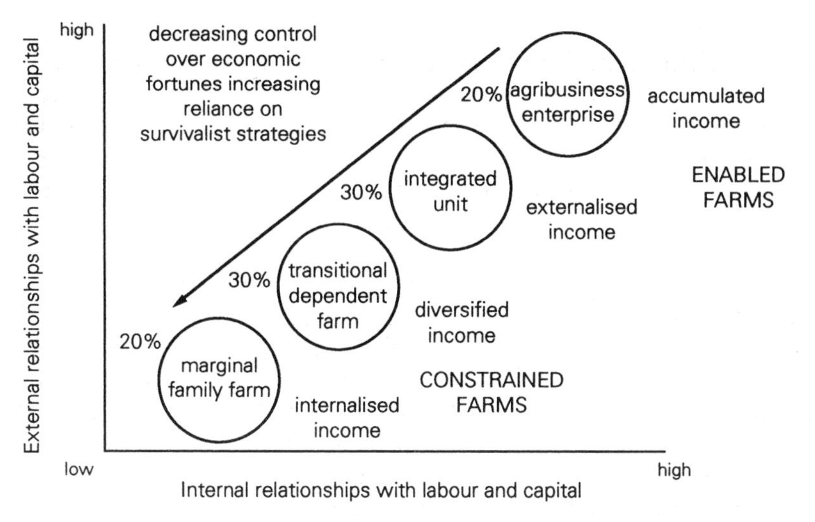

FIG. 12.1. "Ideal types" of modern UK farm.

adjustments. Yet their presence holds the key to much of the more precious landscapes and rural economies. Direct income support coupled to a well-defined stewardship role is one possibility. But the state has not been good either at providing charity or at directing private economic effort in such a comprehensive manner to promote the public good. The danger is that agricultural support policy is likely to become a real mess. Those who are most in need will not be given adequate help. Those least in need could well usurp the new conservation cash on offer. This will help them pay to restore the damage that the state financed them to wreak only ten to fifteen years ago.

This tension between state spending to fix a mess and private entrepreneurship is also exhibited in the changes affecting environmental regulation and in energy planning and management. Nowhere is this more evident than in the dramatic change of fortunes over the nuclear industry. Three factors have caused the mothballing of Britain's one proud nuclear development programme: Chernobyl, privatization, and climate warming scares. Chernobyl proved to many that nuclear power could never be wholly safe, and anything less would be unacceptable. A Chernobyl-type disaster in a rich nation with energy choices would be an unmitigated political disaster. As it is the Soviets will have to lose 6 per cent of their whole economy to pay for the consequences (Medvedev 1990).

Privatization forced the nuclear industry to its Waterloo in the form of city financiers. They looked at escalating decommissioning costs and the never ending saga of opposition to radioactive waste disposal, and realized that this was an industry that would not pay its way in open competition. The two ideologies of the Conservatives favouring free energy markets and state buttressed nuclear power development clashed head on. The aborted privatization of the nuclear industry finally made public what analysts knew all along, namely that big, base load nuclear power is uneconomic (Mackerron 1988).

Climate warming has put the main pressure on energy conservation, not new generating capacity of whatever kind. In this regard the Thatcher government misread the public mood. That mood favours subsidized energy saving investment. Thatcherist approaches to public spending and subsidy kill it. There is no more money available for energy conservation than there was in 1980. The "spend to save" paradox is just as evident in the struggle between a desire to ensure that the environmental damager pays and the wider political containment of rises in consumer prices and the safeguarding of industrial competitiveness. The need to price energy, fertilizers, water, mineral extraction in sensitive locations, and the disposal of toxic and persistent bio-accumulative wastes with regard to their environmentally disruptive side effects has never been greater. This argument has been admirably presented by David Pearce and his colleagues in their much cited report, *Blueprint for a Green Economy* (Pearce *et al.* 1989). Yet the government persistently refuses actually to levy environmental taxes on the grounds that it is electorally dangerous, at odds with macroeconomic policy, and potentially inhibiting to industrial enterprise when there can be no guarantee that other countries will follow the same path.

Here we see critical theory in its full glory. Environmental policies are in a fascinating state of flux. Economics, law, international relations, social conscience and principles of individual freedom versus collective well-being are all undergoing change. The old way of looking at these things is no longer tenable in the modern world of environmental crisis. The government is grappling with the changing demands on the state: how far should it lead, how much should it follow public opinion? To what extent should the state become the conscience for future generations? What is the appropriate mix of private pricing or taxation and public investment to ensure that the management structures and technologies of tomorrow are ready for when they are required? The free market has never been free, nor socially just. The environmental invisible hand cannot operate outside of strong national and international legal commitment and political guidance. Critical theory and environmental change are focused on the educative and liberative aspects of the rewarding tensions between appropriate role for the private and public spheres set in a flux of changing social values.

Dry Greenism and Critical Theory

It has never been easy to define environmentalism, and it is nowadays even more difficult to do so. This is because the environmental message has begun to permeate all aspects of daily behaviour, from absorbing messages in the media, through political rhetoric at all levels of government, via finance, marketing, manufacturing, consumer choice and leisure. Contrary to the judgement of Habermas, environment itself is becoming part of the commodification exercise, potentially threatening to undermine the very essence of the modern market economy.

Beforehand, environmentalism was ideologically separable. It could be accepted or rejected without fundamentally changing world view and social morality. An earlier distinction between ecocentrism (an earth caring mode) and technocentrism (an earth transforming mode) (see O'Riordan 1981, Pepper, 1984, and Dobson 1990: pp. 86-87) was based on the principle that environmental ideologies were not central to value formation and behaviour guidance. Such ideologies were more peripheral, dislodgeable when the pressure to retain material standards became very great.

Figure 12.2 illustrates a slightly different formulation (see O'Riordan 1990). Nowadays, we are all green to some extent, but the depth of greenness varies considerably. Thatcherism remains at the right hand end of the spectrum, in the "dry green" mode. Here there is great emphasis on the earth as a set of physical and chemical processes which need to be understood, in order to be mastered. Hence the emphasis on fundamental scientific research and theory building. The aim here is that once understood, meddling with these processes holds the key to global manipulation in the interests of both the earth and humanity. Just as science forms the basis for national action, so "sound" economics provides the method by which scientifically grounded policies can be valuated for the costs of taking various courses of action, including doing nothing, set against the benefits of putting the earth to rights or not messing it up in the first place.

In this respect the government's White Paper on environmental strategy is enlightening. Under the sub-title "fact not fancy" the

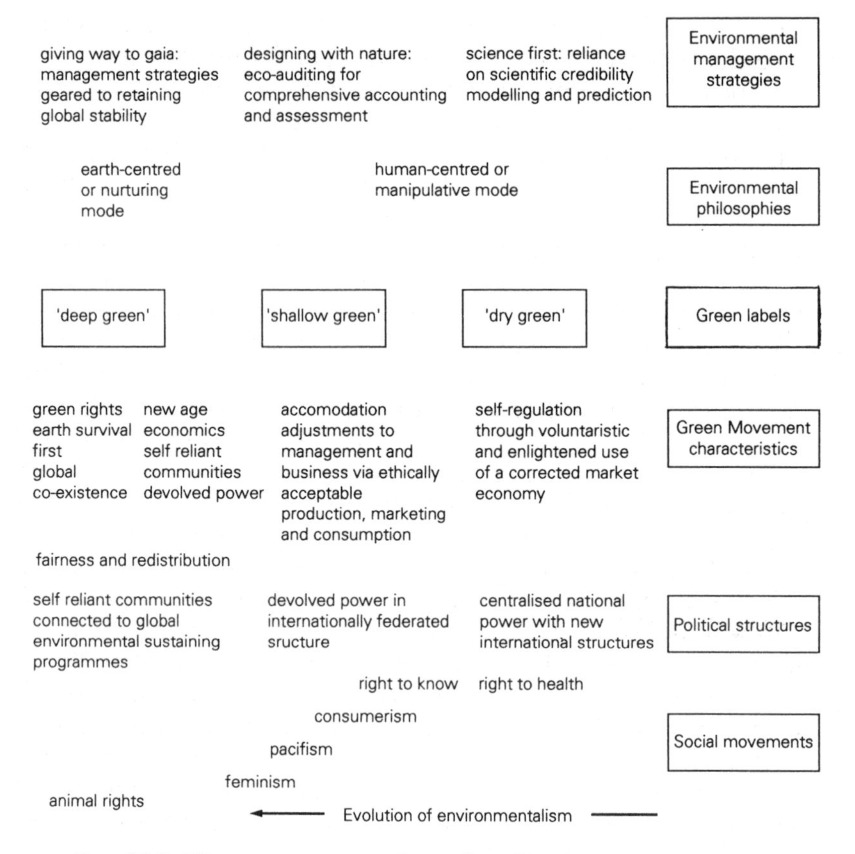

FIG. 12.2. The contemporary dynamics of environmentalism, social change and environmental management

government takes the view that in environmental decisions, as elsewhere, there is a need "to look at all the facts and likely consequences of actions on the basis of the best scientific and economic information available. Precipitate action on the basis of inadequate evidence is the wrong response" (HM Government 1990, para 1.17, p. 11). With regard to the precautionary principle, the issue which still divides Britain and the US from continental Europe, the government backed away from the ministerial declaration at a UN regional conference in Bergen in May 1990 where it agreed that lack of full scientific certainty should not be used as a reason for postponing measures to prevent environmental degradation, where there are threats of serious or irreversible damage. In its White Paper (ibid., para 1.8) the government believes that it will only take precautionary action "where the balance of likely costs and benefits justifies it".

This position assumes that science and economics can arrive at predictions, analyses and policy judgements in good time to ensure that "sound" advance decisions are made. To this end, the Thatcher administration places some store on British global environmental science, notably on climate warming research, ozone depletion appraisals, and practical measures to monitor and to understand the rich ecosystems of tropical rain forests. It is also in this vein that the administration has welcomed a centre for global environmental policy research, reliant on a strong input of environmental economics (HM Government 1990; para 17.9).

There are important features of the Thatcherisque variant of dry greenism. The former Prime Minister's concern with global warming, and global change generally, as first announced in her important door-opening speech to the Royal Society in September 1988, was a feature of her genuine scientific interest, her belief that sound science must form the basis of any political action, and her desire to lead the world stage on environmental matters. It was also the reason why she would not readily be budged on the policy of stabilizing carbon dioxide emissions only by 2005. Given prudent housekeeping in the meantime, this need not cost the UK economy very much, except possibly in a leaner, privatizable, coal industry. There is money in energy conservation nowadays, even without a carbon tax, or similar levy, and the normal practices of industrial prudence, coupled to a voluntaristic greening of key industrial sectors and well-known companies (see Elkington and Burke 1987, Cairncross 1990), should almost do the job without the need for heavy handed government regulation. However, if the German preference, namely for a reduction of carbon dioxide of 25 per cent of 1990 levels by 2005, were to become European Community policy, then the role of regulation and pricing would have to come far more prominent. Such a position is also advocated by the Dutch and Danish governments, and now supported by the Commission of the European Communities. This would almost certainly be quite contrary to the former Prime Minister's wishes.

Shallow Greenism and Critical Theory

This chapter is all about the tension between Thatcherism and a wider environmental political and social imperative. Figure 12.2 suggests that dry greenism is only a comforting start of a process of more radical ideological and structural change. In the middle is shallow greenism, the fashionable centre ground of most Liberals, the bulk of environmental scientists and far sighted industrialists and academic economists. Here the environment is visualized as a bundle of processes, all of which have natural functions that serve the interests of human survival and contentment. Forests absorb excess water, and release it gradually: silt from regular and predictable floods nourishes alluvial soils: coral reefs provide harbour for fish, and physical protection against stormy seas: wetlands soak up nutrients, recycle chemicals, and act as sinks for carbon: stratospheric ozone shields the world from lethal ultraviolet rays which might otherwise destroy the marine food chain: and so on.

This perspective forms the basis of a philosophy of designing with nature (see McHarg 1969), namely constructing, transforming and replacing the natural world in a manner that is consistent with the inherent life protecting functions. It is also the basis of the emerging science of ecological economics, outlined by Pearce and Turner (1990) and promoted in the relatively new *Journal of Ecological Economics*. The aim is to combine natural and economic science to provide a more secure approach to valuing the intrinsic merits of natural processes and functions. This has a twin purpose. The first is to provide a better indication of what ecosystems, habitats, species mix, scenic views, cleansing properties are worth in their present state. The second is to illustrate, again by the most informed analysis, how much it might cost to abuse or usurp these values now and create large costs to future generations in the form of repair and restoration.

In the shallow green mode, environmental accounting in the form of side-by-side national economic and environmental accounts, in the guise of industrial environmental audits, and via more comprehensive environmental impact assessments, becomes the essential tool for future management. In shallow greenism, however, voluntarism and good business practice are insufficient safeguards. Regulation needs to be tough, independent, professionally competent and accountable. Regulation must be seen to be the public safeguard, the visible hand of the state guiding the uncertain and untrustworthy invisible hand of the free market.

In critical theory terms, therefore, shallow greenism takes environmental politics a number of steps further than is acceptable to dry greenism. Rights of access to information are paramount for all aspects of health and safety, environmental change, and proposed policy development on executive action. Notification of intent cannot rest on voluntarism and good will: it must be legally enshrined and enforced when incompetently or mischievously misapplied. This goes for the removal of Saxon hedges just as much as for the introduction of genetically modified organisms. In this respect, the Labour Party (1990), ever anxious to catch the middle ground vote, has recently committed itself to a comprehensive Freedom of Information Act that would make rights of access to information a statutory agreement. This is not a position yet endorsed by the Conservatives.

Similarly, accountability of policy and action first to Parliament and second to the courts also becomes paramount. No longer should it be possible for departments of state to avoid a statutory duty of environmental care, laid down by Parliament and subject to parliamentary scrutiny and judicial review. Otherwise the mouthings of environmental concern remain the distorting rhetoric that fuels the legitimation crises alluded to earlier.

Third, regulation must be seen to be independent of those who are being regulated. The actual practice of regulatory enforcement should also be free of meddling by government. This suggests that the regulatory agencies responsible for health and safety and pollution control, on the one hand, and the custodial agencies responsible for nature conservation, scenic beauty, historic buildings and landscapes and public enjoyment of amenity and heritage generally, on the other, should be clear of governmental influence, at least to the point of articulating policy and pursuing objectives (see O'Riordan and Weale 1990).

Once again, the role of critical theory is relevant here. Such agencies should *educate* via information, consultation and the seeking of consent for their actions and their economic consequences. They should *elucidate* choices for regulatory action. Examples of such choices include the option of taking action now or delaying to action later (precaution). Another is the scope to dilute and disperse versus to contain and eliminate where the determining factors as to which route to take will be the comparative costs and the strictures of international regulatory conditions imposed on countries by collective consent. A third arena for policy choice involves voluntary compliance compared with strict liability coupled to built in protection via "superfund" levies. These may be necessary to pay for possible long term public or ecosystem ill health effects arising out of hazard or toxic contamination that is unforeseen. Finally there is nowadays the more discussed option of command and control versus economic incentives and market based compliance.

This suggests a role for custody and regulation that goes beyond standard setting, emissions permitting and enforcement of licences or agreed practices. It suggests that, in order to offset the inherent legitimation crises of environmental degradation usurping future corporate profitability and, in the shorter term, corporate public relations and consumer and shareholder backing, the regulatory agencies need to adopt an proactive educative, elucidative and policy evaluative role that is both informing and participatory. To date the various agencies concerned, with the possible exception of the former Nature Conservancy Council and the Countryside Commission, have not seen this as their function.

In the difficult areas of environmental risk from radiation, waste disposal sites, incinerators and genetically modified organisms and foods, this elucidatory and participatory role is becoming ever more necessary. Here science in its conventional form cannot provide unambiguous answers regarding long term safety and sustainability. In the absence of that assurance, the regulatory process needs to incorporate legitimate public anxieties and demands for compensatory safeguards in the event of unforeseen calamity or accident. This can be done by opening up the regulatory process to a wider representation of consumer interests, by ensuring that adequate safeguards are built in, and by creating local risk information services to allow the community living nearby hazardous facilities to have a greater say over standards of safety and public health protection.

The emerging character of environmental custody and regulation is an important tension zone in contemporary British environmental politics. Until the mid 1980s the tradition for regulation lay in secrecy, paternalism and close client-regulator relations (see Ashby and Anderson 1984, Hawkins and Thomas 1984). Since 1987 important changes have taken place, notably in the area of environmental protection.

To begin with the government has created a unified inspectorate of pollution control, known as Her Majesty's Inspectorate of Pollution (HMIP), to prepare a single integrated permit for certain classes of especially awkward industry. Similar reforms have been introduced for local authority environmental health regulation for air pollution control (advance notification procedures and more formal practices according to best practice guides), for waste disposal (independent waste disposal executives), and for monitoring and enforcement. These are contained in the Environmental Protection Act 1990. The history of the formation of HMIP is written up by O'Riordan and Weale (1989) and by O'Riordan (1989). It is largely a result of a power struggle within Whitehall between Environment and Health and Safety, between the public environmental sphere and the commercial management sphere, between the dictates of administrative efficiency against the dangers of time consuming and cumbersome bureaucracy, and because of a desire on the part of industry to be regulated by competent people who could commit themselves to a licensing regime that is predictable well in advance.

This last point is crucial and has a significance beyond the role and responsibility of HMIP. The contemporary drive for tougher and more independent regulation comes from the responsible element of industry itself. British industry is well aware that the European Community is determining the critical standards for air, water and land protection, via an onslaught of directives, new legal safeguards and the whims of an environmentally concerned European Parliament. Industry is also well aware that environmental regulation is no longer a purely British matter. So it is looking for a secure basis for regulation that will allow it to determine its processes, product mix and abatement technology years in advance. This combines good practice with necessary environmental safeguards. The really powerful companies and trade associations are even seeking to establish standards that are more advanced and protective than the best technology guidelines put forward by HMIP and its sister organizations.

This is another aspect of the changing relationship between modern environmentalism and legitimation of the survival of capitalism. The private sector does not want merely to rely on voluntary compliance. It is looking for an acceptable regime of regulation that will justify in the eyes of the consumer and the shareholder that it is following the very best practices covering energy conservation, recycling, non-hazardous product manufacture, environmentally benign waste flows and strict liability procedures in the event of accident. To date only a few lead corporations are taking this line. But others will have to follow.

Shallow Greenism and Regulatory Reform

Lying in wait in shallow greenism are three fundamental, and internationally binding, policy measures that will force the state to take a much more proactive role, but which can only be achieved by strict compliance at the industry and household levels. These three measures are (i) national regulatory "bubbles"; (ii) best practice and strict liability; and (iii) public trust and equivalent compensation. In each of these three important measures three principles are at stake. One is the legitimation of regulation in relation to good science and public support. A second is the legitimation of international control over national domestic environmental and economic policies—a highly controversial area that is still in a state of early transition. The third is the legitimation of environmental sustainability as an organizing concept for economic management generally. Environmentalism is taking on the big guns of society and development.

National regulatory "bubbles" have become a standard tool of European Community environmental policy (see Rebinder 1989). The idea is to establish a total Euro-pollutant load for each class of emissions, and to assign to each member state a suitable proportion of that load in the form of a national emission bubble. The idea is central to the directive on large combustion plants, which fix the national emissions of sulphur dioxide and nitrogen dioxide, and it will emerge in the forthcoming municipal water treatment directive and directive on civil liability for damage caused by waste.

In each case, the Commission's approach is to set the national "bubble" and leave it to each member state to decide just how to meet the target. In the past, the line taken by the British government is to do the least that is necessary in the hope that general industrial productivity advances will do the trick. Rose (1990) covers this general point very well (see also Friends of the Earth 1990). Nowadays that is an unacceptable position to take, so targets for emissions are being set.

An extension of the bubble approach is the application of the *critical loads principle*. This has been announced in the white paper (HM Government 1990, p. 144). Figure 12.3 describes the process. The aim is to try to establish an ecologically feasible total acceptable load for each class of pollutants, mathematically modelled for sensitive regions. This can then be set against targets for emission controls set to cost-benefit calculations of achievement indices. The critical loads idea is fine in principle. It will be useful if it can provide a tough yardstick to set against present performance. But if it becomes an excuse for sloppy science and abatement control it could be counterproductive. Time and experience will tell.

The trouble is that these targets fly in the face of the two recent major privatizations in electricity and water. The newly privatized electricity generating companies, National Power and Powergen, cannot meet the SO_2 and NO_x emission reduction targets without the need to finance major new investment costs that would possibly frighten potential investors. Yet the new, muscle-bound HMIP is looking for *best available technology not entailing excessive costs* (BATNEEC), as already practised according to the highest standards elsewhere, to be the basis of regulating integrated

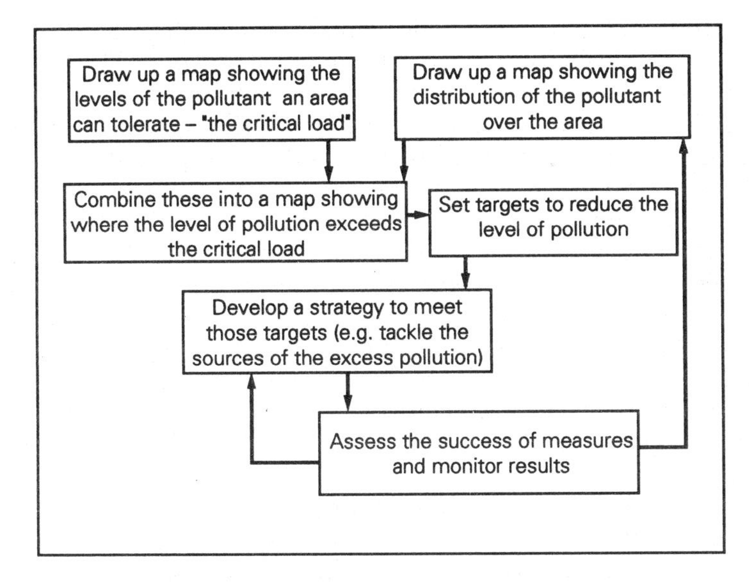

FIG. 12.3. The processes leading to the application of the critical loads concept.
Source: HM Government 1990, p. 141.

pollution control. This means expensive but effective flue gas desulphurization, nitrogen oxides elimination and containment of toxic materials in the resultant sludge. Advanced technologies already exist in Germany and Japan, and it is at these expensive but efficient processes HMIP is looking (see Environmental Data Services 1990). Under the Environmental Protection Act, HMIP would be liable to prosecution if it did not follow BATNEEC principles. A court action is now more likely because the authorization process is now much more open. Similarly in the water sector, the privatized utilities will have to face up to over £5.5 billion of new investment over the next 20 years simply to meet the minimum environmental standards imposed by the European Commission and already agreed to by British ministers (Bowers 1989).

In both these cases there will be a clash between private commercial interest, privatization, political protectionism, and the new look arms length regulatory agencies (in this case HMIP and the National Rivers Authority (NRA)). It is likely that in the resulting fudge and nudge, the regulatory agencies will prevail, accepting a longer time period of compliance than is wanted by the Commission, but requiring more costly levels of investment than the new electricity generation companies and the private water utilities would like.

Look for the fine print of the final prospectuses of the electricity generation companies. As was the case in the water industry, a greater level of debt write off will have to be financed by the government in advance of final flotation to allow for the share price to be attractive. The legitimation crisis, as so often is the case, will be temporarily resolved by means of taxpayer baleout, whereby the state has to intervene to protect the private capital it has created.

The strict liability doctrine is altogether more worrying for the private sector. This will apply especially to hazardous waste reduction. It will mean that not only the waste disposal company, but also any body "holding" financial control over that company, will be liable for any environmental or public health effects resulting either from accidental misdemeanours or unforeseen chemical contamination. This liability will apply, regardless of fault, even when best practice is in place, and the companies concerned have complied with all regulatory licences.

These tough proposals emanating from Brussels fly in the face of British waste management strategy, so carefully crafted for industry in the Environmental Protection Act of 1990. That statute makes it difficult for the NRA to pre-empt action likely to pollute a water course in advance of nuisance. It also retains the *caveat emptor* (buyer beware) principle which relieves a discharger of the duty to disclose knowledge of contamination. This will make it difficult for planning authorities to use the precautionary principle when considering waste disposal applications (see Reid 1990).

It is possible that the strict liability doctrine will extend to consumer safety generally and not just to toxic waste disposal. The implications both for regulation and for industrial practice are formidable. As the regulatory agencies begin to charge for their licensing administration, so industry may seek to make them jointly liable for any resulting legal action on strict liability grounds. This is bound to increase further the pressure on the regulatory agencies to be much more accountable for their actions, and to allow a little more daylight between their own policies, and broader policies of environmental protection set by the Department of the Environment. This in turn may lead to a more policy and organizationally independent regulatory regime than even that outlined in the white paper where only a small step in independence is proposed for HMIP alone, (HM Government 1990: p. 232). Such a regime could well become a co-ordinated Environmental Protection Executive, with sufficient cash and staff resources to undertake a strict compliance approach (see O'Riordan and Weale 1990). This would also have to involve much more publicity concerning policy formulation, standard setting, enforcement practices and financial control of the whole process, probably before strengthened parliamentary select committees.

The scope for regulatory agencies, together with their back up advisory committees, to be more open and revealing over the public interest aspects of their work is considerable. So far few of these advisory agencies have taken such responsibilities seriously (Everest 1989). However, the political climate is changing, and it is ever more necessary for such organizations to "prepare the ground" via public consultation and incorporation of consumer representatives amongst their number, in order to remain credible and accountable.

The *public trust doctrine* is not yet officially accepted in British land management practice. Its roots lie in Roman law, and it has been developed in the States with remarkable effect (see Sax 1972). The essential feature of this doctrine is that natural resources are truly a common inheritance and heritage, so they should be passed on in good heart to future generations. This is one feature of the sustainability principle, about which so much is discussed nowadays (see Brundtland Commission 1987, Turner 1989, Engel and Engel 1989).

The twin principles of this doctrine are:

1. Where an ecosystem, or a natural process generally, or a human culture, is irreplaceable if damaged, and vital to the understanding and functioning of the earth's life-sustaining processes, it should be safeguarded against any molestation irrespective of cost. This is the *biodiversity principle.*
2. Where ecosystems, processes or cultures are significant, but not vital for global sustainability, damage to their integrity must be compensated for by complementary investment in kind or other resources that provides at least as much satisfaction or viability of process as was the case beforehand. This is the *equivalent compensation principle.*

This approach is now being followed in US wetlands, and may become the cornerstone of a revived tropical rainforest strategy (see, for example, Winterbottom 1990). It hinges on good scientific assessment of ecological and anthropological criticality, coupled to powerful negotiating techniques of both developers and the custodial planners and land managers. The role of mediation is also significant in this regard, as are the power and influence of the international conservation non governmental agencies such as World Wide Fund for Nature, the various bird protection organizations and the International Union for the Conservation for Nature.

All this suggests a form of plea bargaining between developers and spokespeople for the larger global interest. It also suggests that private sector short termism will have to give way to a broader definition of a commercial environmental conscience. At present, certainly on the international stage, this seems most unlikely. But as the power of ethical investment groups influences shareholder concerns, as the international media coverage of major issues trigger environmental consciences more profoundly, and as a new cohort of environmentally more sensitized corporate managers come to the fore, so the tensions between old style capitalism and some neo-liberal capitalism may begin to be resolved.

Shallow greenism provides the setting for the acting out of the legitimation crisis between the respective roles of the individual, the local communities, the corporation and the financing institutions, the regulatory and custodial agencies, the international environmental diplomatic community and the state generally. At present the various relationships involved are all in flux. The individual is only beginning to be mobilized, and mostly in areas, such as the choice of "ozone friendly" aerosol propellants, which can easily be accommodated with no change of values or lifestyles. The much more radical changes have yet to be discussed, let alone enacted. Industry has barely begun to wake up to the challenge, especially in the UK. The environmental audit is still seen as a financial management exercise, or at best new public relations angle. It is not yet regarded as a fundamental basis for reorientating and restructuring the whole ethics and practice of production, though, to be fair, the Business in the Environment Green Guide for Managers is a step in the right direction.

On the regulatory side, the Thatcher legacy has been to leave a paradox. This is in the form of a halfway house of administrative independence, some element of charging, though mostly on a cost recovery basis with only a promise of proper environmental charging in the future, and serious lack of cash for reorganization, recruitment and the retention of senior and experienced officials. The new National Rivers Authority as well as the HMIP are beginning to lose good people and are desperately short of funds for proper surveillance. The local environmental health authorities are penalized by poll tax restrictions and the constraints of annual budget accounts that can neither be exceeded nor found to have shortfall at the end of the financial year. Long-term capital investment in, say, energy conservation measures or pollution control equipment is simply not possible in many local government departments, despite the need for long-term environmental investment, and the probability of tougher environmental charging.

The result is an uneasy and shifting coalition of uncertain interrelationships between a state that is recognizing its public interest role but which is unable to exercise it properly, an industrial sector that is becoming more proactive environmentally, but is uncertain how far to go, and an international political arena that will increasingly have to take the lead simply to ensure compliance. It will be around this triangular pivot that the next phase of legitimation will take place. What will be the role of the citizen and the consumer in this process?

Deep Greenism and the Environmental Crisis

So far we have been looking at the next ten to twenty years. In this phase there is nothing on the environmental horizon that should upset the basic power structure of the rich northern countries, assuming that they will remain largely anaesthetized to the growing pain and suffering in the Third World. Beyond 2010, however, the future looks somewhat grimmer for the globe as a whole. In a nutshell the largely cosmetic changes outlined in shallow greenism will by then have been shown to fail. It is a feature of critical theory that distortion and legitimation work hand in hand. Right now the industrialist, the politician and the citizen are being persuaded that modest levels of reform will somehow do the trick, that capitalism will essentially survive, and that wealth creation and an element of sharing can continue in the shadowy state of sustainable development. It is doubtful that the environmental conscience movement will puncture this "dream" picture in the foreseeable future, since the evidence of calamity is not anywhere overwhelmingly present. Even Third World environmental tragedies can be explained away in terms of corruption, insupportable tax and subsidy regimes favouring squandering by the rich, and by marxist or at least socialist governments which fail to make the private sector work.

So distortion of the real non-sustainability crisis continues unabated. Deep greenism takes a more radical view of the world. It draws its perspective from a series of loosely connected ideas that depart from mainstream science, economics, politics and philosophy (see Dobson 1990: pp. 135-152 for a readable review). Because their ideas diverge from established professional wisdom, and because proof of conjecture into the real generation is all but impossible, so deep greens remain socially and politically peripheral. Irvine and Ponton (1988) provide a reasonable statement of the green manifesto.

At the heart of deep green thinking lie three fundamental concepts. The first is that humans are marginal to the real well-being of the earth, so should see their role much more as a tenant in the process of co-evolution, than as master and steward. This position is enhanced by philosophical misinterpretation of the gaia thesis advanced by the geochemist James Lovelock (1989). Lovelock is anxious to convert the gaia thesis into a scientific doctrine, namely that the earth acts as a physiological whole, purely by random interactive processes that maintain homeostasis, just as the physionomy of the human body achieves similar results so long as the body and mind are healthy. Lovelock's ideas are not wholly dismissed by scientists, though there is still general unease as to the merits of the argument (see Schneider 1990). Deep greens like to use the gaia idea as a metaphor for an all powerful life support hypothesis which humans must adhere to because of their own, inbuilt, gaian imperatives.

Second the deep green credo is based on the idea of communal self reliance within a federation of global co-operation. The idea is to give to the lowest level of government the scope for life support, communal co-operation and trading of services between families and neighbourhoods, yet fit this all into some grand global survival plan (see Ekins 1986 for an early statement: fuller analyses are expected shortly).

Third the deep green philosophy extends to a much greater sense of social fundamentalism than is nowadays found in left of centre parties who nowadays search for new liberal social democratic issues to remain viable. This social fundamentalism has its roots in both the idea of communal sharing and the provision of basic needs to retain the essential fabric of survival. It encompasses such notions as negative income tax, a land rent based on the real environmental value of resources, and on the state provision of essential social services such as health care, family planning, education, the mobilization of civil liberties, and the removal of debt. Many of these ideas are becoming part of official thinking at the international environmental diplomatic level (see IUCN 1990) and some will undoubtedly be raised at the 1992 UN Conference on Environment and Development to be held in Rio de Janeiro to set the basis for a sustainable future.

Deep greenism is radical in that it encompasses rights of minorities to be protected, it demands that civil liberties are extended, it expects that the peace dividend will be directed at sustainable development, and it looks to rights of nature as being on an equal footing as rights of humanity. It also seeks federation of nation states into larger co-operating entities, and the denationalization of power into local community structures that are broadly socialist in principle but allow private initiative to flourish at the points of fine detail (see Weston 1986 for an exposition of this principle).

Figure 12.4 outlines the main challenge of deep greenism, and the five fundamental barriers to its achievement. The diagram rests on the principle that there is, at present, no superhuman religious morality, whether via traditional religion or through a variant of the gaian theme (see Engel and Engel 1989 for a good review of religious views and environmental sustainability, but also for a sensitive analysis of how and why this rhetoric is not transmitted into practice).

The point of the diagram is to suggest that almost all people, wherever they live, at whatever they do, are alienated from the environmental disruption they in part help to create. Alienation in this sense is part of a critical theoretic concept. It suggests that people are misinformed, that crucial information is not available, that various authoritative structures are designed to thwart and to obscure, and that one crisis leads to various structure and

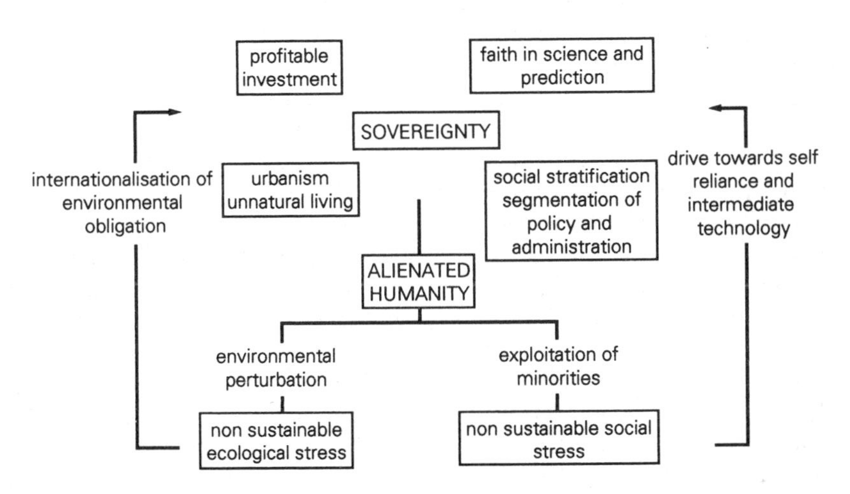

FIG. 12.4. Environmental alienation.

power maintaining outcomes that fail to resolve the underlying dilemma.

National sovereignty still holds sway, even in the confederated structures of the European Community or in federated states such as the old Commonwealth, the US and Germany. Struggles over ownership of resources and rights to control pricing and trade flows result in distortions to natural resource pricing and gross manipulation of resource trading markets. Nationalism also appears in the form of ecological sovereignty. It will not be easy to force the tropical forest owing states to adopt protective measures, even with compensatory financial and legal arrangements, unless the sovereignty issue is handled with considerable care and diplomatic delicacy. This means recognizing much greater sovereign rights than merely to ownership of forests, and will have to embrace trade patterns, debt write off and social improvement investment.

The other four boxes in the upper part of the diagram are relatively self explanatory. Science is not always able to serve in the cause of global survival, as this area of scientific understanding has hardly begun to be developed. Similarly, regulation in the cause of elucidating options and identifying long-term outcomes is still in its infancy. Bureaucracies that divide wholes into parts, and chop patterns of programme spending into inconvenient annual segments, are equally to blame. Finally the sense of individual culpability, the belief that personal action is vital and that the cause of collective well-being will only be pursued by a trust that everybody else has to play by the rules, all of these are still lacking, largely because, as yet these principles have been obscured from education and the general pattern of awareness raising.

So the deep green perspective is to couple global responsibility with defederated individual and communal action. This requires freeing peoples from the tyranny of markets and short-term expediency to the liberating pastures of communal co-operation, basic needs provision and constructive experimentation in sustainable development, all set within a neo-liberal approach to regulation, custodial management of resources, and international sharing regimes.

So far this is pie-in-the-sky thinking, despite some good ideas from the concerned environmental community (see World Resources Institute 1989, IUCN 1991). After all, the essential political maxim is that one will not achieve one's ends if the opposing minority is seriously bent on resistance. All the evidence to date is that the big players, namely the US and Japan, are not prepared to shoulder the burden of global financial sharing until the environmental crises is shown to be upsetting world economies, and most Third World governments rid themselves of corruption and financial mismanagement generally. In this cause, the other major economic powers, Germany, Britain, France, hold a similar line.

The environmental crisis on a global scale will have to get more obvious before anything serious is done about it. No amount of liberal bleeding hearts will change that. In the meantime shallow greenism will play an important role at the national level, and will open up avenues for elucidation and awareness raising. This is certainly no panacea, but is a necessary realism unless the political and educational transformation outcomes demanded by critical theory are somehow speeded up.

Critical Theory and Environmental Futures

At present critical theory provides a basis for analysis, but little else. Despite the potentially alarming prospects for environment and economy generally, it is unlikely that critical theory will provide the powerful force for evolutionary change that is fundamentally required. Nevertheless, in its role of seeking to classify how the environmental crisis is occurring and why it is likely to get worse before it gets better, critical theory can at least provide a perspective for other more radical movements to follow.

The centre for action in the longer term must lie in the non governmental movement. This is the only basis for communal involvement that combines education, enlightenment and experimentation beyond the confines of official government that is perforce sectorized, narrow minded and inherently corruptible. Already the non governmental movement is gratifyingly activated at the international level in what is known as the Brundtland process—the follow up of the World Commission on Environment and Development process that began in 1987 and will continue beyond the Rio meeting in 1992. There are encouraging signs of genuine international NGO co-ordination of effort which will embrace the young, education, industry, science and the trades unions. This will take time, and needs nurturing, but some reasonable amounts of private philanthropic money is in the offering to help this process.

At a national level, the NGO movement is also beginning to make waves on such issues as experiments in sustainable development, alternative energy schemes, community environmental audits and the opening up of self-help co-operatives for women and ethnic minorities. At present this is still on the small scale. But the fact that it is expanding and that it is now benefiting from the experiences of others, is a sign of hope for greater co-ordination in the future.

At the local level, too little is still being done. This is not a topic for "trickle down" politics, quite the reverse. The NGO movement is just becoming activated on a community basis, but at present more so in the Third World than in the richer world. This is understandable given the relative complacency built into the structures depicted in Fig. 12.4, but it is not an arrangement that can continue if genuine awareness raising is to achieve fundamental changes in behaviour and outlook.

Maybe the solution here lies in greater regulatory pressure, especially from international protocols, that force governments to establish local structures for implementation in areas such as best practice, strict liability provision and the public trust doctrine. Maybe it will be through the force of co-operative compulsion that local initiatives will begin to spawn—over energy conservation, resource pricing, nature protection and community sharing that could become the hallmarks of twenty-first century environmentalism. In this transition, critical theory does have a role to play, but as collaborator rather than a subversive force.

Finally, to repeat the words of caution spelt out earlier. Environmentalism is currently the flavour of the month. It will not go away, but it cannot afford to push its luck. It will not succeed by frightening or by threatening, nor will it prevail by demanding social reform that is ahead of its time. To push too hard may well prove counterproductive. One must always remember that the death knells to past environmental movements have been recession and war. Both occurred in late 1990. Environmentalism will need to be contained in broader political and social movements aimed at justice, compassion, harmonious relations with people and the natural world, and slow but steady decentralization of power within internationalizing government.

In this process a mixture of social spending, state direction, private initiative and communal self help will set the pattern for a post Thatcher legacy of environmental reform. Thatcherism laid down vital markers for choice and initiative with an attempt to put the state in its proper (secondary) place. In reassessing the future role of the state, we must never forget the immense significance of that legacy. The acid test is to resurrect the public interest role of the state as broker and regulator beyond the national boundary yet within a positive climate of personal initiative, and global conscience.

References

Ashby, E., and Anderson, M. (1984) *The Politics of Air Pollution*. Clarendon Press, London.

Blowers, A. (1987) Transition or transformation? Environmental policy under Thatcher. *Public Administration* **65**: 277-294.

Bowers, J. (1989) *Liquid Costs*. World Wide Fund for Nature. Godalming, Surrey.

Bowers, J., and Cheshire, P. (1984) *Agriculture, the Countryside and Land Use*. Methuen, London.

Brundtland, G.H. (Chair) (1987) *Our Common Future*. Oxford University Press, Oxford.

Cairncross, F. (1990) Cleaning up: A survey of industry and the environment. *The Economist* 8 September, 30pp.

Country Landowners Association (1989) *The Environmental Land Management Service Scheme* (The Greenwell Report). CLA, London.

Dobson, A. (1990) *Green Political Thought*. Unwin Hyman, Hemel Hempstead.

Ekins, P. (ed.) (1986) *The Living Economy*. Routledge, London.

Elkington, J., and Burke, T. (1987) *The Green Capitalists: Industry and Environmental Excellence*. Gollancz, London.

Engel, J.R., and Engel, J.G. (eds) (1989) *Ethics of Environment and Development*. Belhaven Press, London.

Environment Committee (1987) *Pollution of Rivers and Estuaries*. HC Paper 183. HMSO, London.

Environmental Data Services Ltd (1990) Green bill rocks the boat for electricity privatisation. *ENDS. Report*, No. 188, pp. 3-4.

Everest, D. (1989) The provision of expert advice to government on environmental matters; the role of advisory committees. *Science and Public Affairs* **4**: 17-40.

Friends of the Earth (1990) *How Green is Britain? The Government's Environmental Record*. Hutchinson Radius, London.

Habermas, J. (1976) *Legitimation Crisis*. Heinemann, London.

Haigh, N. (1987) *EEC Environment Policy and Europe*, 2nd edition. Longmans, London.

Hawkins, K., and Thomas, J.M. (1984) *Enforcing Regulation*. Kluwer Nijholt, Boston.

HM Government (1990) *This Common Inheritance: Britain's Environment Strategy*, Cmd 1200 HMSO, London.

International Union for the Conservation of Nature (1951). *Caring for the Earth. A Strategy for Sustainable Living*. IUCN, Geneva.

Irvine, S., and Ponton, A. (1988) *A Green Manifesto: Policies for a Green Future*. McDonald Optima, London.

Johnson, S.P., and Corcelle, G. (1989) *The Environmental Policy of the European Communities*. Graham and Trotman, London.

Kemp, R.V. (1986) *Power in Planning Decision Making*. PhD. Thesis. University of Wales, Institute of Science and Technology, Cardiff.

Kinnersley, D. (1988) *Troubled Water: Rivers, Politics and Pollution*. Hilary Slipman, London.

Labour Party (1986) *Jobs and the Environment*. Labour Party, Walworth Road, London.

Labour Party (1990) *An Earthly Chance*. Labour Party, Walworth Road, London.

Lovelock, J. (1989) *The Ages of Gaia*. Oxford University Press, Oxford.

Lowe, P., Cox, G., McEwen, M., O'Riordan, T., and Winter, M. (1986) *Countryside Conflicts*. Gower Publishing, Aldershot.

McHarg, I. (1969) *Design With Nature*. Harvest Press, Montreal.
MacKerron, G. (1988) Alternative energy. In MacKay, L. and Thompson, R. (eds.) *Something in the Wind: Politics after Chernobyl*, pp. 161-181 Pluto Press, London.
Marsden, T. (ed.) (1990) Key issues in the political economy of pluriactivity, *Journal of Rural Studies* **6**.
Marsden, J., Munton, R., Whatmore, S., and Little, J. (1986) Towards a political economy of agriculture: a British perspective, *International Journal of Urban and Regional Research* **10** (4): 498-521.
Medvedev, Z. (1990) *The Legacy of Chernobyl*. Basil Blackwell, Oxford.
Nature Conservancy Council (1984) *Great Britain Conservation Strategy*. NCC, Peterborough.
O'Riordan, T. (1981) *Environmentalism*. Pion, London.
O'Riordan, T. (1989) Best practicable environmental option: a case study in practical bureaucratic adaptation, *Environmental Conservation*, **16** (2): 113-122.
O'Riordan, T. (1990) Major projects and the environment, *The Geographical Journal*, **156** (2): 141-148.
O'Riordan, T., and Weale, A. (1989) Administrative reorganisation and policy change: the case of Her Majesty's Inspectorate of Pollution, *Public Administration*, **67** (3): 277-294.
O'Riordan, T., and Weale, A. (1990) *Greening the Machinery of Government*. Friends of the Earth, London.
Pearce, D.W. Markandya, A., and Barbier, E. (1989) *Blueprint for a Green Economy*. Earthscan, London.
Pearce, D.W., and Turner, R.K. (1990) *Economics of Natural Resources and the Environment*. Harvester Press, London.
Pepper, D. (1984) *The Roots of Modern Environmentalism*. Croom Helm, London.
Porritt, J. (1986) Beyond environmentalism. In Goldsmith E. and Hildyard, N. (eds.) *Green Britain or Industrial Wasteland?* pp. 340-350. Polity Press, Cambridge.
Porritt, J., and Winner, D. (1988) *The Coming of the Greens*. Collins Fontana, London.
Rebinder, (1989) U.S. Environmental policy: lessons for Europe? *International Environmental Affairs*, **1** (1): 3-11.
Reid, J. (1990) Contaminated land: a vast inherited problem, *The Planner* 9 November, p. 17.
Rose, C. (1990) *The Dirty Man of Europe*. Simon & Shuster, London.
Royal Society for the Conservation of Nature (1990) *The Health of the Nation*. Lincoln.
Sax, J. (1972). *Defending the Environment*. Knopf, New York.
Schneider, S.H. (1990) Debating gaia, *Environment Magazine*, **32** (4): 4-9, 29-32.
Thompson, J.B., and Held, B. (eds.) (1982) *Habermas: Critical Debates*. Macmillan, London and Basingstoke.
Turner, R.K. (ed.) (1989) *Sustainable Environmental Management*. Belhaven Press, London.
Weston, J. (ed.) (1986) *Red or Green?* Pluto Press, London.
Winterbottom, R. (1990) *Taking Stock: The Tropical Forest Action Plan After Five Years*. World Resources Institute, Washington D.C.
World Resources Institute (1989) *Natural Endowments: Financing Resource Conservation*. WRI, Washington.
World Resources Institute (1990) *World Resources 1990-91*. Oxford University Press, Oxford.

13

Redressing the Balance: Labour, the National State and Spatially Uneven Development

DAVID SADLER

1. Introduction

In the course of the 1970s and the 1980s, social scientific debate on and investigation into the relationships between systems of production and processes of uneven development grappled at first uncertainly, then with growing confidence, over a number of closely related concerns. One of these involved a recognition that the organization of production—the precise combination of productive machinery and labour, and the way in which this was managed and ordered—was integrally engaged in questions to do with the geographical location of production. *How* a good or service was produced or delivered was intimately related to—both affecting and affected by—*where* such processes took place, and this held true at a variety of spatial scales. A second focal point was the increasingly apparent interlinking of the global economy, as long-standing international investment flows seemingly gained ever greater fluidity and the worldwide circulation of capital accelerated. This heightened degree of international connectivity was evidenced also in the emergence of new centres of accumulation, and the challenges which they posed to an established order. And a third (closely related) theoretical and practical agenda entailed consideration of the multitude of ways in which regional trajectories of socioeconomic development were interwoven (via corporate and state policies) as part of a broader national and international fabric: simultaneously product of and condition for global change.

One way of interpreting uneven regional development, that emerged as part of such concerns, lay within a framework wherein different periods or rounds of investment were associated with the creation of regional industrial structures, which overlapped through time in a changing mosaic of economic opportunity and were associated at any one time with particular spatial divisions of labour (see especially Massey 1984). There were a number of contentious aspects to this geological analogy of a layering of regional industrial structures. These included the primacy attached to economic change, and the relationship between economic, social and political transformation. It was nonetheless a widely adopted and useful conceptual device, especially in the extent to which it directed attention to capital's requirements for different kinds of labour supply, and the national state's role in ordering this process. Such issues form the starting point for this chapter.

For instance, regional patterns of growth and decline in the UK could be related to its changing international prospects through different phases of state intervention, with particular implications for waged labour (see especially Massey 1986). Nineteenth-century expansion in the old industrial regions such as North East England, South Wales and Central Scotland (based on industries like coal, steel, shipbuilding and mechanical engineering) hinged on the Imperial dominance of British manufacturing. In this period, work forces were actively constructed in such regions, often through widespread migration and the creation of a wholly new built environment. This process was typified in the one-industry company town. In these places, and more generally, workers became placed in a highly dependent and precarious waged-labour relationship.

During the first half of the twentieth century, the decline of the British Empire was clearly reflected in collapse in these sectors and the first signs of deindustrialization in those regions. Then in the 1960s decentralization from the core regions of the national economy (the West Midlands and the South East, and large urban agglomerations) along with new international investment flows led to a new layer of (temporary) growth being added to peripheral regions such as North East England. There, branch plant operations of multinational capital, attracted by government regional policy incentives and plentiful labour reserves (including incorporation of women into the waged labour force), overlapped the declining heavy industrial complexes and coal-mining areas. This layer or round of investment proved no more able to cope with heightened international competition and its decline only worsened the unemployment crisis in the 1980s, as the older industrial structure went into near terminal collapse. At the same time British financial capital became integrated into a highly sensitive, internationalized circuit, one small cog in a wheel rather than the engine of the system (though London remained an increasingly computerized control room).

Such emphases on the national state dimension in the mediation of international market forces, and the significance of capital's different forms of control over labour, were partly overshadowed during the later 1980s by a welter of claims that a new organizational form was emerging in the global economy, one which was characterized by flexible production. This type of account had many origins, often not necessarily compatible. For Piore and Sabel (1984) the shift was necessitated by a heightened diversity of consumer demand, requiring a much more differentiated product and hence more flexible production processes. To other authors often grounded more or less explicitly in the work of the French regulationist school[1] (see Scott 1988a, Storper and Christopherson 1987), the new system rested on a fragmentation or vertical disintegration, as the economies of scale which had characterized an earlier, Fordist era, began to break down and were replaced by economies of scope. Proponents of this model of flexible specialization also claimed that it was associated with a tendency towards spatial reconcentration, as clusters of small firms emerged in new industrial districts, again in stark contrast to the process of decentralization which was held to be the locational hallmark of the Fordist model.

Such proposals generated a heated response (see, for instance, Amin 1989, Hudson 1988, Lovering 1990, Pollert 1988, Sayer 1989). It was argued that it was not clear how widespread a phenomenon "flexible specialization" was even supposed to be, let alone might be, despite the bold claims advanced for the scope of the model, which was criticized for overgeneralizing from a limited range of evidence. As well as these issues of empirical substance, the model appeared seriously flawed in three further respects which are developed further in this chapter. It conceptualized a particular form of spatial change as some kind of inevitable, abstract constituent of organizational (or social) change; in this way it grossly oversimplified the relationship between organization and location. The characterization of the new regime as "flexible" conflated *system* flexibility with *labour* flexibility; and the latter was most definitely not necessarily a liberating phenomenon from the point of view of the individual employee, but often rather a prelude to intensification of the production process. Finally—and at first sight oddly given the regulationist school's emphases—the national state dimension was selectively disregarded.

Yet the national state remained one of the key building blocks of the world economy. The long post-1945 boom in most advanced countries was ordered around a social consensus in which the national state played a central part in securing some of the new preconditions for profitable production, such as currency stability, free trade and growing consumer demand, in return for commitments to welfare provision and relatively full employment. As the boom faltered to a close, this regulatory model was increasingly replaced by a neo-conservative version, epitomized in the elections of Margaret Thatcher as Prime Minister in the UK in 1979 and Ronald Reagan as President in the USA in 1980. The new reactionary orthodoxy held particularly strong views on the role of the state in regulating capitalist markets (or, to cast it in the terms of the new right, the role of the market in regulating the scope of the state), which marked a sharp break with the earlier basis for agreement.

In the UK, cutting back the rate of increase of public expenditure became a policy priority of the 1974-79 Labour government in the face of balance-of-payments difficulties and soaring inflation, and was targeted as an early policy of the new Conservative government after 1979. Authority was increasingly centralized as a necessary step to "freeing the hand" of market forces (to use a phrase much favoured by government ministers; see Gamble 1988), but this power was that of the *international* market place, which rapidly proved to have catastrophic consequences for manufacturing and production within the UK. A long-standing decline became a rout; in 1984 the UK recorded a trade deficit in such goods for the first time since records began, and this widened sharply in the rest of the decade (partly because of changes in income distribution precipitated by new taxation arrangements). The extent of the decline in manufacturing, coupled with the spatial concentration of (largely higher-order service sector) growth in a broad arc from the "M4 corridor" west of London through to East Anglia, was captured in concern for a growing north–south divide within the country. Regional employment and unemployment differentials were echoed in vast differences in socioeconomic conditions (see Lewis and Townsend 1989, Martin 1988, Mohan 1989).

Perhaps the clearest expression of this new government policy emphasis was with regard to the nationalized industries. In an attempt to recreate the conditions for capital to invest profitably, capacity was cut back drastically, with scant regard for the strategic role of many of the industries concerned to the UK economy. Sectors such as coal and steel came to be a major proximate cause of economic collapse in the regions where they were formerly concentrated (see Hudson 1986). Such policies also fulfilled another role for the government, as part of its assault on the power (whether perceived or real was not at issue) of trade unions; for the nationalized industries had been amongst the strongest points of organized labour. Major national disputes were entered into and pursued with a ruthless determination; for instance in steel in 1980 and above all in coal in 1984/85.

At the same time (and at first sight paradoxically) the UK government actively courted inward foreign investment in manufacturing, most especially from Japan. This pursuit reflected a recognition not only of the new and increasingly powerful role of the Japanese multinational corporation on the world stage, but also of the particular hallmarks of Japanese state-guided industrial success. These included the exceptionally organized character of interfirm production relations, and a particular form of mass production which depended upon relatively weak trade unionism. They came to be subsumed under the label "Just-In-Time", often contrasted to its Western counterpart "Just-In-Case". A distinction was drawn between the tight stock control and regular deliveries of JIT (entailing minimum production disruption at any part of the chain), and the high stock levels held at great cost against the uncertain delivery of components in JIC production. JIT was, however, more than just a system characterized by low stock levels, but extended more deeply to a continuous learning about the production process and a never-ending search for efficiency (see Sayer 1986).

The proclaimed superiority of JIT production systems was one argument used forcefully by the UK government in support of a growing tide of Japanese investment in manufacturing in the UK in the 1980s. This was concentrated in a few sectors, principally electronics and motor vehicles, and a few regions. The extent of the government's welcome was apparent from the clean sweep which the UK made of the first round of full-scale Japanese car assembly plants in Western Europe: Nissan at Sunderland, Toyota at Burnaston (with a separate engine plant at Shotton), and Honda at Swindon. For these companies, location within the European Community provided a means of leapfrogging restrictive trade barriers; for the UK government these plants brought employment, new production techniques and, crucially, new patterns of industrial relations.

Whilst it is easy to over-emphasise the absolute significance of Japanese investment in manufacturing in comparison to the number of jobs in US-owned factories (see also Dicken 1988), there is no doubt that Japanese investment became seen as at the leading edge of changes to do with productivity and efficiency. As debate on the impact of such investment intensified (see Dunning 1986, Morris 1988, Oliver and Wilkinson 1988), labour relations became an increasingly central focus. The JIT concept was being selectively re-interpreted in a way which facilitated legitimation of developments taking place elsewhere in manufacturing by reference to the threat of "Japanization". This enabled far-reaching changes to be introduced more readily and with less opposition from the shopfloor than might otherwise have been expected (see Graham 1988). The standard representation of the Japanese employment situation as an ideal masked a number of far from idyllic labour practices (see Briggs 1988). It was apparent that the UK government's enthusiastic welcome to Japanese investment rested heavily on a coincidence of views with regard to labour relations.

In this chapter, therefore, the interaction between Japanese direct foreign investment and UK state policies is used as one way of providing an insight into some of the points of encounter, or the critical edges, between different production systems and national state policies, particularly with regard to their conception of the role of labour. These edges are apparent not just (inter)nationally but also regionally, for Japanese investment was heavily concentrated in regions such as North East England. In this way the focus here is upon the interaction between different "layers" of investment, as new employment practices (exemplified in but by no means confined to Japanese factories) have been and are being introduced into old industrial regions (drawing on Sadler 1991).

These themes are illustrated first by reference to national changes in the 1980s in three key sectors: coal mining, iron and steel production, and automobile assembly. The loss of 0.5m jobs in these industries during the decade represented nearly one-quarter of the overall decline in production employment (see Fig. 13.1). In coal and steel this collapse was orchestrated by state owned corporations. In automobile production, decline at Rover and in other, foreign owned concerns such as Ford, Vauxhall (GM) and Peugeot in the early years of the decade contrasted markedly with an upswing in *production* (employment

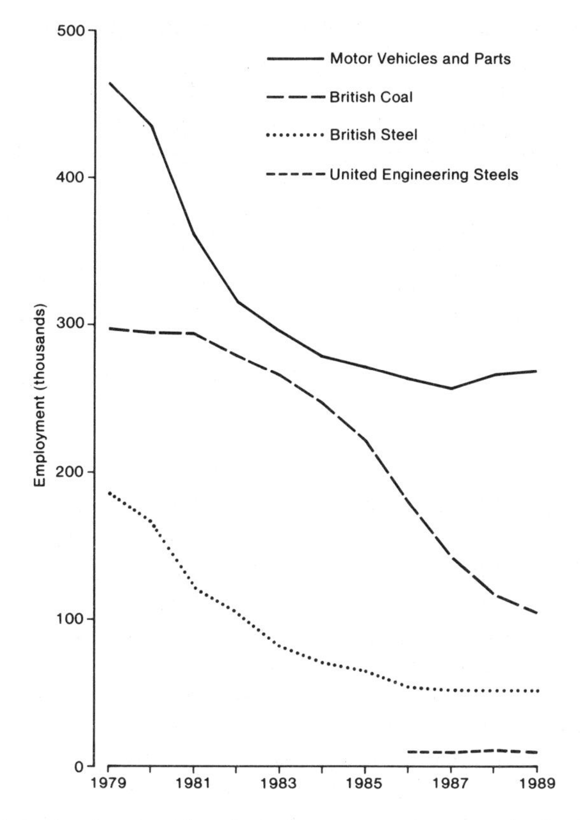

FIG. 13.1. Employment in selected sectors and companies in the UK, 1979-89.

roughly stabilized) associated with changing corporate policies and the arrival of Japanese producers towards the end of the decade. These industries are revealing, then, for the character of UK state policies, and for the precise mediation within the UK of international market forces.

The analysis is then developed further by examining these same sectors in the case of one region, North East England. The decline of coal and steel became interwoven with a whole host of changes to do with labour relations, epitomized in the new Nissan complex at Sunderland but also evident more generally in the growth of low wage, often part-time or casual service sector employment. At this scale, it is possible to examine in more detail the full implications of production reorganization and shifting international patterns of investment for people living and working in the region, through their changing experience of labour market conditions.

2. International Markets and National State Policies

One of the most important factors affecting the pattern of spatially uneven development within the UK in the 1980s was the pace and extent of collapse in the country's economic base of production industries.[2] This decline had been long-standing; there was nothing new in the deindustrialization of the UK. What was striking, however, was the precise form which government policy took during the course of the decade, as it became increasingly apparent that the power of international market forces was being allowed—even encouraged—to penetrate practically all sectors of industry, regardless of—indeed arguably because of—the catastrophic slump in employment which followed. This section examines some of the ways in which state policies were instrumental, in many senses even decisive, to the path of three key sectors—coal mining, iron and steel production and automobile assembly—and outlines some of the paradoxes of these policies in the 1980s.

Nationalization of the UK coal industry in 1947 in the form of the National Coal Board (NCB) had partly represented a recognition of the broader strategic significance of this domestically produced energy source. Until around 1958 the UK remained effectively a single fuel economy, and that fuel was coal. Thereafter, especially during the 1960s, in response to the availability of low cost imported oil, the use of coal began to fall both relatively and absolutely, and the NCB's employment contracted sharply. In 1947 the NCB had employed 718,000 men at 958 collieries to produce 200mt of coal; by 1974 its workforce was down to 246,000, its collieries to 246 in number and its output to 127mt. In that year, however, *Plan for Coal* was agreed between the Labour government and the National Union of Mineworkers (NUM). This foresaw an apparently brighter future for coal, with output expected to rise again to somewhere in the region of 135-145mt by the mid-1980s.

One reason for this newfound optimism (apart from the evident consensus of views which the NUM found with the government of the day) was a fourfold rise in oil prices during 1973 and 1974. Coal, all of a sudden, appeared once again to be a relatively low-priced, highly competitive fuel, with the added advantage in the UK that it could also be produced domestically. Internationally, too, coal appeared to have become a premium fuel, and many oil multinationals invested heavily during the second half of the 1970s in coal deposits in the USA and Latin America. In the event, however, demand for coal (and for energy more generally) failed to expand at anything like these anticipated rates—global recession and fuel conservation largely saw to that. So instead of investing in a newly profitable commodity, the new producers and the NCB alike found themselves faced with a situation of vast global oversupply. During the first half of the 1980s coal prices tumbled seemingly ever lower.

These pressures were behind the Conservative government's insistence on cost reduction and capacity closure in the UK coal industry in the 1980s, which led to and in many ways provoked the 1984/85 miners' strike (see Beynon 1985). After this, the pace of decline quickened. In the second half of the decade colliery employment slumped from 171,000 to 65,000 as the number of collieries fell from 169 to just 73. Some of the peripheral coalfields (such as Scotland, North East England and South Wales) faced the threat of extinction; even the so-called central coalfields in Yorkshire and Nottinghamshire saw massive redundancies.

Capacity cutbacks were not the only response pursued by British Coal (as the National Coal Board was renamed in the wake of the 1984/85 dispute), even if they were the most dramatic. Driven on by government imposed financial restrictions, BC followed other routes to cut its costs in an attempt to improve its profitability. A search for improved capital utilization led to the opening of some new collieries, the increased use of more capital efficient mining techniques (including the computerization of mine operating systems and the provision of a greater proportion of coal faces with heavy duty equipment) and pressure for more flexible working practices. Finally, and perhaps most contentiously, BC sought dramatically to expand the proportion of its output which was produced from opencast sites as opposed to deep mines, for this gave it a far greater return on capital investment. In the course of the decade, despite environmental opposition, the proportion of output which came from this source practically doubled, to reach one-fifth of total production.

The biggest single problem facing BC, though, was in its *market*; for by the 1980s it had come to depend heavily upon the electricity supply industry (ESI) for its sales. As the state owned Central Electricity Generating Board (CEGB) in particular sought to cut its own costs in preparation for privatization, it used the threat of low cost imported coal as a strong bargaining counter. In 1986 the CEGB and BC signed a new five year "understanding" which incorporated a guaranteed annual sales volume of 70mt (a previous deal had been for 75mt p.a.) in return for a virtual freeze on prices. As the ESI moved closer to privatization, though, the pressure on BC really began to bite. In the process, the extent of many of the contradictions inherent in UK energy policy became fully apparent (for a fuller account of these issues see Hudson and Sadler 1990).

The original proposals for electricity privatization (see Energy Committee 1988, HMSO 1988) envisaged the creation of two major generating companies, National Power and PowerGen, from the old CEGB, with National Power taking the existing nuclear power stations and obliged to continue to produce a similar proportion of electricity from this source as the former CEGB. It soon became evident, however, that the costs of nuclear power had been subject to systematic manipulation over several decades, and the private sector would be unwilling to shoulder the burden of (now vastly increased) estimated decommissioning costs (see Energy Committee 1990a). In consequence, during 1989, the nuclear stations were withdrawn from the privatization prospectus and a freeze on new nuclear plant construction was ordered until 1994 (apart from the completion of what had been intended as the first of a new generation of Pressurized Water Reactors, Sizewell B).

The pressures on British Coal inspired by international overcapacity continued, however, and were made worse by the impact of environmentalist opposition to the combustion of coal. For coal burnt in UK power stations contributed substantially to the problem of acid rain, and also to the greenhouse effect. In 1988 the UK agreed to cut its emissions of sulphur dioxide from power stations from the 1980 level by 40 per cent before 1998 and by 60 per cent before 2003 (see Commission of the European Communities 1989, Energy Committee 1989). To this end the CEGB proposed to install sulphur-removing equipment (flue gas desulphurization or FGD) at coal fired power stations with 12,000 MW capacity, at a cost of £2,000m. This was an unattractive proposition to potential investors in a privatized ESI, and the burden of FGD investment by National Power and PowerGen was cut back to 8,000 MW capacity at a cost of £1,200m. Instead, the new generating industry proposed to produce a much greater proportion of its electricity from gas-fired power stations, and to purchase greater quantities of low sulphur content imported coal. Faced with these threats, BC signed a further three year supply deal with the ESI for the period 1990-92, allowing for a reduction of total coal sales to 65mt in the final year of the agreement and a continued freeze on prices.[3] One forecast suggested that taken together, such developments could effectively cut BC's sales to the ESI much further, down to 50mt by 1998 and 38mt by 2003, entailing 20,000 further job losses by 1998 and 32,000 by 2003 (see Energy Committee 1990b).

All of this also largely ignored a final set of questions to do with coal's impending virtual demise in the UK—the longer term strategic implications. Whilst the price of internationally produced coal was undoubtedly low throughout the 1980s in comparison to that of British coal (with the exception of much Western European production), the availability of sufficient volumes of internationally traded coal was a matter of dispute. Some expressed fears that a sudden expansion in imports by the major UK consumers would in itself push up the price of such coal (see Prior and McCloskey 1988).[4] Even without such problems, increased imports would add heavily to the UK's balance of payments deficit (just 25mt of coal a year at £30/t would add £750m to the import bill). Probably most significantly for the longer term, the premature decimation of much of the UK's indigenous energy production capacity would leave the economy open to similar wild fluctuations in international market price as had happened in oil in 1973/74, with (potentially at least) equally devastating consequences.

A similar story of intensified international competition and state mediation dominated the UK steel industry during the 1980s. After the recessionary slump of 1973/74, a geographical shift in the global balance of iron and steel production intensified (for details see Hudson and Sadler 1989). As demand, output and profitability slumped in practically all of the advanced countries, the greater steel intensity of development programmes in several Newly Industrializing Countries (NICs), most spectacularly Brazil and South Korea, meant that the proportion of global steel production accounted for by NICs more than doubled to reach 20 per cent by the end of the 1980s. For companies in the advanced economies, this new environment (exacerbated by a growing tendency to substitute for steel with other, lighter, materials such as plastics) entailed massive contraction. Employment in steel production in OECD countries halved, involving the loss of 1m jobs. Much of this global shift was state backed, both in the NICs (to secure expansion) and in the advanced economies (to offset the worst impacts of contraction). From 1980 to 1988 the European Community authorized state aid to steel producers amounting to a staggering £25,000m (Commission of the European Communities 1990). Over this same period too the EC deployed some of its strongest institutional powers, in itself a further indication of the depth of the problem. Following a declaration of "manifest crisis" in the industry, the EC was enabled to set detailed production quotas for each steel company in an attempt to smooth the path of restructuring.

Such were the devastating international forces which swept the UK, and in particular the state owned British Steel Corporation (BSC). In the early 1970s zealously optimistic forecasts had indicated its annual capacity would increase from 27mt to the range of 36-38mt by the early 1980s (HMSO 1973). These plans, like those of the NCB, were rapidly overtaken by events, and the emphasis switched instead to one of savage retrenchment (see Bryer *et al.* 1982, HMSO 1978). From 1979 to 1982 capacity was effectively cut from 21mt to 14mt, as employment almost halved from 186,000 to 104,000. Equally (and again the parallels with the NCB are strong ones here) BSC followed other routes to meet government imposed financial targets. From 1981 to 1985 there was no national pay rise (following a prolonged national strike in 1980): rather, increases were wholly dependent on works level, locally agreed productivity improvement schemes. Numerical and functional flexibility were widely introduced, particularly through the greatly increased use of subcontracted labour, and employment continued to fall. At the same time the government pursued a drive to reintroduce private capital to the industry through a series of joint ventures known as the Phoenix schemes, involving the formation of companies such as United Engineering Steels, Allied Steel and Wire, and Sheffield Forgemasters in the more profitable special steels sector. In these businesses, new patterns of industrial relations were amongst the most dominant concerns—with a clear demonstration effect to the rest of industry.

In 1986, after a decade of losses, BSC produced an operating profit. In a steadily (if only temporarily) improving market environment, the corporation (with a workforce down to 52,000) was privatized intact in 1988. Five main integrated sites remained —at Llanwern and Port Talbot in South Wales, Ravenscraig in Scotland and Scunthorpe and Teesside in England—but the future of these was far from secure (see Sadler 1990). On privatization BSC guaranteed the continuation of steelmaking at all of the main sites until 1994 (crucially, this provision was subject to market conditions), but the future configuration of rolling mill capacity was not even accorded this limited assurance. The closure of the Ravenscraig hot strip mill in 1991 was widely interpreted as confirmation of this plant's impending (and long heralded) total demise. Despite a protracted decline the continuation of steelmaking in the UK continued to be at risk, largely due to the weak demand occasioned by cutbacks elsewhere in manufacturing. Like the coal industry, steel had been exposed to the forces of the international market, and the state owned corporation had been used as a vehicle for reorganization, contraction and the reintroduction of private capital to the sector. Any sense of rational planning for the longer-term future of key industrial sectors had been cast aside.

Within the international automobile industry, a range of subtly differing processes was apparent. The key actors within the UK were not state owned enterprises (although British Leyland, later renamed Rover, went through a period of similarly traumatic decline as British Coal and British Steel) but multinational corporations. Worldwide automobile production was heavily dominated by a few companies (see, for instance, Beynon 1984): the top five controlled over one-half of total output, and the top ten some three-quarters. Vehicle assembly was vital to many national economies. The interplay between national states (seeking to influence locational decisions) and the global strategies of multinational capital was a distinguishing hallmark of automobile manufacture.

Equally significant was the dramatic rise during the 1970s and, especially, the 1980s of Japanese vehicle producers. Toyota and Nissan increasingly challenged the US giants General Motors and Ford for global dominance. From a mere 1 per cent of world output in 1960, Japanese companies grew to control over one-quarter by the end of the 1980s. This initially entailed wholesale exports from Japan. From the early 1980s, however, there was a growing tide of Japanese direct foreign investment in automobile factories, especially in North America, where by the end of the decade Japanese owned capacity amounted to over 2m vehicles annually. In the second half of the 1980s, too, Japanese corporate strategy switched to the vast and growing Western European market (which peaked with sales of 13.5m units in 1989). Japanese producers took around one-tenth of this market (largely through exports), but as the EC prepared to remove internal trade barriers by 1992, and in anticipation of greater external trade restrictions, Japanese companies also began to invest in new production facilities there. The pioneer in this regard was Nissan, which began production at its new plant at Sunderland in the UK in 1986. By the end of the 1980s, both Toyota and Honda had also announced plans for new car assembly plants within the UK.

The UK automobile industry had, until the mid-1980s, been in a protracted slump. Output fell as low as 0.9m vehicles in 1982, compared to a 1972 production of 1.9m. Steady withdrawal by multinational corporations had enmeshed with decline in the domestic state owned producer British Leyland to draw in imports of finished vehicles and components. This created a first ever motor vehicles trade deficit in 1982, which broadened dramatically in subsequent years. By 1988 it amounted to £6,000m, or 30 per cent of the visible UK trade deficit. As sales grew in the later years of the 1980s, though, and as multinationals re-evaluated their European corporate policies, output picked up, to reach 1.3m vehicles by 1989. With the anticipated addition of around 0.5m vehicles annual capacity at the three Japanese factories, it was confidently being predicted that UK automobile output would rebound to over 2m by the mid-1990s.

The growing Japanese presence in the UK automobile industry was vitally significant. It owed much to the lack of a strong national producer (in contrast to say Volkswagen in Germany or Fiat in Italy; and it should be noted that this in turn partly reflected government policy attitudes towards the national producer Rover—as British Leyland was renamed in 1986—from the mid-1970s to its privatization by sale to British Aerospace in 1988). An extremely supportive national government attitude was also important. The first and second phases of Nissan's factory, for instance (building up to an output of 100,000 vehicles annually and a workforce of around 2,500), cost an estimated £390m, of which £110m was recouped via government grants. Effectively, the Japanese plants initiated a transformation in the geography of vehicle production in the UK (see Fig. 13.2), and in the social organization of automobile manufacture: and the linkage of these was far from coincidental. For in their assault on the Western European market, Japanese companies sought to transplant their systems of production and industrial relations styles. In this process they actively avoided old established traditions.

The trade union agreement at Nissan in Sunderland, for instance, incorporated four features which, taken together, were wholly new to the UK automobile industry: single-union status for the Amalgamated Engineering Union (AEU) (in contrast to Nissan's plant at Smyrna in the USA, which was non-union), no-strike pendulum arbitration, common conditions and complete flexibility. Partly inspired by its partnership with Honda, Rover introduced radical changes to working practices in 1990, including agreement for continuous, round the clock production at its Longbridge plant. Other companies such as Ford and GM also sought changes in work organization in response to

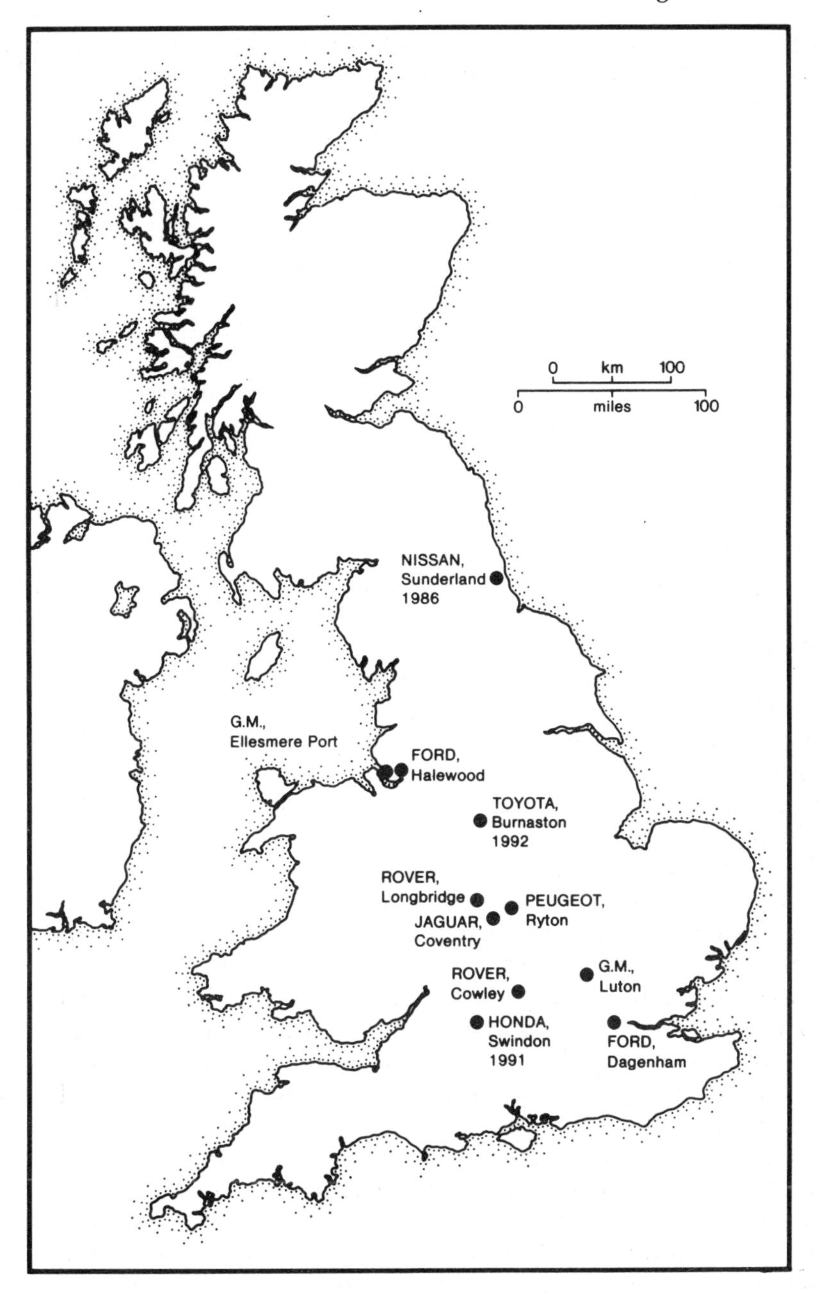

FIG. 13.2. Automobile assembly plants in the UK.

the perceived Japanese threat. There were, of course, limits to this process of Japanization. The heightened interdependence of different plants brought about by low stock levels as part of a near JIT system meant that supply disruption at any one point could ripple rapidly outwards (see Turnbull 1987). Ford experienced such problems in its European operations as a result of industrial disputes in the UK in 1988 and 1990 (see also Starkey and McKinlay 1989). Nonetheless, it was hard to escape the conclusion that a wide ranging shift was underway in work organization and labour relations, largely, if not entirely, inspired by the Japanese example.

In the longer term, too, the impact of this Japanese investment was anticipated, by some at least, to run deeper than changing working conditions and into the whole basis of organization of the production system. It was argued that adoption of JIT would require much shorter delivery lines and lead to a reconcentration of production in complexes akin to Toyota City in Japan (see Schoenberger 1987). In the USA, Mair *et al* (1988) found evidence of growing clusters of newly arrived Japanese automobile component manufacturers around the Japanese assembly plants, although Hill (1989) argued that such operations both in Japan and North America still drew in some measure on components produced in low wage NICs. Clearly, some combination of decentralization and reconcentration was still being practised: the two strategies were by no means incompatible.

This question of component supply was of pressing importance in the UK in the context of the new Japanese assembly plants. The first phase of the Nissan complex at Sunderland involved assembly of kits produced in Japan. Only later did "local content" (meaning EC produced) rise first to 60 per cent, then towards the ultimate target of 80 per cent. The definitional basis of this agreement was very imprecise, even though it was the model followed in negotiations with Toyota and Honda; especially problematic was the calculation of local content on the basis of proportion of ex-works price, for this incorporated a wide range of indirect production costs and also included corporate profits (see Trade and Industry Committee 1987). Inspired by Japanese practice, though, there were clear signs in the European automobile components industry during the late 1980s of the emergence of a "first tier" of suppliers, capable of participating with the assemblers on a preferred basis from the earliest design stages through to full production (see Sleigh 1989). From the standpoint of British capital, this was a particularly troubling development, for many component manufacturers were small and depended exclusively on the UK market. Very few had internationalized and were large enough to absorb some of the initial costs associated with Japanese demand (see Sleigh 1988).

Underpinned by government support, then, companies such as Nissan were instrumental in fashioning new industrial relations practices and patterns of work organization, re-shaping the geography of the UK automobile industry (and note also that in this process they displayed a clear grasp of its existing geography). In this sense there was a strand running through the three sectors considered above (and the same could also be argued about the economy more generally)—that of control over the production process and the significance of corporate labour management. Much of the character of UK state policies towards industry in the 1980s can only be understood with this in mind. The formulation and implementation of state policy was significant, despite arguments to the contrary on the part of some in government: self-evidently so in the drastic refashioning of coal and steel production via the abolition of drastically restructured state owned corporations as a means of reintroducing private capital, but also in the contrasting attitudes towards Rover on the one hand and Japanese vehicle manufacturers investing in the UK on the other. State policies were in many ways decisive, in other words, to the path of large parts of industry (more precisely, in their mediation of international market forces) and the associated (re)creation of particular processes of spatially uneven development. This was nowhere more apparent than with regard to the control of labour. The following section therefore considers this question of labour management in more detail, focusing on the same processes within one region, North East England.

3. State Policies and Labour Relations: the Reorganization of Production in North East England

The changing geography of production in North East England provides a revealing insight into the nature of spatially uneven development, in part because the region has played a central, on occasion even leading, role in many phases of the UK's integration into the global economy. This section examines the reorganization of production and the creation of new forms of uneven development there during the 1980s, using the same sectors once again to provide a lens which can focus attention on some of the key changes taking place. It is precisely in old industrial regions such as the North East, where long established working traditions and forms of social reproduction were so entrenched (if increasingly anomalous) that the policy thrust of the 1980s faced both its greatest challenge and its biggest opportunity. Tackling this task was one of the central agendas in the decade. It is impossible to understand the decline of the national industrial base without some regard for this attempt at redefining social relations in the workplace; equally, it is impossible to do full justice to the character of such changes without recognizing their heavily state imbued nature.

The extent of this state intervention in the North East regional economy was nothing new. It had a long history, so much so that the region was in many senses a "state managed" one (see Hudson 1989). Immediately after 1945 the region's economy was relatively prosperous and near full employment was not exceptional, largely built on the strength of the emphasis placed on coal by the UK's single fuel policy. After 1958 this began to change, and by 1963 the region faced what appeared at the time to be a major crisis of unemployment, as coal-mining and shipbuilding redundancies coincided with a cyclical downturn in the national economy. In response the government appointed Lord Hailsham as the first (and last) Minister for the North East. His regeneration programme (HMSO 1963) envisaged selective public investment in the region's infrastructure, with a new road network and enhanced development of New Towns such as Peterlee and Washington.

For a time, at least in the 1960s, these measures, along with a strengthened regional policy, appeared to be working, as there were substantial increases in manufacturing output, and some (limited) gains in employment. In this period the region was particularly attractive to certain forms of investment, in existing heavy industry such as steel and chemicals on Teesside, and in new factories established in response to the reconstitution of labour supply following run-down in coal and increased encouragement for women to work for a wage. In the main, though, these factories tended to be branch plant operations with limited skill requirements, which in recession proved to be the first to close. From the 1970s onwards the story of the North East economy was essentially one of steadily rising unemployment and factory closures, as the region—aptly characterized as a global outpost of multinational capital, but suffering also from the effects of state policies—saw declining employment in both the new employers of the 1960s and the staple industries, the latter increasingly underpinned by state supported investment in new, capital intensive production methods.

By the 1980s the North East had become one of the UK's most intractable "depressed" regions. Even national recovery towards the end of the decade had only a limited impact, as the traditional industries—especially coal, steel and shipbuilding—continued to decline. Some 44,000 jobs were lost from British Coal and British Steel in the course of the decade, equivalent to one-third of the relative decline in the region's production industry employment. Such a collapse was far from uncontested: the demise of the Consett steel works in 1980 was the subject of a protracted, largely trade union-led anticlosure campaign (see Hudson and Sadler 1983) and in 1984/85 North East coal miners participated in the year-long (and ultimately, equally unsuccessful) national strike against pit closures (see, for instance, Hudson *et al.* 1985, Hudson and Sadler 1987). These were nonetheless deeply significant protests. In their defeats, the national miners' strike (in particular) and (works based) anticlosure campaigns like that at Consett signalled the extent to which the state (via the public corporation) was prepared to go to crush opposition and the power (such as it was) of organized labour. And once having established the proclaimed "right to manage", labour relations were recast with a vengeance.

The full scope of the use of state owned corporations to underwrite the decimation of large parts of the North East coalfield and the truncation of the Teesside steel industry, in stark contrast to the (largely flawed) expansion plans of the mid-1970s, has been explored in detail elsewhere (see Beynon *et al.* 1986, 1991). In an environment of mounting unemployment, British Steel and British Coal moved to consolidate newly found strength. At BSC Teesside, for example, far-reaching changes began almost immediately after the defeat of the three month long national pay strike in 1980.[5] Many workers were clear that the Iron and Steel Trades Confederation (ISTC, the main steel union) had been selected as a soft target for the Conservative government's anti-union strategies, pointing to the management style of new chairman Ian MacGregor. Much of the new climate was associated with the spectre of redundancy and closure, possibly even of the whole complex, creating an atmosphere of fear and uncertainty. A sense of competition between different BSC sites was actively fostered by management. Ron Agar, AEU convener, described this collective dread of greater "success" at other BSC plants:

> The BSC divisions now are running businesses separate from each other. If Ravenscraig were to close, that would be to our benefit, because on certain items customers would come to us. The same goes for Llanwern. As a trade unionist I never wish to see these works close. But from a purely selfish

> point of view it would help us—and you'd get the same reaction from my counterpart at Ravenscraig. That's how MacGregor got it organized. Every business must be self-financing.

A central element in this approach lay in the devolution of responsibility for labour costs, via an emphasis on locally agreed productivity bonuses; a clear indication of management's newly found strength. A further factor was a drive on labour force flexibility, both in functional terms and, through the greatly increased use of subcontracted labour, in numerical terms. On Teesside this was supposed to be regulated by an agreement signed between BSC and the local unions in 1981; but much evidence suggests that this was observed only in passing. Ron Agar described some of the abuses as follows:

> A lot of the men who come in to work are claiming DHSS benefits. I have proof of this, and I'm in close contact with management about it. BSC claim not to know. Certainly they wouldn't condone it. But they've used the economy of this country to help the profitability of the steel industry. They've used the black economy, indirectly—although they wouldn't admit it. There's no way that a contractor coming in for one day would sign off—he'd lose all his benefit. And in a week he could earn more than a skilled craftsman. That's a sore point.

Whilst BSC spokesman Mr Adamson argued that "at present no one who is on the dole is on this site" (quoted in *Middlesbrough Evening Gazette*, 17 June 1986), others were less than convinced. A four week enquiry by a special team of Department of Employment investigators concluded, in the front page headline words of the local newspaper, with a "dole swoop on 100 at BSC". The article went on:

> More than 100 people face prosecution for false benefit claims after an anti-fraud swoop on men working at British Steel. Some of the men netted by Department of Employment investigators were allegedly being paid up to £180 a week working for subcontractors. But they were also receiving as much as £60 a week in unemployment or supplementary benefit (*Middlesbrough Evening Gazette*, 28 August 1986).

Such a high profile enquiry (its findings were formally announced by a government minister) was significant in a number of ways; not least in the message it sent out to the rest of Teesside's unemployed about the burgeoning surveillance activities of the state, and the apparent vindication of many of the steel unions' claims. But the deeper reasons behind the growing informal economy remained shadowed from public view. For a large part of the potential for abuse lay in the fact that subcontracted labour was casual work; and the transition from stable to casual employment in the steel industry had been actively and positively encouraged by BSC.

Part of the reason for this lay in the use of outside labour to encourage changes within the remaining core workforce. In the minds of many core employees, the subcontracted labour force, not the system under which subcontracting had grown, became the challenge. This was by no means unwelcome to either BSC or the subcontracting companies, especially in that it led to even greater fragmentation within the remaining workforce. For example, one of the few women branch officials of the ISTC described the consequences of the transfer of catering services to Gardner-Merchant:

> Our girls don't like to fight. They don't want to argue. You get the area manager telling our girls what to do and they'll do it, because they're frightened to lose their jobs. When we were with British Steel, the men backed us. They don't today, they say we're contractors. I believe they would come out if it came to a real fight, but only some of the men back us now. We're on our own, more or less, and the girls are frightened of that. The managers play on the fact that the girls are frightened. They're splitting us up into little families.

At the same time active trade unionists like this woman found themselves increasingly discriminated against:

> We were all interviewed for our jobs by Gardner-Merchant. Some of us had been there for ten or twenty years. It was a case of "if your face fits". Mine nearly didn't. They offered me a shift job and said if I didn't take it, I was out. It took me two years to get off shift work. The night shift was no good for my union work, and they knew it.

Such active discouragement of trade union activity was a further clear manifestation of the reassertion of managerial power. This is what many of these changes in steel on Teesside were about (and note also that similar processes were evident in the coal industry, especially after 1984/85 with the creation of the breakaway Union of Democratic Mineworkers, an emphasis on flexible working in the deep mines and still greater fragmentation within the workforce occasioned by the expansion of opencast mining). Competition between and within works to stay in employment was buttressed by the fear of unemployment in a jobs crisis area and the knowledge that some workers were on short-term contracts or ignoring skill boundaries, probably for an outside contractor. The reward to individual core employees for increased labour productivity was only too tangible, in the form of lump sum bonuses. The price, in terms of individual job control and quality of work environment, was one that many workers were prepared to pay because they saw, and were offered, no alternative.

In other parts of the North East, including large parts of the coalfield (see Fig. 13.3), such once staple industries had completely departed. New labour market conditions were the mainstay of government supported reindustrialization programmes. These were typically delivered via bodies such as enterprise agencies,

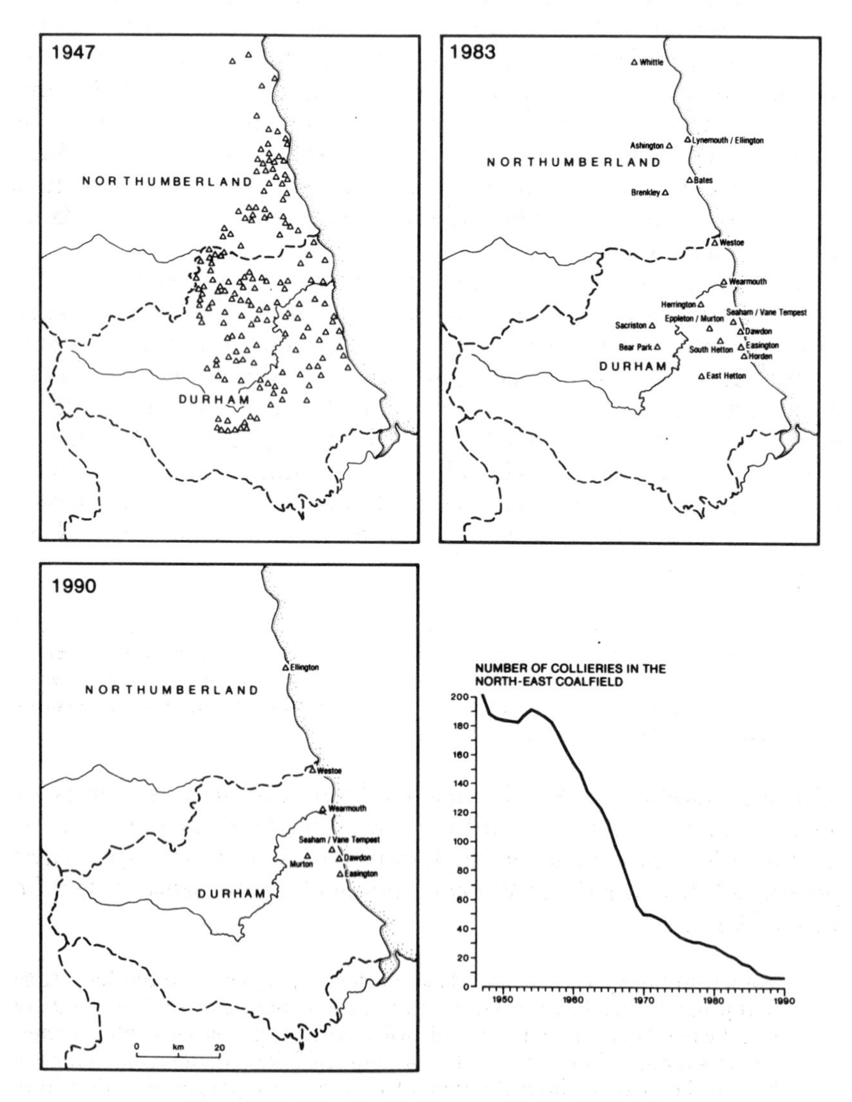

FIG. 13.3. The North East coalfield, 1947-90.

Urban Development Corporations and Enterprise Zones (and note too that British Steel and British Coal played no small part in this process via their job creation subsidiaries, BSC Industry and BC Enterprise). These various bodies aimed to create a new "enterprise economy" through the emergence of a new generation of small businesses, in an attempt to "rejuvenate" the economic base. Within such companies, however, working conditions were often markedly different to previous norms and expectations. Many—especially in industries such as textiles and clothing, and in the service sector—depended on low paid, highly exploitative employment, often taken by women as their one chance of earning a wage. A declining old economy was steadily being overlain in many parts, in other words, by a new, small firm-centred manufacturing base and a growing, but equally insecure, service sector, as new employers sought to take full advantage of readily available labour reserves.

It was in major new investment projects such as Nissan, though, that the full extent of new labour relations styles and working practices was most clearly heralded. Announcing the selection of the Sunderland site, company vice president Kaichi Kanao indicated Nissan's concern to install just one trade union and to negotiate a wide-ranging labour flexibility agreement. He placed particular emphasis on Nissan's desire to implant Japanese style industrial relations procedures and made it clear that further development of the plant to a second stage would depend on success in this regard:

> I am confident that we will have the type of labour management and industrial relations that we have in Japan when we settle here. Whether we have good working relationships with the unions will be a big factor in determining whether we go on to the second stage (quoted in *Newcastle Journal*, 31 March 1984).

The amenability of North East trade unions to new forms of agreement in the motor industry was arguably a major factor in Nissan's choice of location. Later that year, newly appointed personnel director Peter Wickens made clear the kind of deal he was seeking:

> We would hope to create a package under which people would have faith that problems can be resolved through the negotiating procedures, and not feel the need to go on strike. People will have to be prepared to adapt to new and changing technology. We do not want rigid demarcations, and they will have to be flexible about the type of jobs they are prepared to do within their capability (quoted in *Newcastle Journal*, 8 August 1984).

In April 1985 the company (in its own words) "appointed" the AEU as its union, under an agreement which incorporated wide-ranging changes. As Joe Cellini, North East divisional organizer of the AEU, picking up the challenge laid down earlier, said of the deal:

> Our aim is to make it work constructively and to justify the second phase (quoted in *Newcastle Journal*, 23 April 1985).

Clearly, from the AEU's viewpoint at least, the price—in terms of further investment and jobs—was well worth acquiescence to Nissan's terms and conditions.[6]

Nissan's other major early concern was to fashion a workforce that was prepared to adapt to its rigorous demands. This was achieved through a complex recruitment and screening process, which was made all the more legitimate and competitive by the sheer volume of employment applications received from the job starved North East. The first appointments after the managerial team were twenty-two "supervisors", selected in 1985 from over 3,000 applications. Each successful candidate was interviewed several times, put through a series of practical and written tests, and medically examined. They were sent as a group to Japan for a two month period of intensive training at the Nissan plant at Oppama. On their return they participated in the process of interviewing and recruiting forty "team-leaders" from 1,000 applicants; these in turn were sent to Japan and participated (along with their supervisors) in recruiting the two grades of manual employee, manufacturer and technician. Each team leader was responsible for some fifteen employees. The whole approach was carefully designed to build considerable team loyalty, as described by one manager, Clive Griffiths:

> The man (*sic*) who does the interviewing is recruiting his own team. He tells the people that he sees that they will not just be working for Nissan UK, but for him. He then passes them on to his manager and I decide if they are right for my team (quoted in *Newcastle Journal*, 29 August 1986).

Competition for employment at Nissan was intense. The first 240 manufacturing jobs prompted 11,000 applications. Workers recruited were typically young, fit, agile, and previously in employment elsewhere; in 1987 the average age of the workforce was just 27 and only one quarter had been recruited from the unemployment register. Their inculcation with Japanese values was exemplified as follows by Clive Griffiths:

> We have to beat the Japanese. Many of us have been to Japan and seen how things work there. We are deliberately looking for quicker and easier ways of doing the job, that can be taken back to Japan (quoted in *Financial Times*, 29 August 1986).

Such attitudes epitomized Nissan's long-term strategy, as it sought to transplant not just production, but also whole production systems, to a Western European context.[7] It was evident that the single most important factor to the Nissan project was the way in which the company secured control of the labour process. The essence of the Japanese production method involved close managerial control both inside the factory and, as far as possible, out of it down the supply chain. This was imposed through continuing, detailed changes to work organization, and the use of techniques designed to create loyalty to corporate goals. Adopting such procedures in a different context to the Japanese environment—where they rested heavily on relatively weak trade union representation—was (from Nissan's viewpoint) one of the most potentially difficult aspects of its internationalization strategy. Nissan's great care to screen its workforce so as to minimize potentially disruptive elements and develop a "team spirit" neatly illustrated the significance of such concerns.

The broader impact of the Nissan investment extended well beyond its own affairs. Within the North East, it was treated—in many senses quite correctly—as a mark of the extent of a radical break with the past.[8] By the start of the 1990s a substantial shift had indeed taken place in the North East regional economy; not just in the volume of employment in different sectors, but also in conceptions about the *nature* of employment. This shifting balance of power—heavily backed in a whole variety of ways by the UK state—involved a complex interaction between new employers and the region's existing industrial base. Companies such as Nissan were only too aware of the subtlety of some of the changes taking place. So too was the chairman of the Northern Development Company, Sir Ron Dearing, who remarked in 1990 that:

> What has happened is the recreation of a new industrial society. In that sense we can sell the North not as the old industrial economy but as the new one (quoted in *Newcastle Journal*, 23 January 1990).

In this new industrial society, flexibility, adaptability and—all too frequently—insecurity had become the new key words.

4. Concluding Remarks

In analysing patterns and processes of spatially uneven development, it is vital not to underestimate the significance, firstly, of the national state as a mediating element in the global organization and location of production and investment; and, secondly, of labour as a component of the social relations of production. A focus on production organization in terms of the relations between companies (as epitomized in the notion of flexible production) has the unfortunate consequence of blurring a vision of what is happening in terms of the balance of power within individual companies, regardless of their role in the productive system. Within the UK, the 1980s was a decade in which state power was used selectively to unpick many of the fragmentary threads of an earlier consensus, and begin to rebuild a new (possibly rather shaky but certainly more aggressively exploitative) conception of the employment relation. The UK's disproportionate share of Japanese direct foreign investment in Western Europe was in itself partly a reflection of the "success" of the Conservative government's policies in tackling overall labour costs to industry. This project was integrally connected to a recognition on the parts of capital and the national state of the significance of the *geography* of production, leading to the active (re)creation of new forms of uneven spatial development. The recent experience of economic change in North East England clearly reflects a particular social and political agenda. Regional reconstruction to a particular blueprint has been an indispensable accompaniment to a chosen path of mediation of international market forces.

One of the reasons (indeed, arguably the key factor) for the Thatcher governments' successes—in their own terms, at least—lies in the dearth of alternatives which were on offer. Such questions are essentially ones of the limits to and possibilities for national state policies in an international environment. They are of growing significance as old barriers come down in Eastern Europe and new power structures open up in and around the European Community. International changes in the political arena are creating new possibilities—not just for capital but for labour (for instance, in the context of the limits to new, internationally organized close-knit production strategies), even though to date internationalization of the latter has far from matched that of the former. In these (and other) ways, the (spatially uneven) legacies of the Thatcher years—when the history of this period comes to be written, and if the balance is to be redressed—will probably prove to have been challenging ones indeed.

Notes

1. The regulationist school evolved in France in the 1970s (see Aglietta 1979, Lipietz 1986). It focused on the idea that any given national social formation was characterized by a particular form of accumulation, or an approximate stabilization over time of the balance between production and consumption. This was secured by a mode of regulation, a body of rules and social processes that governed and secured the smooth running of accumulation. To the regulationist school, the crisis of world capitalism in the mid-1970s was a reflection of the breakdown of the Fordist regime of accumulation, as the balance between production and consumption disintegrated and the postwar consensus built on the welfare state fell apart.

2. To say this is not to understate the significance of the growth in different kinds of service sector employment in the decade. There is no doubt that the internationalization of financial services in the 1980s, for instance, was vital to the booming growth of some parts of South East England; or that the spread of low wage service sector employment in activities such as retailing and tourism was integral to the increasingly insecure labour market conditions emerging in many parts of the peripheral regions.

3. The impact of these effective price reductions was particularly apparent in BC's own accounts. As Sir Robert Haslam, chairman of BC explained in 1990, the price freeze agreed with the ESI cost BC an estimated £850m of lost revenue in that year if compared against prices in 1986. The new three year deal meant a further progressive loss of income of £150m each year, so that (on this basis) by 1992/3 BC would be experiencing a loss of income of £1,300m annually.

4. In addition to this there were other substantial difficulties in the way of an all-out import policy. In 1987 the CEGB imported just 1mt of coal; orders contracted for 1990 amounted to 6mt. Obstacles to further expansion included lack of dedicated port capacity and the inland location of many coal-fired power stations.

5. This account draws upon interviews conducted by the author with trade unionists and management at BSC Teesside during 1985 and 1986.

6. Although the two biggest motor industry unions, the TGWU and GMBU, also offered a single-union package, the final deal between Nissan and the AEU met with some criticism from other union leaders. Joe Mills, northern regional secretary of the TGWU, complained of being "forced to parade before prospective employers like beauty queens" (quoted in *Sunday Times*, 28 April 1985). He subsequently expanded on these views as follows:

   > Many trade union officials in the North East are facing tremendous pressure from within their organisations because they are allowing companies who are moving into the region to treat unions like supermarket products. Because of high unemployment and in des-

> peration to co-operate with inward investment, some unions are ignoring their traditional role to organise workers and are standing back and allowing companies to choose which union they want, similar to choosing washing powder from a supermarket. (Quoted in *Newcastle Journal*, 26 November 1986).

It should also be noted that Nissan's deliberate choice not to adopt a non-union policy (as it had in North America) displayed a clear grasp of the way in which it could work within existing North East traditions.

7. This also involved questions to do with component supply, as Nissan tested the limits to existing European standards of quality and reliability. As "local" (that is, EC produced) content built up, it was clear that some Japanese companies were following Nissan into the UK as suppliers (although not on the same scale as had rapidly followed the earlier Japanese vehicle makers' investments in North America).

8. For example, Jim Gardner, who had led the negotiations with Nissan on the part of the North of England Development Council, heralded the project as follows:

> We have sown the seeds for what will be a major public relations exercise as more and more people move to the north east. As word gets round so the region will be revitalised. I regard the arrival of Nissan as the most significant industrial landmark in the history of the north east in the last twenty years. And I remain convinced it will be the single biggest factor in the regeneration of the region (quoted in *Newcastle Journal*, 8 September 1986).

References

Aglietta, M. (1979) *A Theory of Capitalist Regulation*. New Left Books, London.

Amin, A. (1989) Flexible specialisation and small firms in Italy: myths and realities, *Antipode*, **21**: 13-34.

Beynon, H. (1984) *Working for Ford*, 2nd edition. Penguin, Harmondsworth.

Beynon, H. (ed.) (1985) *Digging Deeper: Issues in the Miners' Strike*. Verso, London.

Beynon, H. Hudson, R., and Sadler, D. (1986) Nationalised industry policies and the destruction of communities: some evidence from north-east England, *Capital and Class*, **29**: 27-57.

Beynon, H. Hudson, R., and Sadler, D., (1991) *A Tale of Two Industries: the Contraction of Coal and Steel in North East England*. Open University Press, Milton Keynes.

Briggs, P. (1988). The Japanese at work: illusions of the ideal, *Industrial Relations Journal*, **19**: 24-30.

Bryer, R. A. Brignall, T. J., and Maunders, A. R. (1982) *Accounting for British Steel*. Gower, Aldershot.

Commission of the European Communities (1989) *Energy and the Environment*, COM (89) 369. Brussels.

Commission of the European Communities (1990) *General Objectives Steel 1995*, COM (90) 201. Brussels.

Dicken, P. (1988) The changing geography of Japanese foreign direct

investment in manufacturing industry: a global perspective, *Environment and Planning A*, **20**: 633-653.
Dunning, J. (1986) *Japanese Participation in British Industry: Trojan Horse or Catalyst for Growth?* Croom Helm, Beckenham.
Energy Committee (1988) *The Structure, Regulation and Economic Consequences of Electricity Supply in the Private Sector*. House of Commons paper 307, session 1987/88.
Energy Committee (1989) *Energy Policy Implications of the Greenhouse Effect*. House of Commons paper 192 (3 vols), session 1988/89.
Energy Committee (1990a) *The Cost of Nuclear Power*. House of Commons paper 205 (two volumes), session 1989/90.
Energy Committee (1990b) *The Flue Gas Desulphurisation Programme*. House of Commons paper 371, session 1989-90.
Gamble, A. (1988) *The Free Economy and the Strong State: the Politics of Thatcherism*. Macmillan, London.
Graham, I. (1988) Japanisation as mythology, *Industrial Relations Journal*, **19**: 69-75.
Hill, R. C. (1989) Comparing transnational production systems: the automobile industry in the USA and Japan, *International Journal of Urban and Regional Research*, **13**: 462-480.
HMSO (1963) *The North East: a Programme for Regional Development and Growth*. Cmnd 2206. London.
HMSO (1973) *British Steel Corporation: Ten-year Development Strategy*. Cmnd 5226. London.
HMSO (1978) *British Steel Corporation: the Road to Viability*. Cmnd 7149. London.
HMSO (1988) *Privatising Electricity: the Government's Proposals for the Privatisation of the Electricity Supply Industry in England and Wales*. Cm 322. London.
Hudson, R. (1986) Nationalised industry policies and regional policies: the role of the state in capitalist societies in the deindustrialisation and reindustrialisation of regions, *Society and Space*, **4**: 7-28.
Hudson, R. (1988) Uneven development in capitalist societies: changing spatial divisions of labour, forms of spatial organisation of production and service provision, and their impacts on localities, *Transactions of the Institute of British Geographers* **13**: 484-496.
Hudson, R. (1989) *Wrecking a Region: State Policies, Party Politics and Regional Change in North East England*. Pion, London.
Hudson, R., and Sadler, D. (1983) Region, class and the politics of steel closures in the European Community, *Society and Space*, **1**: 405-428.
Hudson, R., and Sadler, D. (1987) *Easington Undermined? An Up-date of Undermining Easington: Who's Paying the Price of Pit Closures?* Easington District Council, Co. Durham.
Hudson, R., and Sadler, D. (1989) *The International Steel Industry: Restructuring. State Policies and Localities*. Routledge, London.
Hudson, R., and Sadler, D. (1990) State policies and the changing geography of the coal industry in the United Kingdom in the 1980s and 1990s, *Transactions of the Institute of British Geographers*, **15**: 435–54.
Hudson, R. Peck, F, and Sadler D, (1985) *Undermining Easington: Who'll Pay the Price of Pit Closures?* Easington District Council, Co. Durham.
Lewis, J., and Townsend, A. (eds.) (1989) *The North South Divide: Regional Change in Britain in the 1980s*. Paul Chapman, London.
Lipietz, A. (1986) New tendencies in the international division of labour: regimes of accumulation and modes of regulation. In Scott, A. J., and Storper, M. (eds.) *Production, Work Territory*, pp. 16-40. Allen & Unwin, London.

Lovering, J. (1990) Fordism's unknown successor: a comment on Scott's theory of flexible accumulation and the re-emergence of regional economies, *International Journal of Urban and Regional Research*, **14**: 159-174.

Mair, A. Florida, R., and Kenney, M. (1988) The new geography of automobile production: Japanese transplants in North America, *Economic Geography*, **64**: 352-373.

Martin, R. (1988) The political economy of Britain's north-south divide, *Transactions of the Institute of British Geographers*, **13**: 389-418.

Massey, D. (1984) *Spatial Divisions of Labour: Social Structures and the Geography of Production*. Macmillan, London.

Massey, D. (1986) The legacy lingers on: the impact of Britain's international role on its internal geography. In Martin, R., and Rowthorn, B. (eds.) *The Geography of De-industrialisation*, pp. 31–52. Macmillan, London.

Mohan, J. (ed.) (1989) *The Political Geography of Contemporary Britain*. Macmillan, London.

Morris, J. (1988) The who, why and where of Japanese manufacturing investment in the UK, *Industrial Relations Journal* **19**: 31-40.

Oliver, N., and Wilkinson, B. (1988) *The Japanisation of British Industry*. Blackwell, Oxford.

Piore, M., and Sabel, C. (1984) *The Second Industrial Divide*. Basic Books, New York.

Pollert, A. (1988) Dismantling flexibility, *Capital and Class*, **34**: 42-75.

Prior, M., and McCloskey, G. (1988) *Coal on the Market: Can British Coal Survive Privatisation?* FT International Coal Report, London.

Sadler, D. (1990) Privatising British Steel: the politics of production and place, *Area*, **22**: 47-55.

Sadler, D. (1991) *The Global Region: Production, State Policies and Uneven Development*. Pergamon, Oxford.

Sayer, A. (1986) New developments in manufacturing: the just-in-time system, *Capital and Class*, **30**: 43-72.

Sayer, A. (1989) Post-Fordism in question, *International Journal of Urban and Regional Research*, **13**: 666-695.

Schoenberger, E. (1987) Technological and organisational change in automobile production: spatial implications, *Regional Studies* **21**: 199-214.

Scott, A. J. (1988a) *New Industrial Spaces*. Pion, London.

Scott, A. J. (1988b) Flexible production systems and regional development: the rise of new industrial spaces in North America and western Europe, *International Journal of Urban and Regional Research*, **12**: 171-186.

Sleigh, P. A. C. (1988) *The UK Automotive Components Industry*. Economist Intelligence Unit, Automotive Special Report 10, London.

Sleigh, P. A. C. (1989) *The European Automotive Components Industry* Economist Intelligence Unit Special Report 1186, London.

Starkey, K., and McKinlay, A. (1989) Beyond Fordism? Strategic choice and labour relations in Ford UK, *Industrial Relations Journal*, **20**: 93-100.

Storper, M., and Christopherson, S. (1987) Flexible specialisation and regional industrial agglomeration: the case of the US motion picture industry, *Annals of the Association of American Geographers*, **77**: 104-117.

Trade and Industry Committee (1987) *The Motor Components Industry*. House of Commons paper 143, session 1986/87.

Turnbull, P. (1987) The limits to Japanisation—just in time, labour relations and the UK automotive industry, *New Technology, Work and Employment*, **3**: 7-20.

14

Social Divisions, Income Inequality and Gender Relations in the 1980s

LINDA MCDOWELL

Introduction

The 1980s have been a decade of uneven development and widening differentials in Britain. As the previous chapters have demonstrated, the three terms of Conservative governments presided over by Margaret Thatcher have witnessed growing social and spatial divisions in the country. Economic restructuring and the growth of a service based economy has led to a labour force that increasingly is divided between a core of well paid, highly qualified workers with secure employment prospects and an expanding periphery of low paid, often part-time and casualized workers with little or no job security. The model worker of the Fordist era—a family man who expects to work for a single employer throughout his life—is being replaced by a new model worker of these post-Fordist, post-modern times—the single, the rootless, women and ethnic minorities, whose attachment to the labour market is constructed as marginal or casual and who, correspondingly, can be expelled in times of recession.

The old universal institutions of collective welfare provision that accompanied Keynesian economic policies are also being dismantled. The health and welfare of working class people *in situ* are less relevant to the new mobile capital and employers who increasingly shift their investments between industrial and financial sectors and between places, within and between countries in their search for profit. Not for them the old paternalist strategies, concerned with the health and welfare of their workers and his family (the gendered terms are used here intentionally).

In association with a government throughout the 1980s that regarded basic welfare entitlements as creating a culture of dependency on a "nanny" state among the impoverished and unfortunate and aimed to construct a newer, leaner Britain of morally responsible individuals by rolling back the state, rights to social income and a range of goods and services have been reduced, increasing the social divisions between those in work and those out of work, between the young and fit and the elderly and disabled people.

Earlier chapters have illustrated the impact of changes in the provision of housing, health and transport in the 1980s. In this chapter I want to assess the net impact of economic restructuring—the changing world of waged work—and of changes in the sphere of social reproduction on social divisions, seen through the particular lens of the changing position of women and the family in contemporary Britain. For despite strong appeals to the ideal of the traditional nuclear family and an emphasis on the familial roles of women, particularly in social policies, the 1980s have seen a rapid acceleration in the recruitment of women to the waged labour force and a concomitant decline in the numbers of women whose sole role is a domestic one within the home. This has been one of the most marked social changes of the Thatcher era.

A Family Crisis?

1990 may come to be characterized as the year when the family became *the* social issue of the time. Politicians of the left and the right are struggling to come to terms with the enormous changes that have taken place over the 1980s in the position of women, particularly their increased labour market participation, and in the structure of the conventional nuclear family that appears to be being rocked to its foundations by rising divorce rates, illegitimacy and single parenthood. The right, in particular, is finding the contradiction between its rhetoric of individual rights and responsibilities and its economic policies on the one hand, and its commitment to traditional family life shored up by the unpaid labours of women as wives and mothers at home on the other, difficult to resolve. While women are needed in the labour market, in part because their typical patterns of participation mirror the desire for "flexibility" but also to meet the shortages caused by the decline in the number of young people available for work—the so-called demographic time bomb—they are also needed in the home and in the community where their unpaid labour continues to be essential to prop up and supplement services available from the state and in the market to ensure the relative health and well-being of the population as a whole.

For individual women, struggling to reconcile the competing demands on their time, the Thatcher decade has been an era of increasing work, declining leisure and, for many, declining standards of living. For a minority of women, however, the decade has been one in which a wider range of opportunities opened up, particularly as they gained access in growing numbers to relatively secure and well-paid occupations in the professions and in some areas of the service sector, in business and financial services for example. Professional incomes bring with them the ability to pay for goods and services that individual women may previously have provided themselves in their homes—childcare is the classic example—and for some of these women increased labour market participation may entail a form of emancipation rather than increased drudgery. The 1980s may, therefore, have been a decade of widening social and economic differentials between women, as well as greater inequality between households and the social classes. Whereas these latter dimensions are more commonly the focus of assessments of the Thatcher decade than are gender differentials (that is divisions between men and women), differences among women are barely discussed at all.

Some of these issues are explored below. First, the changing gender composition of the labour force is examined, followed by an assessment of the implications for the distribution of income between individuals. This is followed by an outline of the changing structure of households and families, patterns of births and divorces. The two sections are then combined by a focus on the distribution of household income, assessing whether inequalities have also increased between families and how the proportion of families and households with below average incomes has changed over time. In particular, the impact of women's wages and of changes in benefit levels is addressed.

This focus on women's work and on income inequalities is not to deny the widespread social changes that have occurred in other areas in Britain throughout the 1980s. On the negative side, racial intolerance, discrimination and harassment in the labour market and in the community appears to have deepened during this decade. Similarly tolerance of other than a heterosexual sexual orientation has declined, culminating with the notorious clause 28 banning the dissemination of information about homosexuality in the arts and in schools. AIDS was a significant factor in the general hardening of moral attitudes in the mid eighties. Religious fundamentalism and intolerance of others' points of view also has become a more significant feature of the political and cultural landscape of Great Britain, from the deepening of sectarian political divides in Northern Ireland to the reaction to Salman Rushdie's novel *The Satanic Verses* in the Muslim community. In this upsurge of religious and nationalist feeling, of course, Britain has not been alone. The world at the end of the 1980s was faced, among other movements, with the *intifada* in Palestine, the dissolution of the Soviet Union, the end of state socialism in Eastern Europe and the associated rise in nationalist feeling, and in 1991, war in the Middle East.

Within Britain during the 1980s social attitudes generally seem to have hardened. There is a greater emphasis on market values, on individualism rather than on collective provision, a focus on the spurious "choices" available in the market, be it of life style accoutrements from diaries to cars, or of more essential needs such as housing, education and social services. Attitudes vary, of course, by region, between the classes, by gender and by political belief. For example, only 47 per cent of Conservative supporters, according to the 1990 British Social Attitudes Survey (SCPR, 1990), believe that "there is quite a lot of poverty in Britain today", compared with 81 per cent of Labour supporters, and the former are far more likely to attribute the cause either to laziness or lack of willpower (30 per cent Conservative, 9 per cent Labour supporters) or regard it as an inevitable feature of modern societies (39 per cent Conservative; 30 per cent Labour). But despite these differences and the eleven years of Conservative governments committed to the reduction of state spending and the widening of social inequalities documented below, there is evidence that in 1990 there is a growing groundswell of support for a switch back to welfarist rather than individualist policies on tax and social spending. Despite growing income inequalities and substantial redistribution towards the better off in "the Thatcher years", the Social Attitudes Survey has documented an annual increase in support among all sectors of the population, including the better off, for the welfare state. Space precludes all but the consideration of questions related to income and welfare changes in this chapter, and even these are treated in an aggregate fashion. Interesting work remains to be done on the spatially uneven form of these social changes.

The Gender Composition of the Labour Force: A Decade of Change?

Rather than being a specific 1980s phenomenon, the rising participation of women in waged labour has been one of steady progression over the entire postwar period, apart from the slight decline that occurred during severe recession of the early eighties—a period during which men's labour market opportunities seemed to be hit rather more badly than women's. The inadequacy in the recorded figures for female unemployment, however, make it difficult to make accurate statements about the differential impact of the recession on men and on women. What distinguishes the 1980s, however, as far as women's labour market participation is concerned, is the enormous and unprecedented increase in the numbers of mothers of young children who have become waged workers, particularly in the later years of the decade. The figures are really quite remarkable. Whereas 24 per cent of women with children under 5 were in employment in 1983, 36 per cent were in 1988 and 41 per cent by 1989. Although the increases are somewhat less marked for women with older children, there were also significant rises in these women's participation rates between 1983 and 1989. Thus, 69 per cent of women with children between 5 and 9 years of age were employed in 1989 compared with 54 per cent six years previously and among women whose youngest child was 10 or older, 75 per cent were working for wages in 1989 compared with 66 per cent in 1983.

Many of these women work part-time—a feature of women's labour market participation that is particularly noticeable in Great Britain in comparison with other advanced industrial nations. However, in 1989, one in five women with dependent children—those under 16 or under 19 in full-time education and living at home—was employed on a full-time basis. Not surprisingly, this proportion is positively related to the age of the youngest child—that is it declines as does the age of the child. Thus, 19 per cent of women with children between 5 and 9 and 12 per cent with children under 5 worked full-time in 1989.

In 1989 59 per cent of mothers and no less than 70 per cent of all women of working age (between 16 and 59) were employed on some basis. As a group women accounted for almost 46 per cent of waged workers, almost one in two of all workers compared with less than one in three at the end of the fifties. Clearly, these figures are an immense challenge to established notions of the gender division of labour, the idea of waged work as a man's

TABLE 14.1
Trends in the Gender Division of Labour 1971–88 Great Britain Employees in employment (June)

	Men	Women	Women as a % of total	Women full-timers as % of total	Women part-timers as % of total	Women part-timers as % of all women
	(millions)					
1971	13,424	8,224	38.0	25.3	12.6	33.5
1976	13,097	8,951	40.4	24.3	16.3	39.6
1981	12,278	9,108	42.6	24.7	17.8	41.9
1986	11,643	9,462	44.8	25.2	19.6	42.4
1988	11,978	10,096	45.7	26.2	19.5	42.8

Source: *Department of Employment Gazette*, various years.

world and the home as the place for women. At a time when 6 out of every 10 mothers work and nearly half of all employees are women (indeed on current trends the number of women in the labour market is set to overtake that of men by the end of the century), a reassessment of domestic and familial responsibilities for child care provision. However, as will be demonstrated later, this reassessment and renegotiation of responsibilities has largely failed to materialize.

Table 14.1 shows the changes in men and women's labour market participation rates since the early 1970s. Since this time the number of men in employment in Great Britain has fallen by 1.5 million and the number of women has risen by over 1.8 million. However, as the table reveals, almost half of all women work part-time so whereas the last two decades have witnessed a large rise in the overall numbers of women in employment, the total numbers of hours worked in the economy, especially with the declining numbers of men in employment, has not increased correspondingly. Rather there has been a *sharing out* of total hours between a greater number of workers. Indeed, the activity rates for full-time female employment fell during the 1970s, and remained static until 1986 when they began to rise again.

It is frequently assumed that women prefer to work on a part-time basis as this enables them to combine their family responsibilities with waged employment. However, in addition to the obvious fact that part-time employment is only paid *pro rata*, women on such contracts are paid at a lower rate than women in full-time employment. On average women in part-time employment earn only 80 per cent of the hourly rate paid to women in full-time employment (and, of course, women's average wages are lower than men's). Further, the statutory position of part-time employees is an inferior one, in which their entitlement to both employer-provided and state benefits is significantly poorer than that of full-time workers. This makes part-time employees a cheap and exploitable labour force for employers—the quintessential "flexible" labour force (Blanchflower and Corry 1989). For individual women, however, the benefits are not so obvious. Hakim (1987) found that many women took part-time or temporary jobs for lack of alternatives, while continuing to search for full-time employment and Evans (1990), in a recent survey of labour market trends, has warned that "one should be wary of endorsing the view that women have a 'taste' for part-time jobs, which are demonstrably exploitative jobs. It may be that the 'taste' for part-time jobs is actually that of employers" (p. 53).

Women's increased integration into the labour force has been associated with the shift to a service based economy in Great Britain. Some of the fastest expanding areas of the economy, such as retailing, sales, clerical work and some white collar and professional occupations, particularly in the public sector expansion throughout the 1970s, have traditionally been feminized occupations. Women have increased their predominance in these areas, with the exception of the public sector where women accounted for 85 per cent of job losses in the 1980s, and have also gained access to certain private sector services, such as banking and finance, although even here in jobs at the lower end of the occupational heirarchies. The net result of the big increase in female employment has not therefore been to decrease the differences in the industrial and occupational patterns of men and women. Gender segregated patterns of employment remain marked (Rubery and Tarling 1988) and are reflected in gender differentials in pay.

Earnings Differentials

One of the effects of women's increased labour market participation rates has been to accelerate Britain's shift towards a low wage economy. As Rubery and Tarling (1988), among others, have argued, it is the social and institutional conditions of women's labour supply that constructs them as low paid workers and makes them attractive to employers. Those who argue that it is the shift towards a low paid, low skilled economy that has drawn women in increasing numbers may have their explanation the wrong way round. Rather "... it is clear that these lower rates of pay (*for women compared with men: comment added*) do not derive from the characteristics of the jobs but from the conditions under which women supply their labour. Exclusion from particular forms of skilled work still prevails, ... but not all women's jobs are low skilled, even though they may be so defined for purposes of job and pay grading" (Rubery and Tarling 1988: p. 119). Examination of the changes over time of women's hourly pay rates compared with men's is instructive (Table 14.2). Neo-classical economists would argue that as the demand for women's labour rises, their rates of pay should do so too, if not absolutely in relation to men's, until the gap is closed. However, despite the rising demand for women's labour, the gender differential has not been gradually declining but has remained constant apart from a one-off rise in the early seventies. Between the end of the Second World War and the early seventies, women's earnings stubbornly stuck at around 60 per cent of men's and then rose to 70 per cent where they have remained since that date. The rise was a partial result of the implementation of the Equal Pay Act and the trade unions' policy of implementing it through raising women's minimum earnings, but also of the incomes policies then in operation that gave the same absolute increases for all workers.

The table is based on a comparison of women's and men's full-time hourly earnings. While the gender discrepancy between

TABLE 14.2
Ratio of Hourly Earnings of Female to Male Full-time Adult Employees, Great Britain 1971–89

1971	**1972**	**1973**	**1974**	**1975**	**1976**	**1977**	**1978**	**1979**	**1980**
63.3	63.4	63.2	65.4	69.7	73.2	74.2	72.9	71.3	72.4
1981	**1982**	**1983**	**1984**	**1985**	**1986**	**1987**	**1988**	**1989**	
72.6	72.4	75.0	74.2	74.7	74.1	73.4	74.9	76.0	

Until 1983 male adult employees were those aged 21 and over, female adult 18 and over; from 1983 onwards the figures are for all those on adult rates. The 1983 estimate on the former basis would be 73.1. All figures exclude overtime payments.

Source: *New Earnings Survey*, various dates.

full-time workers gives no cause for celebration, at least not by employees, the position for part-time women workers is much worse. The data on part-time earnings are, however, not completely satisfactory for comparative purposes. The *New Earnings Survey*, for example, only includes employees earning enough to pay income tax. As well as excluding women who fall below this threshold, there is, in addition, an unknown percentage of women who work in a range of casual jobs and do not declare their earnings. Women employed in other people's homes as cleaners, nannies and casual domestic workers (an expanding group throughout the 1980s) are likely to fall in this latter group, and homeworkers (those employed in their own home) in the former. These women are amongst the most exploited and low paid workers in the country (Allen and Walkowitz 1987).

Table 14.3 shows that, even excluding the most poorly paid women employees, part-time women workers' average hourly rate relative to men's falls to 57 per cent. Women in non-manual occupations fare particularly badly. The comparisons in this table are based on women over 18, and it seems that the position of young women is worse as there was a significant deterioration in the youth to adult pay differentials for girls between 1979 and 1986 (Rubery 1986). The current decline in the numbers of school leavers and the abolition of young workers under 21 from the wages council legal minimum wage regulation which was effected by the 1986 Wages Act as an incentive to employers to hire young workers may partially redress this balance, but young women remain disproportionately concentrated among the lowest paid.

The 1980s has been a decade when differentials between workers *of the same sex* have widened rather than between men and women. Economic restructuring, the decline of manufacturing

TABLE 14.3

Women's Hourly Earnings Relative to Men's in manual and non-manual Occupations, Great Britain, 1989, %

	Wages relative to men employed full time: women full-timers	women part-timers	Wages of women: part-timers relative to full-timers
All occupations	76	57	75
Manual	71	63	88
Non-maual	63	49	78

Source: *New Earnings Survey*.

TABLE 14.4
Distribution of Gross Hourly Earnings of Full-time Adult Employees

	Ratios to median				Ratio of women's wages to men's	
	Men		Women		%	
	1980	1989	1980	1989	1980	1989
Top decile	175	200	169	193	71	76
Top quartile	130	140	126	139	72	78
Median	100	100	100	100	73	78
Lowest quartile	81	76	81	78	76	80
Lowest decile	68	60	70	64	76	83
Mean					72	76

Source: *New Earnings Survey* (1980 sample: men 21 and over, women 18 and over 1989 sample workers on adult rates).

and the growth of the service sector, the attack on union regulated employment and the growth of temporary and casual work, for men and for women, the divisions between adult and young workers, and the reduction of tax burdens for the better paid have in combination extended the difference between the best and the worst paid workers of both sexes. As Table 14.4 shows, the top decile employees now take home a larger proportion of total wages than in 1980. Among women workers, these divisions are partly a consequence of the increased access by a minority of women to better paid occupations as their possession of the requisite credentials improved during the 1980s (Crompton and Sanderson 1986). The extent of inequality in the distribution of earnings between women as a whole now more nearly mirrors that among men. The table does, however, reveal some slight overall improvement of the position of women within each decile relative to that of men.

What are the consequences of these changes as a whole? It is clear that for men and for women the Thatcher years have been ones in which economic restructing has profoundly affected their labour market opportunities. Men as a group, but particularly working class men, have seen their access to secure and reasonably paid employment in the manufacturing sector reduced without parallel opportunities being created in the expanding service sector. Here the majority of new jobs have been for women. However, many of these jobs are low paid and women workers in the main have found that their earnings have not resulted in an increased level of total family income, but have been an essential element in maintaining a standard of living previously attainable on the basis of one industrial wage, typically a male wage. Townsend (1987) has argued that without women's wages, four times as many families would have been poor than the number so defined in the mid 1980s. Thus, while it cannot be denied that economic participation brings with it a range of advantages for women, including greater self confidence and a reduction in the social isolation felt by many women at home, for most women their increased labour force participation over the 1980s has not brought with it a greater prospect of economic independence or the opportunity to live independently from men. Their own earned incomes simply are not high enough for independent living. And many of the poorest households in contemporary Britain consist of women living alone or with their children.

In common with the distribution of individual incomes, inequalities in the distribution of incomes between households has also increased over the 1980s, partly as a consequence of women's rising economic participation rates but also because of changes in the structure of families. Before assessing the extent of poverty and the widening structure of household inequality, demographic and social changes in the population and the ways in which it is grouped into households will be examined.

The Changing Structure of the Family

It seems somewhat ironic that three terms of a Conservative government committed to "traditional" family values has coincided with a rapid rise of all those features that their supporters would see as marking the breakdown of family life. Thus over the decade people have married later if at all, more people cohabit, more people have divorced, illegitimacy rates have risen, more women are bringing up children alone, and cohabitation after divorce lasts longer. To right wing commentators these trends constitute a crisis in family life which, bad enough in itself, is moreover, in their opinion, also the cause of a range of societal ills from increasing violence to, less explicably, inner city decline. Charles Murray (1990), for example, a US researcher, whose article based on brief studies of Liverpool and Glasgow has been published by the Institute of Economic Affairs, has claimed that illegitimacy is the best "predictor of an underclass in the making". In fact, as will be made clear, simple measures of illegitimacy are not all that they seem, let alone any correlation between this and future prospects or behaviour.

Political commentators on the left have had less to say during the 1980s about the links between the social trends briefly outlined above and the ideal family, although they have continued to rely very strongly on traditional notions of the heterosexual couple as the basic unit in social and economic policy and in their publicity material. Witness the marketing of the Kinnocks as a cuddly twosome during and between election campaigns. However, partially in response to the Conservative focus on the family as a key political issue, in 1990 the Institute for Public Policy Research, the independent charity with impeccable Labour credentials headed by Baroness Blackstone, published *The Family Way* (Coote *et al.* 1990)—a document that recommended putting the interests of children first. Despite its consistent argument that families take a variety of forms, none being better than the other, the heterosexual couple featured large in the policy recommendations. The ideal future proposed in the document seemed to be based on a combination of "strong self-reliant women" (p. 34) and men prepared to take emotional responsibility (p. 37) in an interdependent partnership. In a stringent critique of this Fabian idealism, Ann Oakley (1990) pointed out that "these moral prescriptions arise uneasily like a phoenix from the ashes of statistics which paint a picture of corrosive female dependency, dangerous male violence, and enduring material and domestic inequalities between the sexes" (p. 45).

Less traditional, and more optimistic, interpretations of the current trends are uncommon in Britain. However, an interpretation of similar changes in family and household forms in the United States by the noted feminist scholar Heidi Hartmann (1988) leaves scope for thought and comparison. She argued, on the basis of women's greater autonomy from men indicated by rising rates of economic participation and women living alone or as household heads, "that to the extent (that) there is a family crisis, it is by-and-large a healthy one, particularly for women" (p. 49). This, of course, is a controversial conclusion that fails to take into account class and ethnic differences. The costs and opportunities of the current social changes in family and household relations differ for women in different positions. Black women, for example, in both the USA and Britain, have been very dismissive of the critique of family life in the academic feminist literature, charging it with both ethnocentric and class bias and failure to recognize the strengths of different black family forms. Partly in response to this, British feminists have modified their position on the family, recognizing the contradictions in its significance as a site of loving and emotional interdependent relationships as well as an arena of abuse and oppression.

Households, Families, Births and Divorces: Contemporary Changes

The 1980s were a decade of increasing diversity in household and family forms in Britain. The number of single person and female headed households rose in response both to the continuing ageing of the population and rising divorce rates. In 1987 just over a quarter of all households consisted of the "traditional" unit of a married (or cohabiting) couple and dependent children. Nevertheless, more than two-fifths of all people still lived in such households (see Table 14.5).

Over the decade birth rates have risen slightly from their lowest point in the mid seventies, although they remain lower than the peak rates in earlier years (the early sixties for women over 20 and 1971 for women aged 15-19). The patterns are quite complicated, however with the rates for women over 25 rising, those for women between 20 and 24 stable and those for very young women continuing to fall. Rates for women from ethnic minority communities—or at least those born abroad, as black British women are included in the statistics for all British women—are continuing to fall. The most marked feature about births, however, is the rise in the number of births outside marriage. They accounted for 25 per cent of all births in 1988 compared to only 12 per cent in 1981 and 6 per cent

TABLE 14.5
Households by Type of Family and People in Households
Great Britain, %

	Households		Persons	
	1981	1987	1981	1987
1 person only	22	25	8	10
Married couple:				
no children	26	27	20	21
with dependent children	31	28	47	44
with non-dependent children	8	9	10	12
Lone parent:				
with dependent children	5	4	6	5
with non-dependent children	4	4		
Other households	6	4	9	8

Source: Office of Population Censuses and Surveys.

in 1961. However, this rise has been paralleled by an increase in the proportion of births outside marriage registered by both parents, from 45 per cent in 1971 to 70 per cent in 1988. Further, in 1988 the mother and father gave the same address as their usual place of residence in 71 per cent of these joint registrations. This suggests that at least half the children born outside marriage at the end of the decade had parents who were living together and, in the measured tones of the Central Statistical Office, "were likely to be bringing up the child within a stable non-martial union" (*Social Trends* 1990, p. 46)—viz. marriage in all but in name or, rather, legal status. Thus statistics of "illegitimacy", that apparently reflect a shocking decline of moral standards, in some commentator's eyes at least, in fact reflect no such thing. And the recent revelations about the extent of child abuse, and longer term statistics on maritial violence, reveal that the notion that all is rosy within conventional families is far from correct.

Despite the figures for births outside marriage, and a rise in the rate of cohabitation (for women aged between 18-49 years the rate doubled between 1981 and 1988—but only to 7.7 per cent), marriage continues to be popular in the United Kingdom. Indeed, in 1987 of all the EC countries, the UK had the highest marriage rate (shared with Portugal), but it also had the highest divorce rate (shared with Denmark). The rate of divorce has risen from 2.1 per 1,000 existing marriages in 1961 to 12.8 in 1988. Part of the explanation of the rising marriage rate lies in people getting remarried after divorces. Interestingly, the remarriage rate for eligible men in 1988 was two and a half times the corresponding rate for women. The number of divorce petitions filed by women also far exceeds that by men (134,000 compared with 49,000 in 1988). It seems that the advantages of marriage may be differently perceived by men and women—perhaps supporting Hartmann's contention that the so-called family crisis is not necessarily entirely to women's disadvantage.

Lone Parents

One of the consequences of the rising divorce rate has been an increase in the number of single parents, particularly women bringing up children alone. The proportion of all families with dependent children which are lone parent families has increased from 8 per cent in 1971 to 14 per cent in 1987. The rise is entirely accounted for by the rise in lone mothers; the proportion of families with dependent children headed by a lone father has remained relatively unchanged at around 1 per cent of all families with dependent children. Nine out of 10 lone parents are women, almost all of whom are divorced or single (in similar number). The number of widowed lone mothers has declined. The geographical distribution of one parent families is uneven. Perhaps a consequence of housing and job opportunities, or of social attitudes, higher than average proportions of single parent households are typical in Inner London and in the other major urban conurbations.

It has perhaps been the rise in the number of single mothers, above all the changing features of families, that has been singled out for adverse comment by the Conservative governments. Single parents have been variously blamed for causing inner city poverty, youth unrest, vandalism and delinquency, and falling educational standards, as well as young women being accused of becoming deliberately pregnant to gain access to local authority housing. However, this ignores the limited opportunities available to many young women in inner city areas and, as research has shown, many young women chose to become mothers as a way of asserting their individuality and independence in the absence of labour market opportunities and have a clear view of the consequences of their actions (Campbell 1984, Phoenix 1989).

Employment prospects for single mothers are restricted, partly as a consequence of the inadequate childcare facilities in Great Britain, which, of course, affects all women. Good quality, affordable and accessible childcare is virtually non-existent. In England and Scotland, day nursery places were available for 2 per cent of under fives in 1988 and for less than 1 per cent in Wales (EOC 1990). While 24 per cent of 3 and 4 year olds were in nursery schools or classes in the same year, this was on a part-time basis for a restricted number of hours, making waged work difficult for women without additional childcare arrangements. These problems seem to be reflected in the employment participation rates of single mothers which differ from those of other women with young children. Single mothers are less likely to be employed overall, but of those who are working for wages they are more likely to be employed on a full-time basis, which at least gives them the prospect of an adequate income (Table 14.6).

For many single women, because the earnings disregard is low (i.e. the sum from employment that may be retained before state benefits are cut) and because women's earnings from part-time employment are poor, as the previous section demonstrated, there is a strong disincentive to seek employment in circumstances where there is no childcare provision. Thus a large number of

TABLE 14.6
Economic Activity Rates of Mothers, Great Britain 1986, %

	Married women	Lone mothers
Youngest child under 5		
Working full time	7	13
Working part time	24	9
Youngest child 5 or over		
Working full time	22	22
Working part time	44	31

Source: *The General Household Survey 1986*. HMSO, 1989.

single parents are solely reliant on the state for income support. Over 70 per cent of lone mothers are reliant on the state for their main source of income, compared with 7 per cent on maintenance payments and the remainder on earnings. The cost of this provision, combined with a strong desire to see men accept their financial responsibilities for their children, led to the introduction of a White Paper *Children Come First* in October 1990. The proposals of this White Paper included an obligation for women to identify the father of their child and earnings attachments to men's wages to ensure that maintenance payments are received. Women on state income support who refused to disclose the identity of the man involved would incur financial penalties, thus deepening their poverty.

Many single mothers would prefer not to be permanently tied to a man with whom they no longer, or indeed never, lived and surveys have demonstrated that a far higher proportion of single parents than are actually employed would be interested in a job immediately if childcare were available. The current proposals, however, do not address the question of childcare. Indeed, far from improving access to the labour market, a report from the National Council for One Parent Families in November 1990 revealed that training schemes for the long-term unemployed are effectively closed to lone parents as managers of the Employment Training scheme are unable to pay childcare allowances after recent government cuts. The ET programme was cut by £350 million (to £1.2 million) in 1990 and in the autumn statement a further cut of £365 million was announced for 1991.

Household Income Inequalities

Single mothers and their children are thus over-represented among the poorest households in Great Britain (Glendinning and

Millar 1987). Indeed, the rising labour market participation rate of married women over the eighties has increased the differences in living standards between married women and single women, particularly single mothers, and concomitantly the gap between the living standards of the majority of children (86 per cent) brought up by two parents and those in single parent families. Two-thirds of all married couples were dual income households by the mid eighties (Table 14.7)

The table reveals a further source of income inequality between households, in this case between dual headed households rather than between dual and single headed households. Women with husbands who are unemployed are significantly less likely themselves to be in waged work. It is commonly argued that this is the result of the disincentive effect of welfare benefit regulations (Cooke 1987) as a wife's earnings are deducted £1 for £1 from her husband's entitlement to unemployment benefit, apart from the first few pounds. However, work in Rochdale by Stanley and Temple (1989) has suggested that there may be geographical variations in the "typical" response, depending not only on local labour market opportunities for women but also the development of long standing traditions, beliefs and assumptions about the "proper relationship" between the sexes. A complete examination of the structure of these geographical variations remains to be undertaken, although McDowell and Massey (1984) have sketched in the broad outlines of the variation.

Of the third or so of married women in full-time employment,

TABLE 14.7

Dual Earner Households: Economic Activity of Married Women whose Husbands were Economically Active, Great Britain, %

	1973	1986
Women with husbands in employment		
Working full time	26	31
Working part time	29	36
Unemployed	1	4
Economically inactive	43	29
Women with unemployed husbands		
Working full time	19	9
Working part time	15	15
Unemployed	1	6
Economically inactive	65	70

Source: *The General Household Survey 1986*. HMSO, 1989.

it is those women who have gained access to professional and other well-paid employment who bring the greatest financial contribution to the household budget. Given the propensity for such women to marry men in similar or higher status jobs (in so-called cross-class marriages it is usually the man who marries a woman of lower social status—hardly surprising given the relative occupational structures for men and for women), a distinction between dual career and dual income households is helpful. This distinguishes between a first group of households who have benefited from the economic restructuring of the Thatcher years and a second who have not, but who have had increasingly to depend on two earned incomes to maintain the standard of living previously obtainable on one in previous decades. This reflects, in particular, the decline of relatively well-paid jobs for men in the manufacturing sector.

The redistributive effects of the changes in total family and household incomes (earnings, pensions, investment and other income and state benefits) over the 1980s are difficult to calculate with any certainty. There are, for example, no longitudinal statistics that monitor the changing position of households with different structures over time, so it is difficult to know whether families have moved in or out of poverty over the decade, what the effects have been of changes in income support regulations and levels of payment compared with average incomes, the effects of unemployment and of women's increasing participation in the labour market. However, it is clear that inequalities in household incomes have increased during the 1980s and that increasing numbers of people are living on very low incomes. Thus in 1986, by comparison with a decade earlier, the rich were richer and the poor were poorer. Of total *original income* (that is all pay, pensions, investment interest, gifts and alimony) the top fifth of households received 50.7 per cent, compared with 44.4 per cent in 1976. Figures for the bottom fifth were 0.3 per cent in 1986, compared with 0.8 per cent in 1976. Of total *disposable income* (including state benefits and income tax) the figures were 42.2 per cent of the total in 1986 for the top quintile, compared with 38.1 per cent in 1976; for the bottom quintile 5.9 per cent compared with 7.0 per cent. Of total *final income* (allowing also for indirect taxes and the imputed benefits of state spending) the richest fifth had 41.7 per cent in 1986, 37.9 per cent in 1976 and the poorest fifth 5.9 and 7.4 per cent for the same years (*Social Trends* 1990).

The total number of households with incomes of less than half the average also expanded throughout the 1980s. So, as well as a widening of differentials between the richest and poorest households, the absolute numbers of those on low incomes increased. Just how big the number actually is is disputed. The figures published by the Department of Social Security exclude housing costs, and show that 8 million people lived in households with below half the national average income in 1987. However, the Institute of Fiscal Studies have estimated that if housing costs are taken into account the figure rises to 11 million. Not surprisingly the DSS disputes the basic latter estimate, preferring their own.

The quintile group with the lowest original income derived over 96 per cent of gross income from cash benefits in 1986. Half of the adults in these households were pensioners and of the other half negligible numbers were in waged work. By comparison, in the top quintile 89 per cent of gross income was derived from earnings and the majority had more than one salary coming in. Recent figures from the Family Expenditure Survey (1990) show the importance of more than one earner in positioning households within the overall income distribution (Table 14.8). The positive correlation between number of workers and average incomes is hardly surprising. These figures, of course, do not reveal the distribution of income between individual household members within households. Research has demonstrated that there are significant gender inequalities in this (Graham 1984, Pahl 1983).

For the families at the bottom end of the distribution, changes in the value of state benefits relative to earnings over the decade have had a crucial impact on their living standards. The gap has widened. For example, between 1981 and 1988 the state pension for a retired couple fell from 43.3 per cent of average earnings to 32.7 per cent and for single pensioners from 27.0 to 20.5 per cent. Unemployment benefit for a single person fell from 21.5 per cent to 16.3 per cent and the invalid care allowance from 26.0 to 19.6 per cent. (Average weekly earnings for a

TABLE 14.8
Households at Different Levels of Income, Average Household Size and Average Number of Workers, UK 1988

	Decile group of household income distributions									
	Lowest	Second	Third	Fourth	Fifth	Sixth	Seventh	Eighth	Ninth	Highest
Av. number of persons	1.179	1.184	2.133	2.176	2.530	2.850	2.970	3.021	3.140	3.340
Av. number of workers	0.074	0.167	0.371	0.704	1.154	1.390	1.688	1.842	2.069	2.220

Source: *Family Expenditure Survey: Report for 1988*. HMSO, 1990.

man in full-time employment in 1988 were £235.) In addition, state benefits remained an important share of total household income throughout the 1980s (around 13 per cent throughout the decade) compared with earnings which fell from 64 per cent to 60 per cent of average household income between 1981 and 1988.

Thus during the 1980s the fall in the value of state benefits relative to average earnings, the widening of individual incomes differentials and the entry of growing numbers of married women into the labour force have all contributed to a widening differential in household incomes. The net result is that Britain in the early 1990s is a significantly more unequal society than it was ten years earlier and, indeed, than it has been for several decades.

The Dependent Population, "Community Care", Domestic Work and Gender Relations

One of the questions that women's increased labour force participation rates raises is whether they have increased or reduced women's dependence on men. In the absence of systematic information about the changing structure of gender relations in Britain, it is only possible to give a speculative answer to this question. While there can be little doubt that for many women entry to the labour market brings with it increased independence in the sense of earned income and greater social contacts in the workplace, it is also clear that for most women their level of earnings is low and that their financial contribution is an essential element to overall family budgets in a time of high inflation and rising housing costs rather than money to spend on themselves. In a Mintel survey of why women work, reported in *The Guardian* (27 September 1990), 60 per cent of the respondents replied that they needed the money. The next two highest response rates were 43 per cent "to keep mind active" and 42 per cent "money for extras" (the categories were not mutually exclusive). It seems clear from these results and the distinction between needing money and money for extras that for many households women's earnings were crucial to basic budgets.

It is often suggested that women's entry to waged work may result in the renegotiation of household tasks and a reduction in the gender inequality in the division of domestic labour. However, in a comparison of the results of the annual British Social Attitudes Surveys between 1983 and 1987 (*Social Trends 20*, HMSO 1990) little change was evident over the years.

Domestic responsibilities remain primarily in women's hands, despite protestations of greater equality. For example, among married couples in 1983 the washing and ironing was done by women in 89 per cent of cases, the evening meal prepared by women in 77 per cent of cases, the cleaning done by women in 72 per cent of cases. In 1987 these figures were 88, 77 and 72 per cent respectively, but when questioned about who should do these tasks 54 per cent of couples felt that cleaning should be shared equally, 45 per cent cooking and 30 per cent washing and ironing. Even these figures are hardly the expression of a strong belief in equality!

Two other related changes—one demographic, the other in social policy—seem to be reinforcing women's responsibility for unwaged work and diminishing the prospect of greater equality between men and women. The first of these is the rise in the number of elderly people, particularly in the over 80 age group. There were 2 million people aged 80 and over in 1988, a 50 per cent increase since 1961. Many of these elderly women are cared for by their daughters or by women volunteers in the community, although a proportion are in residential homes, in both the public and private sector. However, there has been a general shift throughout the 1980s to provide care for the elderly—and for other groups who are unable to lead completely independent lives (including mentally and physically disabled people) "in the community". While in certain cases a commendable reaction to the inadequacies of institutional provision, this movement towards community care has not been accompanied by a transfer of resources to "community" forms of provision, whether volunteer, market or state agencies or the families and relatives of the person requiring care. In a report from the Mental Health Foundation (1990) the gross inequity in the current distribution of resources between institutional and community provision was highlighted. Of the 6 million people who receive treatment for a medically identified mental illness each year, all but 60,000 live in the community, but the vast bulk of resources goes towards funding psychiatric hospitals. Whereas care for an in-patient costs £72 a day, expenditure on the mentally ill in the community is 29p each day.

For a government openly committed to cutting the cost of public services, community care has overwelming advantages. Indeed the Community Care White Paper *Caring for People* published in November 1989 established a programme of de-institutionalization for the old, physically and mentally disabled people and the terminally ill. Community provision was to be established through the market with local authority co-ordination and with women's voluntary labour identified as a crucial component of provision. That this flies in the face of current labour market trends was conveniently ignored. Seven months after the White Paper the funds for the programme were slashed and the introduction of new forms of provision deferred until 1993. Meanwhile the closure of institutions continues and individuals are left to cope as best they may—in many cases individual women in their own homes continue to struggle to care for dependent relatives virtually unaided. The feminist critiques of community care as a euphemism for women's unpaid labour appear to be amply justified (Finch and Groves 1983, Finch 1988, Langhan 1990).

Conclusions

It is clear that the Thatcher era—dramatically brought to a close by her resignation in late November 1990—was neither one of untrammelled social progress for women nor entirely one of negative change. Women entered the labour market in unprecedented numbers in the 1980s, gaining a modicum of independence. However, they entered in the main in their traditional place in low wage, low skill and low paid employment, frequently on a casual or part-time basis, in a labour market that itself had been restructured in such a way as to produce a greater reliance on these typical features of women's participation. Some women gained, of course, entering professional occupations in greater numbers as the rise in the possession of educational qualifications by girls and young women was reflected in improving job prospects. But these women remain the minority among women employees.

Outside the arena of waged work, the changes seem unambiguously to have been to the detriment of all women and their dependents who rely on state goods and services. State income support was cut during the decade; and, as previous chapters have demonstrated, the provision of housing, health and transport services became more inequitable. Although education has not been discussed in detail in this book, the enormous changes in funding arrangements and curriculum requirements have placed severe burdens on the teaching profession, already demoralized by falling relative pay rates and by vacancies. These changes have had an uneven impact but have hit hardest working class families in the more deprived areas of the country. For most women the combination of waged labour with an increasing burden of unpaid work in the home and in the community has resulted in a declining standard of living, especially if measured by available leisure hours, over the 1980s. For a minority of women, benefiting by the increased differentials in individual incomes demonstrated in the earlier part of this chapter and so able to purchase the labour power of other, low paid women to perform part of their domestic work or goods and services in the market, the 1980s have been marked by higher standards of living and a reduction of male power in the home and, probably, in the labour market. To what extent the election of a more "caring" government of whatever political complexion will be able to extend these benefits to greater numbers of women remains an open question. However, the current contradiction of an economy increasingly reliant on women's labour and a welfare system that remains firmly based on the patriarchal family and women's unpaid labour means that the answer is not straightforward nor the policy conclusions obvious.

References

Allen, S., and Walkowitz, C. (1981) *Homeworking*. Macmillan, London.

Blanchflower, D., and Corry, B. (1989) Part-time employment in Great Britain: an analysis using establishment data. *Research Paper* 57. Department of Employment, London.

Campbell, B. (1984) *Wigan Pier Revisited*. Virago, London.

Cooke, K. (1987) The withdrawal from paid work of the wives of unemployed men: a review of research, *Journal of Social Policy*, **16**: 371-382.

Coote, A., Harman, H., and Hewitt, P. (1990) *The Family Way*. Social Policy Paper 1. Institute for Public Policy Research, London.

Crompton, R., and Sanderson, K. (1986) Credentials and careers: some implications of the increase of professional qualifications among women, *Sociology*, **20**: 25-42.

Equal Opportunities Commission (1990) *Women and Men in Britain 1990*. HMSO, London.

Evans, L. (1990) The "demographic dip": a golden opportunity for women in the labour market? *National Westminster Quarterly Review*, February 1990, pp. 48-69.

Finch, J. (1988) Whose responsibility? Women and the future of family care. In Allen, I., Wicks, M., Finch, J., and Leat, D. (eds.) *Informal Care Tomorrow*. Policy Studies Institute, London.

Finch, J., and Groves, D. (eds.) (1983) *A Labour of Love: Women, Work and Caring*. Routledge, London.

Glendinning, C., and Millar, J. (eds.) (1987) *Women and Poverty in Britain*. Wheatsheaf, Brighton.

Graham, H. (1984) *Women, Health and the Family*. Wheatsheaf, Brighton.

Hakim, C. (1987) Trends in the flexible workforce, *Employment Gazette*, **95**: 549-560.

Hartmann, H. (1987) Changes in women's economic and family roles in post World War II United States. In Benaria, L., and Stimpson, C. (eds.) *Women, Households and the Economy* pp. 33-64 Rutgers University Press, New Jersey.
Langhan, M. (1990) Community care in the 1990s: the community care White Paper: "Caring for People", *Critical Social Policy*, Autumn 1990, pp. 58-70.
McDowell, L. and Massey, D. (1984) A woman's place? In Massey, D., and Allen, J. (eds.) *Geography Matters!* Cambridge University Press, Cambridge.
Mental Health Foundation (1990) *Mental Illness: the Fundamental Facts*. London.
Murray, C. (1990) *The Emerging British Underclass*. IEA Health and Welfare Unit Choice in Welfare Series 2, London.
Oakley, A. (1990) Family friends, *New Statesman and Society*, **3**(121): 45.
Pahl, J. (1983) The allocation of money and the structuring of inequality within marriage, *Sociological Review*, **17**: 237-262.
Phoenix, A. (1988) Narrow definitions of culture: the case of early motherhood. In Westwood, S., and Bhachu, P. (eds.) *Enterprising Women*. Routledge, London, 1988.
Rubery, J. (1986) Trade unions in the 1980s: the case of the United Kingdom. In Edwards, R., Garonna, P., and Todtling, F. (eds.) *Unions in Crisis and Beyond: Perspectives from Six Countries*. Auburn House, London.
Rubery, J., and Tarling, R. (1988) Women's employment in declining Britain. In Rubery, J. (ed.) *Women and Recession*, pp. 100-132 Routledge, London.
Social and Community Planning Research (1990) *British Social Attitudes Survey* 7. London.
Stanley, L., and Temple, B. (1989) Male unemployment, the benefits system and female labour market participation: some Rochdale SCEL data. Paper given at the Work, Employment and Society conference, University of Durham, September 1989.
Townsend, P. (1987) *Poverty and Labour in London*. Low Pay Unit, London.

INDEX

Index